IAN CAMPBELL

T0333297

The Addis Ababa Massacre

Italy's National Shame

HURST & COMPANY, LONDON

First published in English in the United Kingdom in 2017 by
C. Hurst & Co. (Publishers) Ltd.,
41 Great Russell Copyright, London, WC1B 3PL
© Ian Campbell, 2017
This paperback edition, 2019
All rights reserved.
Printed in Great Britain by Bell and Bain Ltd, Glasgow

A Cataloguing-in-Publication data record for this book
is available from the British Library.

ISBN: 9781787382237

This book is printed using paper from registered sustainable
and managed sources.

www.hurstpublishers.com

This book is dedicated to the innocents who died in the Massacre of Addis Ababa, Ethiopia.

February 1937

CONTENTS

CONTENTS

CONTENTS

LIST OF MAPS

LIST OF TABLES

LIST OF FIGURES

Permission to publish all photographs has been sought and granted in all cases where the source of the photograph can be identified and the copyright is still in force.

In some instances the source cannot be identified—particularly where several prints were made from the same negative—or has been forgotten. In such cases, if readers can bring the source and the owner of the copyright to the attention of the author, permission will be sought and credit provided in subsequent editions of this book.

Comments on the provenance of the photographs and the circumstances in which they were taken are to be found in Appendix V.

ABBREVIATIONS

AAU	Addis Ababa University
ACS	Archivio Centrale di Stato, Rome
AIP	Archivio Fotografico INSMLI, Milan
IES	Institute of Ethiopian Studies, Addis Ababa University
MAI	Ministero dell'Africa Italiana, Direzione Affari Politici
PAAA	Politische Archiv des Auswärtigen Amts, Berlin
PNF	Partito Nazionale Fascista (Fascist Party)
UNECA	United Nations Economic Commission for Africa, Addis Ababa
USNA	United States of America National Archives II, Maryland, USA

NOTES ON TRANSLITERATION

The following system has been used for the transliteration of Amharic words into English.

VOWELS

The seven orders are represented as follows:

1. be ('e' as in 'open'). The 1st order 'h-' is represented by 'ha'; the open vowel form is represented by 'a'.
2. bu ('u' as in 'rude')
3. bi ('i' as in 'piano')
4. ba ('a' as in 'fast')
5. bé ('é' as in the French 'détente')
6. bi ('i' shortened; similar to 'eu' in the French 'peu'). Where this vowel is silent, no vowel is shown.
7. bo ('o' as in 'core')

EXPLOSIVES

To minimise the need for diacritical markings, no distinction has been drawn between the explosives and non-explosives except for the use of 'q' for explosive 'k', and 'ts' for explosive 's'.

'jh' is pronounced as 's' in 'pleasure'

'ñ' is pronounced as in 'señor'

The use of double consonants normally employed in English to indicate pronunciation of the preceding vowel (such as the double 's') is retained. Double consonants are also used to indicate gemination in Amharic names, as in 'Iyyasu'.

When an Ethiopian name consists of two words, these are hyphenated to indicate to non-Ethiopian readers that they are inseparable (e.g. Hayle-Maryam).

All proper names have been transliterated according to the above system, with the exception of the following common names, which have been written as conventionally spelt: Menelik rather than Minilik, Haile Selassie rather than Hayle-Sillassé, Lorenzo rather than Lorénso, Addis Ababa rather than Addis Abeba, Dire Dawa rather than Diré Dawa, Harar rather than Harer, Massawa rather than Mitsewa, Hamasien rather than Hamasén, and Bale rather than Balé.

Names and other words already transliterated within quoted text have generally been adjusted to be consistent with the system adopted for this book, unless otherwise stated.

It should be noted that when the name of an Ethiopian author of a European-language publication or affidavit cited in this book appears in that publication or affidavit using a different system of transliteration (such as Tamasgen Gabre or David Oqbazqui), the original spelling has been retained in the citations, and thus will be different from the way the name appears in the text of this book (i.e. Temesgen Gebré and Dawit Oquba Igzi'i).

GLOSSARY AND EXPLANATORY NOTE

(All terms are Amharic unless otherwise stated)

Abba	(title) Father, used particularly for monks
abun	bishop
Abune	(title) Bishop
adarash	traditional meeting hall, esp. for banquets
Afa Negus	(title) Chief Justice (lit. Mouth of the King)
Agefari	(title) Superintendent of Banquets
Aleqa	(title) Administrative Head of a Church
amba	steeply sided natural fortress
angach	retainer, usually assistant to Patriot fighter (pl. *angachoch*)
arbeñña	resistance fighter (pl. *arbeññoch*)
ye wist arbeñña	undercover (typically urban) member of the resistance
askari	(Swahili) native soldier, guard
Ato	(title) equivalent to Mr
awraja	district
Azajh	(title) Commander; Chief of the Imperial Court
bahtawi	ascetic cleric; hermit
balabbat	hereditary land-owner; roughly equivalent to country squire
Balambaras	(military title) Head of a Fort (lit. Head of an *Amba*)
banda	(Italian) a group. In particular:
bande militari:	uniformed Ethiopian regulars fighting for the Italians;
bande irregolari:	Ethiopian irregulars fighting for the Italians;
banda	(coll.): Ethiopian collaborating with (esp. fighting for) the Italians (derogatory term commonly used by Ethiopians)

GLOSSARY AND EXPLANATORY NOTE

Basha	(military title) derived from Turkish *pasha*
Bejirond	(title) Royal Treasurer; Guardian of Royal Property
ber	gate
bermél	barrel, drum (large container for liquid)
bét	house
Betwedded	(title) 'Beloved'; high-ranking government official
Blatta	title signifying learning (lit. 'Youth'), generally awarded to government officials at director-general level
Blattén Géta	title awarded to officials at ministerial level (lit. Master of the *Blatta*)
chika	simple construction of wood plastered with a mixture of mud and grass
Dejazmach	(military title) rank just below *Ras* (lit. Commander of the Gate; Commander of the Threshold)
Dyakon	(title) Deacon
Fitawrari	(military title) rank normally (but not always) below *Dejazmach* (lit. Commander of the Vanguard)
gibbi	palace or nobleman's residence or compound
Grazmach	(military title) rank normally below *Fitawrari* (lit. Commander of the Left Wing)
Ichegé	(title) traditionally the highest Ethiopian ecclesiastic in the Ethiopian Orthodox Church
Itegé	(title) Empress
Itété	(title) Aunt
Immahoy	(title) Sister
kabba	decorative ceremonial Ethiopian gown, for both men and women
Kentiba	title equivalent to Mayor of a town or city
Lij	title, roughly equivalent to Prince (lit. Child), but not necessarily indicating royalty
Liqe Liqawint	title (lit. Most Learned of the Learned)
Liqe Mekwas	title given to official serving as the double of the sovereign
Memhir	title employed particularly in churches and monasteries (lit. Teacher)
Neggadras	(title) Head of Merchants; Head of Customs
Negus	(title) equivalent to King
Qebelé	district, section of a city
Qeññazmach	(military title) Commander of the Right Wing; rank generally below *Fitawrari*.

GLOSSARY AND EXPLANATORY NOTE

Qés	(title) Priest
qorqoro	corrugated metal roofing sheets, introduced to Addis Ababa in early 20th century
Ras	(title) roughly equivalent to Duke or Lord
sefer	district, settlement, village
Shaleqa	(military title) equivalent to Major (abbrev. *Shaqa*)
Shambel	military title, below *Shaleqa* (lit. Commander of 250)
shamma	light Ethiopian toga worn by both men and women
shifta	bandit, brigand
shimagilé	elderly, respected man; male interlocutor
Shum	(title) Chief, official
Tenente	(title) Lieutenant
thaler	silver Austrian coin bearing the head of Empress Maria Theresa
Tilinti	(title) Lieutenant
Tsebaté	(title) Official second in rank tot he Abbot of Debre Libanos
Tsehafe Ti'ezaz	(title) Head Scribe; Minister of the Pen; equivalent to Lord Privy Seal
tukul	traditional round thatched Ethiopian house (term used by non-Ethiopians)
wereda	administrative district
Weyzero	(title) roughly equivalent to Mrs
Weyzeret	(title) roughly equivalent to Miss

The terms 'Invasion', 'Occupation' and 'Liberation' (with the initial letter capitalised) denote the Italian invasion of Ethiopia from October 1935 to May 1936, the military occupation that followed, and the expulsion of the occupying forces that culminated in the restoration of Ethiopian government in May 1941, respectively.

The term 'patriot' simply means a patriotic person. However, when the initial letter is capitalised (i.e. 'Patriot'), the term denotes an active member of the Ethiopian resistance.

THE ETHIOPIAN CALENDAR

The Ethiopian calendar is approximately seven years and eight months behind the international, or Gregorian, calendar. It begins and ends in September.

GLOSSARY AND EXPLANATORY NOTE

Unless otherwise stated, all years in *The Addis Ababa Massacre* refer to the international calendar. Where the year refers to the Ethiopian calendar, it is written, for example, 1929 EC. If, for example, an event is recorded as having occurred in 1929 EC, then since this spans 12 September 1936 to 11 September 1937, the year of the event in the international calendar is written 1936/37.

Dates in the Ethiopian calendar are written with the day followed by the month, e.g. 12 Yekatit. The event of that date consisting of the attack on the Italian High Command and the massacre that followed is referred to in italics as *Yekatit 12*.

ETHIOPIAN TIME

Ethiopian time begins at 6.00 am, i.e. more or less when the sun rises. For example, 8.00 am international time is 2.00 am Ethiopian time. However, all times specified in this book refer to international time.

NAMES OF ADDIS ABABA STREETS AND DISTRICTS

At the time of the Italian invasion of Ethiopia most streets in Addis Ababa had no official names. The Italians gave the streets names, but these were generally used only by the Italians, and in any case were dropped when the Occupation ended, in 1941. After the Liberation, most streets were given new names (e.g. Arbeññoch Street, Belay Zeleke Street, Churchill Road), but these names were not in use during the events described in this book. An additional complication arises in that another completely different set of names has recently been allocated to most of these streets, and, further, many of the major roads are actually often referred to using yet other names (such as 'the Gojjam Road').

The question then arises as to how the streets should be referenced, in a manner recognisable to present-day readers, young and old, foreign and Ethiopian. The method adopted in this book is to use the post-Liberation name in most cases (e.g. Arbeññoch Street), but with a reference to what the Italians called it at the time (i.e. viale Tevere) and, where appropriate, to mention today's common name (i.e. the Ambo Road). To avoid unnecessary repetition, subsequent references may be limited to just one of these names. Where possible, both the Ethiopian post-Liberation and Italian street names are shown on the maps.

Before the Occupation most districts of the city were known informally by the names of the most prominent landmark—often a church—in the area concerned. In some cases these have become the official names of those districts (eg. Lideta, Qechené). In other cases new names have emerged in more recent times (e.g. Amist Kilo). As in the case of street names, while every effort has been made to be both faithful to the period and consistent, the later name may be used where the earlier name is either not known or did not exist. Thus, for example, the statement 'He walked to Amist Kilo' does not necessarily imply that Amist Kilo was the name by which that location was known at the time.

The Gennete-Li'ul Palace, built by Emperor Haile Selassie in the early 1930s, which was taken over by the Italians as the headquarters of the Governo Generale, is often referred to in the literature as the Viceregal Palace, although Viceroy Graziani never actually resided there. In this book it is referred to occasionally as the Viceregal Palace, but more frequently as the Gennete-Li'ul Palace or the Governo Generale.

ACKNOWLEDGEMENTS

Many people have generously assisted in the research that has led to this book, commencing with an interview 25 years ago, in 1991, of His Beattitude *Abba* Mattéwos of the Ethiopian Orthodox Church. Formerly Archbishop of Jerusalem, he was at that time member of the Holy Synod and head of the Monastery and School of Meskaye Hezunan Medhané Alem, Addis Ababa. Previously known as *Tsebaté* Hayle-Mesqel of the Monastery of Debre Libanos of Shewa, *Abba* Mattéwos was one of my original sources of inspiration, and I remain most indebted to him.

The interview of *Abba* Mattéwos came about as a result of a study of the Monastery of Debre Libanos and its vicinity that I was undertaking at the time with Degife Gebre-Tsadiq (then librarian of the Institute of Ethiopian Studies, Addis Ababa University), and with the gracious support and assistance of His Holiness *Abune* Pawlos, Patriarch of the Ethiopian Orthodox Church and *Ichegé* of the See of St Tekle Haymanot. The study not only triggered in me a wider interest in the monastery, but also opened my eyes to the Italian occupation of Ethiopia. Although the wars of invasion (1935–6) and liberation (1941) had been documented by several authors, comparatively little—apart from Dr Richard Pankhurst's notable contributions—about the Occupation and the protracted war that was waged throughout the five years of its duration had been published, and this left an important episode of modern Ethiopian history relatively undocumented.

The resultant research, triggered by the apparent connection between the Monastery of Debre Libanos and the massacre of Addis Ababa, which continued until 2014, yielded so much information that it culminated in a trilogy: *The Plot to Kill Graziani* (Addis Ababa University Press, 2010), *The Massacre of Debre Libanos* (Addis Ababa University Press, 2014), and the present volume.

ACKNOWLEDGEMENTS

My reconstruction of the Massacre of Addis Ababa is based principally on Ethiopian testimonies contextualised with published and foreign sources. Following the interview of *Abba* Mattéwos, the most critical sources have been communications or interviews—in several cases on site—with the following informants, to whom I am most grateful. They are listed in the chronological order in which their first interview or communication took place:

Ato Tebebe Kassa of Debre Libanos, who was detained during the Massacre of Debre Libanos in May 1937 and was subsequently incarcerated in Danane concentration camp;

Weyzero Alemash Sibhatu, daughter of Viceroy Rodolfo Graziani's secretary and interpreter, *Ato* (later, *Dejazmach*) Sibhatu Yohannis, who was with the Viceroy when the attack was carried out on the Italian High Command;

Ato Tekle-Tsadiq Mekuriya, historian and former Minister of Culture, who lived through the massacre and was imprisoned in Danane concentration camp;

Ato Taddesse Tiruneh, Patriot and a brother of one of the conspirators in the plot to kill Graziani that triggered the Massacre of Addis Ababa, and who sheltered from the massacre at the Hermannsburg Evangelical Mission at Qechené;

Blatta Mehari Kassa, a friend of three of the *Yekatit 12* conspirators, who sheltered from the massacre of Addis Ababa at Qechené;

Weyzero Yeweynishet Beshahwired, daughter of Beshahwired Habte-Weld (director of finance in the pre-Occupation government, and later executed by Graziani), who as a child witnessed at first hand the early stages of the massacre and was imprisoned in Italy;

Weyzero Welette-Birhan Gebre-Iyyesus (sister-in-law of *Ato* Beshahwired), who witnessed the early stages of the massacre and sheltered from it in Siddist Kilo;

Weyzero Sara Gebre-Iyyesus (wife of *Ato* Beshahwired and mother of Yeweynishet), who witnessed the early stages of the massacre at close hand and was imprisoned in Italy;

Ato Emmanuel Abraham, former government minister, head of the Mekane-Yesus Church, and secretary to Dr 'Charles Martin' Werqineh Isheté (Ethiopian minister in London at the time of the Italian invasion);

ACKNOWLEDGEMENTS

Ato Demissé Hayle-Maryam, Patriot, and relative, companion and assistant of the *Yekatit 12* conspirator *Bejirond* (later, *Dejazmach*) Letyibelu Gebré, who sheltered at the British legation from the massacre, but witnessed its aftermath;

His Holiness *Abune* Birhane-Yesus Demirew Surafa'él, Metropolitan Archbishop (now Cardinal) of the Catholic Church in Ethiopia, and his brother, *Ato* Mombasa Surafa'él, civil servant—both nephews of one of the *Yekatit 12* conspirators;

Shaleqa Éfrém Gebre-Amlak, an Eritrean resident of Addis Ababa who sheltered from the massacre as a young boy in his family home;

Mr Vahak Karibian, a long-time resident of Addis Ababa and a leading member of the Ethio-Armenian community, who as a schoolboy witnessed the early stages of the massacre;

Ato Tekle-Maryam Kiflom, former Deputy Minister of the Imperial Palace, who as a young man was arrested during the massacre, was released, then took shelter in Arat Kilo;

Ato Tamrat Istifanos, Patriot and retired civil servant, who lived through the massacre near the hospital where Viceroy Rodolfo Graziani was being treated;

Weyzero Amsale Letyibelu, *Ato* Habtu Welde-Medhin and *Weyzero* Aselefech Letyibelu, relatives of *Dejazmach* Letyibelu Gebré;

Mr Yervant Semerjibashian, brother of Johannes Semerjibashian (dragoman of the German legation during the Occupation), who sheltered from the massacre at his brother's house in Amist Kilo;

Ato Dawit Gebre-Mesqel, former *Dyakon* of the Church of Ta'eka Negest Be'ata, Addis Ababa, who narrowly escaped execution during the massacre when the adjoining Church of Kidane Mihret was invaded by Fascist troops;

Immahoy Hiruta, latterly of the Church of Ta'eka Negest Be'ata, Addis Ababa, whose relatives were imprisoned during the massacre, and who helped prisoners escape from detention during the days that followed;

Ambassador Imru Zelleqe, who as a boy witnessed the outbreak of the massacre, was imprisoned in Danane concentration camp, and later served as secretary to the Ethiopian Minister of Foreign Affairs during the post-war peace negotiations with Italy;

ACKNOWLEDGEMENTS

Signor Nicola Antonio DeMarco, grandson of Dr Iago Bossi, an Italian military communications expert billeted in Addis Ababa who sheltered Ethiopians in Piazza during the massacre;

Dr Abraham Asnake, son of *Ato* Asnake Jembere and *Weyzero* Zenebech Werqineh, residents of Addis Ababa who survived the massacre despite an arson attack by the Blackshirts in the northern suburb where they were living;

Dr Siyum Gebre-Egziabher, who as a child went looking for his father during the massacre and was arrested and imprisoned during the conflagration.

Invaluable information and assistance were also provided by the following, listed in chronological sequence of their first interview or communication:

Ato Degife Gebre-Tsadiq, a good friend and indispensable co-researcher who collaborated with me for several years in our joint study of the Massacre of Debre Libanos;

Fitawrari Nebiyye-Li'ul, son-in-law of *Ras* Kassa Haylu, and historian of the Monastery of Debre Libanos;

Dejazmach Zewdé Gebre-Sillassé, distinguished politician, diplomat and scholar, who on several occasions kindly reviewed, commented on and contributed to my findings;

Dr Azeb Tamrat, former Deputy Minister of Health, who kindly arranged for me to meet two knowledgeable informants;

Professor Angelo Del Boca, a leading historian of the Italian Fascist period;

Weyzero Alem-Seged Feqade-Sillassé Hiruy, daughter of Feqade-Sillassé ('George') Hiruy, granddaughter of *Ras* Imru Hayle-Sillassé, and stepdaughter of *Blattén Géta* Lorenzo Ta'izaz;

Weyzero Sennayt Siyum and her uncle, *Ato* Seged Abriha, friends of *Blatta* Mehari Kassa;

Weyzero Elené Mekuriya, former BBC representative in Addis Ababa and granddaughter of Dr Werqineh Isheté;

Mr Garbis Korajian, a leading member of Addis Ababa's Ethio-Armenian community, who kindly introduced me to members of the community who lived through the Occupation, and assisted with photography;

Ato Mengesha Werqineh, who kindly introduced me to his cousin, Dr Abraham Asnake;

Herr Cord Heinrich Bahlburg, the son of Hermann Bahlburg (head of the German Hermannsburg Evangelical Mission in Addis Ababa during the Occupation), who graciously shared with me the results of his research into the circumstances of the arrests of Mission employees Sibhat Tiruneh and Hinrich Rathje, and provided copies of important contemporary documents from German national and family archives;

Pastor Jürgen Klein, who, together with Cord Bahlburg, kindly shared his knowledge of the history of the Hermannsburg Mission, and facilitated access to German sources;

scholar and Ethiopianist Dr Roman Herzog, who made available the results of his research into imprisonment during the Invasion and Occupation, provided important documents, and granted me permission to quote from his interviews of informants;

Italian scholar Professor Giuseppe Finaldi, who kindly shared with me his analysis of the influences that gave rise to the massacre in the Fascist and Italian colonial context;

Jeff Pearce, author of *Prevail*, who provided important documents from British archives and rendered valuable assistance;

Professor Christopher Duggan, who directed me towards important Italian sources;

Professor Christopher Clapham, who generously provided a copy of the original list he compiled in 1964 of foreign-educated Ethiopians before 1935, and their fate.

novelist Francesca Melandri, who pointed out to me the existence of Sergeant-Major Boaglio's published memoir, and kindly gave me a copy.

In addition, I am particularly indebted to the following friends, who devoted considerable time and energy to the project:

the indefatigable Professor Richard Pankhurst, prolific writer on Ethiopia and founder-director of the Institute of Ethiopian Studies, Addis Ababa University, and his wife, the librarian, scholar and linguist Rita Pankhurst, who introduced me to informants and provided important information.

ACKNOWLEDGEMENTS

Richard and Rita Pankhurst have been my generous and unflagging mentors throughout this project;

Professor Shiferaw Beqelé of the History Department, Addis Ababa University, who kindly reviewed and commented on several versions of the manuscript, directed me to Amharic sources, provided introductions, and was a vital source of information on 1930s Addis Ababa;

historian and linguist Dr Birhanu Abebe, who identified witnesses, arranged and assisted with interviews, and provided copies of stills from old film clips, as well as hitherto unpublished photographs;

Weyzero Yeweynishet Beshahwired, who was of great assistance not only as an invaluable informant in numerous interviews, but also in providing important details on life in Addis Ababa before and after the Liberation;

my dear friend and former colleague *Ato* Welde-Aregay Tessema, who assisted and encouraged me and introduced me to key informants;

Dr Birhanu Gizaw Hayle-Maryam of the College of Telecommunications and Information Technology, Addis Ababa, and scholar of Ethiopian cultural history, who helped to trace informants and rendered unstinting service in the conduct of interviews;

my good friend and colleague *Ato* Tamene Tiruneh, who provided Amharic translation and transliteration services, as did *Weyzero* Yeweynishet, *Ato* Lemma Argaw and *Ato* Begashaw Woldu Wukaw. Assistance with Italian was generously provided by Rita Pankhurst and Carlo Di Chiara.

I am grateful for the invaluable services provided by the staff of the Institute of Ethiopian Studies, Addis Ababa University, who kindly provided access to the institute's incomparable resources. Thanks are also due to the staff of the US National Archives II, Maryland, and the staff of the British Public Record Office (now The National Archives) at Kew.

Both Professor Shiferaw and Professor Pankhurst generously rendered invaluable services by reacting to key findings as they emerged, reviewing the draft text and providing comments, suggestions and guidance. *Dejazmach* Zewdé Gebre-Sillassé kindly provided critical insights into the events of the Occupation, and his encyclopedic knowledge of modern Ethiopian history proved an invaluable source of information.

Although a great deal of the Ethiopian testimony on which this book is based is oral, use has also been made of the Ethiopian written sources. These range from detailed reports of various aspects of the massacre published

ACKNOWLEDGEMENTS

within Amharic accounts of the Occupation written not long after the event, to brief but valuable anecdotal testimony appearing in autobiographies and biographies published more recently in English. Though relatively few in number, the Amharic accounts are important in that they are typically quite detailed and were written by well-known and highly respected witnesses. The most substantive publications in this category, as far as the excesses of the Occupation are concerned, begin with Kirubel Beshah's *Ke-Hulum Tikit* (written in 1940/41 but published anonymously several years later). This was followed in 1944/45 by Ambassador Birhanu Dinqé's *Ye-Amistu Ye-Mekera Ametat Acher Tarik*, one of the few sources providing partial lists of detainees, deportees and execution victims, and Fitur Abriham's *Armenéw Fashist*. A decade later came Lieutenant Meleseliñ Aniley's *Balefut Amist Ye-Mekera Amatat Fashistoch be Etyopya*, which includes details of the author's personal experience of the massacre. In the 1960s Taddesse Zeweldé's *Ye-Abalashiñ Zemen* and *Qerin Geremew: Ye-Arbeññoch Tarik* appeared. Finally, Temesgen Gebré's personal account, written in the 1940s, was published recently in *Hiweté Gile Tarik*.

While much information on the background of notable Ethiopians mentioned in the text has been gleaned from a variety of cited oral sources, the most valuable published works in this regard proved to be the late Professor Harold Marcus's annotations in his edited translation of Emperor Haile Selassie's autobiography, *My Life and Ethiopia's Progress*; Professor Bahru Zewdé's *Pioneers of Change in Ethiopia*; and Mika'él Bethe-Sillassé's *La Jeune Éthiopie: un haut-fonctionnaire éthiopien Berhanä-Marqos Wäldä-Tsadeq (1892–1943)*.

I have consulted contemporary reports and documents of the British, French and American diplomatic envoys based in Addis Ababa at the time of the Occupation. I have also drawn on Richard Pankhurst's published syntheses of British records regarding the planned trials of Italian war crimes suspects, including parliamentary proceedings as recorded in Hansard.

For the Italian primary sources I have made extensive use of the microfilmed correspondence and associated reports held in the Library of Congress Archives, Maryland, USA, and the Institute of Ethiopian Studies (IES), Addis Ababa University. For critical documents in Rome but not available at Maryland or the IES, I am indebted to Dr Roman Herzog and Andrea Guiseppi for accessing the relevant files of the Archivio Centrale dello Stato. For other Italian sources—both primary and secondary—I have relied principally on the published works of Professor Angelo Del Boca, Professor Giorgio

ACKNOWLEDGEMENTS

Rochat and Professor Alberto Sbacchi. Finally, Professor Christopher Duggan's recent publication, *Fascist Voices*, breaking new ground in examining a treasure trove of personal diaries and letters, has proved to be a valuable resource for the thoughts, beliefs and aspirations of ordinary Italians under Fascism, and those of some of the soldiers involved in the Invasion.

I was able to access contemporary official correspondence in the Politische Archiv des Auswärtigen Amts in Berlin concerning the activities of the Hermannsburg Evangelical Mission in Addis Ababa, through the kind offices of Herr Cord Bahlburg, who also shared with me correspondence between the mission, the German legation and officials of the Governo Generale in Addis Ababa, as well as a personal report by mission employee Hinrich Rathje.

Acknowledgements of the sources of photographs are included in the List of Figures. I am grateful to all copyright owners listed for their kind permission to publish, and would like to acknowledge particularly the generosity of Vieri Poggiali for permission to reproduce the important photographs originally accompanying the publication of his father's private diary. Although every effort has been made to trace copyright holders, in some cases this proved impossible, and any oversight in this regard brought to the attention of the publishers will be addressed in future editions.

Warm thanks are due to the unknown (but probably French) cameraman who took the original footage of the massacre from which stills were provided to me by Dr Birhanu Abebe; and finally, and not without a touch of irony, I have to thank the Italians who provided the most compelling evidence of all: the photographs that dispel any lingering doubts that the events described in this book really took place. These incriminating images were found in the Italian military archives in Addis Ababa and among the personal possessions of the soldiers surrendering to the liberating forces in 1941. These photographs, it must be stressed, were taken not by Ethiopians or their allies wishing to demonstrate the horrors of Fascism, but by the perpetrators themselves, who were looking forward to impressing their relatives and friends at home with evidence of their accomplishments during the invasion and occupation of Ethiopia.

Ian Campbell
Addis Ababa
2016

FOREWORD

by Professor Richard Pankhurst

Ian Campbell, today one of Ethiopia's most eminent cultural historians, arrived in the country as a development economist and environmental specialist in the energy sector in 1988. By 1990 he was on assignment in Northern Shewa to ascertain whether the Siga Wedem River, a tributary of the Blue Nile north of the great monastery of Debre Libanos, was suitable for hydroelectric development. After careful study he concluded that the entire area, on account of its important early Christian antiquities, should rather be preserved as an integral part of the country's cultural heritage. (He also found that many people lived in the valley, which was thought to be largely uninhabited.)

Studying the history of Debre Libanos Monastery, perhaps Ethiopia's foremost religious establishment, Campbell was surprised to learn that the Italians, during their short-lived Fascist occupation of the country (1936–41), had killed many of its monks. The Italians had allegedly done so in retaliation for an attempt on the life of Italian Viceroy Rodolfo Graziani by two young men from the Italian colony of Eritrea, Moges Asgedom and Abriha Deboch. The latter was also under Fascist suspicion because he had taken his wife to the monastery for safety and had fled there after the attempt. On researching further, Campbell became aware that this mass murder had been the personal responsibility of Graziani, who had ordered the execution of the entire monastic community. After their liquidation the Viceroy had proudly telegraphed to Mussolini in Rome to report that 'of the monastery nothing more remains'. In this the *Duce*, Ian discovered, had in fact been misinformed, for one sole monk, *Abba* Welde-Maryam Isheté, had, on the fateful day, gone to town to sell grain, thus escaping execution. He was thus the only monk to survive. As Campbell shows in *The Massacre of Debre Libanos*,[1] some 900 monks and priests of Debre Libanos had perished, together with 125 deacons and around 1,000 visiting clergy, laymen and pilgrims.

Investigations into the causes of the Debre Libanos Massacre, which took place on 20–25 May 1937, led Campbell almost automatically to inquire into the much more extensive three-day Addis Ababa Massacre of 19–21 February, which is irrevocably associated with Graziani's name.

Ian Campbell showed that despite its manifest importance in Ethiopian history, the Addis Ababa Massacre had been largely ignored by scholars. Though it was generally known that it was triggered by an attempt on Graziani's life by the two young Eritreans, both of whom had studied in Addis Ababa, precious little was known of their supporters, and nothing was known about their being members of any organisation.

Meticulous research by Campbell, which included interviews with the families and associates of both Moges and Abriha, revealed, as he explains in his earlier work *The Plot to Kill Graziani*,[2] that the Moges-Abriha attempt on Graziani's life was part of a far more broadly based movement than had previously been suspected. It was supported in particular by a number of the Young Ethiopians—as the modern intelligentsia were nicknamed—as well as by some of the traditional elite.

Campbell's investigations into the Addis Ababa Massacre are no less far-reaching. The event had been widely reported at the time by foreign diplomats and journalists, and had been denounced by Emperor Haile Selassie in his speeches. The main features of the massacre, as well as its scope, were therefore indisputably attested, but no scholar had thus far attempted to study it dispassionately and in detail. Thus no one had established precisely when, where, and in what order the various atrocities had taken place and who was responsible for the various crimes: the shooting into crowds, attacks on 'natives' in their homes and in the streets, the burning down of houses, etc. All this—and much more—is now thoroughly explained by Campbell in the present work.

Despite the careful research he has undertaken over more than two decades, some readers may wish to quibble with his assessment that approximately 19,000 people were killed in and around Addis Ababa during the massacre, equivalent to around 19–20 per cent of the Ethiopian population of the city. Suffice it to say that if the number that perished had been only half as many as Campbell estimates, it would still have been a massacre of tremendous proportions.

* * *

Italian war crimes in Ethiopia were preceded a decade earlier by similar atrocities committed during the Italian conquest and occupation of Libya. Campbell shows that *Hakim* Werqineh, otherwise known as Dr Charles Martin, the Ethiopian envoy in London, having read about that military operation, warned his fellow diplomats that Mussolini's invasion and occupation of Ethiopia would probably be no less ruthless.

Since 1922 Italy had been a strictly totalitarian state in which many of its principal opponents were arrested and prosecuted for propagating subversive ideas. Some were then exiled on penal islands or, like Giacomo Matteotti, a parliamentary adversary, were brutally assassinated.

The Addis Ababa Massacre was almost immediately followed by a series of Italian racial laws. The first, signed on 19 April 1937 by the King of Italy, Vittorio Emanuele III—who was given the additional title of Emperor of Ethiopia—prohibited conjugal relations between Italian citizens and colonial subjects of the Italian 'East African Empire'. Further decrees established rigid racial segregation in both housing and transport, prohibited conjugal relations with Jews, and excluded the Jews from employment in government or semi-government service.

* * *

The early chapters of this book describe a series of atrocities which observers writing prior to the Nazi holocaust compared only with the Armenian Massacres of 1895–6 and 1915, which had shocked the world.

Ian Campbell's book goes much further than this. It shows how some of the Great Powers, and in particular the British, turned a 'blind eye' at the massacre to avoid offending Mussolini and, as was said, pushing him into the arms of Hitler, with whom he was already ideologically allied. Campbell cites evidence of the Foreign Office deliberately suppressing a damning report of the massacre on the convenient grounds that its publication would 'serve no useful purpose'.

Turning to the supposedly more altruistic post-war world, the author shows that the approach to Italy's war crimes in Ethiopia was largely dominated by Great Power politics. The major Allied Powers, wanting to have a right-wing government established in Italy, were thus reluctant to see the trial of Fascist war criminals—especially as this would involve the trial and punishment of whites by blacks.

Everything was done, as Ian Campbell relates, to exclude Ethiopia from representation on the United Nations War Crimes Commission. It was thus argued that the invasion of Ethiopia had taken place in 1935, and was thus too early to allow her membership of the commission. China (a larger and more influential power than Ethiopia) was, however, given membership, though she had been invaded in 1931, several years before Italy's invasion of Ethiopia.

British opposition to the trial of Italian war criminals found expression in a remarkable Foreign Office memorandum, cited by Campbell. It presented the Ethiopian government with the threat that Britain would support Ethiopian claims to the former Italian colony of Eritrea only if Ethiopia abandoned the war crimes issue. Should Ethiopia not do so, British support for the Ethiopian claims would be withdrawn.

Typical of this approach was a secret letter which the British wartime Prime Minister, Winston Churchill, wrote to his ambassador in Rome in 1944. It instructed the ambassador to provide 'safety and sanctuary' to Marshal Badoglio, should the latter be charged with war crimes by the post-Fascist Italian government. Badoglio had been the Italian commander of the northern front in Ethiopia, who used poison gas, and had been listed as no. 1 war criminal by the Ethiopian Government.

* * *

Campbell's detailed research, which cuts much new ground, provides the reader with a daily, almost hourly, picture of the infamous three days, enhanced by many photographic images not previously in the public domain. Some of these shocking photos were taken by the murderers themselves. Campbell also confirms that, in addition to random killings, there was deliberate targeting of educated Ethiopians.

The reader is indebted to Ian Campbell for assembling a considerable amount of little-known information on the tragic events surrounding the Massacre of Addis Ababa. He presents his material clearly and concisely. His book is well served by a name index and an extensive bibliography.

INTRODUCTION

On this cool February morning the coarse, unkempt field grass on the steep slopes above the Qechené River—at this time of year little more than a stream—looks much as it did in the 1880s, when King Menelik of Shewa first broke ground to begin building on the hilltop with its commanding vistas across the vast plain below to accommodate his new capital of Addis Ababa. In the morning mist a distant dog barks, and a few early risers on the road pull their *shammas* tight to keep out the cold. Through a gap in the yellow and green corrugated iron, or *qorqoro*, fence to the south-east can be seen the forbidding walls of the old Police Garage, and beyond, in the early morning light, the 21st century beckons with the imposing edifice of today's Sheraton Hotel.

This is—or was—Sera Bét Sefer: the 'workers' village' below the ramparts of the sprawling palace complex, where the sovereign's masons and carpenters settled in their traditional wattle-and-daub thatched cottages, to be joined in due course by a retinue of imperial servants, cooks and footmen drawn from the far reaches of the empire.

Across the wooded river gorge to the west are the grassy slopes where the royal cattle grazed and, beyond, the Lycée Gebre-Maryam and the bustling Churchill Road come into view—names that evoke a dark period in Ethiopia's history.

This empty, windswept field bounded by the same makeshift multicoloured *qorqoro* that by decree now surrounds all the city's construction sites is not a graveyard. There are no tombstones, no memorials to the dead, and no visitor's book to sign. Yet perhaps there should be, for this is surely hallowed ground. It was here on the night of 19 February 1937, when all God-fearing men and women should have been fast asleep in their beds like the unsuspecting inhabitants of Sera Bét Sefer, that a tsunami of destruction struck, bringing not water, but fire, terror and cruel death.

1

In a crisp morning just like today, the survivors, peering out from their shattered windows, saw only smouldering ruins in what had been a teeming, thriving and dense settlement where men, women and children had worked, laughed and played. Like the aftermath of a terrible battle, charred tree-stumps, bodies and scattered body parts bore witness to the carnage of the night.

This was not, however, Mother Nature at its worst. This was a manmade horror with its centre at nearby Siddist Kilo, and it continued in wave after wave across the city for more than three nights, leaving scarcely a single residential area untouched.

Just as the eucalyptus root sprouts again after the tree is burned, so Sera Bét would rise again, and life and laughter would return as new generations rebuilt their cottages cheek by jowl. In fact, it is only today, three-quarters of a century later, that for the first time since the tsunami one can again see the unbroken expanse, the grass left to grow as it did long ago, its roots now reaching down into the ashes of an evil past.

This time the demolition has been carried out in the name of progress, the occupants moving on for a better life in new, distant suburbs. But can one sense the past here? Only in the emptiness and the silence—the first total silence to descend on Sera Bét Sefer since that fateful morning that followed the raging inferno three generations ago.

The Massacre of Addis Ababa forms but one chilling chapter in a longer story, starting when, in late 1935, in an effort to galvanise domestic support for his cult of Fascism, to be regarded as the leader of a Great Power, and to launch his dream of 'Fascism International', Benito Mussolini engaged Italy in an unprovoked and brutal invasion of the sovereign state of Ethiopia—the first in a series of Italian invasions of vulnerable nation-states that would defy and disempower the League of Nations, inspire and embolden the Nazis, and culminate in the conflagration of the Second World War. Despite brave and dogged resistance by the ill-equipped Ethiopian army for eight terrifying months, in May 1936 the intruders reached the capital, and invasion became military occupation.

The widespread slaughter, burning and pillage of thousands of unsuspecting and defenceless civilians in the city by the Italians nine months later revitalised the Ethiopian resistance, changed the course of the Occupation, and had impacts that reach down to the present time. However, the bloodbath remains largely unknown outside Ethiopia, and is rarely mentioned in published historical literature. Even when it is mentioned, there remain widely divergent opinions about the scale and nature of the massacre, and who was responsible.

Published accounts of the slaughter are generally brief. A few are more detailed, but are usually focused on a particular aspect or episode of the massacre, and do not tell the whole story. Thus they do not, by themselves, provide a framework for either a detailed chronology or a mapping of the events concerned. This dearth of information may be attributed to five phenomena.

(i)   The occupying forces drew a veil over Addis Ababa at the beginning of the massacre by declaring a city-wide curfew, closing down public telecommunications between the city and the outside world, and confiscating cameras from non-Italians.

(ii) A large proportion of the Ethiopian eyewitnesses died in the conflagration, and of those who survived, each typically observed only a small fraction of the totality.

(iii) The locally based Italian officials who presided over the massacre wrote little or nothing about it in their reports to Rome.

(iv) After the Liberation it would have been possible to compile a reasonably complete account of what occurred in February 1937, but Emperor Haile Selassie's government had to operate at that time under the auspices of the British government, which regarded Ethiopia as Occupied Enemy Territory, and blocked documentation of Italian war crimes. Furthermore, by the time the Ethiopian government had managed to prepare the basic documentation required, Britain's opposition to the investigation of Italian war crimes had hardened as a result of Italy changing sides in the Second World War, thereby becoming a British ally.

(v)   Finally, in more recent times, those who carried out the massacre seem to have suffered from the collective amnesia that has afflicted many former members of the Italian civil service and military of the Fascist period, thus leaving the field of the historiography of the Italian occupation of Ethiopia largely bereft of serious source material.

Thus, although several Ethiopian writers mentioned the subject of the massacre in post-war accounts of the activities of the Ethiopian patriotic resistance, there were no comprehensive reports written of the events of *Yekatit 12*, the popular name for the holocaust that was launched on that day of the Ethiopian calendar. Furthermore, the British government ensured that the trials of the Italian officials responsible, which were to have taken place under the auspices of the United Nations War Crimes Commission, and which would have provided exposure and a measure of dispassionate analysis of the events concerned, never took place. Thus, while the German High Command paid the price at Nuremberg for the excesses of Nazism, the Fascists, whose lead Hitler and his henchmen had followed, were never prosecuted. This created a facilitating environment for the spinning of myths about Italy's 'benign Fascism', and the matter of the Massacre of Addis Ababa—along with numerous other excesses—was studiously swept under the carpet.

Fortunately, over the course of the 25 years that this research spanned, I was able to trace a number of credible and articulate Ethiopians who lived through the events of February 1937, and whose stories are told in the pages that follow. This cast of characters, many members of which will already be familiar to readers of *The Plot to Kill Graziani*, hail from various walks of life, but all have one thing in common: they lived through the greatest single atrocity that Ethiopia has ever known. Interviews of these witnesses provided crucial testimony and made possible the development of a spatial and temporal framework to which the published accounts could be attached, thus making this reconstruction possible.

A word must be said about the published sources. Written accounts by Ethiopian witnesses are typically rich, and provide important details, but, as mentioned above, they are brief, few in number, and inevitably have a narrow geographical focus, since no Ethiopians were permitted to move freely around the city at the time. Furthermore, the surviving witnesses tend to be those who were living in areas of the city exempted from destruction because of their strategic importance to the Italians, which means that they often viewed the events they describe from a distance. There are, however, a small number of detailed accounts of atrocities committed in the detention camps into which the able-bodied residents of the city were herded, of which the most notable, written by the well-known author Temesgen Gebré not long after the event, was recently published by his daughter, Sister Kibre Temesgen.

Memoirs by Italians who were soldiers in Addis Ababa at the time of the massacre are rare, the only significant examples known to me being the recently published reminiscences of Sergeant-Major Alessandro Boaglio and Lieutenant Alberto de Turris. Reports by Eritreans working for the Italians during the massacre are also scarce, but a few are quite detailed in parts, such as the affidavit provided for the United Nations War Crimes Commission by the interpreter *Dejazmach* Rosario Gilaezgi.

Some of the most informative documentation is in the form of diplomatic dispatches transmitted throughout the massacre by the British, American and French envoys in Addis Ababa. Despite their diplomatic status not being officially recognised by the Italian de facto authorities, they were the only non-

Italians relatively free to drive in the city and maintain a wide communications network at that time. Based on detailed accounts by the envoys themselves, their staff and other members of their communities, and with access to telegraphic facilities, their reports are authoritative, although they understandably tend to be preoccupied with incidents in the immediate vicinity of the legation concerned.

In addition, there are brief reports by a number of foreign correspondents (though typically not based in Addis Ababa), published in various European and American newspapers, and, finally, accounts in Sylvia Pankhurst's *New Times and Ethiopia News*, particularly those consisting of primary source material gathered by her Anglo-Indian correspondent, Wazir Ali Baig, in Djibouti from Addis Ababa residents fleeing the conflagration. They were gathered through the good offices of *Betwedded* Andargachew Massay, the Ethiopian consul in Djibouti who, despite strong objections from Rome, continued in that office for much of the Occupation.

The most notable exception to this pattern of reporting is the extensive and detailed but little-known eyewitness account by a Hungarian medical practitioner resident in Addis Ababa, Dr Ladislas Shashka (*nom de plume Sava*). His description of what he witnessed during the massacre is the most complete and graphic ever written. His manuscript was for some time in the custody of Professor Stanley Jevons, secretary of the Abyssinian Association in England, who withheld it from publication until Mussolini brought Fascist Italy into the Second World War in alliance with Nazi Germany in June 1940. Then Jevons released it to the *New Times and Ethiopia News*, in which it was serialised.[1] While this delay meant that the report was not disclosed to the international community at a time when it might have had most impact, the advantage to today's student of the Occupation is that, being written soon after the massacre, and then being kept under lock and key, the account could not have been influenced by subsequent reports or speculation, nor could it have influenced them. It thus remains one of the most important and independent accounts of the events of February 1937.

If Dr Shashka's account is the most complete, one of the most compelling reports of the massacre is that of the British representative in Addis Ababa, William Bond, who was acting consul-general at the time. His 13-page dispatch, sent to London less than two weeks after the event, is explicit and pulls no punches. Bond speaks with authority, and the fact that his report confirms much of what Dr Shashka has to say is a compelling endorsement of the doctor as an honest rapporteur. However, Bond's report was deliberately suppressed by the British government under Prime Minister Neville Chamberlain, in accordance with Britain's policy of appeasement towards the rising tide of Fascism in Europe. Thus, despite appeals by the post-Liberation Ethiopian government, it was never published; in fact, its existence was at one time denied in Parliament by the Foreign Office.

So far as information on the nature of the atrocities carried out during the massacre is concerned, the bronze reliefs on the *Yekatit 12* monument at Siddist Kilo in Addis Ababa are not to be disregarded. It is clear from the accuracy with which the events are depicted on these reliefs that their design was guided by serious research, the result being that they have historical integrity. Commissioned by Marshal Tito, the President of Yugoslavia, only 18 years or thereabouts after *Yekatit 12*, when there were still many living eyewitnesses to be consulted, the images constitute an important source of information on the massacre.

It is not the intention of this book to suggest that the behaviour of the Italians towards the population of the countries they invaded was necessarily any more barbaric and cruel than the behaviour of other nations in similar circumstances in the past. Nonetheless, owing to the generally low awareness of the impact of the occupying forces on the nation-states that Fascist Italy invaded, it may be difficult for some readers—particularly younger ones—to accept the facts of the Massacre of Addis Ababa, let alone believe that it was perfectly in accordance with the norms of contemporary Italian socio-political culture. Morally outrageous though the tenets of Fascism may seem to the 21st-century reader, the fact is that a substantial proportion—probably the majority—of the population of Italy came to believe in them. Certainly, the brutal and pitiless invasion of Ethiopia—or what some modern writers describe as the rape of Ethiopia—was immensely popular with Italians at the time, once it was clear that the invasion was likely to succeed. For this reason, despite the fact that this book is basically a narrative account, I decided to include a discussion of these norms and an overview of the policy context in which the Massacre of Addis Ababa was conducted—while not suggesting that understanding why the perpetrators acted as they did absolves them of guilt for having done so.

In 1978, at the Fifth International Conference of Ethiopian Studies at the University of Illinois, the late Professor Alberto Sbacchi pointed out that there were no reliable estimates of how many people lost their lives during the massacre of Addis Ababa.[2] In this book I have attempted to respond to Professor Sbacchi's concern by including a section in which I endeavour to arrive at a credible estimate of the number of victims. I am aware that, given the absence of records and the passage of time, any estimates made now are bound to be only indicative. Nonetheless, I have tried to make the best use of the information available, and should readers be in a position to point out significant gaps or shortcomings in the data or the analysis set out here, or indeed if they have any testimony or photographs that could be included in a second edition of this book, I would be grateful to hear from them via the publisher.

1

BACKGROUND

PRELUDE

Ethiopia and Italy had a lot in common. By the early 20th century they were both inheritors of an ancient culture and an empire dating from pre-Christian times that over the centuries had shrunk and lost its prestige and glitter, although, unlike the ancient Roman empire, the Ethiopian empire had never ceased to exist. Both had a written language that dated back several millennia, was the root of their contemporary language, and was still used in ecclesiastical rites.

Both powers had adopted Christianity as official state religion in the 4th century, but it was Ethiopian Emperor Ezana at Aksum whose head appeared on the world's first coin to carry the Christian cross. Both became theocracies, although Rome lost its pre-eminence to the 'new Rome' at Byzantium, while Ethiopia could claim unbroken adherence to the earliest canons of Orthodoxy. Rome boasted the relics of St Peter, while Ethiopia pronounced itself to be the guardian of the True Cross and the Ark of the Covenant. Both theocracies persecuted heretics during the 15th century, although the Ethiopian holy fathers never descended to the level of barbarity of the popes in burning them en masse and in public.

Both empires had been subject to invasion, had fallen on hard times and had fragmented into warring states. They had both made strenuous efforts at reunification in the mid-19th century, and had both been recognised internationally as nation states only in the second half of that century. By then many of their citizens were living off the land as illiterate subsistence farmers in a largely feudal system, scratching a living from the soil as their oxen pulled antiquated ploughs around crumbling monuments of a bygone age. And by the 20th century both were monarchical sovereign states, although the Ethiopians could claim a far longer royal bloodline than the Italians.

For more than two thousand years these two ancient powers coexisted peacefully. Indeed by the 15th century a Pontifical Ethiopian College was operating in the Vatican, King Alfonso VI had dispatched artisans and artists from Naples to adorn the churches of Ethiopia, and a marriage pact had been proposed between the two royal families. And by the early 16th century a number of Venetians and their compatriots had achieved acclaim and distinction as members and employees of the Ethiopian imperial court.

Yet by the late 1930s, the despairing Emperor of Ethiopia was moved to declare, 'The Italians have always been the bane of the Ethiopians.' So what occurred in the interim to turn these two fading imperial powers with such a long history of peaceful cooperation into mortal enemies?

Paradoxically, the root cause of Ethiopia's problems with Italy actually had nothing to do with Ethiopia. They originated with concerns in 19th-century Rome that the newly created nation-state of Italy was viewed as 'the poor man of Europe', and had been left behind in the European scramble for colonies and dominions overseas. The resultant inferiority complex led to a desire for expansion and conquest, and the roots of what was to become a pattern of unprovoked aggression towards Ethiopia can be traced to the opening of the Suez Canal in 1869. For the first time, Italians had direct access from the Mediterranean to the Red Sea, and this led to the purchase of the Red Sea port of Assab in 1885 by an Italian Lazarist missionary named Giuseppe Sapeto, on behalf of the Rubattino Shipping Company of Genoa. The transaction meant that the Italians now possessed a tiny and faraway but strategic outpost on a hot and humid coastal strip traditionally tributary to the Ethiopian emperors.

By 1884 a revolutionary Islamic anti-Western movement known as Mahdism was coming to power in the Egyptian Sudan, and its followers had besieged a number of Anglo-Egyptian outposts there. The British sent a diplomatic mission to the neighbouring Ethiopian Emperor Yohannis IV (r. 1872–89), requesting military assistance to relieve their outposts. The Emperor agreed, in return for the restoration to Ethiopia of the port of Massawa, an important Red Sea trading hub at that time nominally under Egyptian control but claimed by Yohannis, and certain Ethiopian borderlands that had also fallen under the control of the Egyptians. Thus in June 1884 the Ethiopian and British governments signed a treaty.

Yohannis's forces successfully relieved the Anglo-Egyptian garrison towns, thus allowing the British troops to depart unmolested. However, a few months later, in a shocking act of treachery, the British broke the treaty. Wishing to curb French expansion in Africa, and taking advantage of the fact that Italy now had a foothold (Assab) on the Red Sea coast, in February 1885 they facilitated an Italian occupation of Massawa. In turn, the Italians, who had already started shipping hundreds of soldiers into Massawa, took advantage of Britain's strategy by seizing adjacent coastal areas, and making armed incursions into the interior. Yohannis had been deceived. Until the Italian occupation of Massawa he had welcomed Italians seeking to establish trade relations with Ethiopia, for he needed European technology and military hardware. However, Italian geopolitical and military imperatives were by 1885 overtaking the desire for purely economic ties. Outraged by Britain's behaviour, and unable to dislodge the Italians in Massawa, Yohannis wrote a bitter letter of protest to Queen Victoria, but to no avail.

Having thus obtained control of Massawa with the connivance of the British, the Italians were not deterred by Yohannis's claims on the port city. Although there was significant parliamentary and popular opposition at that time in Italy to expansion overseas, the government in Rome had already set its sights on the ancient empire of Ethiopia itself. The relatively lush and much more extensive Ethiopian highlands would be a much greater prize than the coastal strip, which consisted only of sweltering and unproductive lowlands. Italy seemed determined to occupy Ethiopia, Ethiopians or no Ethiopians.

By late 1886, the Italian military had penetrated inland and established themselves at a fort named Sahati. Yohannis was outraged. Troops under his redoubtable military commander, *Ras* Alula, twice tried to take the fort, but failed to make headway against the better-armed Italians. Hundreds of the *Ras*'s brave but lightly armed men died in the slaughter, while almost no Italians fell. On the night of 25 January 1887 the surviving Ethiopians withdrew and, after tending to their wounded and taking a few hours' rest, rose to move away towards a location known as Dogali. However, in the early morning light the weary *Ras* and his men were surprised to learn that there were yet more heavily armed Italian soldiers in the vicinity. Climbing a nearby hill to check, *Ras* Alula was stunned to see coming towards him a column consisting of no less than 520 armed Italian soldiers and 50 *askaris* recruited from the coastal region getting into combat position, with machine guns at the ready.

Taken unawares, and having no machine guns himself, the quick-thinking *Ras* positioned his men strategically some 700 metres from the invaders, and not before time, for moments later the machine guns opened fire. Yet another battle had begun.

Fortunately for the Ethiopians, the Italian commander, like several of the military officers sent by Rome to Ethiopia, was a poor strategist. He had led his men across exposed and vulnerable terrain and, despite the advantage of his machine guns, was outmanoeuvred by the Ethiopians. By utilising the topography to their advantage, the ill-equipped Ethiopians managed to turn the tables on the smaller but better-armed enemy force. Staying as far as possible out of sight, and having put the machine guns out of action, the weary but still energetic Ethiopians gradually surrounded the invaders. After two hours of heavy shooting the Italians realised that much of their fire was falling short, they were running out of ammunition, they were outnumbered and in a serious situation. They attempted a retreat, but it was too late, for the Ethiopians chose that moment to make one of their traditional 'do or die' mass onslaughts. Fifteen minutes later it was all over; few Italian soldiers had survived. Although the Italians liked to refer to the incident as 'the Dogali massacre', the fact is that in an extraordinarily gracious gesture the victorious Ethiopians put the Italian wounded in the shade, gave them water, and allowed their compatriots to come from Sahati and collect them the next day.

It transpired that the Italian column had been sent from the coast to reinforce the troops at Sahati, and its destruction shook Italy. But in a move that came to be characteristic of the Italians whenever they overreached themselves in Ethiopia, the government in Rome disguised its aggressive intentions and military incompetence by striking a posture of hurt innocence. Amazingly, the Italians, who seem to have had a penchant for myth-making, managed to project themselves in Europe as the wronged party. The hundreds of valiant Ethiopian patriots who had been mown down at Sahati did not feature in the Italian narrative; it was the invaders, who had no business to be there in the first place, who were presented as the fallen heroes. According to the myth created in Rome, the Ethiopians were 'treacherous', and despite the fact that it was *Ras* Alula who had been taken by surprise by the sudden and unexpected appearance of the armed column advancing through his territory, the story was reversed, suggesting that it was the Ethiopians who had organised a 'cowardly ambush'. The Ethiopians' honourable treatment of the enemy wounded was not acknowledged; rather, according to the Italian media, the Italians had

had to confront 'twenty thousand savage cannibals'.[1] Finally, far from being deterred, the government in Rome presented their defeat at Dogali as a reason to extend their incursions into Ethiopia yet further, and even pressed for compensation. Indeed, the presentation by the Italian government of the débâcle as a 'heroic stand' by the invading force succeeded in stirring up such a groundswell of patriotism in Rome that domestic support for the government was strengthened, and popular opposition towards overseas expansion was largely silenced.[2]

Yohannis was not intimidated, or even moved, by the European reaction. When Britain joined the chorus of condemnation of Alula's 'cowardly ambush', the Emperor treated the accusation with the contempt it deserved. He told Queen Victoria, '*Ras* Alula went down to enquire, "What business have you to do with other people's country?"', and told her envoy, '*Ras* Alula did no wrong: the Italians came into the province under his governorship, and he fought them, just as you would fight the Abyssinians if they came to England.' But Yohannis's logic failed to move the British government, which for political reasons was quite happy to see the Italians installed in the Horn of Africa. No sooner had the dust settled at Dogali than the Italians re-established themselves at Sahati, with the backing of London.

Alula, who told the British that the Italians could occupy Sahati only if he could go as Governor to Rome, was in favour of a military showdown with the Italians. But while the Emperor was apparently preparing to follow his advice, news came that the Mahdists, who since Ethiopia's intervention in the Sudan on behalf of the British regarded Yohannis as their enemy, had swept into western Ethiopia, and sacked the former capital of Gondar. Distracted by the shocking news, the Emperor turned his attention to the Mahdist incursion. Although his armies succeeded in repelling them, the sovereign tragically died in the process, at the border town of Metemma in March 1889.

Meanwhile, desperate for an ally in their battle with Emperor Yohannis, and for an opportunity to see a pliable friend of Italy on the imperial Ethiopian throne, the Italians had entered into a treaty of friendship with King Menelik, then sovereign of the highland Ethiopian Kingdom of Shewa (r. 1865–89). Following the death of Yohannis, Menelik succeeded him as 'King of Kings', or Emperor, of Ethiopia. In 1889, desiring, like his predecessor, trade and the products of European technology—notably guns—the new Emperor signed an agreement with the Italians commonly known as the Treaty of Wichalé. Under the treaty, Menelik's sovereignty was recognised, and he was granted rights to import arms through Italian territory, that is, through Massawa. But the most significant provision of the treaty was the extension of Italian rule beyond the coastal strip to include part of the Ethiopian highlands, thereby creating Italy's first colony and depriving Ethiopia of its own access to the sea—a move for which future generations of Ethiopians would pay a heavy price. Proclaimed in January 1890, the newly acquired colony was named by the Italians Eritrea.

The treaty also gave Ethiopia the right to communicate with other foreign powers through the Italian government. However, in a first step towards hegemony over the Ethiopian empire, but apparently unknown to Menelik, the Italian-language version of the treaty circulated to European governments made it *mandatory* for Ethiopia to conduct its foreign relations through Italy, thereby in effect turning Ethiopia into an Italian protectorate. Claiming he had been deceived, Menelik, now installed in his new capital of Addis Ababa, declared the treaty invalid. But even more alarming was the news that the Italians, whose government under Francesco Crispi had become increasingly authoritarian and militant, had crossed the Eritrean border and occupied much of northern Ethiopia, including most of Tigray. His patience exhausted, in 1895 the exasperated Emperor realised he had no choice but to check the Italian advance. Declaring a general mobilisation, he set out from Addis Ababa to march north in an extended campaign across more than 800 kilometres of Ethiopian territory, rallying around him fighting men from all parts of the empire.

The Ethiopians' first engagement in this campaign was with a Major Toselli, who, in a display of extraordinary incompetence on the part of his superior officers, had been instructed to position just 2,000 soldiers—now mostly Eritrean *askaris* rather than Italians—on a mountain known as Amba Alage in the Ethiopian province of Tigray, to confront Menelik's cousin, *Ras* Mekonnin, who commanded a force of some 40,000. The gentlemanly *Ras*, who had earlier received a royal reception on a state visit to Italy, tried to avoid a confrontation by imploring Toselli to retreat and leave Ethiopia. In the communications muddle that was characteristic of the Italian military, Toselli had reportedly been sent orders to retreat, but they had gone astray. So unaware of his new instructions, the dutiful major stood his ground.

Despite the advanced weapons of the Italians, which included exploding artillery shells that caused heavy losses among the Ethiopians, the outcome of the battle was never in any doubt. The Italian force was surrounded and obliterated. Toselli fought bravely, and despite their own extensive casualties, the Ethiopians buried him with full military honours. But true to form, Italy's invading forces were once again projected in Rome as blameless heroes whose deaths at the hands of the 'treacherous' Ethiopians should be avenged for the 'prestige and honour of the motherland'.

The next move in Italy's comedy of errors was to send 1,200 of its soldiers into Ethiopia under a Major Galliano, to entrench themselves in a hurriedly built fort at the former Emperor Yohannis's capital of Meqele. Arriving with his army of 25,000 victorious Ethiopian warriors straight from Amba Alage, the ever-considerate *Ras* Mekonnin wrote to Galliano, 'I pray you leave this land, otherwise I will be forced to make war.' 'Do what you have to do,' was Galliano's jingoistic reply—not unusual among the Italian commanders, who frequently behaved as if they had the upper hand even when common sense would suggest otherwise. Mekonnin encircled the fort, and in due course was joined by Menelik with his enormous force of another 100,000 men. Criticised by the Emperor for having waited too long without attacking, thereby allowing the Italians to complete their fortifications, the peace-loving *Ras* was obliged by the Emperor to commence battle. The Italians were well armed and well protected behind thick walls; hundreds of Ethiopians died in the attack that followed. This triggered a change of strategy by the Ethiopians. They pulled back, took control of the springs flowing into the fort, and waited.

Surrounded by Menelik's forces, with dwindling food rations and no water supply, the Italians would have all starved to death, were it not for the Emperor's astonishing magnanimity. After several days, despite the loss of life that the Ethiopians had suffered, Menelik allowed the Italians to evacuate the fort unmolested, with their women, children and wounded, all transported on several hundred mules that he personally provided. In Rome Menelik's unparalleled generosity went unremarked and unappreciated. Instead, its beneficiaries became the heroes of the day, and Galliano was promoted *in absentia*.

Menelik resumed his campaign northwards, nonchalantly passing by some of the Italian garrisons, in a clear demonstration of his unquestioned authority as Emperor, and in an implicit rejection of the invaders' claims to any part of Ethiopian territory. Finally, his armies took up a strategically advantageous position near the small town of Adwa—not far from the Eritrean border— and waited. Despite the new arrivals who had been disembarking at Massawa on a daily basis, the Italian force assembled to confront the Emperor was hopelessly outnumbered and, being without cavalry, was slow-moving. Thus one might imagine that having discovered to their cost on several occasions the formidable and agile enemy awaiting them, the Italians would have made a strategic withdrawal back into Eritrea and reconsidered their options. But for the Italian High Command, discretion was not the better part of valour. Commitments had been made, and 'honour' was at stake. The Italians seemed determined to join battle, and decided to advance to a series of small mountain passes only a few kilometres from the Ethiopians, apparently hoping to draw the Emperor's massed armies out onto open ground.

By now even the most generous-hearted commander in Menelik's position would have found his patience wearing thin, and it is testimony to the Emperor's fairness and desire not to shed blood that he once more attempted a peace settlement, only to be met yet again by haughty rejection. Nonetheless, the Ethiopians still did not want to be the ones to open fire. Accompanied by the Empress Taytu, who had never trusted the Italians, as well as other dignitaries of the empire and commanders of the troops, Menelik stood his ground and waited for the Italians to attack.

The earlier humiliating defeats suffered by the Italians had only increased the resolve of Rome for revenge and conquest, thus putting political pressure on the normally cautious commander, General Oreste Baratieri, whose brigadier-generals seem to have been overenthusiastic to engage the enemy, and had almost certainly underestimated the size and capability of the force they were facing. Fed with inaccurate—and sometimes false—intelligence on the geography and the enemy, and beset with jealousies, power struggles and poor communications between their commanders, Baratieri's battalions failed to take up their prescribed positions. Instead, their commanders conducted a series of reckless manoeuvres, resulting in their fighting units advancing far beyond their allocated positions.

On the night of 29 February 1896, for reasons that have never been entirely clear, one of the Italian advance columns isolated itself from the main force, and early in the morning engaged one of Menelik's massed armies. The engagement was a costly mistake, for greatly outnumbered by a wave of spirited, tenacious and well-armed men fighting for their nation's survival on their home ground, the column was rapidly enveloped. Furthermore, instead of staying close to provide back-up, the other Italian columns had also managed to isolate themselves, and one by one they were also overwhelmed. The lessons of Dogali and Amba Alage had not been learned. For many, surrounded as they were, retreat became impossible, and the Italian army dissolved into terror-stricken pandemonium.

By the end of the day the invaders had paid a heavy price for their commanders' recklessness and incompetence: the entire Italian army had been routed, the majority of its soldiers had been slaughtered, and thousands taken prisoner. After marching them back to Addis Ababa, the honourable Emperor sent the Italian prisoners of war, numbering almost 2,000, back to Italy for the most part unharmed, and even allowed the Italians to retain the colony of Eritrea. But the Kingdom of Italy earned the scorn of Europe, for its repeated attempts to invade and subjugate Ethiopia had ended in decisive and ignominious failure. The government fell, and all thoughts of foreign conquest were banished. The humiliation of the Battle of Adwa, together with the shameful fiascos that had led up to it, was to haunt the Italians for decades to come.[3]

The Italians fared little better as a result of their involvement in the First World War (1914–18). Despite their staying out of the war until they were sure of joining the winning side, it left their economy in ruins, and in the Treaty of Versailles that brought the war to a close, their former allies—the French and the British—did not consider that the Italian military contribution had warranted the territorial rewards that the Italians were expecting.

Humiliation piled upon humiliation, the country was thus ripe for revolution, and ready for a hero who would restore national pride. One of the leading champions of socialism in pre-war Italy had been a young anti-war politician named Benito Mussolini. But as the war progressed, he changed his views and joined the army. In 1919, after the war, emerging as a fanatic with a flair for propaganda, he formed a new militant political party: the Partito Nazionale Fascista (Fascist Party), named after the *fasces*—an axe wrapped in a bundle of rods—the symbol of imperial unity and might carried by the magistrates of ancient Rome.

Backed by gangs of armed *squadristi*—largely battle-hardened ex-First World War servicemen for whom violence had become a way of life and who attacked and terrified the opposition—Mussolini won sufficient support to transform the party into a political force. In 1922 King Victor Emmanuel III, overestimating Mussolini's popularity, asked him to form a government. The die was cast; Mussolini was now in control.

Mussolini was not simply a dictator; his aim was to create a totalitarian state in which every individual would fit, and which would be self-perpetuating. The agenda of Fascism, a form of political religion, included militarism, the glorification of war, and the revival of the grandeur of ancient Rome. Thus it is not surprising that the idea of yet another invasion of Ethiopia surfaced several times during the early years of his rule. In a bid for increased influence in Ethiopia treaties of friendship were tabled, and the King of Italy and

Mussolini himself hosted the future Emperor Haile Selassie in a state visit to Italy in 1924. In 1925 Mussolini formally declared Italy a totalitarian state, and in 1926 Minister of Colonies Luigi Federzoni told him that Italy's possessions in north and east Africa (Eritrea, Libya and Italian Somaliland) should be considered as 'a springboard for a vaster and more varied expansion of the influence of Italy in the world',[4] which would inevitably begin with the annexation of Ethiopia. In 1930—the year of Haile Selassie's coronation as Emperor—Federzoni's successor, Emilio De Bono, asked for a large increase in the budget for Eritrea and Italian Somaliland, stating that it would be 'ridiculous to speak of the Romanity of the Empire if expansion beyond the confines of the Fatherland was not considered possible'.[5]

By the early 1930s, with Europe in the throes of the Great Depression, the case for invasion was growing stronger; the *Duce* needed a glittering military conquest to galvanise support for his government. He talked much about the need for more 'living space', and seems to have reconciled himself to the idea that Italians could live successfully only in other people's countries. Indeed, Italy was unusual in Europe in having such large colonies of its nationals eking out an existence overseas; in New York alone there were over a million Italians who had fled their impoverished motherland, and in Argentina there were another million.

Despite Emperor Haile Selassie's programme of modernisation, Ethiopia had not been part of Europe's industrial revolution, and had not focused on manufacturing and the military to the extent that the European countries had managed to do. Ethiopia was thus Mussolini's most obvious choice for an invasion, being a relatively softer target than it had been 40 years before.

Thus by the spring of 1934 Italy was making large-scale preparations in both Eritrea and Italian Somaliland to facilitate yet another invasion of Ethiopia, with the *Duce* presenting a variety of different reasons, depending on the audience. Many jumped at what they saw as an opportunity to restore Italian prestige and raise the nation to the level of the imperial powers of Britain and France. Notwithstanding Mussolini's massive ongoing campaign for higher population growth (based on his claim that the population was far too low), his rationale for the intellectuals was that Italy was overpopulated, and that access to Ethiopia's natural resources was therefore necessary for national development and expansion. Thus for the land-hungry peasants of the south, fertile and virgin farmlands would be theirs for the asking. For the liberals, he declared that conquest would constitute a 'civilising mission' to a 'barbaric' country, while the military was inspired by the prospect of avenging Adwa. Finally, the Catholic Church expected the invasion to 'open the gates of Ethiopia' to penetration of the Catholic faith. There was a story for everybody.

The intended reality, however, was none of these. The attack on Ethiopia would actually launch the first phase in Mussolini's expansionist drive linking Eritrea and Italian Somaliland, to be followed by the conquest of British-controlled Sudan and Egypt, constituting a bridge to Libya and eventually to the French colonies. What the *Duce* would refer to as 'Fascism International' would ultimately provide Italy with hegemony over the entire Mediterranean Sea, with control over its eastern and western access, and annexation of states in central and eastern Europe. To serve this purpose, Mussolini's orders required the nation-state of Ethiopia to be annexed and dismantled, and the land turned into a vast military-industrial complex. One million able-bodied Ethiopians would be drafted into a new 'black army' to fight the other wars of conquest that were to follow, and the thousands of Italian labourers brought in to open up Ethiopia to the invading armies would be deployed to establish countrywide infrastructure to facilitate military and administrative control, including the construction of 'fifty or so airfields' and the development of a 'massive metallurgical industry' to support large-scale armaments manufacture, based on the rich mineral deposits thought by the Italians to exist in Ethiopia. The invasion, which was to be supported by the use of chemical warfare by the Regia Aeronautica, the Italian air force, was scheduled to be launched at the beginning of October 1935.[6]

To meet these geopolitical and military goals, the Ethiopians would have to be 'pacified', that is the existing polity would be destroyed, the ruling class and the intelligentsia would be liquidated, all actual and potential opposition would be crushed, and the consequently leaderless masses would be subjugated. Ethiopian secondary education institutions would be closed, and the major task of the primary schools would be to prepare men for the army.

There was only one problem: Italy had no justification for an attack on the faraway, peace-loving sovereign state of Ethiopia, which had been a member of the League of Nations since 1923, even before countries such as Germany, Russia and Turkey. Furthermore, Ethiopia hosted diplomatic embassies not only of all the major powers, but also Italy itself, which, in addition to its embassy in Addis Ababa, was unique in maintaining consulates in many of the secondary towns. Thus Mussolini needed an excuse to trigger the invasion.

Since the coronation of Emperor Haile Selassie in 1930, the Italians had been making incursions into Ethiopia from Italian Somaliland, while striking

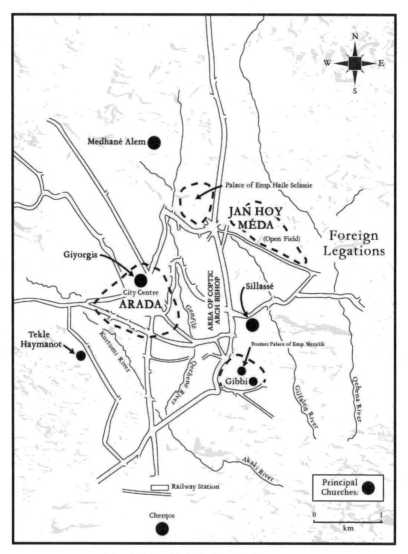

Map 1. Addis Ababa before the Occupation

a posture of innocence under the Treaty of Wichalé. In August 1934 Mussolini, worried that some observers might have seen through the charade, ordered his commanders 'to put an end to the rumours ... which make out the aggressive nature of our aims towards Abyssinia', stressing that 'the line to be adopted with regard to Abyssinia must be such as to create the general impression that we still continue to adhere faithfully to the Treaty'.[7] A few weeks later, in November 1934, there was an incident at a remote desert oasis named Welwel, some 100 kilometres inside Ethiopian territory, where the Italians had unilaterally established a military post. Soon after an Anglo-Ethiopian border survey commission arrived, shooting broke out, in which more than 100 Ethiopians and 30 Italian colonial soldiers died. Once again striking a posture of hurt innocence, the Italians claimed that Welwel lay within their colony of Italian Somaliland, and even went so far as to demand apologies and damages. But the fact is that Mussolini's claims were deliberately intended to provoke the Emperor, for the *Duce* wrote to the commander-in-chief of the Italian armed forces in Africa, 'In case the *negus* [Emperor Haile Selassie] has no intention of attacking us, we ourselves must take the initiative.'[8]

The Emperor, who had a strong belief in the rule of law and, in particular, great faith in the League of Nations, took the case to the League. However, the League procrastinated for eleven months, thus allowing Italy to complete a massive build-up in military capacity. The League applied sanctions on the importation of weapons by both sides in the coming conflict, but since Italy had a well-developed domestic armaments industry, this strategy negatively affected only Ethiopia. The only sanctions that would have constrained Italy's ability to invade Ethiopia were a ban on the sale of oil to Italy and closure of the Suez Canal to its ships. However, neither of these strategies was adopted.

Choosing appeasement in an attempt to ensure that Mussolini's energy was focused on Ethiopia rather than Europe, where he was making threatening noises, the French and British declared themselves neutral, and on 3 October 1935 the Italians launched their long-awaited war of conquest. For his public pronouncement, and taking advantage of the fact that Ethiopia was situated in the Horn of Africa, Mussolini selected the rationale of colonialism. Although this was illogical, Ethiopia being a recognised nation-state in which Italy herself had diplomatic representation, he said that the justification for war was that Italy deserved to have an empire, and was not satisfied with 'a few crumbs from the rich colonial booty gathered by others'. The Ethiopians, whose country was to be invaded, who were to be subjugated and slaughtered, and whose government was to be destroyed, were not considered. In fact,

1. 13 Sept. 1935: The Emperor broadcasts an international appeal in the face of the impending Italian invasion. From right to left: Lorenzo Ta'izaz; Emperor Haile Selassie; Minister of Foreign Affairs *Blattén Géta* Hiruy Welde-Sillassé; Hiruy's son, Feqade-Sillassé Hiruy; unidentified adviser

Ethiopia was not even mentioned, other than in the bizarre statement 'With Ethiopia we have been patient for forty years! Enough!'

ADDIS ABABA ON THE EVE

Addis Ababa of the early 1930s was centred on the Emperor's palace, or *gibbi*, with an urban 'core' to the north-west, and a collection of villages scattered far and wide on and around the surrounding hills.

In the city centre, known as Arada, were a number of public and commercial buildings of permanent and semi-permanent construction, several of which still stand. Taxis—of American or European manufacture and driven by Ethiopians or Eritreans—operated from taxi stations, but the majority of Ethiopians travelled on foot or, in the case of the nobility, by mule, followed by retainers. The Emperor and his courtiers travelled by limousine or mule, depending on the occasion.

2. 'Downtown' Addis Ababa in 1935. The sleepy ambience of the city centre is highlighted by the number of vehicles on the pavements and the number of pedestrians on the roads—a pattern that still prevails in much of Addis Ababa today

The Emperor's Swedish military adviser, General Virgin, captured in his memoirs a typical street scene in the city, observed from his house, which stood on a road just west of Amist Kilo. 'Along the street', he wrote, 'among hooting cars, bleating flocks of sheep, sedately advancing camels and half-running pedestrians, comes a grand lady ... riding slowly on her richly caparisoned grey mule.' Wearing a white dress, the lady has her *shamma* drawn up over her face and she is protected by a retinue of servant-girls and armed men. From the opposite direction a man comes riding, and they meet outside the General's house. 'Both stop, take off their hats, and bow deeply in the saddle.' The lady's servants hold up their *shammas* to hide her completely from the eyes of passers-by while she is lifted from the saddle, and meanwhile the man has dismounted. They stop and bow several times, a conversation begins which lasts a few minutes, then after many more bows they return to their steeds. 'With bared heads and renewed deep bows', the General concludes, the parties pass each other, and proceed on their separate ways.[9]

Although most photographs of early Addis Ababa show the relatively modern buildings and streets of the urban centre, the majority of the approximately 100,000 Ethiopians in Addis Ababa lived in urban and peri-urban 'villages', clustered into *sefers*. They or their parents before them had moved from the rural areas to the city and dwelt in traditional thatched cottages, which they built largely as they had done in the countryside. The destruction of houses and their occupants during the massacre of Addis Ababa would be focused principally on these communities.

Viewed from above, Ethiopia's capital city looked like a large cluster of villages hidden in a vast forest, for the area had been planted with fast-growing eucalyptus trees imported from Australia by Emperor Menelik.

It is not suggested that Addis Ababa was a paradise. Nonetheless, the fact remains that the country was free, and Menelik's original capital was now a rapidly expanding metropolis, with significant Armenian, Greek and Indian communities. A resident Hungarian doctor said of Ethiopia, 'I think there is no country in the world where aliens have enjoyed greater liberty and more polite treatment.' All the major powers had legations in Addis Ababa, and it was a reflection of the magnanimity of the Ethiopian government towards Italy that it allowed the Italians to establish consulates throughout the countryside.[10] As the British war correspondent George Steer put it, 'When I first came to Addis Ababa it was a peaceful town ... Everybody was friendly, the

3. In the 1930s, most residents of Addis Ababa lived in traditional thatched cottages and preserved their rural way of life. The massacre of Addis Ababa was concentrated mainly in 'urban villages' such as this one

town was orderly, prosperous, happy; the ... population of Addis Ababa was healthy, for it had room to spread and breathe the uncontaminated air. Ethiopia was still free, and when the Emperor drove through the town the people applauded him ...'

Ethiopia's principal exports were hides, skins and coffee, and the main economic activity of Addis Ababa was trade. Near the Cathedral of St George was the city market, set out in three sections surrounding an area occupied by the customs administration. There was no armaments industry; one could scarcely imagine a city less equipped to face the onslaught of a military juggernaut such as the one now heading for its gates.

* * *

INVASION AND OCCUPATION

The invasion of Ethiopia was notable for its ferocity and brutality. Emperor Menelik's fair and honourable responses to Italy's earlier unprovoked attacks on Ethiopia's sovereignty were rewarded by an almost complete disregard for even the most basic tenets of civilisation. Furthermore, unlike Ethiopia, Italy had been able to take full advantage of the upsurge in science, technology and manufacturing that had taken place in Europe since the Battle of Adwa, and so this time around the invaders were far better equipped than the Ethiopians.

In late 1935, as the invasion was launched, the Ethiopian government, in accordance with its international legal obligations, allowed the Italian ambassador, his several consuls-general and other diplomatic staff, to peacefully pack and depart the capital by train.

Virtually abandoned by the world, the Ethiopian barefoot levies, armed with little more than a few guns remaining from Adwa, put up a stubborn resistance to the invasion. But their bravery and pride were not enough. Using long-outdated military strategies, and with their traditional white clothes making them easy targets, they faced an enormous modern army that included elite Italian regiments as well as numerous battalions of well-armed colonial (mainly Eritrean) soldiers who constituted a formidable fighting force, the principal livelihood open to Eritrean men being the military. The Ethiopians were also confronted with overwhelming military superiority in the form of new weapons of mass destruction with which most Ethiopians were unfamiliar: tanks, machine guns, flame-throwers and, above all, a massive air force equipped with chemical weapons. In the world's first mass aerial bombard-

4. Emperor Haile Selassie, a firm believer in protocol and international conventions, permitted the Italian diplomats and their families to leave the Italian legation in Addis Ababa peacefully and depart from the country as their government's invasion of Ethiopia was launched

ment of civilians[11]—a harbinger of what would become commonplace in Europe a few years later—entire settlements with their inhabitants were obliterated, with no distinction made between combatants and non-combatants, or between men, women and children. Despite vigorous and dogged resistance, which often slowed the invading forces to a crawl, ultimately all was lost in Tigray at the decisive Battle of Maychew, where, on 31 March 1936, led by Emperor Haile Selassie himself, the Ethiopians faced defeat. The sovereign's retreating army was then methodically drenched by the Italian air force with asphyxiating gases.[12]

The journalist George Steer later summarised in a brief but bitter cameo the suffering and sacrifice of the Ethiopians in their desperate defence that cost a quarter of a million Ethiopian lives:

> Remember the bombs, remember the sprayed *yperite*, the smoking circle of artillery and machine-guns that burnt the blood out of the Ethiopians as they sat on their mountains defending their country and their women. Remember the destruction of the Red Cross in the plains of the North and along the shallow rivers of the

South. Remember the revolutions, how western money was used to turn Ethiopian against Ethiopian; the villages in flames, the flies fat with man's putrefaction, the paths stagnant with corpses, the caravans scattered and destroyed. Remember the tens of thousands that died in battle and bombing and the bitter retreat. These fell, remember, that civilisation should prevail.[13]

Having led his armies at Maychew, and having personally suffered from the effects of Italy's chemical weapons, the Emperor realised that the enemy had launched an offensive beyond all the international rules of war, and that the fall of Addis Ababa was inevitable. Thus on 2 May 1936 he left to play the only card he had left: the pursuit of Ethiopia's cause on the international stage. Departing by train, he travelled with a small entourage to Jerusalem and then on to exile in Britain.

Three days after Haile Selassie's departure, General Pietro Badoglio arrived in Addis Ababa at the head of his invading forces. On 9 May 1936, following the fall of the town of Dessie, Mussolini appointed Badoglio Viceroy of Ethiopia, and on the same day General Rodolfo Graziani, who had been commanding on the southern front, was promoted to Marshal. The Occupation had begun.

For the Italians, Badoglio was the hero of the hour. As Mussolini appeared on a balcony in Rome's Piazza Venezia the tumultuous crowd was delirious with joy and adulation. Fascism had finally launched its programme of international conquest, Pope Pius XI was overjoyed by what he declared to be a 'beautiful victory by a great and good people', Italians felt they now had an 'empire', and Adwa was avenged. It was the *Duce's* finest hour. In characteristic style, King Victor Emannuel of Italy proudly but paradoxically assumed the title 'Emperor of Ethiopia', Ethiopia, according to the Italian government, having ceased to exist (being absorbed into Italian East Africa).

A few days after the Occupation began, in an unexpected turn of events, Badoglio's proposals for running the newly conquered territory, based on governance through traditional local leaders—a policy consistent with that of the ancient Roman empire—was rejected by Alessandro Lessona, Minister of Colonies. Knowing Mussolini's plan to use Ethiopia for strategic military purposes, he not surprisingly replaced the proposals with a strategy based on direct totalitarian rule. The rejection was followed by Badolglio's resignation, and on 21 May Graziani was appointed Viceroy in his place.

The *Duce* now declared 'demographic expansion' as the purpose of the invasion. The *modus operandi* of the European scramble for Africa had been based on the taking over of large tracts of land where no nation-state was deemed to exist, and establishing a polity with law and order that would be welcomed by the ignorant and grateful—and thus loyal—natives. Then a colony of Europeans in need of 'space' would arrive. The fact is, of course, that the Italian attack on Ethiopia was not a colonial expeditionary force taking over an unclaimed tract of land; it was nothing less than an unprovoked and ruthless armed invasion by one nation-state of another. Thus, not surprisingly, the idea never took root in the age-old empire of Ethiopia, any more than it would in any of the other countries that Mussolini would invade and pronounce to be Italian 'colonies'. With the exception of a handful of souls who tried unsuccessfully to make a living in remote and besieged homesteads, the overwhelming majority of Italians fleeing the slums of Naples and the poverty of Sicily continued to seek their fortune in New York and South America rather than in the killing fields of occupied Ethiopia. That was, however, of no great concern to Mussolini, who actually had no real interest in Ethiopia per se, and never even visited the land he claimed to have conquered. For him the invasion had served its purpose. He had his glittering victory, and Graziani's iron fist would ensure the necessary 'pacification'. The *Duce*'s popularity was never greater, and his attention soon turned elsewhere. Albania would be next; it was announced that Nice, Corsica and Tunisia would follow;[14] and before long Greece and Yugoslavia would resound to the cry of '*Duce! Duce!*'

The de facto acquiescence that the invasion received from the League of Nations constituted a critical test case. It was an assurance not only for Mussolini, but more importantly for Adolf Hitler, who at that time held the *Duce* in high esteem and modelled his Nazi movement on Italy's Fascism, that there would likewise be no resistance to Italy and Germany invading their weaker neighbours—an assurance that the international community was to bitterly regret having given, as Haile Selassie became only one of many forlorn heads of state gathering in exile in London in the years that followed.

Throughout the Occupation, Italian control in Ethiopia was limited principally to the locations where they were able to maintain garrisons, for while some of Ethiopia's military commanders and traditional leaders submitted to the invaders soon after the beginning of the Occupation, many of the submissions were opportunistic, and several never submitted. As happens in any invaded nation, Ethiopian resistance groups dug in for a long war of attrition in the countryside.

Though poorly coordinated, the war of resistance was hard fought and brutal, for, upon his appointment as Viceroy, Graziani was given virtually unlimited powers by Mussolini, whereby any Ethiopian soldier who continued fighting after Addis Ababa had been occupied, and any civilian who resisted in any way or was simply suspected of not welcoming Italian overlordship, was branded a 'rebel' and was either shot or hanged in public. It was the beginning of a five-year military occupation underpinned by a policy of terror—the creation of extreme fear—the technique used extensively by Graziani to 'pacify' the Libyans, used by Badoglio to cow Ethiopian civilians during the invasion, and now brought to perfection once again by Graziani.

POLICIES OF REPRESSION

The military machine that carried out the invasion of Ethiopia consisted of Italian officers and soldiers of Italy's regular army, Blackshirt militia, *carabinieri* (military police), and colonial troops (Eritrean, Libyan and Somali *askaris*). The regulars were conscripts; the Blackshirts were volunteers. In all, including militarised workers, the invading forces totalled around a quarter of a million men. All Italian men over the age of 18 years were liable for compulsory military service, and the conscripts, some of whom were reluctant soldiers, were subject to quite tough military discipline. On the other hand, the Blackshirts had more freedom of action, higher pay, and were subject to considerably less discipline. So who were these Blackshirts, or Camicie Nere?

Mussolini had established the Milizia Volontaria per la Sicurezza Nazionale (MVSN) in 1923, based on the 'action squads' he had used since 1919 to attack communists and destroy opposition to his Fascist Party. Initially the movement was made up of ex-servicemen aged 21 to 36, including many First World War veterans, supported by reservists up to the age of 56. Whereas regular army soldiers were conscripted into full-time service, the Blackshirts were called upon only when required. Nonetheless, in the second half of the 1920s they were increasingly deployed as a military fighting force, and by 1930 were being attached as a combat force to regular army divisions. The invasion of Ethiopia in 1935 provided a boost to the evolution of the Blackshirts as a military entity, deploying 97,500 of them to fight alongside 70,500 regular soldiers.[15] In all, six Blackshirt divisions were deployed for the invasion of Ethiopia, incorporating several flame-thrower units.[16]

Having a semi-permanent structure with divisions and battalions that were created only after they were mobilised, the Blackshirts were mainly deployed as light infantry, and were largely limited to the weapons and equipment that they could carry.[17] Of all their weapons, the dagger, or *pugnale*, was their pride and joy. Generally hanging from the belt in a scabbard on the left, it not only symbolised the Fascist glorification of violence, but also had been a favourite of the soldiers of ancient Rome, who discovered that a quick stab to the soft parts of the body was more likely to be fatal than the sweep of a sword. Similarly the bayonet, suspended from the belt like a long sheathed dagger next to the *pugnale*, ready to be fixed to the barrel of the rifle, was another essential weapon. The dagger and bayonet would be used extensively against Ethiopian soldiers and civilians during the Invasion and Occupation.

While most of the regular military stayed on in Ethiopia during the Occupation, encountering continued resistance from the Ethiopians on a daily basis, most of the Blackshirt divisions were disbanded and sent back to Italy in 1936, many of them for redeployment in Spain. However, on 9 June 1936, Graziani, concerned about the extent of resistance around the capital, gave orders for the largest of the Blackshirt divisions—the 6th Blackshirt Division named the 'Tevere', which had fought under his command on the southern front—to move from Dessie to Addis Ababa, where it remained.[18]

The majority of the 14,567 men originally forming the 'Tevere' were stationed in the north of the city at the former Teferi Mekonnin School, which backed onto the French legation. The 'Tevere' also included a transport section garrisoned at the northern corner of the open field of Jan Méda (see Map 1), as well as many militarised labourers, the Centuria Lavorati, who were engaged in road-building and construction and were issued with shovels.

5. Blackshirts of the 6th 'Tevere' Division, 219th Legion, mobilised for action in Ethiopia

It is clear from the crimes against humanity that have been perpetrated during the 20th and early 21st centuries that no single race or nationality has a monopoly on wanton violence. Yet the astonishing level of brutality and cruelty of the Italians towards defenceless civilians during the Invasion and Occupation is at first sight baffling, and calls for an explanation. It is thus instructive to examine the extent to which Fascism provided the essential ingredients for war crimes: nationalistic fervour, the glorification of war, dehumanisation and demonisation of the enemy, and a culture of brutality and impunity.

Patriotism, Adulation and Policies of Terror

There was certainly no shortage of patriotic fervour. Although some Italians had earlier expressed reservations about the wisdom and morality of invading Ethiopia, by the time the invasion was announced, the Italian public was, in the words of Professor Angelo Del Boca, so possessed by nationalistic frenzy that 'when the sirens sounded and the church bells pealed, its people rushed shouting and cheering into the streets and squares in a passionate patriotic stampede unique in our history'. He continued, 'thirteen years of Fascist propaganda and indoctrination had made an indelible mark on the Italians, particularly the younger generation'.[19]

As Professor Christopher Duggan points out, much of the enthusiasm for the invasion of Ethiopia stemmed from feelings that it would expiate the trials and tribulations suffered by Italy. He quotes a young recruit writing to Mussolini in early August 1935 a letter that shows how completely the young generation had swallowed the *Duce*'s propaganda. The invasion would gain a 'most beautiful victory' for Italy, would 'avenge the error of Versailles', and would make Italy a great nation. 'Today', he added, 'the youth of Italy has leapt forward as one man, ready to bear arms and carry into the barbarian land the symbol of Rome, symbol of greatness, civilisation and strength.'[20]

Although Ethiopia did not participate in the First World War and thus had nothing to do with the Treaty of Versailles, the idea that annexing Ethiopia and handing over its resources to Italians would 'avenge the error of Versailles' was widespread among Italians. The vast majority of the invaders, many of whom were from poor peasant families, actually believed, absurd though it may seem today, that they were each entitled to a piece of far-away Ethiopia.

Furthermore, by the time of the invasion, there was no shortage of precedents in the Italian armed forces for atrocities against civilian populations. Although many of the more recent Blackshirt volunteers were too young to have fought in the First World War and had no prior military experience, most of their commanders (normally seconded from the regular army) were well versed in a tradition of cruel and brutal operations against civilians, particularly in the subjugation of Libyans. In pre-Fascist times Italy's predilection for invading existing polities rather than focusing on 'unclaimed' lands had drawn them to invade and attempt to conquer Libya, then a polity of the Ottoman Empire. Carried out in 1911, the invasion represented the world's first military use of airpower and aerial bombardments. Later, under Fascism, in its attempts to 'reconquer' Libya, which had proved a hard nut to crack, Italy was the first country to widely use chemical weapons in violation of the 1925 Gas Protocol.[21]

Together with mass detentions, such aggressions laid the ground for what was rapidly to become a national tradition of extraordinary brutality in the suppression of unarmed civilian populations.[22] In the initial conquest of Tripoli, the Italians had acquired a reputation for large-scale and indiscriminate civilian massacres,[23] and in the 1920s under Fascism, which as we have seen glorified militarism and war, Graziani built on that reputation by the use of implacable force and the establishment of his favourite technique for separating a subject population from the potential influence of 'rebels': concentration camps. Graziani's infamy in Libya as a champion of civilian abuse earned him appellations such as 'the Butcher of Tripoli' and 'the Hyena of Libya'.

In fact, during the span of Fascism, from 1922 to 1943, with the exception of some of the fighting against Russia, the Italian army forces would be concentrated principally on attacking civilians and makeshift armies cobbled together to resist the invasion of their countries. Herding unarmed women and children into concentration camps, reprisals in the form of civilian massacres whenever they met resistance, and looting and burning of villages were the order of the day. From Libya to Ethiopia, and from Greece to Yugoslavia, the principal modus operandi of the Italian army was 'counter-insurgency'.

6. Viceroy Rodolfo Graziani was a career soldier. Having fought in Libya and Austria during the First World War, he went on to achieve notoriety as military commander in Libya

To understand the ease and speed with which the Italians incarcerated innocent Ethiopian civilians during the Occupation, it is necessary to digress briefly into the question of the role of penal camps in Italian colonial governance. All European colonial powers adopted, from time to time, measures of varying degrees of severity as instruments of control and punishment of colonial subjects, but the widespread use of penal camps, along with the deportation of subjects to such institutions, was a remarkable phenomenon in the countries that Italy invaded. It was a cornerstone of Italian government policy in Libya long before Fascism, and was subsequently written into the public security laws of 1926 and 1931. Used to 'free a territory from its inhabitants' as well as to separate subject populations from the possible influence of 'rebels', the camps were widespread, and many were very brutal. About half of the population of eastern Libya was interned in 16 concentration camps operating in the Cyrenaica region (north-eastern Libya) between 1930 and 1933. Considered to have constituted one of the grimmest aspects of Italian history, these camps experienced a death rate of around 40 per cent. Mandated by Mussolini, the camps were ordered by Badoglio and organised by Graziani.[24] Thus the incarceration of Ethiopians in concentration camps did not constitute an isolated episode, for, far from being wartime improvisations, these camps had their origins in the well-established policies of pre-Fascist Italy.

Terror being one of the pillars of Italian governance in Cyrenaica, mass executions, deportation and internment of civilians were standard practice. However, under Fascism they were elevated to previously unknown levels. And even if they were not designed to be death camps, the conditions in many of the concentration camps were appalling, with death by starvation and disease, punishments and public executions daily occurrences. Explaining the principle that Italy's subject populations were expendable, Badoglio offered as a rationale in Libya the need to create 'a broad and clear territorial separation' between 'rebels' and the general population. He declared, 'I do not deny the extent and gravity of the decision which will amount to the ruin of the so-called subject population. But by now the path has been marked out and we must follow it to the end *even if the whole population of Cyrenaica should perish*' (emphasis added).[25]

The experience gained by Graziani in Libya was promptly applied to Ethiopia. The principal concentration camp to be used for incarcerating Ethiopians—Danane, in Italian Somaliland—had been built by late 1935, when the invasion of Ethiopia was launched, and was thus ready for use before the Occupation had even begun.

The tradition of civilian abuse was maintained during the resistance that continued in Ethiopia after 9 May 1936. Once Haile Selassie's military commanders with their outdated strategies had been vanquished, their successors began adopting guerrilla tactics. In many ways, albeit on a limited scale, the Italians had now met their match, and their response was determined but shameful. Contempt for the enemy had been generated by the demonisation of the Ethiopians through the state-controlled media; the dapper, dignified and highly acclaimed Ethiopian Regent who had charmed the crowds and been given a royal welcome by King Victor Emmanuel and Mussolini on his official state visit to Rome in 1924—the Emperor to whose imperial court Italian diplomats had long been proud to be accredited—was transformed by Mussolini's propaganda machine into a caricature. Haile Selassie was now a hideous, subhuman creature with an enormous beaked nose and gigantic deformed feet—a monstrous potentate ruling with revolting brutality over a horde of ignorant savages, who for their own good needed to be forcibly subjected to what Rome called 'Italian civilisation'. Many of the Blackshirt volunteers swallowed the propaganda, and against such a background the Italian military commanders' numerous written instructions for suppression of the local population through the spreading of terror, and demands for 'merciless rigour' and 'the destruction of everything', rapidly created a culture of brutality and impunity. It is not surprising that Italians who might not have been predisposed to abuse the Ethiopians often did so with enthusiasm, as can be seen from some of the photographs in this volume.

For those who might otherwise have pitied their victims, the high-flown objectives of Italy's purported civilising mission meant that no pangs of conscience were felt, particularly as the Ethiopians were now claimed to be a grossly inferior species. In any case, the Blackshirts were, in effect, above the law. A recruit named Dom Pietro, who joined the Blackshirts at the age of 28, quickly rose to the level of sub-officer, and was deployed in Ethiopia in 1937. Recalling the impunity with which the Blackshirts behaved, he admitted that they maltreated Ethiopian women, and 'quelled those poor people with force'. Citing an instance in which a Blackshirt had killed an Ethiopian for not cleaning the soldier's boots, he said that he was unable to punish the soldier 'because the *militia* couldn't be punished, couldn't make a mistake and were the living examples of the Roman legions—the glory of the "Empire"'.[26]

And if the required brutality proved too much for delicate Italian sensibilities, there were always the Libyan *askaris* standing by. A 26-year old medical officer, Manlio La Sorsa, wrote that the Italian soldiers delegated their 'barbaric, ferocious and inhuman' methods to the Libyans, owing to the apparent inability of Italians to bring themselves to commit the heinous crimes required. 'We Europeans,' he wrote, 'who are easily moved and readily forgive, would never have been capable' of committing the 'vandalic acts' required.[27] Although La Sorsa does not deny that the Italians authorised the 'barbaric and inhuman' excesses that characterised the invasion of Ethiopia, his claims that his fellow countrymen were not directly engaged in such excesses are belied by the numerous photographs showing them gleefully carrying out the most sordid and cruel atrocities.

Terror from the Skies, and Attitude Towards International Conventions

The Italian air force, or Regia Aeronautica, played a critical role in creating terror among the Ethiopians. As early as 1932 Emilio De Bono, then Minister of Colonies, was arguing that the invasion of Ethiopia would depend on having 'a powerful Air Force, one that can bring terror to the [Ethiopian] empire's capital and major cities'. In response to a letter from Mussolini in December 1934, he advised that the invasion should be prepared 'by a violent bombing action on all the principal Ethiopian cities', including Addis Ababa. 'Everything must be destroyed with incendiary exploding bombs,' he wrote. 'Terror must be disseminated throughout the Empire.'[28]

When the time came, terror from the air was indeed the cornerstone of the invasion strategy. It was further strengthened during the Occupation, for the most common method of fighting the Ethiopian Patriots was to follow what had been done to their counterparts in Libya: blackmailing them into surrender by terrorising the civilian population. This was accomplished largely by the bombing and aerial spraying of Ethiopian men, women, children, animals, crops and drinking water with toxic chemicals provided by the Asmara-based Chemical Warfare Service known by the Italians as Section K. The use of these chemical weapons was not, however, an isolated decision or a panic reaction. Neither was it, as was later claimed, a response to atrocities committed by pastoralists against two Italian pilots who had had to make an emergency landing after carrying out a horrific and deadly bombardment of their remote community. The deployment of chemical weapons was all along intended to be a key component of the invasion strategy, to be deployed in the event that the Ethiopians put up serious resistance. To this end, as early as August 1935, before the invasion had begun, and despite Italy's being a signatory of the Gas Protocol, Section K had set up an advance unit near Mogadishu in neighbouring Italian Somaliland. By October, when the invasion of Ethiopia was launched, an extensive chemical weapons facility covering 12.5 hectares had already been established, with facilities for preparing deadly liquids and gases for the invasion. It contained no less than 17 warehouses for storage, together with 35,000 gas masks and decontamination materials for the protection of Italians.[29]

By December 1935, the Italian advances on both northern and southern fronts had virtually ground to a halt in the face of Ethiopian resistance, despite the fact that many of the Ethiopian rank and file were barefoot and often armed only with antique rifles or spears. The Italian response was the deployment of poison gas and the systematic bombing of Red Cross field stations.[30]

Until 1996, when the Italian government finally admitted having used chemical weapons, the reaction in Italy to charges of having used such weapons in Ethiopia was denial and, indeed, self-righteous indignation at such a suggestion. Yet the intention to use such weapons was common knowledge by September 1935, when Mussolini was being exhorted by members of the public to demonstrate to Britain Italy's power and military might by displaying 'diabolical savagery' in Ethiopia, and 'saturating the plains of Somalia and the forests of the Tigray in a week with gas bombs'.[31]

For the Italian military the great value of chemical weapons was as a means of destroying Ethiopians—soldiers and civilians—en masse from a safe distance without having to confront the enemy directly, but only from aeroplanes. That this policy was public knowledge in Italy is illustrated by the fact that in early October a group of Bologna university students, having swallowed the propaganda put out by Mussolini regarding Ethiopians, exhorted him to conduct 'a war to the limits', against the 'inhuman, vile … bestial Abyssinian people', and insisted that in the process the Italians should deploy chemical weapons to ensure that they themselves would not be put in harm's way. In a telling admission of Italian martial spirit that probably infuriated the *Duce*, who always proclaimed multiple deaths on the battlefield as positive expressions of Italian valour, they wrote, 'We are Italians, and we want to keep our sacrifice to a minimum—especially when it is a question of fighting animals like the Abyssinians.' The students knew that chemical weapons were expensive but regarded them as the most effective method of dispensing death from a safe distance, in order to preserve the lives of young Italians 'who will be needed as the productive forces of tomorrow's empire'. Dismissing international treaties as applying 'only to weak states', they went on to reassure the *Duce* that, in any case, 'How can anyone check if Italy does or does not use gas?'[32]

By January 1936 the application of poisonous chemicals had been further refined by the Regia Aeronautica to provide for high-volume discharge during low-flying aerial spraying of Ethiopian civilians and their crops, animals and water sources, bringing the number of Ethiopian deaths during the invasion to an estimated total of more than a quarter of a million. After the Italians reached Addis Ababa in May 1936, chemicals were also used liberally on the remaining fighting units, as instructed by Mussolini in telegrams to Graziani marked 'Secret' and passed on, in, for example, Graziani's orders to General Alessandro Pirzio-Biroli to secure the surrender of the Ethiopian commander *Dejazmach* Wendwessen Kassa in September: 'Since it is now impossible to use troop columns owing to the rains, ... the goal can be attained by use of all means of destruction from the air day after day, mainly using asphyxiating gases.'[33] Poison gas, administered from the air, was used extensively and, after the Occupation began, became the principal weapon used against the resistance.

The reluctance of the Italians at the time, and for the next half-century, to admit the use of chemical weapons against the Ethiopians appears to have stemmed not from fear of being accused of breaking international law—of which, after all, the invasion of Ethiopia itself was already a massive breach. Rather, it was the shame of having to admit that they were deploying a weapon widely viewed in Europe as one of last resort. Thus, given the poorly armed Ethiopian army, and the absence of an Ethiopian air force, resorting to chemical weapons would suggest military incompetence in conventional warfare on the part of the Italians, or even cowardice. Since documentary evidence now shows that during the Occupation much of the gas was used on civilian targets, the reluctance to admit its use becomes even more understandable, as does the Italians' decision not to use gas against the British during the war of liberation in 1941, which they would not have been able to hide from the international community.

One of the remarkable features of Mussolini's government was its posture regarding the principles of the International Committee of the Red Cross (ICRC), and the international conventions to which Italy was signatory—not only the Gas Protocol, but also the Geneva Conventions, which included the 1929 Convention on the Treatment of Prisoners of War. Even before the invasion of Ethiopia, it was clear that there was a fundamental incompatibility between such conventions and Italian government policies. The *Duce's* creed exalted war; chivalry, compassion and humanitarian service were regarded as weakness and cowardice. As Dr Edoardo Borra, who was director of the Ospedale Italiano (Italian Hospital) in Addis Ababa and representative of the Italian Red Cross during the Occupation, admitted many years later to the historian Rainer Baudendistal, there was at the time a widespread view in Italy that 'the Hague and Geneva Conventions and the Gas Protocol had no value, because this was a war that had to be fought'.[34]

Italy's breaches of the Geneva Conventions in terms of her disdain for the symbol of the Red Cross in Ethiopia have already been analysed in meticulous detail by Baudendistal. While neither side can be said to have been above reproach, the Regia Aeronautica deliberately attacked Ethiopian, Swedish and British Red Cross field hospitals and facilities whenever it suited them for military reasons, for the carrying out of reprisals, or to silence doctors who might reveal Italy's use of chemical weapons. And when later challenged by the international community, officials such as Graziani, in a face-saving exercise for Mussolini, had no qualms in falsifying pilots' flight reports to make it appear that the strikes had been unintentional.[35]

Under Fascism, any service rendered to the Ethiopians—including the activities of the Red Cross—were viewed as acts against Italy, and thus both the Ethiopians and the foreigners working in the national Red Cross field hospitals in Ethiopia were treated as the enemy. As Dr Borra put it, many Italians considered the foreign doctors 'as mercenaries, sell-outs and against us'.[36]

This belief is illustrated by the Italians' treatment of two Polish Red Cross workers encountered on 16 February 1936, during the invasion of Ethiopia, when Blackshirts of the '23rd March' Division overran a cave in an area they had raided the day before. The head of the Red Cross field hospital, Dr Maksymiljan Stanisław Belau, and his assistant, Tadeusz Medyński, were arrested, in contravention of the Geneva Conventions. Under threat of execution, they were chained and beaten, thrown to the ground, and made to kneel, before being photographed. After being put on a starvation ration and subjected to a series of mock executions, Dr Belau had a nervous breakdown. Detained and interrogated, they were both imprisoned in Massawa. Ironically, Belau was threatened with execution unless he retracted his previous reports of mistreatment of Red Cross staff by the Italians. Disavowing the reports under threat of death, both men fortunately survived.[37]

While theoretically the Italians adhered to the Convention on the Treatment of Prisoners of War, the reality was a far cry from the principles they expounded. Conditions in the prison camps were typically abominable. But although thousands of Ethiopian civilians would be herded into camps, there were actually very few Ethiopian prisoners of war; during the Invasion none of the camps held more than a few hundred of them. Thus the question is: What happened to all the Ethiopians missing in action? It is a mystery. The Ethiopian army totalled between 250,000 and 350,000 men in the field, and in many of the battles tens of thousands of Ethiopians lost their lives in action. One would thus expect that the Ethiopians taken prisoner would be numbered in many tens of thousands, yet the Italian sources confirm only a handful becoming prisoners of war. Baudendistal points out that *in one day* in the Battle of Adwa (1896) the Ethiopians took more prisoners than the Italians did in the *entire war of invasion*, which lasted some seven months.[38]

So far as the present author is aware, this issue, referred to by Baudendistal as an intriguing discovery, has never been closely examined. It is well known, and attested by numerous written instructions, that from the beginning of the Occupation in May 1936 combatants who surrendered or were taken prisoner by the Italians were shot. But were prisoners of war also killed en masse during the war of invasion, in flagrant breach of the Geneva Convention?

Dr Ladislas Shashka, a Hungarian medical practitioner who had been living in Ethiopia for three years before the Italian invasion, spoke fluent Italian, Amharic and Oromifa, and was to write a detailed account of the massacre of Addis Ababa under the pseudonym Dr Sava, attended and interviewed many wounded Ethiopians during the war of invasion, and also met many Italians during the Occupation. In the process, he was shocked to learn that indeed the Italians massacred their prisoners. He concluded that the Invasion was 'a war of extermination', and described the mode of Italian warfare as mass murder.[39]

Statements made by high officials of the Italian military confirm Dr Shashka's conclusions, and give the impression that the Italians regarded the killing of prisoners as perfectly normal. For example, Graziani made a chilling comment in his report of a battle in the Ogaden in April 1936, when thousands of Ethiopians were slaughtered: 'Few prisoners, as is custom of Libyan troops [fighting under Italian command].'[40] Badoglio himself informed Minister Lessona that had the two captured Polish Red Cross medical staff been soldiers, they would have been killed. He wrote, 'Your Excellency can rest assured that had they been combatants, there would be no need to talk about them now.'[41] And according to none other than Mussolini's son-in-law Galeazzo Ciano, the Fascist Party secretary Achille Starace, a leading architect of Fascism throughout the 1930s and military commander responsible for occupying Gondar, not only shot Ethiopian prisoners, but used them for target practice, aiming at their hearts. Concluding that the victims were not suffering enough, 'he shot them first in the testicles and then in the chest. Eye-witnesses reported these details.'[42]

Impunity

It is not the purpose of this book to dwell on the atrocities carried out during the Invasion and Occupation prior to, or after, the massacre of Addis Ababa. However, the methods of implementing the Fascist policy of terror throughout Ethiopia constitute an essential part of the context in which the massacre of Addis Ababa was conducted, and so they cannot be ignored. These methods, for which written instructions were repeatedly issued, included the massacre of civilians, the destruction of entire villages, and execution on the slightest pretext. Neither were these atrocities committed in the 'heat of the moment'; they were often ordered in writing, and frequently photographed at leisure.

The most common forms of execution were hanging, and shooting by firing squad. Other methods included skinning alive; beheading, followed by public displays of the severed head on a pole in the medieval manner; putting victims into aeroplanes and throwing them out alive; hanging victims in stress positions, leading to slow death by gangrene; and the burning alive of families in their houses using flame-throwers.

7. An Italian soldier and two *askaris* pose for the camera beside their Ethiopian victim, who is dying from gangrene

BACKGROUND

The atrocities, carried out with revolting barbarity, are well chronicled, for the Italians left behind numerous written official instructions authorising them. It is not surprising that none of the many photographs of these excesses betray any sign that the perpetrators thought they were doing anything to which their superiors might object. On the contrary, those responsible were usually behaving with impunity, smiling, and clearly wanted the scenes to be photographed.

A modern Italian scholar, Professor Giuseppe Finaldi, identifies removal of the risk of punishment as one of the key contributing factors to a massacre. In the case of the massacre of Addis Ababa it was made clear that the perpetrators would not be held accountable for anything they did; their actions would, in fact, be lawful: 'The more Ethiopians murdered, and the more brutality shown, the more one's loyalty to the Italian viceroy was affirmed.' 'The Graziani killings', he wrote, were 'permitted on the direct authority of Rome'.[43]

Graziani himself frequently made it clear that when it came to dealing with his perceived enemies, there should be no restraint on the licence given to the

8. 'We Europeans, who are easily moved and readily forgive, would never have been capable of committing the vandalic acts that were indispensable for keeping this treacherous and ignorant people in check.'—Manlio La Sorsa. Nevertheless, we see here Italians happily entertaining themselves with the grisly trophies hacked off their Ethiopian captives

rank and file—both regulars and Blackshirts—to commit atrocities. On the contrary, he made it abundantly clear in his written instructions that they must suppress any residual feelings of sympathy, mercy or compassion, or what he referred to in his written orders as 'false pity'.

That the Viceroy's subordinates typically had no qualms in passing on such instructions may be judged from orders such as the one given by Captain Corvo, the *Residente* in Bahir Dar, to the chief of a group of *askaris* fighting for the Italians during the Occupation (in an area where for centuries all men traditionally carried guns, however ancient, albeit that few of them were serviceable): 'You are to punish without pity all persons found in possession of arms and ammunition. I instruct you to burn not only their houses, but also the persons themselves.'[44]

Turning the Tables

It is often said that people who have lived at the lowest echelon of society, with no power over anyone, sometimes become cruel and notorious when put in uniform and given the power of life and death over others. So it was that in the 1930s, when Mussolini's soldiers, many of whom were illiterate and from impoverished backgrounds, found themselves overnight superior in the pecking order to even the most distinguished and educated Ethiopians: 'Suddenly removed from the deadly monotony of Italian provincial life, from dull drudgery, starvation wages, and unemployment, they found in Africa a breathtaking spaciousness and the individual right to at least a small measure of power.'[45]

Eager, like the Vikings of old, to swap their inconsequential lives back home for the adventure and plunder of the marauding invader, all that was now required to turn the party rank and file into warriors worthy of Mussolini's 'New Fascist Man' was encouragement to be tough and assertive, as befitted their newly acquired 'master race' status. And such encouragement—and, indeed, compulsion—was definitely provided. As Christopher Duggan puts it, under Fascism every effort was made to get Italians to be 'less nice' and more masterful.[46]

The Graziani Factor

A significant factor throughout the Invasion and Occupation was a marked tendency on the part of the Fascist civilians, and particularly the lower ranks of the Blackshirts, for hero worship of the Viceroy. To understand this phenomenon and its impact on the culture of impunity during the Occupation, we must digress briefly into the subject of Graziani's background, appearance and character. As the scholar Dr Fabienne Le Houérou states, no general was ever as popular as Graziani. 'Fascist supporters were very fond of heroes ... The most amazing stories were told about him ... Journalists liked to underline his romantic and exotic destiny in the desert.' She points out that the international press was always flattering Graziani, and presented his image like a beautiful Latin medal. 'Graziani was strong, slim, and his features were of marble.'[47]

Graziani shared with Mussolini an obsession with ancient Rome, and cast himself as, in effect, a reincarnation of a Roman emperor. In an Italian archive Le Houérou found a notebook in which Graziani's worshippers endlessly praised and congratulated him, gave him noble titles and ranks, imagined being related to him, or called him a genius.

After interviewing Italian ex-soldiers who had fought during the invasion, attempted to become colonists, then stayed on in Ethiopia in reduced circumstances after the collapse of Italian East Africa, Le Houérou concluded that their social frustrations had led them to their extreme fascination for the Viceroy. 'They deny their own mediocrity in liking an exceptional character. The feeling of being such losers—powerless, marginal, forgotten in a mental desert—leads to passion for strength and brutality.'[48]

Thus Graziani's image of a handsome and heroic ancient Roman emperor fed Fascist values to the hilt, and in turn the rank and file of the party projected onto him the attributes of a superman—a 'real man', as one of Le Houérou's interviewees put it. Nothing could have been more effective in exacerbating a culture of impunity among the Blackshirts, each seeking to outdo the other in demonstrating their commitment to the party ideal.

Accountability

Finally, the existence of two parallel institutions, both reporting to Mussolini, complicated the situation in Addis Ababa, confusing the lines of responsibility and accountability. The military government of Mussolini in the 'new empire' was headed by Graziani (who as Viceroy also represented the King of Italy), while the Fascist Party was headed independently by a young but senior Blackshirt named Guido Cortese. Although Graziani was a member of the party, and would prove to be one of Mussolini's most loyal supporters, he was never comfortable with the party apparatus that gave Cortese a direct channel to Rome, and which complicated the position of the regular army vis-à-vis the buccaneering, freebooting Blackshirts. Although at times of military engagement the Blackshirts could be, and were, commanded by regular army officers under Graziani's command, for the rest of the time Cortese had as much control over them as—and often more than—Graziani did.

Another, related factor was the position of the Italian civilians who had been shipped to Ethiopia, the majority of whom were labourers or drivers. Almost all them—at least those who had accompanied the invading forces—were card-carrying party members, and in fact had to be in order to obtain work on the government-financed projects. Furthermore, their 'rest and recreation' activities were organised overwhelmingly by the party. Their primary loyalty was to Cortese rather than Graziani. Thus, while on ceremonial occasions in public the two men would stand shoulder to shoulder, there was always an uneasy relationship between them, in addition to the generation gap (Graziani was 54 years old; Cortese was 34).

* * *

9. Graziani borne on the shoulders of his admiring soldiers during a military campaign he personally commanded in southern Ethiopia shortly before *Yekatit 12*

BACKGROUND

WARNINGS AND FOREBODINGS

As we have seen, any Ethiopian soldier who continued fighting after Mussolini's declaration of the Italian empire on 9 May 1936, and any civilian who resisted in any way or was suspected of not wishing to submit to Italian overlordship, was branded by Graziani a 'rebel' and was shot. Since many Ethiopian soldiers were still in the field fighting under their commanders, this policy led to the cold-blooded slaughter of thousands of Ethiopian soldiers taken prisoner during battle. Even those who surrendered were executed, and civilians who in due course joined hands with the remnants of the Ethiopian army to continue the struggle suffered the same fate.

As early on in the Occupation as 5 June 1936, by which time many Ethiopian soldiers, lacking radio and telegraph, would not even have been aware that Addis Ababa had been taken, Mussolini was instructing Graziani, 'All rebels taken prisoner must be shot.'[49] The Viceroy's liberal interpretation of what constituted a rebel meant that he gave himself carte blanche to kill almost any Ethiopians he desired—whether military or civilian—for the flimsiest of reasons. Indeed, as we shall see, under Fascism the Italians routinely executed not only soldiers but even military commanders who surrendered, after solemnly promising them in the name of the King and government of Italy that they would not be harmed.

Werqineh Isheté (aka Dr Charles Martin), the Ethiopian minister in London, well aware of the implications of Graziani's policy and familiar with the Italians' strategies for civilian control in Libya, was outraged. The day after Mussolini's telegram insisting that soldiers taken prisoner must be shot, he protested, 'General Graziani has declared all Ethiopians still fighting for their country as "brigands" to be shot immediately, not combatants to be treated as prisoners of war. Against this illegal conduct, I make the strongest possible protest.'[50] The envoy's protests were to no avail, but he was right to be concerned. The Italian policy of killing prisoners is another factor critical to an understanding of the civilian slaughter that took place during the Occupation, and in particular the massacre of Addis Ababa.

Knowing the reputation of the Italian military in Libya, Dr Werqineh produced a pamphlet in London drawing attention to the likelihood of similar atrocities being conducted in Ethiopia. Published anonymously in the first half of 1936, the booklet stated that during Italy's unprovoked invasion of Libya in 1911, the Italians had 'disgraced and degraded themselves by committing shameful cruelties and atrocities on their defeated opponents', and its

10. In 1936, Dr Werqineh Isheté, Ethiopian minister in London, published a warning that Ethiopian civilians were likely to suffer atrocities similar to the 1911 three-day massacre of Tripoli

account of the massacre of Tripoli was to prove chillingly prophetic. It related how on 25 and 26 October 1911, the Italians began an indiscriminate civilian slaughter. 'The troops seem to have gone mad with the lust for blood. All the Arabs they met, men, women and children, even babes at the breast—were shot down without trial ... 4,000 Arabs perished in this way, in the space of three days.'[51] Dr Werqineh was explicit in his fears for Ethiopia: 'judging from the horrible events of the war in Tripoli ..., repetition of wholesale massacres of unarmed men, women and children is likely, only too likely, to occur.'[52]

The Ethiopian envoy's fears were widely echoed, for Italy's reputation for civilian massacre as a means of 'pacification' was well known. It was certainly a cause for concern for the British legation in Addis Ababa, as may be gathered from a statement by the chief of the Division of Near Eastern Affairs in the US State Department, in July 1936, just a few weeks after the Italians had announced the conquest of Ethiopia. In a memorandum reporting a conversation he had had with the British envoy regarding the difficulties that the foreign legations in Addis Ababa were having with Graziani's administration, the official wrote that the British ambassador fully expected 'a first-class massacre' in Addis Ababa in the not too distant future, and had said that one had only to recall the experiences of the Italians in subduing Libya to realise that 'they were given to drastic action in times of near panic'. 'It was the Latin way of doing things', he said, 'to resort to massacre in order to impress native populations with the authority of Rome.'[53] As we will see, these fears, as expressed by both Ethiopian and foreign diplomats, turned out to have been well founded.

YEKATIT 12

In December 1936, seven months after the beginning of the Occupation, former Ethiopian government officials in Addis Ababa, in collaboration with members of the Emperor's entourage in exile in England, recruited a number of activists to make a public strike against Graziani's seat of power in the capital, the Governo Generale. The sovereign's position in the League of Nations was precarious at the time, owing to the number of countries that were beginning to recognise the Occupation, and it was hoped that a dramatic public attack on the Italians would convince wavering members of the League that they were not in control of the country.[54]

When Graziani decided to imitate the former Emperor by holding a public alms-giving ceremony on Friday, 19 February 1937 (12 Yekatit 1929 EC), the plotters targeted this date for their strike. They had managed to recruit 'insiders' to lead the attack: two Italian colonial subjects of Eritrean origin who had left Eritrea for Ethiopia before the Italian invasion to pursue secondary education, which was prohibited for Eritreans in the Italian colony. Named Moges Asgedom and Abriha Deboch, both were employees of the Italian occupying authorities in Addis Ababa. In fact, Abriha was a member of Graziani's

11. The site of the attack of *Yekatit 12*, Emperor Haile Selassie's newly built Gennete-Li'ul Palace had been commandeered by the Italians for use as the seat of the Governo Generale early in the Occupation. The 3,000 Ethiopians present at the time of the attack were standing facing the portico at the front of the palace

Political Office, which was responsible for clandestine intelligence-gathering from local informers. But, disgruntled, he had become a double agent.

The activists threw a number of hand grenades at the Italian officials on the dais. Apart from the intended killing or maiming of Graziani, the objective seems to have been temporary immobilisation of the Italian High Command, either to encourage a civilian uprising or to facilitate an attack by *Ras* Desta's forces, or perhaps to trigger follow-up action such as hostage-taking.[55]

As a strike against the enemy in military terms, *Yekatit 12* was unsuccessful; there was no uprising, and no follow-up. Furthermore, no Italians died—at least no senior officials of the Governo Generale, although some, including Graziani, were injured. Moreover, despite his injuries, which triggered the temporary appointment of his deputy and ten weeks of hospitalisation, Graziani remained as Viceroy.[56]

The strike of *Yekatit 12* certainly met the requirement for a dramatic and public attack on the Italian High Command, but it was followed by a series of atrocities against the civilian population of the city that together constitute what became known as the Massacre of Addis Ababa. It is the story of those fateful days that is the subject of this book.

* * *

2

THE TRIGGER

SPEECHES AND SHOCKS

When the Italians made the arrangements for the alms-giving of 12 Yekatit, they were expecting trouble. Tipped off that there might be an attack, they put in place an extraordinary amount of fire-power—certainly more than they had previously mounted for a public meeting. The Gennete-Li'ul Palace had been turned into a fortress. Consisting largely of priests, the blind, the disabled, and mothers with their children, the crowd could scarcely have been less threatening, but the Governo Generale had deployed an unprecedented level of military force. Three senior military officers were reportedly on hand, commanding a force of no less than 93 heavily armed soldiers stationed around the inner courtyard,[1] supplemented by 30 armed *carabinieri*, and 25 *zaptie*, or colonial soldiers, under two junior officers.[2]

Lieutenant Meleseliñ, one of the Ethiopian officers of the Colonial Police on duty at the event, was to recall his amazement at the sight: 'Around the fence you could see those special guards fully armed with machine-guns, and looking as if they were hunting elephants.'[3] They were most likely Breda Model 30 automatic rifles—a light machine gun capable of 400–500 rounds per minute.[4]

But that was not all. The Italians had also mounted heavy machine-guns on the balcony above the dais, where they, too, were aimed at the defenceless crowd.[5] These were almost certainly water-cooled 6.5 mm Fiat-Revelli Model 14s, as shown in Figure 12, which were in common use by the Italians in

12. An Italian machine-gun company armed with 6.5 mm Fiat-Revelli Model 14 heavy machine guns for use in Ethiopia. Each gun had a small tank to hold the recirculating water used to cool it while in operation. The ritual of blessing of weapons was a popular one in the Italian armed forces

Ethiopia at that time. Mounted on a tripod with a revolving barrel, the Model 14 had been used with devastating impact during the First World War. Although not the most modern of machine guns, it was capable of between 400 and 500 rounds per minute, and was a terrifying weapon to mount against unarmed civilians.

When Graziani spoke, he delivered his speech with such fury and passion that Lieutenant Meleseliñ, who was apparently standing to the Viceroy's far right, some distance from the loudspeakers on the other side of the palace front, looked around to see how he might get away quickly, should the soldiers open fire. He was to recall, 'When we saw Graziani talking emotionally, throwing his arms in all directions, the veins visible on his neck, most of us stopped looking towards him and started to glance behind looking for an escape route.' From the tone of Graziani's voice and his 'frantic gestures', it was clear to Meleseliñ that the Viceroy 'wanted to force his message into everyone, not only with his powerful speech, but also with the guns of his guards'.[6]

The speeches over, the crowd began queuing to collect their *thalers*. After the first few beneficiaries had received their alms and returned to the crowd, the Italians started relaxing and chatting to each other. But at around 11.40

13. Following the attack of *Yekatit 12*, the camera catches dignitaries, soldiers and civilians in a state of shock running between the palace building and the crowd, amid noise, confusion and clouds of dust

am they were caught unawares. A grenade exploded out of their line of vision, above the portico. They heard the noise but were not sure what had happened. This was followed by another explosion, which created confusion on the dais, and then a third one which caught Graziani in the back as he turned to run back into the palace. A total of nine grenades were thrown.[7]

Having no idea where the grenades were coming from, or what was coming next, the Italians paused for a few moments and waited for the explosions to cease. Then, nothing happened. There was no follow-up; no uprising. There was a brief silence, as the unconscious Graziani was picked up and taken off the dais, to be carried to the car park and rushed to hospital.

At that moment Guido Cortese, the hard-line federal secretary of the Fascist Party, reportedly reached for his pistol and opened fire on some of the Ethiopian notables. That shot was the trigger for the Massacre of Addis Ababa.

SLAUGHTER AT THE PALACE

As Cortese let loose with his pistol, his Fascist colleagues followed suit, and *askaris* started attacking the crowd. Once the smoke and dust from the hand grenades had cleared, and the Viceroy's convoy had left the premises, it was obvious that the unarmed elderly and dispossessed posed no threat to the Italians, but at that point bloodlust took over from panic, as *carabinieri* and regular Italian and Eritrean soldiers, in a state of fury and excitement, added to the pandemonium by firing repeatedly into the Ethiopians.

Was Graziani dead or alive? At that moment no one at the palace knew, but the Italians had seen their hero felled, and their fury knew no bounds. Panic started breaking out among the shocked Ethiopians, but none could move, apart from those on the fringes of the crowd, a few of whom tried to run away.

However, it was too late. Had the commanders taken stock at that moment and brought the firing to an end, disaster could have been averted. But the high officials—some of them injured—were in disarray, and the initial shooting turned out to be the prelude to an onslaught from which there would be no escape, for within seconds the unthinkable happened. Over the heads of the injured Italians now being carried off the dais, the heavy machine guns above the portico burst into action, sending volley after volley into the defenceless throng. From the moment of that fateful decision there was no turning back.

14. *Askaris* start attacking the Ethiopians. Here the camera captures the moment that an *askari*, viewed from behind, begins an assault on the crowd, apparently with a long-handled whip. Trying to back off, those at the front are unable to escape from the tightly packed throng. Seconds later, the soldiers open fire

15. Apparently filmed from the balcony of the Governo Generale, people at the back of the crowd (in this section consisting mainly of Orthodox priests) are trying to run away as shooting begins and panic breaks out

Only a handful of the 3,000 Ethiopians at the palace that morning survived. For this reason, eyewitness accounts of the slaughter in those awful moments are rare. But one such report is that of Temesgen Gebré, a young Ethiopian Protestant who had been befriended and strongly influenced by Alfred Buxton of the British Bible Churchmen's Missionary Society, who had arrived in Ethiopia in 1934. Temesgen was trapped in the crowd as it was mown down. Eight years later, as a well-known writer, he told of his confusion, and how he was protected from the machine-gun fire by bodies falling on top of him: 'As the machine guns were firing from the balcony of the Palace, I looked at the Palace, to learn from which direction the bullets were coming. The heavy machine guns were firing exactly from the first floor of the Palace, and it seemed to me the Palace was moving backwards.'[8]

The use of machine guns in the palace grounds is well attested, and is confirmed in the memoir of Sergeant-Major Alessandro Boaglio of the Granatieri di Savoia (Savoy Grenadiers).[9] The well-known Ethiopian female Patriot Shewereged Gedle also reported that after the grenades were thrown, 'the

16. Temesgen Gebré was one of the few survivors of the carnage in the palace grounds

17. Ciro Poggiali, correspondent of Corriere *della Sera*, was on the dais when the bombers struck. His personal diary covering his time in Ethiopia, which he had kept secret during the Fascist period, was published in the 1970s

Italians then lost their heads and turned machine guns onto the crowd, killing indiscriminately.'[10]

The slaughter, originally triggered by panic and fear that an attack was imminent, was exacerbated by a general breakdown of discipline and order. The upshot was that, watching horrified as events unfolded in front of them, and unable to get away, the majority of the Ethiopians died where they fell in the palace courtyard, in tangled heaps of bodies.

Horror-struck but unable to do anything other than attempt to save himself, Lieutenant Meleseliñ watched in disbelief: 'The dead fall upon the dead. Human blood streams like floodwater from the rain. The priests and the deacons fall to their death carrying the cross.'[11] Amid the infernal din of the machine guns, the shouting, the screams, the dust, the smoke and the general pandemonium, a few at the front of the crowd tried to reach the safety of the palace building; those at the back tried to run away. Some tried in vain to hide; the elderly and infirm, and those trapped in the crowd, died where they stood.

But the killing was not confined to the regular soldiers, nor was shooting the only method of execution, for Blackshirts were beginning to turn up, chasing any Ethiopians they saw trying to escape. Some were carrying guns; others were pulling out their daggers. According to one eyewitness, 'All the Ethiopians found on the premises were killed by the Fascist militiamen, with revolver shots, bayonets, and daggers, whatever came readiest.'[12]

In the panic, the few Italian civilians present also seized whatever weapons they could find. One of them was an Italian journalist named Ciro Poggiali, who was standing on the dais behind Graziani when the putative assassins struck, and whose son later published his father's personal diary of the events in Ethiopia of 1936–7. Poggiali related how he quickly found himself a weapon as he—like many others—feared that armed 'rebels' had arrived in the city.[13]

The onslaught was so severe that few Ethiopians escaped the bullets, and most of those who did so were felled by daggers or shovels that were lying around at the side of the palace building where construction work was in progress. As the French envoy, Albert Bodard, put it, the scene was 'an indescribable *mêlée* ... Every Ethiopian was presumed guilty and had to be struck down.'[14]

A few managed to reach the gates, only to find their escape barred: the gates had all been slammed shut. No one was to escape the bullets. The *carabinieri* report released the following day was explicit:

> even the nobles [Ethiopian notables who had formally submitted and now accompanied Graziani's entourage] sought a way out. Meanwhile the park gates were closed by the police service [as a result of which] almost all of the defendants—

indigenous people—the poor and the notables—were trapped ... Meanwhile the *carabinieri* patrolling outside the park became aware of what had happened [and] took care to prevent the escape of the natives who were in the park.[15]

This report is, however, also remarkable for what it does *not* say. Not a word is said about the deadly purpose of trapping the crowd inside the compound— not a word about the machine guns. The 3,000 men, women and children simply disappear from the record.

Although most of the Ethiopians were dead within the first few minutes, it took time to hunt down and kill those who had scattered. Antonio Dordoni, an Italian who was in Addis Ababa at the time, told Professor Angelo Del Boca, 'In the courtyard the shooting continued almost three hours, according to one witness. When it ceased, the square in front of the *gibbi* was literally covered with corpses.'[16] The Ethiopian author Kirubel Beshah wrote, 'Because of that [grenade attack], shooting broke out. A great number of people died right there.'[17] Hundreds of men and women, including many elderly, blind and disabled, and children, lay dead in heaps all over the courtyard.

Sylvia Pankhurst, redoubtable daughter of the British suffragette Emmeline Pankhurst, had been a committed anti-Fascist since the movement began and, in order to keep the Ethiopian cause in the public eye, had been publishing an anti-Fascist weekly newspaper, *New Times and Ethiopia News*, at her house in Woodford Green, Essex. This newspaper, which devoted more coverage to the massacre than any other, confirmed that of the Ethiopians in the palace grounds, only a few succeeded in climbing the fences and disappearing.[18] This report is consistent with both eyewitness and diplomatic accounts. Furthermore, the handful who did escape managed to do so only during the first few moments of the mayhem, and most of those were chased and shot on the street outside. As the *carabinieri* report stated, 'Other police applied themselves to the pursuit of those few who were able to climb over the fence.'[19]

One of the few individuals fortunate enough to avoid the bullets was a young Ethiopian named Mekonnin Denneqe, who was working for the *carabinieri*. Despite being only 24, he had received military and police training at the Gendarmerie Royal College in Belgium, and in 1934 had served as police commissioner in the Ethiopian town of Dire Dawa. While fighting the Italians in the Ogaden, he had been captured, and in due course had been recruited by the *carabinieri* as an interpreter.

In an interview in his old age, Mekonnin recalled that when the grenades were thrown he was one of the first to run. He said that he took to his heels as soon as he saw what was happening. Realising that as an Ethiopian his position in the *carabinieri* would not necessarily protect him, he had the presence of mind to flee towards the south-east corner of the palace grounds (near today's Church of St Mark). As he ran, he could see people falling on top of each other in their attempts to escape the gunfire. It appears that he jumped over the outer fence.[20]

The overwhelming majority of the 3,000 Ethiopians who had gathered in the courtyard on St Michael's Day were dead by noon; most of those who escaped the initial onslaught were executed in the 'mopping-up' operation that followed.

As sporadic shooting continued in the compound, some of the few remaining survivors were herded together and shot; the others were tied up and dragged away. At the same time, the violence spread outside and around the palace, and many spectators who had been watching the conflagration were shot as they peered through the railings. The British acting consul-general, William Bond, was to report, 'Wholesale executions followed at once in the grounds and adjoining field, and a large number of mere spectators, most of whom were entirely innocent, thus paid for their presence with their lives.'[21]

* * *

3

AN HOUR OF MAYHEM

THE CIRCLE OF DEATH

Within minutes of the catastrophe at the Governo Generale, any Ethiopian found in the vicinity of the palace—and there were many sightseers, given the scale and importance of the occasion—was beaten or killed and, soon, houses in the vicinity of the palace and the adjoining Itégé Menen School were being set alight.

Contrary to what is often assumed, it was not only a case of the mayhem within the walls of the imperial palace spreading uncontrolled into the surrounding area. Because the Italians feared that an attack on Graziani would be followed by an armed assault on the capital by rebels (as had occurred a few weeks after the beginning of the Occupation), within minutes troops had hurried to their alarm posts, and a prearranged procedure had swung into action.[1] Soldiers from the nearby Regia Aeronautica headquarters at the former Menelik II School[2] were summoned urgently to the palace, and flung a cordon around the area, creating a circle of death within which any Ethiopians found on the streets were liable to be killed. Thus, within minutes, people in this area were being slaughtered by Italian civilians, who were grabbing any object within reach that could be used as a weapon, by soldiers of the regular army and the air force, and by militarised labourers with their shovels. And soon those assailants were supplemented by Blackshirts, who were now pouring out of their barracks at the nearby former Teferi Mekonnin School.

Taddesse Zeweldé, who worked at the public telegraph office and was in Addis Ababa at the time of the massacre, was a man of principle and integrity. A reliable source of information, he was a well-connected member of the underground resistance, and was in a position to interview eyewitnesses after the event. Later, in his historic book on the Shewan Patriots, *Qerin Geremew*, he reported, 'Those who were able to escape the courtyard were received by murderers holding shovels, axes and hammers. They were beaten to death with such tools.'[3]

This was also confirmed by the witness Kirubel Beshah: 'A lot of people were murdered after being repeatedly hit with big sticks, swivels, axes, hammers, stones or vehicle starting-handles. They were killed like mad dogs.'[4] A report published by the London *Times* stated, 'Immediately after the bombs were thrown at Marshal Graziani, Italian troops surrounded the area, and every Abyssinian within the circle was killed.'[5]

18. Taddesse Zeweldé, who worked in the Addis Ababa telegraph office, was well informed and, after the Liberation, published an account of the killings within the Circle of Death around the Gennete-Li'ul Palace

The first eyewitness account to reach the French government, written by one of its Addis Ababa legation staff, made an assessment of the number of victims inside the Circle of Death: 'Immediately after the attempt, the Blackshirts, acting under official orders, surrounded the district and massacred the 1,500 natives found therein.'[6] The Hungarian medical practitioner Dr Ladislas Shashka made similar observations, estimating that the circle 'where the ground was covered with the dead' extended to a radius of around 400 yards (about. 360 metres) around the palace.[7] The doctor's description of the area cordoned off concurs with all the available evidence. The British acting consul-general reported 'wholesale and indiscriminate execution of Abyssinians found in the neighbourhood of the Palace and elsewhere, immediately after the event.[8] As we shall see, Emperor Haile Selassie in due course also made reference to the Circle of Death: 'Italian military forces encircled the area of the incident. All Ethiopians found therein were killed.'[9]

At the time of *Yekatit 12* there was a field between the inner railings of the palace and the Intotto Road (unlike today, when the palace compound reaches the road, encircled by just one set of railings). A few people managed to reach the field, and run down Tewedros Street through the Siddist Kilo residential area to the steps near the Ras Mekonnin Bridge. But a contingent of Libyan *askaris* was rapidly mobilised, and a terrifying manhunt began. Italian eyewitness Domenico Cerutti told Professor Del Boca, how 'the Tripolinis [Libyan *askaris* fighting under Italian command], like lightning, with bayonets thrust forward' chased after the Ethiopians who had reached the field and were running in the direction of the steps, towards Arada.[10]

At this point another eyewitness takes up the story. At the top of those very steps, near the Ras Mekonnin Bridge, was a young demobilised soldier named Tekle-Maryam Kiflom, who had fought at the Battle of Maychew. Tekle-Maryam, who in the post-Liberation government would rise to the level of Deputy Minister of the Palace, was an articulate witness. He described to the present author how around midday he and his friend *Shaleqa* (Major) Yohannis,[11] of the Holetta Military Academy, were walking up the Ras Mekonnin steps after 'window-shopping' in Piazza. Having heard the sound of gunfire and a general commotion coming from the direction of the palace, they were on their way to find out what was going on, only to be shocked at the sight of a stranger, wounded and bleeding, hurtling down the steps towards them and obviously being chased. He was one of the few to have reached the steps alive, and the Libyans were hard on his heels. 'Run for your life!' the man cried. 'Don't you know they're killing all black people?'[12]

Tekle-Maryam wasted no time. Leaving Yohannis to run to his house near the Teferi Mekonnin School, he hurried back down the steps (which were on the periphery of the Circle of Death), across the road, and headed for the safety of his home in Arat Kilo. But he was not safe yet, for a few minutes later, he heard a shout: 'Halt!' Behind him was a *carabiniere*, accompanied by an Ethiopian member of the Colonial Police (that is working under Italian command). Tekle-Maryam's heart sank. However, luck was on his side, for the Ethiopian had recognised him. 'Don't run,' he was cautioned. 'Walk slowly. But for your own good, disappear quickly!' Somehow suppressing the temptation to break into a run, Tekle-Maryam slowed his pace to what he hoped look like a casual walk, arrived home safely, and lived to tell the tale.

* * *

Few Ethiopians who witnessed the devastation within the Circle of Death survived, but a striking and strong-willed woman named Sara Gebre-Iyyesus was an exception, because she was under armed escort at the time. Wife of the Director of Finance Beshahwired Habte-Weld, who had been educated in India and America and was one of the notables at the palace when the grenades were thrown, Sara never forgot those traumatic days of February 1937.[13] Knowing nothing of the attack on Graziani, she was arrested together with her children, Yeweynishet and Sahle-Mika'él, and two house guests at the family villa near the Teferi Mekonnin School by a group of Italian and Eritrean soldiers soon after midday. The family were victims of the Italian policy 'arrest of kin', which would in due course be emulated by the Nazis to deter domestic opposition to Hitler.

19. Seen here in 1941, Tekle-Maryam Kiflom, who had returned to Addis Ababa after fighting at Maychew, fled down the Ras Mekonnin steps when killings began inside the Circle of Death

20. Pictured here in 1939, *Weyzero* Sara Gebre-Iyyesus was arrested immediately after the strike of *Yekatit 12*, and witnessed numerous killings as she was made to walk through the Circle of Death

The front door flew open and in burst five uniformed soldiers—two Italians and three Eritrean *askaris*. Although she was unaware of it at the time, they had been ordered to arrest her because her husband was suspected of having been involved in the attack on Graziani. They started slapping, punching and kicking her. One Italian and one Eritrean administered the beating, while the other Italian watched. But nothing was said, and no questions asked.

Meanwhile, the other two *askaris* started looting the house. Reaching Sara's bedroom, they found a wardrobe containing valuables—gold and silver items—which they proceeded to load into a bag. As the looters cleared the shelves, Sara was repeatedly kicked and knocked about in front of her two terrified children. 'I was trying to protect and hide my children behind me and the wall. Then the Italian kicked me in the buttocks with his heavy boot.'

Having no idea why all this was happening to her, Sara saw one of the Italians tying up the two male guests, and binding their necks together with a shawl. 'Having filled the bag with [my] gold and silver, they told me to carry it, which I did, although it was so heavy, I was afraid I might drop it. It contained many silver *thalers*. Then they told everyone to leave the house.'

Exhausted and frightened, and accompanied by her two petrified children, five military personnel and the two visitors who had also been arrested, the 24-year-old Sara made her way outside onto the main street. As they turned towards the palace, with one of the Italians holding the shawl and leading the two men like the reins of a horse, she was thunderstruck. The scene was a nightmare; hundreds had been killed. 'All around the palace I could see dead bodies. There were many, many bodies inside the palace grounds. There were also bodies in front of the premises [outside the railings]. They had all been shot by the time we reached there. It was then I realised that something terrible had happened, and I was very worried about my husband.'[14]

21. Yeweynishet Beshahwired, photographed here at the age of around 6, not long after accompanying her mother through the Circle of Death

Recalling that surreal journey, Sara later remembered the horror, the noise, the smells, the screams. 'It must have been around one o'clock in the afternoon by the time we were passing the palace. The shooting was still going on. People were running and being killed as we watched. After having to stop several times to avoid bullets, we reached Siddist Kilo square, where there were many bodies strewn around.' Yeweynishet, who was six years old at the time, still recalls seeing Italians armed with spades and shovels, and grievously injured people dead and dying.[15]

Arriving at the great field of Jan Méda (Map 2), where the Emperor used to hold imperial parades and watch horse-racing, Sara was stunned by what she saw. 'In those days, there was a daily market in Jan Méda, near the [Siddist Kilo] square. Many people had been shot as they tried to run away from the market. I saw the bodies of many men, women and children who had been shot there.'

At the Siddist Kilo junction, in front of the Béta Sayda (now Yekatit 12) Hospital, Sara was distraught to see men being beaten and her young brother Sibhatu being dragged along the street together with other boys and men who had been rounded up. But there was nothing his sister could do. The sorry

22. Many Ethiopians were indiscriminately slaughtered inside the Circle of Death around the Viceregal Palace between noon and 1.00 pm. This photograph appears to have been taken in the vicinity of Jan Méda

party was led beside the hospital (renamed by the Italians Ospedale Vittorio Emanuele), down the street that later came to be known as Tewedros Street (Via Vagabur) (see Map 2).

Sara and her family—by now in a state of complete shock—were escorted past a row of military trucks that had been parked on the right of the street, before reaching her mother's house, which was on the left down the hill just before *Bejirond* Letyibelu's residence. Although Sara did not know it at the time, these trucks were being used to collect men who were being dragged out of the houses nearby.[16] The *Bejirond's adarash*, or banqueting house, which adjoined his residence, was said by the Italians to have become 'a house of bandits', and had been commandeered and turned into a detention centre.[17] '*Dejazmach* [then *Bejirond*] Letyibelu's house was just beyond my mother's house. We had to stop so many times to avoid being shot, that it took much longer than it would normally have done to get there.'[18]

However, before they arrived at the detention centre, Sara's sisters, Welette-Birhan and Welette-Haymanot, happened to see them. Welette-Birhan, an independently minded young woman, worked as a nurse under the Swedish

23. Seen here in her Béta Sayda Hospital nurse's uniform, Welette-Birhan Gebre-Iyyesus met Sara and her children on Tewedros Street, on their way to detention.

24. Zenebech Belachew, the wife of *Qeññazmach* Belihu Degefu, was arrested, and detained with her friend Sara Gebre-Iyyesus in the *adarash* of *Bejirond* Letyibelu Gebré

Dr Hanner at the Béta Sayda Hospital. She had spent the night at Sara's house, then at around 10.00 am had set out for their mother's house, where she met up with her friend Aboniza. Together they had walked to Arada, but turned around when they realised there was trouble in the city, and returned to her mother's house in Tewedros Street. There they found that Italian soldiers had burst into the house and dragged out her brother Sibhatu. She and Welette-Haymanot had just stepped outside to look for Sara, when they saw the little procession coming down the road:

> I set out to look for my sister [Sara], but there was a lot of shooting, and Italian soldiers were everywhere. They were wearing black headgear with a tassel.[19] I was ordered, 'Get back!' But instead of going back into the house, after talking to my mother, I stayed on the road. Then I saw Yeweynishet's mother [Sara] walking down the road. Despite them being under arrest, I was happy to see them.[20]

The two sisters walked alongside Sara and her children, and it was then that Sara learned what had happened at the palace. Welette-Birhan was afraid that her husband might have been killed, but was unable to discover anything about his fate.

Passing a great Armenian villa on the right—the home of Agop Bagdasarian[21]—and her own mother's house on the left, they finally arrived at Letyibelu's

25. Seen here in 2004, *Bejirond* Letyibelu's *adarash* in Tewedros Street was commandeered by the Italians and used as a detention centre. The verandah at the front where Sara's children were detained is now closed in and used as a local drinking-house

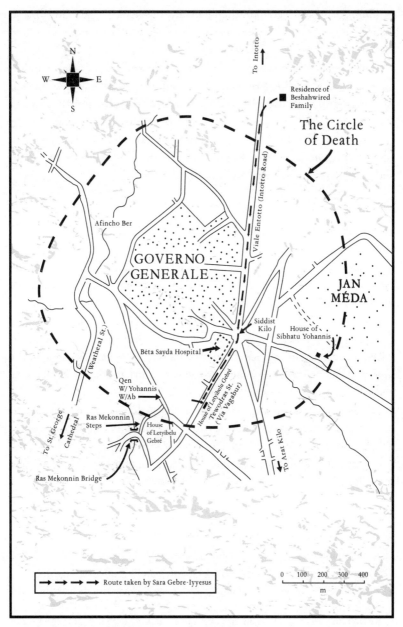

Map 2. The Circle of Death and the route taken by Sara Gebre-Iyyesus. Within this cordon an estimated 1,500 people were slaughtered between noon and 1.00 pm, Friday, 19 February 1937

adarash. As they turned onto the verandah, a military truck rumbled past, loaded with household possessions that Sara immediately recognised as hers. Her home had been completely looted.

The children were told to stay on the verandah, while Sara was taken inside. There she found a fellow prisoner, Zenebech Belachew, wife of *Qeññazmach* Belihu Degefu,[22] a close friend of her husband. Then the Italian who had beaten Sara made an appearance, and took away the bag of gold and silver.

Sara was to spend the rest of the day at the detention centre, following which she was imprisoned at the Governo Generale, where prominent figures and other 'political prisoners' were being held.

* * *

Shortly after the strike at the palace, the Italian journalist Ciro Poggiali had been taken to hospital for treatment, along with 42 other injured people. He does not say which hospital it was, but it was most likely the Béta Sayda Hospital, just across the road from the Gennete-Li'ul Palace, and inside the Circle of Death. Injured in one leg, he found what he called an 'indescribable hubbub' in the hospital, had his leg bandaged, then went outside to see what was going on. He found that 'all the [Italian] civilians in Addis Ababa' had 'taken on the task of revenge', forming squads 'with lightning speed, in the most authentic *squadristi* manner'. Armed with iron bars, they were attacking and killing any Ethiopians they encountered.

Dead bodies lay everywhere. In his diary Poggiali tells how he watched, to his horror, a driver strike an Ethiopian to the ground with a blow from an iron bar, then split the man's head open from one side to the other with the stab of a bayonet—a procedure that would be repeated countless times over the next three days.[23]

* * *

Temesgen Gebré, whose eyewitness account concurs with that of Sara Gebre-Iyyesus, summed up the carnage in graphic terms:

> Every kind of weapon—hand grenades, explosives and incendiaries, rifles, revolvers ... as well as machine-guns and daggers—were used and found their victims. The heads of caught Ethiopians were split with picks and shovels. Blackshirts ran through the streets, looking and seeking for new victims and killing any still breathing. Every [Ethiopian] in town was a welcome prey to those bloodthirsty soldiers under the 'Roman Eagle'. Corpses of men, women and children were lying everywhere.[24]

Men, women and children were taken unawares and killed indiscriminately and without explanation. Going home for lunch or stopping for a chat, unsuspecting and defenceless, they were ruthlessly struck down in broad daylight in the main streets of Siddist Kilo, among the eucalyptus groves and the hedgerows, around market stalls, on bridges, in tiny lanes and narrow alleys.

The devastation around the Governo Generale, and particularly the Jan Méda area, is well attested, and is not surprising, given that most of the Blackshirts were located near the former Teferi Mekonnin School and at a barracks adjacent to Jan Méda. The present author was fortunate in being able to interview another reliable female witness, *Immahoy* ('Sister') Hiruta, who explained that the house-burning at Jan Méda started only a matter of minutes after the attack at the palace. While it is common knowledge that thousands of houses were burned down during the onslaught organised at night, what is less well known is that numerous residences around Jan Méda were burned—many with their occupants inside—in the early afternoon. 'The Jan Méda area was burned to the ground. They were closing homes and fastening the doors. People were burned to death. Children were thrown into the burning homes.'[25]

One notable feature of the Massacre of Addis Ababa was indeed the killing of children—particularly horrifying when carried out by a people often considered to be lovers of children, and especially given that, unlike the young conscripts of the regular army, the 6th Division 'Tevere' Blackshirts included many married men in their thirties and forties, several of whom had children of their own. The killing of children began in the area of Jan Méda, as *Immahoy* Hiruta described, within minutes of the strike of *Yekatit 12*. As children came running out of the burning houses, the Italians lifted them up and threw them back into the flames.

Lieutenant Meleseliñ, the Ethiopian policeman on duty at the Governo Generale when the putative assassins struck, was one of the eyewitnesses to write a book about his experiences during the Occupation. In it he describes how the marauding Italians caught occupants unawares in their houses while they were 'as usual eating food and drinking coffee'; then with cries of '*buongiorno!*' the 'children, women and the elderly' would respond in Italian in good faith, only to be bayoneted, gunned down or burned to death.[26]

* * *

As a general rule the higher-class residential areas such as Siddist Kilo were not burned, because the Italians wanted the houses for themselves. However, the Ethiopian families inside were not immune from attack, and many of them were within the Circle of Death. The Blackshirts, armed mainly with their regulation daggers, accompanied by militarised labourers with their shovels and pickaxes, wanted to claim these houses, and so they were not destroyed. However, they were looted, and many of the occupants were killed. In 2004, the Italian historian and publisher Milena Battistoni, visiting the historic Siddist Kilo home of *Qeññazmach* Welde-Yohannis Welde-Ab, which he himself had built in addition to several others in the area, reported, 'The four daughters of the *Qeññazmach* told us that he was killed on 19 February 1937 in the massacre that followed the assassination attempt against Rodolfo Graziani. The Fascists took him and hundreds of other men from their houses, brought them to Siddist Kilo [junction] and slaughtered them with pickaxes and shovels.'[27]

Indeed, the reader will recall that the military trucks that Welette-Birhan and Sara saw parked near Letyibelu's residence were being used to collect these victims for execution. Siddist Kilo square, where Sara saw her young brother Sibhatu being beaten, had become the first execution site and, in effect, the centre of the massacre.

* * *

One of the first respondents to the conflagration around Siddist Kilo was the Addis Ababa fire brigade. Not knowing the cause of the alarm, *Tenente* (Lieutenant) Mafui, the commanding officer, acted quickly. Rounding up a team of firefighters under Captain Toka Binegid, he sped to the scene of the fire. However, upon arrival, the firefighters were shocked to see Italians deliberately setting fire to the houses. Mafui soon realised what was going on, and told his men not to take any action. But as they stood there helplessly, they were shocked to see Ethiopians being killed as they fled from their burning homes.[28]

Inside the Circle of Death the killing and burning was intense. Houses to the north and west of the Itégé Menen School were being burned wholesale, in addition to the dwellings south-east of the palace, below the field of Jan Méda. Consistent with what Sara Gebre-Iyyesus would later recount, British Intelligence reported that the area between the Gennete-Li'ul Palace and Menelik Hospital (which stood beyond the eastern end of Jan Méda, and thus indicated an expansion of the massacre beyond the Circle of Death) was completely destroyed.[29]

The British Intelligence report was accurate. It had not taken the mob long to start attacking Ethiopians and their property further afield, outside the cordon. Although the *carabinieri* and the regulars seem to have limited themselves to the killing of the 3,000 Ethiopians in the palace grounds and the

1,500 inside the Circle of Death, there were now hundreds of Blackshirts on the streets, some running and others riding on their military 'Trenta Quattro' trucks. Together with numerous Italian civilians they were fanning out across a wider area and pouncing on any Ethiopians they encountered. Refugees from the massacre who managed to reach Djibouti told the Ethiopian consul there what they had seen: 'Terrified men, women and children ran in turmoil in all directions, only to be butchered by groups of ten, twenty, fifty and hundred Italian militia-men and Blackshirts. Soon the streets were strewn with dead bodies ... No one dared venture out.'[30]

Edouard Garabedian, a young Armenian businessman who lived in Arada, knew what he was talking about when he said that the perpetrators he watched were civilians, because as a long-time resident he was familiar with the city like the back of his hand and, since the Occupation began, had come to know many of the Italians personally. In sworn testimony he stated, 'I saw them with my own eyes, beating every Ethiopian they met in the street with anything they could find. *These Italians were civilians.* They were using what they could find, as cudgels, etc. This was going on until the circulation of people had finished' (emphasis added).[31]

* * *

Meanwhile, in the palace grounds a few victims who were still alive but were lying below their fallen comrades had pulled themselves clear and managed to stand up. Among them was Temesgen Gebré, part of whose account was published in 1945. His torment continued as the gunfire finally died down: 'When the machine-gun fire was almost stopped, I tried to get up, but I found myself under several dead bodies, the weight of which I had not felt before.' He was then accosted by Italians who were rounding up and robbing the few survivors. 'When we were ordered to hold up our hands, I stretched mine straight towards heaven, and they searched for papers in our pockets ... If we had money, or a gold watch, we would give it if they did not kill us ... However, the Italians were in a hurry to kill us, for if they killed us, all our watches, money, gold necklaces, gold crosses, gold rings and food would be for them.'[32]

Here Temesgen put his finger on an important objective of the massacre of Addis Ababa that is often overlooked: theft. As noted earlier, the slaughter was led by young men for whom joining the Blackshirts or the Fascist labour force meant a good regular income and the opportunity for personal gain. In addition, many of the Blackshirts were common criminals who had been freed from jail under an amnesty for prisoners willing to join the troops in Ethiopia, and they were often struck by the relative wealth of some of the better-off Ethiopians in Addis Ababa—particularly those who had been based for some time overseas. Murder and mayhem were thus almost always preceded by the robbing of the victims of anything and everything of value. There were few Ethiopian homes that escaped pillage during the massacre, and many Ethiopians were stripped of everything they possessed.

By the time Temesgen had been taken out of the palace, the killing in the Circle of Death was well under way. However, as we shall see, this little group of survivors was taken through the pandemonium to the area of St George's Cathedral. The epicentre was moving.

SLAUGHTER IN ARADA

At the time of the Occupation, Addis Ababa had no obvious city centre. However, the first road constructed when the city was founded led from Menelik's palace, or *gibbi*, to the Gennete Tsigé Giyorgis (St George's) Cathedral, which according to tradition had been built on the site of an earlier church demolished in the 16th century. In terms of its pivotal and prestigious position, the section of this road between the cathedral (known as Menelik Square) and the junction at Piazza Littoria a short distance away (named Charles de Gaulle Square after the Liberation) could for all practical purposes be regarded as the city centre of Addis Ababa of the 1930s.

In the centre of Menelik Square, Haile Selassie had installed a great equestrian statue of Emperor Menelik mounted on a massive plinth, which added to the grandeur of the centre. The Italians had removed the statue and renamed the junction Piazza Impero, but the area retained its prominence and importance as the major hub of Addis Ababa's 'downtown' district, known to the Ethiopians as Arada.

Menelik Square was connected to Adwa Square—another junction just 200 metres to the north. Between these two major road junctions was St George's Cathedral to the west, and a number of buildings to the east, of which the largest and most prominent was the Municipality Office building, commandeered by the Italians for use as the Tribunale Civile (Civilian Courthouse). Formerly the residence of the wealthy notable *Neggadras* Hayle-Giyorgis Welde-Mika'él, it overlooked Adwa Square (see Map 3).

Radiating from Adwa Square were several streets. The two most important were the Gojjam Road (Via Padre R. Giuliani; later, *Dejazmach* Belay Zelleke Street) to the north-west, and the road to Siddist Kilo and the Governo Generale (Viale Regina; later, Weatherel Street) to the north-east (see Map 3).

26. The Cathedral of St George viewed from the north-west, with Menelik Square in the background

Around noon, Dawit Oquba Igzi'i, an educated Eritrean resident of Addis Ababa who had been on the staff of the Teferi Mekonnin School and who would be appointed Governor of Adwa after the Liberation, was making his way home when a member of the *carabinieri* caught hold of him. Had the Italian been a Blackshirt, and had Dawit not been an Eritrean, he could well have been killed. Instead, he was asked where he was going, and taken to a *carabinieri* station near Ras Mekonnin Bridge. 'As I passed through the streets I noticed that there was some disorder. People were running up and down and troops were moving, especially the Fascists.'[33]

At the *carabinieri* station Dawit was questioned as to whether he had been at the Governo Generale in the morning. After the interrogation, he was ordered into the station compound, which had been turned into a prison, holding around a thousand other people who had also been detained there. Dawit was to remain in that police station, without food or water, for the next three days.[34]

Many more people were rounded up and detained near the Ras Mekonnin Bridge, as the Fascist squads made their way from Siddist Kilo, across the bridge towards Arada. But by now not only were the Blackshirts running on foot, yelling and attacking any Ethiopians they met; hundreds of them were also arriving in military trucks, because it was in Arada, just north of St George's Cathedral, that many Amharas—the principal targets of the onslaught—lived.[35]

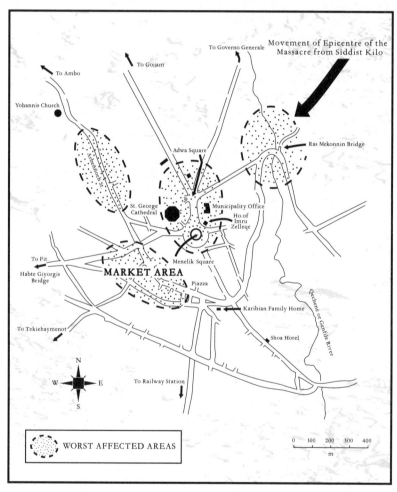

Map 3. Arada, showing areas where the massacre was principally focused from 12 noon to 1.00 pm Friday, 19 February 1937

Some of the trucks contained Ethiopian captives as well as Blackshirts, and it was in one of these that Temesgen Gebré and his little group of survivors from the slaughter at the Gennete-Li'ul Palace were taken to Menelik Square, where he saw a truck containing dead and injured Ethiopians. It was then that he realised that the killing had spread beyond the Circle of Death: 'From St John's [Yohannis] Church, a truck came through Patriots [Arbeññoch] Street to the highway on which we were, and stopped near us. The truck was covered with [a] tarpaulin, and I was not quite sure whether the persons who were inside the truck were dead or wounded, but I saw fresh blood dropping on the ground from the truck.' From the front and back seats of the truck a dozen armed Italian soldiers appeared. Temesgen noted that their shoes and black shirts were blood-stained. 'They did not salute each other but they began to speak, and their speaking was as a flame.' Realising he might be about to die, Temesgen wondered, 'Is this the foundation and height of human life?' He whispered to his companion *Ato* Qenna, saying that maybe they were going to be killed. 'The soldiers ordered us to stand in line. There were some priests among us, and they confessed by praying in the name of St Mary and other saints.'

Were they going to be executed there and then? It seemed so, for 'the machine guns which were there had been brought nearer to us ... Four of us turned our faces towards the truck, the machine guns were pointed at our backs ...' But luck was with Temesgen. He and several others were ordered to get into the truck, which they did, leaving behind about ten for whom there was no room. They were not so lucky. 'After many days, I heard that many of those who were left out were made to dig the ground for their burial place and were shot; but I do not know where they were taken.'

The truck carrying the dead, the injured and the new prisoners continued on its brief journey to nearby St George's School, where prisoners were being detained and executed. What was to transpire—the use of vehicles, shovels and daggers by the Blackshirts as weapons and instruments of death—would become commonplace over the next three days. 'When we arrived at the gate of the school named after St George, they stopped us, and they beat us with shovels, axes and picks. An old man bowed down before the feet of an Italian, seeking mercy; the Italian became angry and told him, "Do not waste my time asking me for mercy" ... that old man, while still bowing down, was killed.'[36]

By that time the burning of houses had also spread from Siddist Kilo to Arada, and the smoke was so dense that even from St George's School Temesgen could hardly see the cathedral, a distance of only 200 metres. He recalled, 'To assure myself that I was not dreaming, I looked carefully at the things I knew before in Addis Ababa, but I could distinguish only the dome of St George's Church, because the city of Addis Ababa was covered with smoke. Even if the Ethiopian Parliament [one of the city's largest buildings] had been in front of us I would not have been able to see it on account of the smoke. When the eucalyptus trees were burning and the blaze was spreading all over the city, then I knew that Addis Ababa was aflame. So I knew that I was not in a dream; also, I did not know why all these things happened.'[37]

If Temesgen did not comprehend why these things were happening, despite having been at the Gennete-Li'ul Palace in the morning, how much less did the majority of the population of Addis Ababa know what was going on. This is one of the particular horrors of the massacre: most of the victims had no idea why they were being attacked. Men, women and children were taken by surprise, with no time to protect themselves or prepare in any way for the terrible end that was to befall them. And they had no authority to which to appeal, for the authority was the perpetrator. The much vaunted law and order of the Italians had proved to be a sham; the Ethiopians were defenceless. Temesgen described a shocking scene in which the Italians set fire to a building where Ethiopians were sheltering. He wrote that one of the victims—

clearly a member of the Orthodox Church—called out for help from the saints. However, he was thrown into the fire, and as the flames reached him, he cried out, 'I am sorry for the Ethiopians who are going to have to live with the Fascists—for me, I am now free of them!'[38]

* * *

Temesgen was not the only witness of what was happening outside the Municipality Office on Menelik Square. At a house on the corner of Menelik Square and what was later named John Melly St, overlooking St George's Cathedral, a 13-year-old boy was looking out of the window, stunned by what he saw. Young Imru Zelleqe, whose late father, *Bejirond*

27. Photographed here at the age of 6, Imru Zelleqe watched the killings near St George's Cathedral when he was 13

Zelleqe Agidew, had held several ministerial positions in the Emperor's government, and whose mother was related to the Emperor, had returned to Ethiopia after several years in Switzerland. When it seemed as though the Italians were going to reach Addis Ababa, the family had left for Djibouti but, following the death of the *Bejirond*, had returned to the city. When they arrived they found the Italians in control of Addis Ababa, and *carabinieri* installed in the family property in Arada.[39]

Later, in his retirement, Ambassador Imru would talk about the events of that terrible day, stating that the Italians used guns, bayonets, knives, and even picks and shovels to kill people, regardless of age or gender. 'One day suddenly we heard a lot of shouting, and then there was a big movement of troops. And then we saw people being arrested and getting killed and so forth ... You could hear shooting, you could hear people running around. You know, it was a riot ... A lot of people were killed in the streets'.[40]

In his memoirs, he wrote, 'The *Camicie Nere* (Blackshirts), the *Legione di Lavoro* (Workers Legion) and the *Polizia Coloniale* (Colonial Police) had a field day. Our house overlooked Menelik Square. From the second floor I

28. From his family home (top left of photograph) on Menelik Square, at the corner of what later became known as John Melly Street, young Imru Zelleqe watched the outbreak of the massacre in Arada. Detail from Fig. 26

could see many Italian military, civilians, and policemen killing and beating people who in panic were trying to take refuge in the Municipality.'[41] 'They were shooting people, and you could see people beaten to death and so forth … not very far, maybe 200 [or] 250 metres away.' Asked if he was terrified, Ambassador Imru went on: 'Terrified? Yes, but sometimes you get mesmerised … I was shocked but I was not terrified because I didn't understand really what was going on. It was the first time I saw people being killed. It was a terrible experience. There were several people next to me. They were in a trance; [it was] almost impossible to imagine such a thing. We thought the sky was falling, and the terror continued for three days.'[42] Looking back, the retired diplomat and banker recalled his shock and bewilderment at the brutality of the Italians: 'In my young mind what shook me to the core was the extreme and indiscriminate violence inflicted on peaceful people, which even today after witnessing the unfolding of so many dramas, I find difficult to rationalise.'[43]

Another potential victim of the slaughter at the Governo Generale who survived being taken to the killing fields around St George's Cathedral was *Ato* Rahmato Muktar. Supervisor in charge of a team of Gurage workers employed in Addis Ababa by the well-known French businessman Antoine Besse, Rahmato was described by Besse's Belgian manager, Maurice Weerts, as 'one of the noblest people I have ever met in my life'. According to Weerts, *Ato* Rahmato was trapped in the palace grounds when the strike of *Yekatit 12* took place and, together with many others, was transferred to the open area near St George's Cathedral. Fortunately, however, Weerts was in a position to bribe the Blackshirts, and Rahmato's being a Muslim might have helped, for among his many bizarre declarations, and notwithstanding the horrific slaughter of Libyan Muslims conducted by his forces, Mussolini claimed to be 'the protector' of the followers of the Prophet. Moreover, the Italian military and civil administrations were renowned for their corruption. 'His [Rahmato's] son, Mohamed, came to tell me about it, and after having examined the site, we managed with the help of some money to arrange for his escape from captivity and almost certain death.'[44]

Captain Toka Binegid of the Addis Ababa fire brigade, witnessing horrors at St George's Cathedral, reported, 'While a priest was trying to hide himself at St George's Cathedral compound in a tomb, I saw, while standing at the Fire Brigade [on Adwa Square, just north of the Municipality Office], a certain Italian sergeant pursuing the priest, and he killed him with a pistol.'[45]

* * *

29. 'Throughout the city they were massacring many people ... Horrible. A shame for Italy'—Ciro Poggiali. Correspondent for the Italian government newspaper *Corriere della Sera*, Poggiali, who witnessed the outbreak and early stages of the massacre at Menelik Square, published this photograph of some 24 massacre victims

After receiving treatment for his injuries, the journalist Ciro Poggiali witnessed the slaughter at Menelik Square. Despite having himself written several pro-Fascist tracts and monographs, in his private diary he wrote that he was stunned to see the extent of the killing: 'Throughout the city they were massacring many people.' Expressing amazement at the terrible things that human beings could do to others, he judged the massacre 'really shameful ... Horrible. A shame for Italy ... I myself will testify to this.'[46]

Another person who had a close brush with death in Arada at this time was Sara's sister, Welette-Birhan, who, the reader will recall, was in Arada with her friend Aboniza: 'At around 1.00 pm, when walking from Giyorgis down to the square in Piazza, near the cinema, we could see that there was a commotion. People were running in all directions, in fear and panic. There was obviously trouble, but no one knew where to run to, to be safe. There was confusion. I decided to walk home immediately.'[47]

* * *

Vahak Karibian, a young Armenian boy, lived with his mother, brothers and sisters in a house behind what the Italians called Piazza Littorio, a triangular piazza at the end of Via Tripoli (later, Cunningham Street), in what is now known simply as Piazza, behind today's Karibian carpet and curtain shop (see Map 3).[48] Mrs Karibian rented the house from an Indian named Mr Kikubhai.

Vahak was a student at the Italian School on Via Consolata, which changed its name to Viale Tevere (later renamed Arbeññoch Street) as one went south-wards some 1.5 kilometres from St George's Cathedral. On that fateful Friday, when class broke up early, Vahak's mother, who had discovered that there were serious disturbances in city, decided it would be best to arrange a taxi to bring him home. Fortunately, Kikubhai had a small fleet of taxis of American manu-facture, which were garaged in the compound of the house where the Karibians lived. A driver was found to go and fetch Vahak, and when he arrived at the school, he told the boy to jump in quickly. There was no time to lose. He said there had been an attack on Graziani and that Addis Ababa was in turmoil. Ethiopians were being attacked and killed all over the city. The driver feared for his life, for, while having a white person in the taxi might offer some protection, as an Ethiopian he could be attacked at any time.

The journey home was not long, but it was a trip that Vahak would never forget. As the car made its way along Arbeññoch St towards Arada, they were forced to take a detour to avoid the Italian Hospital (today, Ras Desta Hospital), to which Graziani had been taken. The boy observed Ethiopians being attacked in the street, and, approaching Piazza, he could see several houses around the market district in flames, the smoke rising in the sky. It was a terrifying sight, and the driver was shaking with fear. When finally they reached home, the driver went to join his colleagues in the compound at the back of the house, and together they begged Mrs Karibian to be allowed to stay there, pleading that if they left the house they would be killed.

Fortunately, like many members of the Armenian and Greek communities in Addis Ababa, Vahak's mother was appalled by what was going on. Her sympathies lay with the Ethiopians, with whom the family had built a close relationship over many years. She not only agreed that they could stay where they were, but, by sheltering them for the duration of the massacre, she risked incurring Italian fury for harbouring 'enemies of the Fascist state'. In fact, the houses of Europeans were now being searched by the Italians, who were going from door to door dragging out Ethiopians wherever they found them. As a contemporary Ethiopian writer put it, 'Forceful onslaughts were also made …

on the houses of the few Europeans who remained in Addis Ababa after the Italian occupation.'[49] But thanks to Mrs Karibian, Kikubhai's drivers survived, as did her two Ethiopian servants, who were allowed to take refuge in the house, and were thereafter forever grateful to the Karibian family.

* * *

ESCAPE TO QECHENÉ

On 12 Yekatit, 13-year old Taddesse Tiruneh was living with his elder brother, Sibhat, at the German Hermannsburg Evangelical Mission at Qechené (now Qechené Children's Orphanage), some 2 kilometres due north of Menelik Square, and about 700 metres north-west of the nearest gate of the Governo Generale. Since the beginning of the Occupation, Taddesse had been enrolled at the Italian Consolata School on Arbeññoch St.[50] While sitting in class that day, he heard several explosions, rather like the sounds he used to hear when the workers at the stone quarry at Qechené were splitting rocks. This was at around 11.40 am, the noise interrupting the lesson well before the normal closing time of 12 pm.[51]

After about 15 minutes, just before noon, the teachers, who had just received by telephone the news about the attack on Graziani, told the boys to gather in the assembly hall where they had to sing Fascist Party songs at the beginning and end of each school day. There they were told that something serious had happened, they must leave the premises, go home, close the doors, and not return to school until instructed to do so. So Taddesse made his way back home to the Hermannsburg Mission in Qechené, but on the way he was surprised and frightened to see hundreds of people running away from the general direction of Siddist Kilo, where smoke and flames were rising into the sky.

Taddesse made haste along the forest tracks between Arbeññoch Street and Dejazmach Belay Zelleqe Street,[52] then on past the Church of Qechené Medhané Alem to the mission, where he was relieved to find Sibhat, who was a resident teacher there, at home. As the two ate their lunch in the relative calm of the mission compound, Taddesse told his brother all about the trouble in the city and the early closure of class.

* * *

When the Italians occupied Ethiopia in May 1936, Eritrean Éfrém Gebre-Amlak, like Taddesse Tiruneh, was 13 years old. Soon this young Italian colonial subject became a member of the Fascist Youth organisation called the

30. Taddesse Tiruneh, seen here as a
Patriot later on in the Occupation

Opera Nazionale Balilla, referring to it in later life as the 'Boy Scouts'.[53] *Shaleqa* (Major) Éfrém, as he later became, was one of a large group of boys who staged a gymnastic display and singing for Viceroy Graziani at Casa Fascio, built as commercial centre before the Occupation by *Ras* Adefrisaw in the western part of Arada. Éfrém always remembered that event, for it was not long before *Yekatit 12*.

On 12 Yekatit Éfrém was at home with his father, on the Gojjam Road (in this section, Via Padre R. Guiliani) some 270 metres north of today's Semien Hotel. The house had a clear view to the east across Zebeñña Sefer below, where the city police used to live, to the wide valley of the Qechené River and Afincho Ber, at the back of the Governo Generale. Suddenly he heard explosions and gunfire from the general direction of the palace, and shortly afterwards he could see from his window people 'running in all directions, in panic', in the vicinity of Afincho Ber, the area immediately west of the palace. As we shall see, Éfrém spent the next three days at home, none of the family daring to venture outside.[54]

FOREIGN DISPATCHES

Sitting after lunch in his residence built in the English country-house style in the vast, 90-acre British legation on the eastern outskirts of the city, a journey of some 6 kilometres from the Governo Generale, William Bond, acting consul-general, decided to send a dispatch to London reporting in somewhat amusing vein on the Viceroy's recent reception for the international community of the city to celebrate the birth of the Prince of Naples.[55] However, no sooner had he sent the telegram for transmission than he began receiving disturbing messages from his staff. There was trouble in the city. He was briefed about the incident at the palace—though the details were not yet

31. Eritrean Éfrém Gebre-Amlak was one of the *balillas* (Fascist Youth) in this photograph of a gymnastic display for Graziani outside Casa Fascio

clear—and, sure enough, standing at the top of the steps at his entrance hall, he could see in the distance palls of smoke rising above the city.[56]

As fragments of information trickled into the legation, Bond began to compile them, with a view to dispatching another, considerably less pleasant telegram to the Foreign Office. Sent later in the evening, it explained what had happened at the Governo Generale and how the Italians had reacted to it: 'Immediate repercussions were wholesale executions of Ethiopians present, burning of native huts over a wide area, many instances of beating to death with staves and otherwise killing of Ethiopians found in the town.'[57]

The legation, occupying land granted to Britain by Emperor Menelik, and providing offices and living quarters for both British and Ethiopian employees, stood comfortably remote from the hustle and bustle of the metropolis, but that remoteness had its drawbacks, for it required an effort to stay abreast of affairs of state. The envoy relied on telephone, telegraph and information provided by the much-reduced British community and members of foreign legations whom he would meet at diplomatic functions.

Over the days that followed, the difficulties were to prove even greater than usual, as the Italians closed down public communication services, and soon few people were on the streets. Fortunately, however, the principal legations—

British, French and American—had access to privileged telegraphic services, and for this reason their reports following the attempt on Graziani were to constitute some of the most reliable documentation of the holocaust that was to unfold, in a city that had been largely cut off from the outside world.

* * *

The American consul-general and resident minister, Cornelius Van H. Engert, was a seasoned diplomat, having held foreign service posts in Turkey, Iraq, Syria, Palestine, the Netherlands, Iran, Cuba, E1 Salvador, Chile, Venezuela, China and Egypt.[58] He was a man of judgement and not easily moved. It is also apparent from the manner in which he was to stand up to the Fascist authorities in Addis Ababa that he was also a

32. William L. Bond, British acting consul-general during the massacre of Addis Ababa

33. The Emperor meeting with Minister Cornelius Engert at the American legation before the Italian invasion

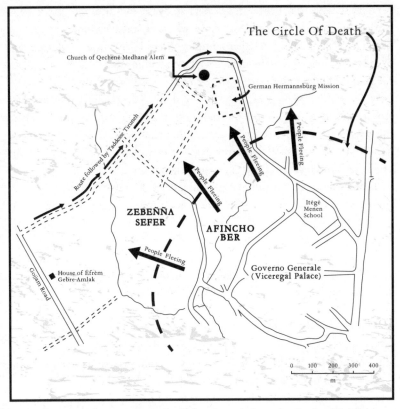

Map 4. Qechené, showing the flight of people from the Circle of Death

man of principle, to whom may be attributed, as we shall see, the saving of many Ethiopian lives.

Unlike the British legation, which was several kilometres from the city centre, the American legation was situated immediately west of Arada, just beyond Fitawrari Habte-Giyorgis Bridge, to the north of the Tekle Haymanot area.

Not only did Engert quickly develop a close relationship with Emperor Haile Selassie, but he persuaded the Emperor to agree to the city's first independent telegraphic facility—at the American legation—which was to prove an invaluable lifeline for the foreign community when the city fell into chaos following the departure of the Emperor in May 1936.

During the Occupation communications between Addis Ababa and the outside world were tightly controlled by the Italians; the only relatively independent systems were by that time operated by the four principal legations—British, American, French and German—whose diplomatic immunity was not, however, recognised by the Italian administration. Telegrams needed to be sent by radio transmission, and in July 1936 all such transmission facilities other than the Italian public radio station were closed by a decree from the Governo Generale. Furthermore, even telegrams sent through the public system could no longer be in cipher (that is coded). Following Engert's discussions with Graziani, this requirement was lifted for America alone, thus permitting the legation to use a cipher. In August 1936 this privilege was extended to all the legations, but none was allowed to resume use of its own broadcasting station.[59]

Though successful in following his mandate of establishing friendly relations between Graziani and the American legation, Engert knew when to adopt a firm attitude towards the Viceroy. However, this sometimes upset his superiors in Washington. In September 1936, following the public execution and burial of a number of Ethiopians near the legation, Engert dispatched a strongly worded message to Graziani complaining about the Italians' 'complete disregard of the most elementary feelings of decency and propriety', and warning the Viceroy that he 'will not in the future tolerate the perpetration of such horrors at the Legation's doorsteps'. He received abject apologies from Graziani, but for such 'violent language' in his protest he was promptly admonished by Washington.[60] Moreover, unknown to Engert, a State Department official noted that following the envoy's 'tactless' letter, there was a feeling in the Division of Near Eastern Affairs 'that Engert should not remain on longer than absolutely necessary in Addis Ababa'.[61]

Fortunately, Engert was permitted to stay on (at least until the legation was closed down in March 1937), and during the massacre of Addis Ababa he kept Washington up to date with daily dispatches. As an eyewitness of several shocking incidents, his observations and commentary constitute valuable source material on the massacre.

* * *

Although the French legation was several kilometres north-east of the city centre, it was not far from the Gennete-Li'ul Palace, where the massacre began. It was also adjacent to a densely populated area, and uncomfortably close to where many of the Italian military were garrisoned. Immediately to the west of the legation boundary wall were the barracks of the notorious 6th Blackshirt 'Tevere' Division, consisting of four regiments that had been deployed in Italian Somaliland, had fought on the southern front during the invasion, and included

34. The residence of the American envoy Cornelius Engert in 1935. Here Engert compiled and transmitted to Washington detailed accounts of incidents he personally witnessed during the massacre of Addis Ababa. Today this historic building has been taken over by the Yemen Community School

35. M. and Mme Bodard during an official visit to one of the offices of the Fascist Party in Addis Ababa in September 1936. Guido Cortese is on the left of the photograph, with M. Bodard

a machine-gun company. As noted earlier, most of the other Blackshirts involved in the invasion had been sent to Spain after the beginning of the Occupation, leaving the 'Tevere' as the principal Blackshirt division in Ethiopia.

Also quite close to the French legation was the 7th Colonial Brigade, consisting of Eritrean and Libyan *askaris*. Furthermore, the Centuria Autocarria, the Blackshirt company in charge of military trucks, was located just above Jan Méda (see Map 5). The presence on his doorstep of Blackshirts and *askaris*— the forces that took the lead in the massacre—was to create serious problems for the consul-General, Albert Bodard, and his staff. The envoy's problems were further exacerbated by a difficult relationship with Graziani. Despite having been decorated by Badoglio, Bodard represented a country whose relationship with Italy at that particular time was somewhat ambiguous.[62]

Circumstances at the French legation during the massacre would probably have prevented Bodard from venturing out into the city even if he had wanted to do so. Nonetheless, his dispatches to Paris, notably a long report sent on

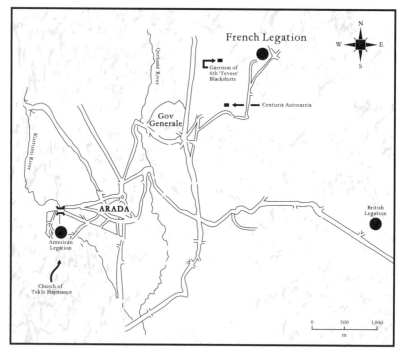

Map 5: Location of the British, American and French legations

24 February[63] and the reports of his conversations with Engert on events in and around the legation, an area known by the Ethiopians as Ferensay Legassion, constitute an important record of the activities of the Blackshirts in that part of the city during the massacre.

All three envoys—Bond (British), Engert (American) and Bodard (French)—played important roles in documenting various aspects of the massacre, but Bond and Bodard were responsible for compiling particularly detailed final reports, which, together with the report of Dr Shashka, remain the most valuable and authoritative accounts.

By 1.00 pm the carnage that commenced at the Gennete-Li'ul Palace before noon, and swept across the city to Arada and beyond, had consumed thousands of lives. It had also left hundreds—if not thousands—seriously injured. Even if it had been brought to a halt at that time, the incident would have gone down as one of the most brutal massacres of modern times. But there was more to come. The Blackshirts were now on the streets in their thousands, and they were not satisfied. The Hour of Mayhem was only the beginning.

4

DEATH IN THE AFTERNOON

CURFEW (1.00–1.30 PM)

At around 1.00 pm the Italian High Command announced a curfew covering the entire city. All the streets of Addis Ababa were now out of bounds to Ethiopians. Rosario Gilaegzi, the Eritrean interpreter of Count Della Porta, who was closely engaged with Graziani's highest officials at the time, explained that this followed a prearranged procedure whereby 'if rebels entered the city, every Ethiopian must stay inside his house; if he was found circulating in the streets, he should be shot'.[1]

The curfew was rapidly implemented. In Dr Shashka's words, 'Blackshirts, *carabinieri* and soldiers were running all over the town, ordering every shop-keeper to close his doors, and everyone else abroad to return to his home.'[2] Thus there were soon few Ethiopians remaining on the streets. But in contrast, groups of excited Fascists were appearing in growing numbers, anticipating orders to conduct reprisals.

This moment represented the official restoration of law and order in the city. Even if it were to be argued that the mayhem of the previous hour was a panic reaction, any crimes or atrocities committed after 1.30 pm can be put squarely at the door of the Italian authorities. Had they wished to do so, the Governo Generale could have terminated the massacre at this stage, and put it down to a temporary breakdown of military discipline resulting from the shock of the incident at the palace. Indeed, reflecting later on the situation, Dr Shashka surmised that if the slaughter had been stopped at the time of the curfew, the Fascist administration could have plausibly argued that their overreaction was the result of panic and fear that an organised rebellion was imminent.

However, despite the fact that no armed rebels had been encountered, and despite the military and *carabinieri* having clearly taken full control of the city, this was not the approach that the High Command decided to follow. Far from putting a stop to any further reprisals, they decided to unleash their *squadristi* across the city.

Thus, although Graziani in his memoirs tried to claim that the massacre was a defence of the city against an imminent uprising, this was a hollow argument. It was actually to satisfy a lust for bloodletting, looting and arson, for which the Blackshirts, militarised labourers and Italian civilians had been prepared and conditioned by Fascism's glorification of militancy and violence. It was also consistent with the tradition of indiscriminate civilian reprisals conducted by regulars as well as Blackshirts that had prevailed throughout the Invasion and Occupation.

While the curfew declared at 1.00 pm and communicated across the city over the half-hour that followed may have followed laid-down procedures to keep the peace, it was actually used for a different purpose. It became the prelude to greater horrors to come, because it made the Ethiopians a sitting target. The men would be taken away from their homes by armed soldiers and killed or detained, leaving the women and children defenceless and at the mercy of the marauding mob. A premeditated and carefully planned pogrom would then be conducted, plumbing depths of bestiality and depravity beside which even the slaughter at the palace would pale by comparison.

* * *

ARRESTS, DETENTION AND MURDER
(1.30–5.00 PM)

On Friday afternoon the city was gripped in fear as thousands of Blackshirts and regular soldiers poured onto the streets. Orders had gone out from the hastily reconvened High Command at the Gennete-Li'ul Palace to round up all potential enemies of the regime. Soldiers went from door to door, dragging out able-bodied adults, who were then herded in batches to the nearest prison or detention centre for screening. All across the city the compounds of public buildings, schools and large houses were being converted into makeshift detention camps, and houses were commandeered as temporary police stations.

Early in the afternoon the soldiers arrived at *Immahoy* Hiruta's house, which was in the area known today as Amist Kilo. Recounting her horrifying experience when a gang of Blackshirts and shovel-wielding militarised labourers—members of the dreaded Centuria Lavorati militia—burst in, she said,

> On *Yekatit 12* I did not hear the bombs, but there was a terrible incident. Soldiers came to the house. My Uncle Hussein was preparing for prayer with his friend Museyin.[3] On that day people were slaughtered with weapons such as shovels. They slashed Hussein with a shovel, cutting his eye. He was blinded, and fell to the ground. But he was forced to walk to prison with Muzeyin.[4]

> The survivors were all collected and taken to prison at the Police Garage. My brother and uncle were imprisoned there. All the men and able-bodied women were imprisoned. Injured people were also imprisoned. I went to the prison camp. (Two or three ladies in each house were left not arrested.) They were transporting dead bodies on open trucks. I saw many dead people. People were crying and shouting.[5]

Soon, hundreds of Ethiopians could be seen being made to walk to detention centres. Lieutenant Meleseliñ wrote, 'Those people who were thought to

36. Detainees rounded up from their houses, including several women, under the watchful eyes of regular army soldiers and *carabinieri* supported by Blackshirts. This photograph appears to have been taken in the compound of the Central Police Station at Fit Ber, most likely when it was just beginning to fill up in the afternoon of Friday, 19 February

be physically capable of fighting were identified and imprisoned.'[6] As Ambassador Imru put it, 'People were arrested and gathered from all over the country. [It was] sheer hysteria.'[7]

Around 1.30 pm the Blackshirts, who, as the reader may recall, had taken Temesgen Gebré with his companions to the St George's School area, moved on, to be replaced by another unit, which had been slaughtering Ethiopians nearby. Armed with eight machine-guns, they surrounded Temesgen's group and started tying them together with chains, arranging them for execution. But at that moment, by a stroke of good fortune, a high-ranking officer arrived who had a somewhat different agenda. It is likely that Temesgen's saviour on this occasion was a regular,[8] and the writer draws an interesting portrait of the senior officer's concerns. As with many members of the regular army, the officer's lack of involvement in the slaughter of civilians stemmed principally from having a different mandate. 'Although he had no objections to mass murder—the burning of people while they are in their houses—even children with their parents—he wanted to investigate and discover who was responsible for throwing the bombs at the Palace.'[9] The situation reflected a degree of confusion between the different arms of the military, with little, if any, coordination between them. The Blackshirts were doing whatever they liked, the regular rank and file were beginning to round up the citizenry, while the officers and *carabinieri* had been instructed to find the culprits of the attack at the Governo Generale.

The senior officer moved around for some time with the trucks, and ordered some of the Ethiopians to be sent to police stations or prisons for interrogation. He told the Blackshirts to untie Temesgen and the other captives, and to line them up for removal to another location. As they walked along the street, explained Temesgen, 'I could see on the ground the heads of Ethiopians split open by spades.'[10]

The captives appear to have been led down past today's Hager Fiqer theatre, across the main road leading to the Ras Mekonnin Bridge, and down into the Qechené River valley behind the shops overlooked by the Greek Church, for Temesgen noted that they ended up in a valley where the holy waters of St George were to be found. On arrival, they were told to line up five abreast. Was this to be their place of execution? Apparently not, for by this time the senior officer seems to have disappeared, and the captives were again at the mercy of the unpredictable Blackshirts, who seemed to have other ideas. They marched the captives back up the hill to the Municipality Building and, arriving at the gate, they were ordered to line up again on the main road outside, all facing forwards.

37. The use of heavy military trucks to kill Ethiopian civilians, depicted here on the *Yekatit 12* monument, began on Friday soon after midday, and was to be a persistent phenomenon throughout the massacre of Addis Ababa. The lower figure with outstretched arms in this close-up is being run over as the vehicle reverses. The truck most commonly used was the Fiat 634N, with double wheels in the rear

Now what were they waiting for? Temesgen soon found out. Standing in line with the other captives, he heard the noise of a military truck being driven at speed behind him, and before he realised what was happening, the vehicle ploughed into the column of prisoners, running them over, one after another along the line-up. The Blackshirts were having 'fun'. Some of the Ethiopians tried to jump out of the way but were bayoneted as they ran. By the time the truck had come to a halt, according to Temesgen, 48 of the captives had been killed outright in the carnage, and 18 had been injured. Among the latter was Temesgen himself, who suffered a painful knee injury. 'When I got up it seemed to me like a dream.'[11]

Though badly injured, Temesgen struggled to reach the safety of the nearby Municipality Office, which stood in a large courtyard. It was now 2.00 pm.[12] Hobbling along in agony, he found that many others were also fleeing the rampaging Blackshirts to reach the safety of the Municipality, and were being challenged by the *askaris* on guard there as they did so (see Figure 38). He managed to persuade the guards to let him in, but, once inside the compound, he was surprised to find that the new arrivals there were being detained—even women, babies, priests and the blind.[13] Nonetheless, despite now apparently

38. 'I sought to reach the gate of the Municipality'—Temesgen Gebré. As Ethiopians run towards the front gate of the Municipality Office to escape the carnage, an armed soldier rushes to stop them, and guards block their way. Other soldiers and Italian civilians look on. An *askari* in the left foreground raises his baton, apparently commanding them to halt. The length of the shadows indicates that this photograph was taken at around 2.00 pm

being a prisoner, Temesgen was at least temporarily safe from the terror on the street outside.

By 2.00 pm Tekle-Maryam Kiflom was back home from Siddist Kilo, in the house at Arat Kilo that he shared with Gebre-Sillassé, a member of the Emperor's Imperial Bodyguard, and Siyum Zenebe, an old friend from his Teferi Mekonnin School days. Along with several other cottages, their home was situated where today stand the apartment blocks owned by the Ethiopian Orthodox Church. But there was no question of relaxing, for no sooner had Tekle-Maryam arrived than he heard a commotion—the sound of roaring engines, slamming doors, shooting, and screaming women. Marauding groups of Blackshirts and Italian soldiers had descended on the area. Amid a cacophony of noise they were going from house to house, bursting in and taking away the men. The noise grew louder, and it was not long before they reached Tekle-Maryam's home. Yielding to swift kicks and rifle butts, the door flew open. Suddenly the room was full of Italian military, and the 18-year-old found himself being dragged outside, flung into the back of a lorry together with other young men, and driven away.

Tekle-Maryam soon realised that once again this was not disorderly conduct on the part of the soldiers; the arrests had clearly been ordered at the highest level. And it was the same story all over town: having told everyone to stay in their houses, Blackshirts and men of the Regia Aeronautica had been sent to scour the Ethiopian residential areas and remove all the able-bodied men they found at home. In each district a public building or fenced open space was used as a temporary prison for their internment.

From the back of the truck, Tekle-Maryam could see that he was lucky to have reached home when he did, for men caught on the street were receiving much harsher treatment than those who had got to their homes. He was stunned to see men being tripped up, knocked down and brutally beaten—in many cases to death—by Blackshirts, who were carrying out indiscriminate killings alongside the relatively orderly arrests of the more disciplined Regia Aeronautica and regular army. In some cases, running unexpectedly into a gang of Blackshirts and Fascist civilians before they realised what was going on, Ethiopian passers-by were accosted, and clubbed or stabbed to death with

39. Violent attacks on Ethiopians continued throughout Friday afternoon. Here a 'repression squad' (as Graziani termed the Fascist vigilante groups of Blackshirts and Italian civilians) looks down on the bodies of its victims, each of whom seems to have had their arms tied behind their back, then tied together with a connecting wire before being killed

40. On Friday afternoon the Italians carried out surprise attacks on Ethiopians on a wider front than before the curfew

daggers on the spot. The American consul-general reported, 'The Italians have ... completely lost their heads. Undisciplined bands of Blackshirts and laborers armed with rifles, axes or clubs have since the incident [at the Governo Generale] been roaming the streets killing all natives in sight even women amidst scenes of revolting savagery.'[14]

In Tekle-Maryam's words, 'After 2.00 pm, when I was under arrest, I saw them doing terrible things in the Arat Kilo district: Men taken from their houses were arrested and detained; men found on the street were beaten. For example, their legs were beaten [to stop them running away]. Some people were just killed when they came across the groups of Italians going around. I witnessed it in Arat Kilo, but I soon learned that this was going on all over town. Orders must have been given. I asked later about the fate of individuals that Friday afternoon, and learned that so-and–so had been arrested or killed in such-and-such an area.'[15]

Tekle-Maryam went on to identify several areas where these attacks were particularly prevalent in the afternoon: the area where the Police Garage or Central Police Station[16] was located, that is Sera Bét Sefer; the western part of Lower Arat Kilo, stretching south from today's Tourist Hotel; the Arada Market area; parts of Piazza; Gedam Sefer (immediately north of St George's Cathedral); Dejazmach Wibé Sefer (around today's Addis Ababa Restaurant); and Serateñña Sefer (east of Piazza, down to the Qechené River). While some of these were the same areas attacked before the curfew was announced, a comparison of Map 6 with Map 3 indicates a general extension of the attacks from Arada. This is, of course, not surprising, given that by now far more troops had come out onto the streets.

* * *

41. The afternoon of 19 February 1937: Ethiopian civilians rounded up are ushered into the Municipality Office, which has been converted into a temporary detention camp

Meanwhile, the large, walled compound of the Municipality Office, to which Temesgen Gebré had managed to drag himself after narrowly surviving the slaughter of the Hour of Mayhem, was now serving as the city's first major detention centre. There were so many people crowding the grounds that the injured Temesgen, squatting on the ground, recalled, 'The compound of the Municipality was not quite large enough for stretching our feet, because there were more prisoners, and more prisoners were still coming. The open spaces between prisoners were used as a lavatory.'[17]

From the length of the shadows it appears that the photograph in Figure 41, showing Ethiopians being herded into the premises, was taken around 2.45 pm—a different scene from the earlier view, when Ethiopians were being hindered from entering in their desperation to escape the carnage outside.

* * *

Some Ethiopians who were fortunate enough to be protected by foreigners escaped the dragnet. It was probably on Friday afternoon that the Greek Lentakis family in Serateñña Sefer gave sanctuary to terrified Ethiopians fleeing the attacks. Michael Lentakis, who was born in the family home in 1932 and wrote about the massacre when he retired, recalled that many ran from St George's Cathedral towards Serateñña Sefer and down towards the river

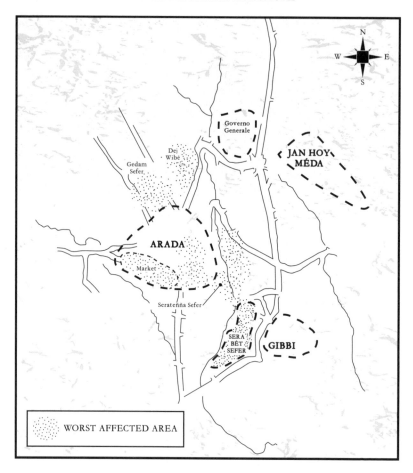

Map 6: Districts particularly subjected to attack on Friday afternoon

Ambesso (also known as the Qechené, or Genfile) in the Eribe Kentu area, which was densely forested. He recalled, 'Five Amharas came into our house [near the Shoa Hotel; see Map 3], and my father hid them in the big store, where we kept firewood and charcoal.' Here these Ethiopians remained in hiding until one day after the massacre, when his father led them down to the river, to safety.[18]

* * *

After a circuitous journey around Arat Kilo collecting men taken from their homes by the military, the truck carrying Tekle-Maryam reached its destination: the former Menelik II School—actually opposite Tekle-Maryam's home—where the headquarters of the Regia Aeronautica had been installed. The prisoners were ordered off the truck, then herded into the school yard, where an officer told them to sit on the ground and await instructions.

On Sunday Graziani would inform Mussolini that 1,000 people had been executed (excluding, of course, those killed by the Blackshirts and civilians). But reports emerging over the next two to three weeks indicated that several thousand men were taken prisoner in Addis Ababa on Friday and the days that followed, and that by the time the detentions and 'official' executions were over, the number of dead exceeded this figure. For example, New York's *Amsterdam News* reported, 'Already, reliable sources in Rome and French Somaliland have admitted that some 1,400 Ethiopians have been executed, that 2,000 more have been rounded up and arrested ...'[19] Another report read, 'As has already been reported, some 2,000 natives were arrested. The majority were shot.'[20] And an Ethiopian writer stated, 'The whole city was in a state of upheaval. People walking the street peacefully were captured and sent to prisons. They killed half of them.'[21]

But Tekle-Maryam was one of the lucky ones. Later that afternoon—probably because he was born in Eritrea—to his surprise and relief he was released, and thankfully made his way across the road to his home. By that time it was around 5.00 pm, and he was pleased to be greeted by the wives and children of his neighbours, who congratulated him on his narrow escape.

* * *

Another survivor was 23-year-old *Dyakon* Dawit Gebre-Mesqel of the Church of Ta'eka Negest Be'ata (often known as the Menelik Mausoleum), who told his story in detail to the present author. The church was, and still is, situated within the periphery of Emperor Menelik's *gibbi*, which had been taken over as the headquarters of the Italian regular army. Thus Dawit, who lived in a nearby church house, was dwelling on the perimeter of a sensitive area exempted from destruction.

Dyakon Dawit, who before the Occupation had by chance been working with *Yekatit 12* plotter Abriha Deboch at St George's School in Arada,[22] was doubly fortunate. Not only was his church located outside the area earmarked later in the day for destruction, but he had also decided not to go to the almsgiving at the Governo Generale. The clergy had been invited, and, being attached to one of the most important churches of the city, he and his colleagues were expected to attend. However, Dawit was due to lead a mass beginning at noon, together with *Dyakon* Kassaye and *Dyakon* Gebre-Sillassé,

42. On the afternoon of Friday, 19 February 1937, following the strike of *Yekatit 12*, the Church of Kidane Mihret (left foreground, in front of the Menelik Mausoleum) was invaded by marauding Blackshirts

and so he had decided to stay in the church. The decision saved his life. The mass was actually to be conducted at the adjoining traditional circular Church of Kidane Mihret, for during the Italian invasion the Emperor had arranged for the Church of Ta'eka Negest Be'ata to be surrounded and reinforced with stones or concrete to help protect it against possible attack, and it was thus not currently in use.

Dyakon Dawit and his fellow deacons went ahead with the mass, unaware that there were disturbances in the city until around 2.00 pm, when he heard the sound of gunshots. As noted earlier, the killing had begun further north, in Siddist Kilo. It spread to Arada shortly afterwards, but had not yet reached as far south as the Menelik *gibbi*. However, the curfew had been announced, and the Italians were entering shops, churches and other institutions all over the city, closing them down and arresting the occupants.

Suddenly there was a disturbance. While mass was in progress, Dawit watched in horror as a gang of Blackshirts burst into the church. There was pandemonium. Some of them were brandishing guns and ordering everybody out, while others, with daggers drawn, forced their way into the sanctuary— the Holy of Holies, which only the most senior clergy were permitted to enter—where they confronted the three priests who were there.

Amid the turmoil Dawit and his two fellow *dyakons* were chased out of the church at gunpoint. They had no idea what was going on, why the soldiers had invaded the church, or whether they were going to be shot. Then they were ordered to stand in a corner of the church compound, which they did, wondering what on earth was going to happen next.[23]

* * *

Meanwhile, the detention centre at the Ras Mekonnin Bridge was filling up, and it seems that it was in the afternoon, during the hours of daylight, that the search for hand grenades, described below by Dr Shashka, was conducted. It was thought at first by the High Command that the grenades used for the attack on Graziani were of Italian 'Breda' manufacture, but his Military Intelligence later claimed that they were British, and used that as a pretext to search and loot houses and burn the occupants to death. One such incident, which, as we shall see, was to be repeated numerous times throughout the city after darkness fell, was described in detail by Dr Shashka:

> In the domiciliary search for British hand grenades a group of Italians entered an Abyssinian hut near the [Ras] Mekonnin Bridge. Of course they found no hand grenades, but there were *thalers* (Ethiopian silver dollars), kept for safety in a money box, and these were confiscated as a trophy of war, victory and civilisation. In the same room they also found a hidden picture of the Emperor Haile Selassie. For the hiding of this symbol the whole family in the hut were condemned to death. They were to be burnt alive. In a few moments' time the house began to burn and with it the members of the family whom the Italians had locked in. Their desperate cries were heard around the hut but the Italians did not move from the place till the cries had ceased; they were anxious that none should escape the fire ... The picture of the Emperor in the incident I have mentioned above was, however, merely a pretext for the burning of the hut and the extermination of the family. Huts were burned and families murdered, with or without the portrait of the Emperor ...[24]

The burning of houses in the afternoon, though not as systematic as it would be after dark, was already quite extensive. In the words of a fire brigade officer who later swore an affidavit as a United Nations War Crimes Commission witness, 'We, the Fire Brigade Section, were specially ordered not to put out the fires in any houses other than Italian ones. Then we understood their scheme for committing atrocities was a big one.'[25]

An Information Blackout

As the afternoon drew to a close, more and more Blackshirts and Italian civilians appeared on the streets. All postal and telephonic communications in and out of Ethiopia had been suspended,[26] a measure designed to put an information blackout over the terror that was about to be unleashed. The result was that the European news agencies were for some time starved of information, and many of their early reports were speculative. Reuters was to complain, 'The Italian censorship does not let pass any telegram from Addis Ababa. No authentic details can be obtained of the attempt on the Viceroy.'[27] This is confirmed by Dr Shashka's report: 'The strictest censorship is maintained, not only on all telegrams, but even on private letters. Everyone leaving by train is searched for letters. The only free communication left open is the diplomatic bag. Journalists are forbidden to send any dispatch mentioning the massacre.'[28]

Furthermore, the order went out for the *carabinieri* and military to confiscate all cameras found in the possession of foreigners. 'If any white person ventured onto the streets he was stopped at every corner, and searched to see if he had a camera on him. The houses of white people were visited by Italian soldiers, who confiscated cameras and then went away as it was still risky to touch citizens of countries under the protection of a foreign embassy.'[29]

With the cutting of telegraphic communications and the confiscation of cameras, a veil descended over Addis Ababa.

* * *

A STATE OF SIEGE

The first indications of the scale of the onslaught to come were the sights and sounds of the Regia Aeronautica flying low and bombing areas on the periphery, to prevent people leaving the city and, presumably, to prevent any 'rebels' from entering. An Ethiopian eyewitness was to speak of 'gigantic birds of death' taking off from the aerodrome at Akaki and, with 'a frightful drone', bombing various districts.[30]

By 1937 Italy's Regia Aeronautica had become one of Europe's most advanced air forces. While not as large as Mussolini's propaganda would suggest, it deployed relatively modern aircraft, and operated hundreds of them. The most numerous was the Caproni Ca 133, which had a wingspan of 70 feet, four machine guns, and a payload of 500 kg of bombs.[31] The Regia Aeronautica operated 205 of these aircraft in Ethiopia.[32] In addition to several hundred other aircraft, they also had a fleet of 57 Savoia-Marchetti SM.81s, which were even larger, with a wingspan of almost 80 feet, a payload of up to two tons of bombs, and seven machine guns.[33]

Overflying the city and dropping incendiary bombs on the outskirts, these machines were indeed terrifying, particularly to Ethiopians for whom aeroplanes were not a common sight, and perhaps even more so for the soldiers who had faced them in battle and had witnessed the horrifying results of their bombing and gas attacks in the countryside. Although the outskirts were bombed, so far as is known no bombs were dropped within the city, for there were thousands of Italians there. However, the Regia Aeronautica overflew the city day and night.

43. Taken looking towards the south-south-east, this aerial photograph shows a Savoia-Marchetti SM.81 bomber flying over the former imperial *gibbi*, which was used during the Occupation as Italian military headquarters. The domed roof of *Dyakon Dawit's* Church of Ta'eka Negest Be'ata can be seen left of centre. In the foreground are the densely populated southern reaches of Beshah Welde Chilot Sefer (Lower Arat Kilo). Between this area and the *gibbi* itself, and stretching to the far right of the foreground, is the even more densely populated Sera Bét Sefer, where traditionally the palace employees lived. During the massacre of Addis Ababa both of these residential areas, full of houses interspersed with eucalyptus trees, were devastated by arson, murder and pillage

Meanwhile, from the outskirts of the city could be heard not only the bombing, but also the sound of artillery—the big guns. Italy's artillery was quite out of date compared to her air force, but nonetheless it had been a formidable force during the Invasion, and certainly more than a match for anything the Ethiopians had been able to bring up to face it. Now the artillery was ostensibly being used to prevent people from fleeing the city. But it was also clearly intended to terrify the city's residents, which, judging from Dr Shashka's report, it succeeded in doing: 'From the fortified positions [around the city] canon and machine-guns vomited a hail of shots without respite ... Very thick smoke darkened the sky. The noise of sharp and hollow blows resounded; they rapidly multiplied, interrupted from time to time by other, yet stronger blows.'[34]

Italian surveillance was intense not only from the air, but also within the city. Several witnesses reported the appearance of tanks and armoured cars on the streets; they had been brought in from the outskirts of the city in the early afternoon, carrying reinforcements for the troops garrisoned in the centre. A French diplomat's eyewitness account that made its way to the authorities in Paris described the situation: 'The capital and its environs then passed into a state of siege. Aeroplanes zoomed overhead and tanks and motorised machine guns patrolled all the roads, shooting down all whom they encountered.'[35]

The most common tank in the Italian arsenal at that time was the CV (Carro Veloce) 33 (brought out in 1933 and also known as the L3 CV-33), as

44. The Italians used L3 CV-33 and CV-35 tanks during the massacre of Addis Ababa

45. Fiat 3000 Model 21 tanks entering Addis Ababa in May 1936

46. The formidable Fiat 611 Autoblinda armoured cars were deployed during the massacre of Addis Ababa. Based on the 'Trenta Quattro' truck chassis, these large and fearsome vehicles weighed 6.9 tons, had a crew of five, and were equipped with three guns, two of which were machine-guns

well as the CV 35 (brought out in 1935). Several hundred of these tanks took part in the invasion of Ethiopia. They were comparatively light, manoeuvrable, and carried a crew of two men. The CV 33 had one 'Breda' machine gun; the CV 35 version was identical but had two machine guns, of which one could be replaced by a flame-thrower. These small but effective tanks were deployed in Addis Ababa during the massacre. They were used not only to shoot Ethiopians encountered on the streets on Friday afternoon, but also, as we shall see, to destroy houses and terrorise and kill their occupants.

The other tank in the Italian arsenal was the Fiat 3000 Model 21. With a weight of six tons, it was larger than the CV 33. It had a crew of two, and was capable of 21 kph.

The streets were also patrolled by armoured cars. These were not, as the name might suggest, armour-plated passenger cars. They were what the French diplomat referred to as 'motorised machine guns', 'shooting down all whom they encountered'. Heavily armed vehicles almost three metres high, they were built on the 6-metre-long Fiat 634N military 'Trenta Quattro' truck chassis and weighed almost seven tons (twice the weight of the CV 33 tank). Although slow when driven cross-country (max. speed 9 kph), they could travel at 27 kph on roads and thus outrun their victims. These formidable machines had no difficulty in 'shooting down all whom they encountered'. Capable of being driven through a house and out the other side without pausing, they brought terror to the residents of Addis Ababa.

The afternoon air raid and the use of artillery were confirmed by the American envoy Engert, who at 4.00 pm sent the Secretary of State a telegram stating that, following an attempt on the life of Graziani, 'Italian authorities at once took dramatic action machine-gunning and beating natives and indiscriminately burning their huts. Bombing planes have been acting with incendiary bombs in the outskirts of the city and at this writing a good deal of rifle and even field-gun [artillery] fire is audible throughout the city. All natives have been driven off the streets and the Italians, including civilian laborers, seem thoroughly alarmed and go about heavily armed.'[36] 'By an odd coincidence', the envoy added, 'the Marshal and Madame Graziani were at their own suggestion to have come to tea at this Legation this afternoon.'

* * *

At the French legation, M. Bodard was worried. By 4.00 pm, when the envoy was dispatching his first telegram to Paris on the subject of the attempt at the palace, he had a lot to report. He described how the gates of the palace had been closed and 'all the natives massacred without pity', and how the city was now in a state of siege, with aeroplanes flying incessantly overhead. He wrote, 'A dark terror reigns across the city and its suburbs, where Blackshirts and labourers are responding like a terrifying whirlwind, machine guns and rifles in their hands. The *carabinieri* and the Army regulars are trying hard to control the Fascist elements, who are ready to murder and pillage.'

Being written at the time, Bodard's report confirms beyond any doubt that by mid-afternoon, without waiting for official instructions, some Blackshirts had already embarked upon reprisals, including burning houses and killing the occupants, 'notably those located near our Legation', while the city was full of tanks and armoured cars. Already, he said, the conflagration had been under way for four hours. It is clear that the consul-general's problems with the marauding Blackshirts, which, unknown to him were to persist for several days, had begun, for he went on to say that shots had been fired into the premises and had injured two of the legation's servants. He added that he was now taking strict security measures, correctly expecting that worse was yet to come.[37]

* * *

5

CARTA BIANCA

'DO AS YOU PLEASE'
(4.30–5.00 PM)

Once the curfew had been declared, and most of the city's men rounded up, all the Fascists knew what was to follow. According to a pattern employed during both the Invasion and the Occupation, these preliminaries were a natural precursor to an orgy of violence, pillage and bloodletting to be triggered by the chilling words *carta bianca* (carte blanche).

The usual procedure was that once *carta bianca* had been declared, the military would swing into action with the support of the Regia Aeronautica. The military telegrams are replete with instructions for such reprisals, in which thousands of homesteads would be attacked. An Italian soldier who fought during the invasion described how *carta bianca* worked in the countryside: 'If by any chance a white was ambushed and killed, the aviation had orders to destroy all habitations within a radius of fifty kilometres. This was called "the order of do as you please" (*carta bianca*). Without mercy all were then killed, unarmed men, women and children ... Many of our "big battles" consisted purely and simply of making great heaps of dead and wounded and burning them with flame-throwers.'[1]

Within a short while of the attempt on the Viceroy, the Blackshirts knew that the announcement of *carta bianca* was only a matter of time. Edouard Garabedian, the Armenian businessman with a shop in Piazza, was to testify, 'I myself heard comments from some of them, saying that they were awaiting orders for reprisals.'[2] Once the order was received, the procedure was sufficiently well known as to follow without delay. Thus the massacre of Addis Ababa would conform to a tried and tested pattern: the looting and torching of dwellings and the shooting, stabbing or burning to death of their terrified inhabitants.

During the afternoon, while the mass arrests were being conducted, the authorities summoned Fascist Party members to Casa Littoria in Piazza. As the High Command conferred and drew up their plans, military and civilian Fascists gathered in the square and waited to hear the announcement as to when and where they should strike. The crowd was in a state of anticipation and great excitement, for once the zones to be attacked had been decided and the order given, it would be 'do as you please'. The person expected to announce it was Guido Cortese, federal secretary of the Fascist Party. So who was Guido Cortese?

As noted earlier, Cortese was a zealous young Fascist who had achieved a high rank at an early age, and had direct communication with Rome. But because so little attention has hitherto been paid to the man who achieved infamy through his commanding role in the massacre of Addis Ababa, it is

47. Fascists at Casa Littoria, housed in the reconstructed Kevorkoff building. Although taken the year after the massacre, this photograph shows the use of Casa Littoria, which today houses Castelli's Restaurant, as a rallying point for the party

worth examining his background in a little more depth.[3] Cortese was born in September 1902. By 1918, at the age of 16, he had joined Mussolini's Fascist Party, and in 1922 he was involved in the March on Rome that led to the *Duce*'s takeover of the Italian government. Having achieved a senior rank as a *squadrista*, and having earned Blackshirt awards, in July 1928 at the age of 25 he was sent to Eritrea as secretary to the Governor. Within a few months he had been appointed federal secretary of the party in Asmara, a position he held until July 1930, when he returned to Italy.

Specialising in Fascist indoctrination of the youth, he was appointed secretary-general of the Ente Nazionale per la Mutualità Scolastica (National Body for Assisting Students). Then a year later, in 1931, he became Secretary-General of the prestigious Fascist thinktank, the Istituto Coloniale Fascista (Fascist Colonial Institute), where he wrote a number of monographs on the Italian colonial experience.[4]

Guido Cortese was an ardent Fascist, but clearly not just a street thug, as were many of the early *squadristi*. A high-flyer, having achieved senior party positions at an early age, he can be regarded as one of the rising stars in Mussolini's constellation. It is thus perhaps not altogether surprising that by June 1936, after five years in the Istituto, at the age of only 33, we find him in Addis Ababa, becoming federal secretary of the party.[5]

He was frequently photographed inspecting schools, and the account of his involvement in the establishment of the first Italian public library in Addis Ababa makes interesting reading.[6] But, above all, as party supremo of the city, given the framework of Fascism that shaped the lives of its members 24 hours a day, Cortese commanded the loyalty of not only thousands of card-carrying Italian civilians, but also more than 14,000 armed Blackshirts. This

48. The Fascist Party federal secretary, Guido Cortese, c. 1935, before the invasion of Ethiopia

gave him, in effect, power of life and death over the Ethiopian residents of Addis Ababa.

Now, in the afternoon of 19 February 1937, the federal secretary, having himself been slightly injured in the attack at the Governo Generale, was beside himself with fury, and gave every sign of being willing to respond to the cries of '*Du-ce! Du-ce!*' with the expected *carta bianca*. The Belgian businessman Maurice Weerts recalled being among the crowd when the Cortese first arrived at *Casa Littoria*: 'I saw Cortese … standing in an open car … with blood on his face, screaming at the top of his voice that Ethiopians had tried to kill the Viceroy and ordering the Italians around him to kill everyone within sight.'[7]

In due course the Eritrean interpreter Rosario Gilaezgi arrived: '[After 4 pm] [*Conte*] Della Porta and [*Capitano*] Bechis took me in a car and I went with them to the headquarters of the Fascists, because Della Porta, who was a Fascist, had received an order to go there. There we met the *Secretario Federale* Guido Cortese, and a good number of Fascists were present.'[8] Having apparently recovered his composure, Cortese disappeared into the building and reappeared on the balcony, looking down on the sea of expectant faces. Clearly, the bloodlust of the last few hours had not satisfied the party rank and file, and neither, apparently, did the officials consider it necessary to turn down the heat. To the contrary, the medieval three days of murder, pillage and arson would now be formally invoked. The massacre of Tripoli was to be re-enacted, with a vengeance. Dr Werqineh's worst fears were to be realised.

49. Proclamation of the massacre of Addis Ababa. This news photograph, taken from a window above the balcony of Casa Littoria, reportedly shows Guido Cortese making the announcement of *carta bianca* to Blackshirts, Italian civilians and colonial *askaris*

Giving the baying crowd unlimited licence to teach the Ethiopians a lesson they would never forget, Cortese met all their expectations, and more. The British acting consul-general summarised the federal secretary's message diplomatically for London: 'I am told that the signal for the slaughter was given by the Fascist Federal Secretary hot from the palace, who in an "injudicious" speech exhorted Italians "'to go to it'".[9] But in his sworn testimony for the UN War Crimes Commission, Rosario Gilaezgi quoted Cortese verbatim: 'Cortese spoke to them, saying: "Comrades, today is the day when we should show our devotion to our Viceroy by reacting and destroying the Ethiopians for three days. For three days I give you *carta bianca* to destroy and kill and do what you want to the Ethiopians."'[10] Then weapons were handed out, and, as the Armenian businessman Edouard Garabedian testified, Cortese announced which residential areas were to be destroyed by designated teams of Blackshirts: 'I heard them [the Fascists] saying that the "Federal" ordered them to call on indicated places in groups. In the evening at about five o'clock they began.'[11]

There was no turning back. From that moment on, the Ethiopian residents of Addis Ababa were doomed. The nightmare was about to begin.

* * *

TERROR UNLEASHED
(5.00–6.45 PM)

Armed with their daggers and guns with bayonets fixed, supplemented by hand grenades and other weapons handed out at Casa Littoria to civilians, the Blackshirts fanned out from Piazza. As Rosario Gilaezgi put it, 'They went out well equipped with their arms, and started their work.'[12] Augmented by armed *askaris*, the militarised Fascist labourers with their shovels, and other Italian civilians who had been handed out weapons such as truncheons, knives and iron bars, the howling mob spilt up into groups of around 50 and attacked like packs of wild dogs every Ethiopian they encountered.[13] From behind rumbled a growing fleet of military trucks, which passed them en route to the 'native quarters', carrying Blackshirts singing and yelling *'Duce! Duce!'* in a state of near delirium.

With the proclamation of *carta bianca* disappeared the last vestige of hope for the citizens of Addis Ababa. If there had been any restraints on the violence of the earlier hours—a few sympathetic and more disciplined regulars or moderate *carabinieri*, a kindly Armenian family, some friendly Greeks—there were now virtually none. The massacre was now official, to be perpetrated by the very organs responsible for law and order. And it would take place in the city's residential 'villages', largely beyond the eyes and ears of any foreigners. Furthermore, there was no possibility of help from outside. The nearest armed Ethiopians willing and able to stand up to the invaders were far away in northern Shewa, and the international community was unaware of what was going on. Furthermore, this situation was not likely to change, since telegraphic communications with the outside world had been cut. With most of their able-bodied menfolk in custody, the women, children and the elderly, many now alone in their houses, would be sitting ducks for the marauding Fascists.

Contemporary records are explicit, consistent, and speak for themselves. Dr Shashka would never forget that day: 'They sped from the Fascio in every direction, fully armed. Everyone in the town was a prey to terrified anticipation, for what really happened was worse than anyone had feared. I am bound to say, for it is true, that blood was literally streaming down the streets.'[14] In 1991, *Abune* Mattewos, then of the Church of Miskaye Hizunan Medhané Alem, told the present author that during the massacre, blood was actually flowing down the Intotto Road outside the church. The full horror took time to reach the outside world, but eventually news started to trickle out. *The Times* of London would describe how 'with rifles, pistols, bombs, knives and clubs served out for the occasion, gangs of Blackshirts and workmen went through the native quarters killing every man, woman, and child they came across'.[15] New York's *Amsterdam News* also announced, 'Following this decision, mopping up parties, made up of young Italians anxious for excitement and slaughter, started out to execute, officially and unofficially, all those they chose to execute, pouncing down on natives who did not even know of the attempt on Graziani's life.'[16] Indeed, those who had already been detained were in some respects better off than those who still knew nothing about the attempt. As Rosario pointed out, 'People who were not [already] arrested by the *carabinieri* and were found in their houses or in the streets were killed.'[17]

As we have seen, house-burning had begun in the Jan Méda area almost immediately after the attack at the palace, and Welette-Birhan Gebre-Iyyesus said that it was still going on there in the late afternoon. 'By late afternoon, by 5.00 pm or earlier, there was house-burning in the daylight. It was especially in the Jan Méda area, close to Menelik Hospital. There the Italians actually threw children into the fires.'

The reader will recall that *Immahoy* Hiruta testified that the Jan Méda area was the scene of particularly horrific brutality. Alemash Sibhatu, daughter of Graziani's secretary and interpreter, Sibhatu Yohannis, whose house was at what is now the Yared School of Music, on the perimeter of Jan Méda, also confirmed that in the afternoon, 'Soldiers were given orders to kill people indiscriminately. They were going to households. Families were sitting [inside] with their children. The Italians put kerosene or benzine—they set fire [to the houses]. There was one house [in particular] near our area which they set on fire ... *tukuls* were burned.'[18]

This particular house is likely to have been one of the two referred to by the French consul-general in the following report: 'I have received from the Superior of the French Sisters of St Vincent de Paul, whose statements cannot be doubted, that in the immediate vicinity of her community [which was in Jan Méda], two *tukuls* were burned with all their occupants, numbering respectively fourteen and sixteen.'[19]

In addition to forwarding to London summaries of Engert's reports, the horrified British acting consul-general reported, 'Ethiopians were hunted through the streets and into their dwellings all over the town and were beaten, shot,

50. In the falling light, following the declaration of *carta bianca*, a gang of armed Blackshirts descend on a house to loot, murder and burn. Note that they have been issued with guns, and bayonets are fixed

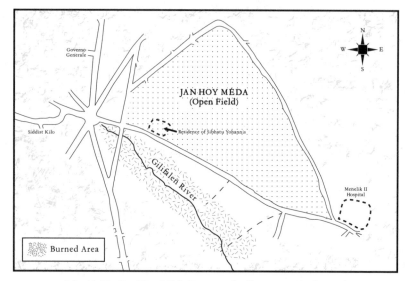

Map 7. The Jan Hoy Méda District, the first area to be burned

bayonetted or clubbed to death ... A band of eight Blackshirts were seen beating, apparently to death, with staves, an Ethiopian whose hands had first been tied behind his back ... A young man fetching water from a well in the middle of the town was struck by an Italian in military uniform and when he started to run off was shot. He fell into a ditch and on attempting to raise [himself,] his head was smashed in by another Italian who had headed him off.'[20]

Being a man on the spot in the city centre, Dr Shashka witnessed several atrocities close up: 'Blackshirts put a stick from behind between the feet of running black men in order to throw them to the ground, the more easily to murder them ... I have seen a man's head split open by a truncheon so that the brains gushed out ...'[21] Witnesses who fled the city arrived in Djibouti to tell their tales of terror: 'Blood flowed on all sides in torrents. Frightful screams of women and children mingled with the diabolical concert of modern arms ... Every Abyssinian man was shot on sight, and those [civilians] who did not have rifles made use of clubs and other weapons.'[22]

The foreign community was aghast. 'A sort of savage anger seized their spirits,' wrote M. Bodard. 'Groups of fierce men, breaking into violence from all sides, armed with guns, grenades and clubs, started, in their turn, to chase the Abyssinians.'[23] The journalist George Steer would relate how 'A friend

51. 'A band of eight Blackshirts were seen beating, apparently to death, with staves, an Ethiopian whose hands had first been tied behind his back'—British acting consul-general. Ethiopians set upon in the afternoon and early evening of Friday were taken unawares, and many were slaughtered with improvised weapons and shovels that were standard issue to the militarised labourers. The soldier in the left background is an officer, as is the decorated soldier squatting on the right

52. 'Every soldier band became a court-martial'—London *Daily Herald*, 8 March 1937. By early Friday evening 'repression squads' of Blackshirts, militiamen and civilians were on a rampage throughout the city

of mine saw a little Ethiopian boy running down a path. Three Italians ordered him to stop. He ran on and they fired at him. He fell down, staggered up, and ran a few paces. They fired at him again. This time he did not get up. One of them walked up to him and clubbed out his brain with the butt of his rifle.'[24]

The residential districts close to the city were the most seriously affected, particularly the Ras Mekonnin Bridge area, which was becoming a systematic killing centre. The Italian journalist Guido Mattioli described how an Eritrean non-commissioned officer positioned himself on the bridge and single-handedly shot dead every Ethiopian who crossed it, 'creating widows all around'. That one soldier, wrote Mattioli, 'could be said to have carried out a massacre of his own'.[25]

Furthermore, as eyewitness Dawit Oquba Igzi'i would testify, the killing was now proceeding on an industrial scale, with Ethiopians being trucked around the city to execution points. 'People were brought in lorries [to Ras Mekonnin Bridge]; they were taken without distinction and most of them were bleeding from hits. The Fascists used to throw them down [from] the lorries. Some of them rolled down to the river, because they were thrown from the lorries, and these the Italians shot in front of us.'[26]

Several days later, when he had had an opportunity to meet witnesses and compile the many reports that had arrived at his office, William Bond at the British legation was to elaborate on the events of Friday. His account included an independent report of the incidents witnessed by Dawit Oquba Igzi'i at the Ras Mekonnin Bridge, and described by Dr Shashka, in which, the envoy reported, Ethiopians 'were thrown over the parapet of a bridge onto the boulders below, a forty foot drop, and those who appeared to be still alive were finished off with rifles from the top'. He added, 'Looting by Italians was general. Even corpses were searched for money.'[27]

Killing with Vehicles

As we have seen, heavy trucks were used to run over Ethiopians at the Municipality Office early Friday afternoon, and later in the day more of these vehicles arrived, as well as several tanks and armoured cars. Many were brought from the barracks near Jan Méda; others were driven into the city by heavily armed militia from the forts constructed around the outskirts a few months before.

The French consul-general, who wrote with a certain literary flair, confirmed the use of heavy trucks as instruments of death: 'The drivers of motor trucks also chased Abyssinians with their vehicles, or fiercely aimed them at natives to crush them. When the victims were reluctant to die, blows from cudgels opened up their skulls and brought the recalcitrants to reason ['*mettaient les récalcitrants à la raison*'].[28]

Apart from driving over and crushing their victims, the practice that earned the Blackshirts notoriety in Italy during Mussolini's rise to power in the early 1920s had been the killing of opponents by dragging them to their death. Given the numerous lorries available to them in Addis Ababa, both from the military and the Italian government transport company, it was perhaps inevitable that they would use the same method during the massacre of Addis Ababa. Kirubel Beshah, an Ethiopian witness who had been a student at the Teferi Mekonnin School

53. An Ethiopian nobleman with retainers crosses the Ras Mekonnin Bridge in the tranquillity of 1935, before the Italian invasion. During the massacre of *Yekatit 12*, the strategically positioned bridge became a killing centre, and here Italians threw men down the steep embankment onto the rocks below. Here also an Eritrean non-commissioned officer stood on the bridge and shot Ethiopians attempting to cross

and who after Liberation would teach mathematics there, reported, 'Ethiopian blood flowed like water everywhere. Saddest of all was that at first they tied dead bodies to the back of their trucks, and pulled them along the road while shouting and singing, but later, they also started to tie the living to their trucks, so as not to waste bullets. It was very disturbing to see human bodies being torn to pieces alive, by stones and bushes.'[29]

George Steer was also aware of these atrocities: 'Others [Blackshirts] in lorries chased Ethiopians down and ran over them; or tied them by the feet to the tail of the truck and pulled them thus along the public streets.'[30] And an Ethiopian witness reported, 'One could see groups of Fascists chaining the lorries and amusing themselves by dragging along poor men from one part of the town to the other until their bodies fell to pieces.'[31]

54. This bronze relief on the *Yekatit 12* monument shows four victims being killed by a military truck with double rear wheels. One victim is being run over (as if the truck is reversing), and the other three have been tied to the back of the truck to be dragged to their death. One, held by his wrists, is being beaten by a truncheon while being dragged. Note that the Blackshirts are shown wearing a soft black 'fez' with a tassel at the back. This was the case on Friday afternoon, when most of them were off duty

55. These two victims have been tied by the ankles, presumably to be dragged to their death, to the apparent delight of their tormentors, all of whom, judging from their uniforms, are Blackshirts

Killing victims by dragging typically entailed tying them to the back of the lorry in one of three positions, as depicted in the tableau on the *Yekatit 12* monument (see Figure 54). Three victims are shown tied to the back of a truck. The man on the left has been tied by his wrists to the back of the vehicle; the central figure is being dragged by his ankles; and the man on the right has had his arms brought up behind him before being tied to the vehicle by his wrists. The photograph in Figure 56 shows a victim tied to the side of a truck in Addis Ababa in the same manner, against the double rear wheels.

At the Church of Kidane Mihret in the relative safety of the Menelik *gibbi* complex, *Dyakon* Dawit and his two colleagues stood in the compound, as ordered, until 3.30 pm. Then they were told to walk across to Dawit's house, which was around 100 metres from the church compound. But on leaving, Dawit learned that people were being attacked: 'On Friday afternoon there were massacres in the streets. Vehicles were driven deliberately over people, and there was shooting.'[32]

The priests in the sanctuary, who had been told to stay there when the soldiers invaded the church, were, in Dawit's words, 'chased out' and told to go home. Among them was *Abba* Welde Samiyat, the highly respected head priest, who, as we shall see, was destined not to survive the massacre.

* * *

Despite the bombing and artillery fire on the outskirts of the city, many people fled the slaughter, as noted in a section of the memoirs of Gebre-Sillassé Oda, son of the dignitary *Qeññazmach* Oda Kelecha hailing from Soddo in Guragé country, south of Addis Ababa. Gebre-Sillassé happened to have set out from Addis Ababa by mule early in the morning of 12 Yekatit with his brother Gebreyes (later, *Fitawrari*) to explore the possibility of moving from the city, where life had become difficult, to the small town of Alem Gena, located on the road to Jimma, some 20 kilometres from the capital.

56. This victim, tied in a tortuous position to the side of a Fiat 634N truck, is about to be dragged to his death

57. Gebre-Sillassé Oda after the Liberation

Friday was market day in Alem Gena, and Gebre-Sillassé and his brother, well dressed as they were, cut distinctive figures in the market, catching the eye of a regular Italian army officer, who approached them and chatted to them in Italian. 'We replied in French', recalled Gebre-Sillassé, 'and he was pleased, because he also spoke French very well. Then he invited us for lunch at his house.' The brothers were happy to accept the invitation, but, unknown to Gebre-Sillassé, the day would turn out to be very different from what they had expected, and before it was over his chance encounter with the friendly officer would save his life.

At around 5.30 pm the two young men, having completed their mission, started their journey back to Addis Ababa. But by the time they reached a settlement known as Rapi, they were alarmed to see people fleeing towards them. Some were on mules, some on foot, and others, seriously injured, were being carried on donkeys. 'They stopped and asked where we were going,' Gebre-Sillassé would recall. '[When we told them,] they cried, "But Addis Ababa is in turmoil! The Italians are killing people! Are you going there just to be killed?"' They pleaded with Gebre-Sillassé and his brother not to continue their journey: 'The Italians are killing people with hoes and spades—regardless of who you are—anyone they encounter! ... Even if you have nowhere to go, it is better to be eaten by a hyena than to be slaughtered by the Italians!'

So, a stunned Gebre-Sillassé and his brother turned around and rode back to Alem Gena. It was around 6.00 pm, and it was getting dark when they arrived at the town. As they drew closer, they were shocked to hear the sound of gunfire. There was shooting in the town—the Italians had heard about the attack on Graziani, they were armed, and they were on the rampage. The brothers were then horrified to see a group of Italians running towards them. 'We could hear them saying, "These could be some of the people involved in the attack on Graziani!"' Gebre-Sillassé feared for his life, but, as the gang closed in on them, he could hear others saying, 'But these people could not be involved, because they were in the Alem Gena market today!' He was then further relieved to hear one of them telling his compatriots that he had seen these two men talking to his captain in the market. That was enough to make the soldiers hold their fire.

It is clear that Alem Gena was now suffering the same indiscriminate slaughter on the streets that had struck Addis Ababa in the afternoon, for Gebre-Sillassé's saviour then told the two men, 'Go straight to where you are planning to spend the night, otherwise if other soldiers who did not see you in the market find you on the street, they will kill you.' So Gebre-Sillassé and his brother decided to seek shelter in the village of Daleti, outside Alem Gena, at the house of *Haji* Mustafa and *Haji* Ibrahim, the sons of a family friend named *Haji* Isma'él. 'We went there because they knew our father and we were confident that they would shelter us.' Fortunately for them, the journey to Daleti was uneventful.[33]

* * *

By 6.00 pm, the French consul-general in Addis Ababa had another serious incident to report. He informed Paris that a group of Blackshirts had forced their way into the legation, pillaged the premises, and taken away two of the legation servants. Bodard had demanded their immediate release. In addition, another group of Fascists tried to get in through one of the main gates of the legation and to set fire to the porter's lodge.

* * *

The holocaust of Friday afternoon was beyond anyone's imagination, but worse was yet to come. The authorities planned a more systematic and even more horrific slaughter to commence at nightfall. In Addis Ababa, dusk lasts no more than a few minutes; by 6.45 pm or thereabouts it would be dark. Thus heavy weapons were distributed, including grenades, machine guns and flame-throwers, and regular troops carried out orders to confiscate cameras. Dr Shashka, who watched events unfold from the window of his house, speculated—and with good reason—that these measures were taken to ensure that what was to occur would be hidden from the eyes and ears of European governments and their citizens.[34]

* * *

FIRE AND FURY
(6.45 PM FRIDAY—6.00 AM SATURDAY)

The urban 'villages' of Addis Ababa typically consisted of an assortment of humble dwellings clustered around the mansion of a great lord, or *Ras*, which in turn was typically situated on a rise within sight of the late Emperor Menelik's royal encampment, or *gibbi*. Full of cottages and huts separated by eucalyptus trees and narrow, winding paths, and with children laughing and playing among grazing cattle and goats, these communities were home to the majority of the city's Ethiopian residents, who had been ordered, on pain of death, to stay indoors. Commencing at sundown, many of these popular housing areas and their inhabitants would be systematically torched by rampaging Italians.

It is not clear whether Graziani, who was in hospital, had recovered consciousness by the evening. However, even if he had, it seems unlikely, given his numerous previous instructions for widespread reprisals in the countryside, that he would have had strong objections to Friday night's fire and fury. As can be seen from the Italian telegrams submitted later as evidence to the War Crimes Commission, the Italian High Command of the 1930s, like the Inquisition of earlier centuries, was not at all averse to burning alive its perceived enemies in what it considered to be a righteous cause.

Houses around the Gennete-Li'ul Palace had been burned sporadically during the afternoon, but systematic house-burning started at dusk and continued throughout the night. The mob would typically enter a house, loot the property of anything of value, herd the family inside, secure the door to stop them getting out, then set the house alight. When it was supposed that a humble dwelling contained nothing of value, it was burned without the occupants realising what was happening until it was too late.

The Techniques

There were basically two techniques of house-burning employed during the massacre: manual and mechanised. The manual method involved dousing the victims' house with kerosene or benzine, then setting fire to the base of the walls and the eaves of the roof with a torch consisting of a burning wad of cloth tied to the end of a long pole. As Dr Shashka testified, 'Ethiopian houses and huts were searched and then burned with their inhabitants. To quicken the flames, benzine and oil were used in great quantities.'[35]

The mechanised method involved the use of flame-throwers. Mussolini himself had been a flame-thrower operator during the First World War, and had made a particular effort to ensure that his army had the best flame-throwers available for the invasion of Ethiopia. Indeed, the flame-thrower turned out to be one of the Italians' favourite weapons for use against Ethiopian civilians during both the Invasion and Occupation.

The Italians had developed two types of flame-thrower. Terrifying weapons, they were actually designed for military assaults on pillboxes, trenches, boulder areas, caves or other enclosed spaces. The first type was portable. Known as Model 35, it was capable of throwing a flaming jet of highly flammable liquid about 20 metres in length, destroying anything in its path and thereby creating an instantaneously uninhabitable zone some 15 metres wide. These portable flame-throwers, which were deployed extensively in the massacre of Addis Ababa, carried enough fuel for 20 seconds of continuous flame or several bursts of a few seconds each. Even a short burst of the flaming liquid was sufficient to cause intense heat, immense damage and horrific death.[36]

58. A member of the Addis Ababa fire brigade setting fire to Ethiopian thatched cottages: Having set light to the bottom of the walls, he moves up and down with his flaming torch, setting fire to another section of wall and then to the eaves

59. Flame-throwers at work in Addis Ababa during the Occupation

Unlike the manual method of house-burning, in which the terrified family inside might hear the sound of scuffling outside the house as the Blackshirts splashed the walls with benzine or kerosene, no such preparation was required when flame-throwers were used. Thus there was not a moment's warning of the use of these weapons; the house was instantaneously covered in burning liquid accompanied by an ear-splitting roar, followed by an agonising death for the occupants.

To appreciate the devastation caused by these fearsome weapons, it is important to realise that flame-throwers did not just throw a flame, but actually hurled a massive volume of burning fuel, which drenched and soaked into its target.

The Italians also operated a flame-thrower version of the L3 CV-33 tank, known as the L3 CV-33 L.F. Weighing 3.5 tons, with a flame-thrower projector mounted at the front together with a machine gun, the L3 CV-33 L.F. could throw a jet of flaming liquid 36 to 40 metres for more than two minutes. The flame could be cut off and on at will.[37] These tank-mounted flame-throwers were used during the invasion of Ethiopia. It is not known for certain if they were deployed during the massacre of Addis Ababa. Nonetheless, it is possible that they were, for a tank of this type is depicted in one of the reliefs on the *Yekatit 12* monument at Siddist Kilo (see Figure 62).

Once the house was aflame, the Italians would surround it, and if any children ran out through the door or through gaps in the wall, they were often pushed back into the inferno with long poles. When crawling babies emerged from the conflagration, they were lifted up and thrown back into the flames through holes in the roof.

Flame-throwers were carried and operated by specially trained soldiers. Untrained men would not have used these weapons, for they could explode and kill the user if not correctly operated. Nonetheless, many Italian civilians did take part in the arson attacks and the atrocities that accompanied them. An Italian civilian eyewitness named Antonio Dordini, who was a resident of Addis Ababa at the time of the massacre, told Professor Del Boca, 'They drenched the *tukuls* with petrol, set them alight, and as the inhabitants rushed out, finished them off with hand grenades.' Dordini had heard one of the mob complaining that his right arm ached from hurling so many grenades, while another boasted that he had 'done' ten *tukuls* with a single can of petrol. He went on, 'Many of these maniacs were known to me personally. They were tradesmen, chauffeurs, officials—people I'd always thought of as law-abiding and respectable, people who'd never fired a shot during the entire war—I'd never suspected that all this hatred was bottled up in them.'[38]

60. 'Children were actually thrown living into the burning houses'—British Intelligence report. On the *Yekatit 12* monument, babies who have escaped from their burning houses are shown being lifted up and thrown back through the roof into the flames

The statements of eyewitnesses such as Dordoni leave no doubt as to the nature of the massacre on Friday night. They also confirm that the killing of occupants by burning alive, shooting, stabbing or clubbing, or by hurling grenades into their houses, was commonplace throughout the city. In many cases Ethiopians were pushed back into the flames, as confirmed by eyewitness accounts received by British Intelligence:

> All thatched and straw huts were burned and their occupants slaughtered. Knives, bayonets, clubs and revolvers were used indiscriminately ... The inhabitants, rushing to escape from their burning houses, were pushed back into the flames with long poles ... Children were actually thrown living into the burning houses. A French lady who endeavoured to save the child of her old servant had it snatched out of her arms, and its throat cut before her eyes.[39]

This phenomenon was also reported by the British envoy himself:

> Ethiopians were hunted, their dwellings burnt and, in some cases, it is reported on evidence that I feel bound to accept, themselves pushed back into the flames and burnt inside. Evidence of the burning of Ethiopians was volunteered to a member of my staff by two Europeans who, hearing that this was going on, themselves inspected gutted dwellings afterwards and saw the charred bodies. In another instance an Englishman saw the native huts burning outside his compound and heard the screams of a person within.[40]

Those who fled the burning homes and could not be pushed back into the flames were shot, bludgeoned to death or blown up with hand-grenades, as confirmed by numerous reports that filtered out of the country over the following weeks. 'Gangs of blackshirts and workmen went through the native quarters ... With flame-throwers and tins of petrol, fired the flimsy huts and houses and shot down those [who] tried to escape.'[41] 'Thousands of native houses were then set on fire, and as the inhabitants tried to flee for safety they were shot or clubbed to death. In some cases no distinction was made between men and women, and many women were killed.'[42] 'From that time a method which was followed out thoroughly during the three long days ... The method consisted of setting fire to the houses, waiting for the inhabitants to be driven out by the fire and massacring them without distinction, with daggers, bayonets, hand grenades, cudgels, stones, and, at times, with guns.'[43] 'Regular troops ... set fire to the "tukuls" or native wooden cabins in several parts of the town, the inhabitants in many cases being burned to death.'[44]

The onslaught went on throughout much of the night, and covered a major part of the urban area: 'in the evening, extensive areas in every quarter were ablaze.'[45] 'The shooting never ceased all night, but most of the murders were

61. 'An Englishman saw the native huts burning outside his compound and heard the screams of a person within'—British acting consul-general. In many cases the families inside were roasted alive

committed with daggers and blows with a truncheon at the head of the victim. Whole streets were burned down, and if any of the occupants of the houses ran out from the flames they were machine-gunned or stabbed with cries of "Duce! Duce!!!"'[46]

Several witnesses report victims being machine-gunned as they tried to flee the burning houses. At first sight this may seem unlikely, as 'machine gun' tends to conjure up the vision of a cumbersome and heavy gun mounted on a tripod. But, as noted earlier, Blackshirt officers often carried a hand-held 'Breda' Model 30 automatic rifle, a light machine gun capable of firing high-speed rounds.

Italian Sergeant-Major Boaglio, who was on patrol during the carnage, recalled seeing scenes 'so frightening that I will never be able to erase them from my mind. Young officers who were models of fairness and education became, out of the blue, vulgar predators and murderers.' Men whom Boaglio had considered fair and honest were raping young Ethiopian girls, and were 'grinning coldly' as they calmly shot the people running out screaming from their burning homes.[47]

Accounts by witnesses in the Feransay Legassion district mention the use of hand grenades. This was confirmed by the French consul-general, who wrote that the killing turned into a pogrom: 'They were killing for the fun of killing; they pillaged for the joy of destroying and getting drunk; they then set fire, through an imperious need to complete the devastation ... The *tukuls*, roofed with thatch and serving as houses for the natives, were burned; sometimes with their occupants inside, due to the impossibility of escaping before the forces liberally unleashed. Flame-throwers and grenades served to exacerbate the evils.'[48]

Testimony from a survivor from inside a burning *tukul* is rare. However, such a case was encountered by the British acting consul-general, who informed London that he had evidence from an Ethiopian who was lined up with others in a hut to be shot. All were shot, one by one, and the hut was then set alight over them. But one man was only wounded and managed to make his way to the American hospital, where he related the facts to the American doctor in charge.'[49] Another case involved an Ethiopian named Werqu Welde-Maryam, who also had a narrow escape from death in his burning house, as we shall see. He survived the massacre, and after the Liberation went on to work for the Djibouti–Addis Ababa Railway. However, he never forgot the horrific sights and sounds of the night of Friday, 19 February. He recalled the city being totally swept with fire. 'Whether it was the skulls of human beings [bursting] with the sound of bullets I don't know, to this date, but there was the noise of explosions here and there from the fires that were raging all across the city.' Memories of that night haunted him: 'When I remember the children I used to play football with, who were trapped by the fire while they were asleep, and burned alive by the Italians, it reminds me of the brutal acts of Fascist Italy.'[50]

Eyewitness Kirubel Beshah put it graphically, capturing the sense of shock and helplessness of victims trapped in a situation in which the self-appointed guardians of law and order were themselves committing the atrocities: 'The poor were burned inside their houses without knowing what was happening. Those who tried to escape the fire were pushed back into it. The others were shot with machine-guns ... The whole city was filled with fire, smoke and screams. Who is going to stop the killers? Who is going to pass judgement on them? After all, the murderers were the Fascists and their brother workers ... They washed the whole of Addis Ababa with human blood.'[51]

62. On Saturday and Sunday nights most of the victims were women, children, and the elderly and infirm. Here mothers and their children are depicted on the *Yekatit 12* memorial dying amid their collapsing home. The man with outstretched arms is desperately trying to shield his family from the tank as it ploughs through their home, reducing it to rubble

House Demolition

One of the bronze reliefs on the *Yekatit 12* monument vividly depicts women and their babies dying amid their collapsing homes. However, in this tableau the houses are of stone; they are not burning. Rather, they are being demolished. In the case of Addis Ababa, the instrument of demolition was often an armoured car or a tank such as the one depicted on the right in Figure 62, which is almost certainly a CV-33 or CV-35. These tanks were driven, it may be noted, not by Blackshirts, but by soldiers of the regular army, as were the military vehicles used by Graziani's forces to destroy houses and their occupants during the civilian massacres in Cyrenaica (eastern Libya)—clearly demonstrating a degree of cooperation between the two arms of the military in the massacre of Addis Ababa.

* * *

View from the Palace

The extensive burning of Friday night was witnessed at a distance by Sara Gebre-Iyyesus, who, the reader will recall, had been arrested, made to walk through the Circle of Death, and then detained in the former *adarash* of *Bejirond* Letyibelu Gebré in Siddist Kilo, which had been commandeered by the Italians as a detention centre. Late on Friday evening, a military truck took Sara to the Governo Generale. In Sara's words,

> I was with *Weyzero* Zenebech, the wife of *Shaqa* Belihu, who was also taken prisoner. We were both in the front. On the way, I didn't really see anything, and I can't really remember the journey. I was exhausted and injured, and it was very dark. I can't say whether bodies were still lying around, as it was dark and I was in no fit state to notice such things.
>
> At the palace, we were put in a big hall on the ground floor together with a lot of other people. The women were kept in a separate section or corner. We were two women, plus two who were already there: Maniyilushal Kassa, daughter of *Ras* Kassa; and Atsede Belay, the daughter of *Dejazmach* Belay Kebbede.[52] Atsede, however, was not there as a prisoner. She had only gone to the palace to sign a legal document.
>
> The palace was full of prisoners. There were hundreds of them. That evening, we were taken upstairs to the roof terrace adjoining the palace bedrooms. While up on the roof terrace that night, I could see many districts of Addis Ababa being burned.[53]

From the terrace of the Gennete-Li'ul Palace, Sara would certainly have seen the city burning. The terrace, which faced east, was completely open and fitted with low railings which did nothing to obstruct the view.[54] It provided a clear vista to the north, east and south, enabling anyone on the terrace to see the burning in Feransay Legassion district and the residential areas around the old *gibbi*.

* * *

Meanwhile, in Sara's mother's house in Siddist Kilo, only a short distance from the Governo Generale where Sara was being held, her sisters Welette-Haymanot and Welette-Birhan were looking after Sara's children, as well as other grandchildren who had arrived earlier in the day, as the family was mourning the recent death of Sara's youngest sister. After dark, Eritrean *askaris* came to the house and told them it was going to be burned down. But, later, Welette-Birhan explained to the present author, when Italian regular soldiers arrived and asked why there were so many children there, 'Someone in charge must have been a bit kind-hearted, because they said that since there were only women and children in the house, they would not burn it. So we could spend the night there.'

In fact, Siddist Kilo had been excluded from the burning programme, but Welette-Birhan was not aware of that, and so to be on the safe side they decided to spend the night outside the house and moved away to a safer area. 'Had the house been burned [while we were inside], no-one would have survived. We could see fire from afar, but they did not burn houses immediately around us [i.e. in Siddist Kilo]. We covered the children with cloth. But they cried that their mother and father [whose whereabouts at that time were unknown] were being burned!'[55]

In the words of Dr Shashka, who watched the city burn from his house, 'Great flames from the burning houses illuminated the African night ... The flames spread from the houses to some of the great trees which graced the streets, and, flaming, collapsed with a tremendous noise.'[56] And as the trees, which grew densely throughout the residential areas, caught fire and collapsed, many people were crushed to death.

Although the reprisals after dark on Friday followed the usual pattern of Fascist retribution, they were on a scale far exceeding anything experienced to date in Ethiopia, and employed methods of killing which were particularly gross and hideous. In Dr Shashka's words, 'There is no means of destroying human life not employed on the night of the 19th of February, 1937.'[57]

The sheer paralysing terror of the night for the victims locked in their burning homes can scarcely be imagined and, since most of them did not survive, personal accounts are almost nonexistent. But from Sergeant-Major

Boaglio's memoir we get a glimpse of the fear that the marauding soldiers engendered when they burst in on the petrified families. Fortunately, his men were regulars of the Grenadiers, not Blackshirts, and their job at that time was to search for weapons, not to kill and burn. But with the two arms of the military wearing similar uniforms, in the darkness it was difficult for Ethiopians to tell the difference.

Boaglio tells how he ordered the occupants of one house to open the door. As he and his four men with bayonets fixed burst into the room, they found shivering and contorted with fear a 'poor man, huddled on the wretched little bed clutching to his chest a little boy screaming while another, bigger boy, clung desperately to his neck, crying incessantly'. 'How can we forget the eyes of that man?' asked Boaglio. 'How to forget that distorted face, that deformed mouth, those reeling hands? And the scene illuminated by the red glare of the fire devouring the city!'[58]

* * *

While the houses were burning, military trucks were on the streets picking up fleeing Ethiopians for execution. Dr Shashka described the process:

> During that awful night, Ethiopians were thrust into lorries, heavily guarded by armed Blackshirts. Revolvers, truncheons, rifles and daggers were used to murder completely unarmed black people, of both sexes and all ages. Every black person seen was arrested and bundled into a lorry and killed, either in the lorry or near the 'Little *Gibbi*' [Gennete-Li'ul Palace], sometimes even at the moment when he met the Blackshirts ... From the lorries in which groups of prisoners were brought up to be murdered near the *gibbi*, the blood flowed onto the streets and again from the lorries we heard the cry, 'Duce! Duce!! Duce!!!', the war-cry of those glorious Blackshirts ... [The] lorries were running with congealed blood all over them ...'[59]

One of the principal objectives was to steal property, but, apart from chickens, livestock was apparently not wanted by the Blackshirts, yet they did not escape the general slaughter. 'Some of the Ethiopian shepherds tried to herd some of the poor beasts into a corner, which appeared to them to offer some protection, but even the animals were not spared from rifles and machine guns'.[60]

But perhaps the most bizarre and sickening aspect of that terrible night of fire and fury was the sight of the wives of Italian officials being driven around the city to view the progress of the massacre, looking for all the world like tourists watching a *son et lumière* performance, 'stopping at some point whence they could have a better panorama of the murdering and the burning'.[61]

However, at least one Italian civilian—a friend of Guido Cortese's wife—was shocked and appalled at the massacre. She later vividly summed up the scene: 'It was an Abyssinian Guernica, the city in flames, people running in all directions, children howling ... Some of them were setting fire to homes and waiting outside, gun at the ready, [to shoot them] as they ran out ... Since these events I never again saluted a Blackshirt for the rest of my life; especially this friend who was married to Guido Cortese.'[62]

63. Addis Ababa burning. 'Great flames from the burning houses illuminated the African night ... The flames spread from the houses to some of the great trees which graced the streets, and, flaming, collapsed with a tremendous noise'— Dr Ladislas Shashka

* * *

It was indeed an Abyssinian Guernica, as Gebre-Sillassé and Gebreyes Oda realised when, having reached the village of Daleti at 7.30 pm, they were transfixed with horror at the sight of the city of Addis Ababa, some 20 kilometres away, on fire. The slaughter 'by hoes and spades' that they had been told about by the fleeing refugees had clearly become ordeal by fire. The blaze was so great that even at that distance they could see it clearly: 'Addis Ababa was on fire, and we saw the flames, like *mesqel chibo* [the great bonfire of tall poles ritually lit by Orthodox Ethiopians to celebrate the finding of the True Cross].'[63]

* * *

VILLAGES OF DEATH

Where did all this Friday night devastation take place? As we have seen, certain districts of the city were singled out for destruction in the directions given by senior Fascist Party officials in the afternoon at Casa Littoria, as confirmed by Edouard Garabedian's testimony: 'I learned from some of the Italians that they had received orders to burn different Ethiopian quarters. They were burning houses during the whole night.'[64] All high-density residential areas were earmarked for attack, but the brunt of the onslaught was borne by the following districts, which fall into two geographic clusters:

- The central cluster: high-density residential areas easily accessible by Blackshirts and civilians, starting from their rallying point at Casa Littoria, comprising Beshah Welde Chilot Sefer (that is Lower Arat Kilo), Sera Bét Sefer, west and south of the Menelik *gibbi*, parts of Arada, Dejazmach Nesibu Sefer, and Fitawrari Habte-Giyorgis Sefer.
- The northern cluster: high-density residential areas readily accessible by Blackshirts from their barracks near Siddist Kilo, including the Ghilifaleñ River valley between the Intotto Road and Jan Méda, Feransay Legassion, and Qechené.

Between the two clusters was the Exemption Zone, utilised by the Italians, where no arson was permitted. While the largest mobs descended on the villages in these two clusters, some suburbs were also attacked, including Qirqos, behind the railway station (not shown on Map 8).

The Central Cluster

Arson in the central cluster was led by the Blackshirts, supported by *askaris*, but it also involved many civilians, who gathered at Piazza during the afternoon, and who were present in their thousands by the time of the proclamation of *carta bianca* at Casa Littoria.

BESHAH WELDE CHILOT SEFER

Beshah Welde Chilot Sefer was the name given to the densely populated district on the western side of the Intotto Road (Viale Entotto), south of Adwa Avenue (Corso Vittorio Emanuele III) and stretching across to Lorenzo Ta'izaz Street (Via Vittorio Bottego), the boundary with Sera Bét Sefer. It consisted of what one might refer to as Lower Arat Kilo. As Tekle-Maryam Kiflom confirmed to the present author, this area—particularly the western section, up to Ras Mekonnin Bridge—was subjected to severe burning on Friday night. For the Blackshirts and their collaborators assembled at Casa Littoria, the district could be reached in a matter of minutes, even without the lorries provided for the massacre after dark. Thus the Italians converged on Beshah Welde Chilot Sefer in large numbers. Being taken unawares, many of the occupants were asleep, with no warning of what was to befall them.

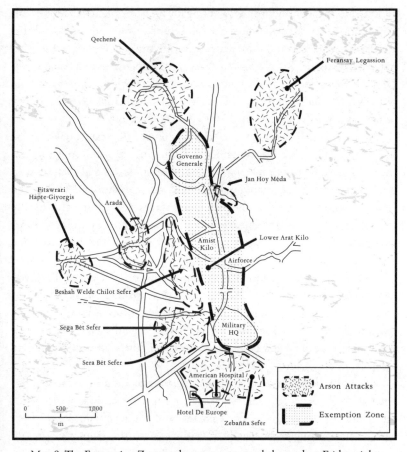

Map 8. The Exemption Zone and areas most severely burned on Friday night

The north-eastern sections of the *sefer*, a little to the north of the Arat Kilo junction where Tekle-Maryam was living, were not burned, but just outside the Exemption Zone there was intense burning, particularly around the Ras Mekonnin Bridge. Dawit Oquba Igzi'i testified, 'All the houses and *tukuls* in front of us [at Ras Mekonnin Bridge] were burning.'[65]

SERA BÉT SEFER

Beyond Lower Arat Kilo the situation was, if anything, even worse. One of the most extensive attacks of Friday night took place in the area originally allocated to the men and women working for Emperor Menelik's former palace, or *gibbi*, which surmounted the hill on the eastern side of the Intotto Road. Indeed, several of the original palace-employee families were still living in the area. Sera Bét Sefer consisted of the steeply sloping eastern banks of the Qechené River (known to the Italians as the Genfile) where it flowed past the old *gibbi*. Densely populated, this 'village' stretched from Lorenzo Ta'izaz Street in the north to where the Hilton Hotel now stands.

This area, which the Italians regarded as one of the residential districts needing to be 'cleaned up', contained few buildings of stone construction, the only notable exception being the police headquarters and garage, taken over by the *carabinieri*, standing in a large, walled compound[66] below the *gibbi* gate known as Fit Ber. The thatched cottages were constructed for the most part with wood and mud, so they caught fire quickly. Since the area was quite congested, the flames spread rapidly through the trees from one dwelling to another.

The housing on the western banks of this section of the Qechené River was considerably less dense, for here the royal cattle herds traditionally grazed, in an area known as Sega ('meat') Bét Sefer, stretching westwards from the river to the back of today's Lycée Gebre-Maryam on Churchill Road (Viale Benito Mussolini). One of the few buildings of any note in this area was the imposing residence of *Ras* Nadew.[67]

For the Blackshirts and their civilian partners at Casa Littoria, Sera Bét Sefer and Sega Bét Sefer could be reached in a matter of minutes, even without the lorries. As in Lower Arat Kilo, many of the inhabitants were asleep, and had no warning of the slaughter. Within a short time Sera Bét *Sefer* and Sega Bét *Sefer* were aflame. The great eucalyptus trees, which were so numerous, crashed to the ground with a terrible noise, adding to the general cacophony, the roar of the flame-throwers, the crackling of the fires and the screams of victims trapped inside their homes.

The burning of Sera Bét Sefer was appalling enough, but, according to one published report, the situation there was compounded by another atrocity. The Djibouti correspondent of *New Times and Ethiopian News*, Wazir Ali Baig, filed a shocking story that he must have heard from refugees arriving there, which was published under the headline '3,000 Butchered at the Abbatoir'. 'Three thousand Abyssinians who were taken prisoner were dragged to Kilas, a place where animals are slaughtered, and butchered there without trial, or even question.'[68] This report could refer only to Sega Bét Sefer, for it was there that the municipal slaughter-house was located. Now known locally as Arogi Qéra (Old Slaughterhouse), it was situated on the southern side of Colson Street (Via Toselli), just before the bridge as one travelled eastwards from Churchill Road (Viale Benito Mussolini) (see Map 8).

The slaughter-house area was indeed burned during the massacre, as confirmed by *Immahoy* Hiruta.[69] However, while there is no doubt that many residents of Sera Bét *Sefer* died in the conflagration, the present author has been unable to verify the report about the use of adjoining Arogi Qéra as a place of mass execution. While eyewitness accounts of specific incidents are usually quite reliable, and can sometimes be verified, 'stand-alone' estimates of large numbers killed based on hearsay can be notoriously unreliable and often impossible to verify. We return to the question of the likely death rate in Sera Bét Sefer in chapter 10.

ARADA

Various reports speak of the burning of the city market, consisting of three areas surrounding the customs sheds south of St George's Cathedral, and covering a significant proportion of Arada.[70] As shown in Figure 64, there was an area of covered stalls, and two other open areas nearby, utilised by traders on market days.[71] Being reserved for commerce, none of these areas was actually residential, but nonetheless they attracted a variety of people that the Italians regarded as undesirables, and, like Sera Bét Sefer, were targets for the Italian 'clean-up' operations.[72]

Watching the city burn from the safety of a car containing Italian high officials, Rosario Gilaezgi drove from Piazza westwards towards Fitawrari Habte-Giyorgis Sefer, which took him through the areas of the city centre being burned. 'I went together with Della Porta and Avolio, director superior of political affairs of all [Italian] East Africa, in a car, and I saw with my own eyes burning houses and heard the Italians cry "Civiltà Italiana!" [Italian Civilisation!] I saw young boys coming out from burning houses, but the Italians pushed them back into the fire.'[73]

Given his direction of travel, *Dejazmach* Rosario's report most likely refers either to the residential area immediately north of St George's Cathedral known as Gedam Sefer, where there were many houses, or the area west of the market area up to Fitawrari Habte-Giyorgis Bridge.

In some parts of Arada there were instances of Ethiopians being protected by Greeks and Armenians. The Greek resident Michael Lentakis tells how the entire family of Yidniqachew Tessema (subsequently the founder of the

64. Aerial view of Arada before the Italian Occupation, showing four areas burned on Friday night: three market areas and one residential area

Ethiopian Sports Association and later general secretary of the African Football Federation) was given asylum in the double-storey house of a certain Mr Mavrikos, near St George's Cathedral, just below the Grar Hotel.[74]

After visiting Fitawrari Habte-Giyorgis Sefer, the Italian officials drove eastwards across the city, then back through Arada to the north-west. Rosario testified, 'From there we went to the ex-Belgian legation where Avolio was living [across the Qebena River, near the British legation], and then to Della Porta's house at the end of the street called Duke of Harar Street.[75] On this trip we saw that they were burning houses. To recollect everything is difficult because I had nearly lost my senses when seeing what was going on.'[76]

* * *

Meanwhile, the Blackshirts had set in motion arrangements for a spectacular event—something designed to strike at the very heart of highland Ethiopia: the destruction of the city's most glorious symbol of the Ethiopian Orthodox Church, the great octagonal Cathedral of St George, founded, as we have seen, by Emperor Menelik, and rebuilt by his daughter, Empress Zewditu.

Traditionally Ethiopian churches were places of refuge, as they had been in medieval Europe, but if Ethiopians expected a reputedly Christian country such as Italy to respect such a tradition, they were in for a shock. In the evening an eager and excited crowd of regulars, *carabinieri*, Blackshirts and civilians gathered at St George's Cathedral to witness the destruction of the great edifice. If the removal of the statue of Emperor Menelik was an outrage, it would pale beside the destruction of the cathedral, which would show the Ethiopians once and for all who was in charge.

There was, however, another reason for the hysteria of the crowd: the razing of the cathedral would also help to bring closure to Italy's open wound, for the Italians knew that it had been built to give thanks for the Ethiopian victory against the previous Italian invasion of 1896, and whenever they passed Menelik Square they were reminded of the shame of that battle—their bête noire.[77]

For the Ethiopians no victory could have been more complete than the Battle of Adwa, and for the Italians no defeat could have been more crushing. Moreover, the cathedral was dedicated to St George, the patron saint of Ethiopian sovereigns, on whose commemoration day the battle had taken place. Furthermore, the paintings adorning the interior included a depiction of the battle, overseen by the Saint, with adjoining portraits of Emperor Menelik and Empress Taytu. Finally, as if to rub salt into the wound, the building, a European interpretation of a traditional round Ethiopian Orthodox church, was the product of an Italian engineer, Sebastino Castagna, who had been taken prisoner after the battle but who liked Ethiopia so much that he stayed on in the service of the sovereign, and married into the Ethiopian royal family.

However, before the ritual destruction, the Blackshirts had business to conduct: looting. They had discovered that in the crypt below the cathedral was a collection of valuable ancient works of art, manuscripts and other treasures.[78] That night was *carta bianca*, so, surging forward, the yelling mob crossed the portals to run amok inside, seizing whatever they could get their hands on, while others organised transport. The loot must have been enormous, for, according to Dr Shashka, they needed a fleet to take it all away: 'they found seven or eight [trucks] to carry the silver and gold vessels, the precious crosses, the prelate's staves and the valuable religious paintings and manuscripts'.[79]

65. The Cathedral of St George at Menelik Square, seen here before the Occupation, was the largest and most important church in Addis Ababa

Meanwhile, other Blackshirts arrived with drums of benzine, which they offloaded. Some they carried into the church and stacked up against the walls; others they opened and splashed the contents over the inner and outer walls. By then the Fascist federal secretary had arrived at the scene with his entourage, and it was time for the fire to be ceremoniously lit. When all was set, Blackshirts hurled incendiary bombs at the edifice,[80] the conflagration being started, as testified by Ciro Poggiali, 'by order, and in the presence of, *Federale* Cortese'.[81]

The Fascists watched, yelling and cheering, as the roaring flames leapt upwards, momentarily lighting the night sky. Inside the cathedral a fierce fire arose and the windows burst from the heat. However, as the benzine burned itself out, the flames died down and the cheering stopped; the crowd fell silent. The attempt had failed. Unlike the traditional Ethiopian thatched cottages, which caught fire quickly, St George's was built of stone. The wall paintings, including the much-hated depiction of the Battle of Adwa, were destroyed,[82] the interior fittings were extensively damaged, and parts of the outer walls were blackened by the flames. However, the building survived, structurally unscathed.

Guido Cortese's reaction to the débâcle at the cathedral is not on record, but we can be sure that he was raised to a fury at the incompetence of his Blackshirts—fury that was to be exacerbated by the humiliation of seeing the job of destroying the edifice being assigned the next day to a more competent arm of the military.

Did anyone die in the flames? The war correspondent Ciro Poggiali, who was well connected with the Italian administration and military, noted in his diary an incident in which a colonel of the Grenadiers saved the lives of 50 *dyakons* who had been tied up with the intention of burning them alive inside the building. Whether the colonel managed to persuade the Blackshirts to release them, or ordered his regulars to do so, Poggiali does not say, but this was one of the few occasions on which the regular army intervened to counter the actions of the Blackshirts.[83] As we shall see, the 65th Infantry Division of the regular army, known as the Granatieri di Savoia, was unusual in having attached to it a Blackshirt unit—the 11th Blackshirt Battalion—which could explain how a Grenadier colonel was in a position to restrain a Blackshirt company.

Nonetheless, there are unconfirmed reports that during the incident some of the clergy *were* burned to death. One such story was relayed to London by the British acting consul-general, who seemed to be satisfied that that it came from a credible source: 'Even priests, it is said, were left to burn in St George's Cathedral, the central part of which was set alight. The report of this came from an Italian officer of standing who, while deprecating the fact that some people had "lost their heads", explained that this occurrence was "a mistake", as orders had been given to avoid damage [during the massacre] to churches and legations,—implying freedom of action in all other respects.'[84] We cannot, however, be certain that any clerics actually died in the fire; the British envoy's report might refer to the *dyakons* who, although 'left to burn', actually received a last-minute reprieve, as reported by Poggiali.

THE MUNICIPALITY OFFICE

We have seen in chapter 4 how the Municipality Office in Arada, where Temesgen Gebré was taken at 2.00 pm on Friday after his lucky escape from the Blackshirts' 'slaughter by truck' conducted on the street outside, was at that moment in the process of becoming a detention centre. In fact, it was the first public building of any significance in Addis Ababa to serve that purpose. Its pioneering role in launching the 'concentration' of potential enemies of the regime in 'protective custody' bears comparison with the objective of the establishment of Dachau in a disused factory on the outskirts of Munich in 1933 as Germany's first detention camp for potential enemies of the newly proclaimed Third Reich. Dachau went on to have a much longer life as a concentration camp, whereas the Addis Ababa municipality compound was closed after a matter of weeks. However, the death rate in the first few days in the case of the municipality compound, where the regime of violence and terror dwarfed anything seen in the city to date, was actually considerably higher than that of the early days of its German counterpart.

From the eyewitness accounts it is clear that by the evening there were well over a thousand people held in the municipality courtyard, and the atrocities being carried out on the premises, within sight of St George's Cathedral, were so appalling that at times Temesgen thought he must be dreaming. It was when soldiers arrived at the compound to select prisoners for execution that the truth dawned: the Municipality Building was not a refuge from the mayhem outside, nor were the authorities interested in bringing the slaughter to a halt. On the contrary, the city was in the grip of what seemed to be total

66. Seen here in the 1960s, the Municipality Office—formerly the residence of *Neggadras* Hayle-Giyorgis, and during the Occupation the Tribunale Civile—was the scene of detention, terror and death following *Yekatit 12*. Today the historic edifice still stands, a sprawling complex of faded grandeur now incongruously hemmed in by high-rise buildings and construction works. Motorists and pedestrians hurry past oblivious to the horrors once perpetrated within its walled compound

insanity. Outside the walls innocent people were being indiscriminately slaughtered, and now the authorities were sending soldiers into the Municipality Building to decide who should be executed.

What was going on? Decisions had been made to execute potential opponents of the regime, and the Italians were targeting anyone who seemed to be educated or of any social standing. Birhanu Dinqé described in some detail what was happening. He explained that the *carabinieri* were ordered to search for those suspected to be in political opposition to the Italian administration, based on a list of names provided by the Intelligence service. The *carabinieri* stood in the middle of the prisoners and called out the names on the list. 'These [people]', wrote Birhanu, 'were taken away and killed in secret.' The Italians then went on to announce that the nobility should identify themselves by title. Birhanu comments that this was to enable them to eliminate the aristocracy, but most of the latter realised what was going on and remained silent. A few, however, thought that, as the elite, they 'would either be freed or held in a better prison, separate from the ordinary people', and identified themselves as titled. They paid a heavy price: '[The Italians] took out the nobility and the youth, and killed them by machine gun.'[85]

It is not surprising that Temesgen found some of the detainees stripping themselves of anything that made them look like members of the urban elite: 'Those of us who were well dressed took off our clothes and shoes and threw them into a pit latrine.' In a desperate effort to avoid being recognised as a dignitary, a certain *Balambaras* Girma, who was apparently wearing an expensive pair of shoes, pleaded with Temesgen to take them and put them on.[86] Some of the prisoners sitting with Temesgen chose not to take off their smart clothes, and paid a heavy price for their decision. Named Nigatu, Gebre Tsion, Semra and Igwala Tsion—apparently brothers—they were taken away, no doubt to their deaths.

The pit latrine in the Municipality Building compound was the focus of a particularly gruesome incident, for it turned out that inside, where the prisoners were throwing their clothes and shoes, were live human beings. The Italians had thrown five of their captives into the pit—a dark, fetid well with vertical sides—and at the bottom the victims were struggling in the sewage in a desperate attempt to escape a horrible death. 'There were five people who were already inside the pit latrine, and they were trying to catch hold of the *inchet* [wooden stakes driven into the wall of the pit, to serve as a ladder]. But they were not able to grasp the *inchet*, and fell back into the sewage.'[87]

It was while Temesgen was incarcerated in the Municipality Building compound that the Blackshirts set fire to St George's Cathedral. Being immediately across the road from the blaze, there was no way the captives would miss the sight. Such desecration heightened their feeling that something unimaginable was happening. Lighting the night sky for miles around, 'The flames looked like a sunset in the west.'[88]

As the evening wore on, in the darkness of the municipality courtyard, Temesgen noted that there were so many prisoners being taken away for execution that they exceeded those left behind. Yet the courtyard was still filling up, because the premises had become a clearing-house for the selection of prisoners for dispatch to execution centres. 'They were bringing in more people through one gate, while they were taking out others to kill them through the other gate.' Temesgen's first night at the municipality detention centre was terrifying, but worse was yet to come.

FITAWRARI HABTE GIYORGIS SEFER

As we have seen, the car carrying Italian high officials with their interpreter Rosario Gilaezgi on Friday evening was driven westward through Arada and across the Habte-Giyorgis Bridge. The area that began at the bridge was known as Fitawrari Habte-Giyorgis Sefer, although the *Fitawrari*, Emperor Menelik's Minister of War, was no longer alive, and his residence, in a park surrounded by many houses, was now rented to the American government to house its legation.

Rosario noticed that beyond the bridge, the dwellings, clustered in villages around the American legation compound, were not burning. 'Up to that bridge we had seen them destroying houses, and killing people. Then on the western side not a single house was burned. The American Legation had assembled all their neighbours in their compound. A *Maresciallo* [Marshal] from the *carabinieri* (who did not like the order from Cortese) stopped us at the bridge, saying, "I do not want any help from the Blackshirts. I will do this myself."'[89]

Indeed, it seems that the *carabinieri* marshal at the Habte-Giyorgis Bridge checkpoint did 'do this himself'—or perhaps he was overruled by the Blackshirts—for, later that evening, the district went up in flames, threatening the legation itself, as reported by the American consul-general the next day:

> Yesterday afternoon and all last night the Italians by way of reprisals set fire to hundreds of native houses including some in the immediate vicinity of this Legation which necessitated our taking special precautions to prevent our buildings from catching too. If there had been a strong wind it would probably not

67. The rear view of the Municipality Office before the Occupation. While the front gate was used for prisoners arriving, the back gate was used by trucks for taking prisoners away either for transfer to other locations or to their death

have been possible and I have this morning [Saturday] pointed out this danger to the authorities.

Many natives whose huts were burning were either shot as they tried to escape or were forced to perish in the flames. Not since the Armenian massacres have I seen a display of such unbridled brutality and cowardice. Besides there have been mass executions in batches of 50 or 100 all over town of wretched people who by no stretch of the imagination could have had anything to do with the incident.[90]

The American legation was too close for comfort to the horrors of the night; it was actually at the centre of the conflagration in Fitawrari Habte-Giyorgis Sefer. As later recounted by staff arriving in Paris following the closure of the legation, the Italians set fire to all of the houses around the legation. As elsewhere throughout the city, when the inhabitants, including women and children, rushed out of the burning buildings, they were either bayoneted or shot down by rifle, revolver or machine-gun fire. Some of the dead, it was noted, were the wives of legation staff who had been allowed to take refuge in the legation, but whose families were still outside.

DEJAZMACH NESIBU SEFER

On the road from St George's Cathedral just before reaching the Habte-Giyorgis Bridge, Via Bengazi, the road to the right, led to a district known as Dejazmach Nesibu Sefer, occupied mainly by Ethiopian military families. This road, today named Dejazmach Nesibu Street, skirted what had earlier become known as the Italian area, or Taliyan Sefer[91] (see Map 9), and led into a large, heavily treed village bounded in the north by the city's Muslim cemetery. At that time, unlike today, there were no other roads in or out of Dejazmach Nesibu village.

In his book on the Occupation, Lieutenant Meleseliñ Aniley described a terrifying but dramatic incident in this area, which was extensively burned on Friday night.[92] Running from the fire, he climbed up a tree to hide, and saw that a strong southerly wind was spreading the flames from the first house to several nearby. Then he saw the fleeing occupants being shot down: 'The people inside were suffocating, and were forced to flee their homes. They thought they would escape death from the blazing fire and smoke. However, the Fascists shot them, one by one. In this manner many people were killed and burned alive inside their homes in this horrifying drama.'

The police officer went on to describe an extraordinary scene: 'In this same village I saw a pregnant woman in her early twenties rushing from these houses, throwing her hands up in the air, towards an Italian officer around two metres tall standing under a big tree. The woman begged for mercy, throwing herself at his legs, and crying, "Please have mercy on me, Señor!" But the soldier simply stretched out his arm and shot her repeatedly, until she died. 'Then a powerfully built man who had been watching what the Fascist had done to the pregnant woman jumped on top of the Italian from a tree around five metres in height, and started to fight him in hand-to-hand combat.' At this point Lieutenant Meleseliñ and two other friends were watching the fight from a tree in which they had hidden. 'The fight continued until the Fascist fighter realised that he was the weaker of the two, and started to call for help: "*Ayuto! Ayuto! Ayuto!*"'[93]

Responding to his cries, five Italian soldiers appeared, coming to the rescue of their comrade. The Ethiopian's face was covered in blood, and for a few moments the Italian started cleaning up his face and clothes, thinking the Ethiopian was dead. But to his surprise the Ethiopian leaped up, 'glaring at him with eyes like those of an angry leopard'. The Italian started running away but fell down. Then one of his colleagues found him, just as he was about to be killed by the Ethiopian. But 'at that moment', recalled Meleseliñ, a young

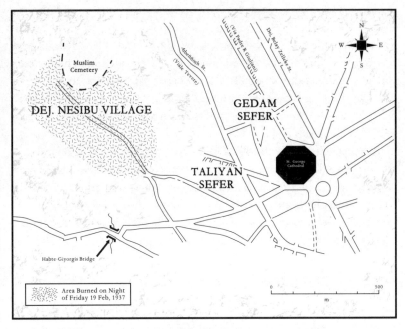

Map 9. Western Arada

man who had been watching from a nearby tree decided to rescue the patriot. 'Just as the Italian was about to grab his weapon, the Ethiopian who had just joined the fight stabbed the Italian to death before he could fire at the Ethiopian patriot.' This enabled the other Ethiopian to strangle the remaining Italian, and the fight came to an end. 'Later we learned that the pregnant woman who was killed so mercilessly by the Italian officer was the wife of the Ethiopian who killed him.' The victorious Ethiopian then explained to Meleseliñ and his friends that he needed the Italian uniform as he was a Patriot en route to the north. Saying goodbye, he struck out for Gulelé and onwards north to Sululta, and the young man from Dejazmach Nesibu village who had come to his aid decided to join him.[94]

The Northern Cluster

As we have seen, the areas close to Siddist Kilo were easily accessible from the Blackshirt barracks in the vicinity of the Teferi Mekonnin School; these consisted principally of the Ghilifaleñ River valley, Feransay Legassion and Qechené.

GHILIFALEÑ VALLEY

The reader may recall that this valley, adjoining the field of Jan Méda, was the first area to be burned in the afternoon, but it was revisited at night. Welette-Birhan noted that this area suffered some particularly horrific atrocities. For example, 'Near today's Mother Thérèsa Home, below [opposite] the Yared School of Music, I know of a family of fourteen who were all burned to death in their house.'[95]

Together with the Genfile River valley of Sera Bét Sefer in the central cluster, these two densely populated areas were two of the most devastated parts of the city during the massacre. Interviewed by Professor Angelo Del Boca, the Italian witness Domenico Cerutti put it bluntly, stating that the agglomeration of cottages along the Ghilifaleñ River valley and the Genfile (Sera Bét Sefer) was 'where the reprisals became a form of genocide'.[96]

FERANSAY LEGASSION

Many houses in Feransay Legassion were burned on Friday night, including some within the legation premises. In the morning the American consul-general was to report, 'French Minister informs me a band of Blackshirts rushed into his compound yesterday [Friday] afternoon, set fire to three huts in his servants' quarters and chased away four of his native servants. He agrees with me that for the last 24 hours the Italians have been behaving like raving maniacs, which bodes ill for the future.'[97]

A French diplomat watching the flame-throwers at work described the scene. 'From the legation we heard uninterrupted firing punctuated from time to time with the sharp rat-tat of machine guns. Bands of Blackshirts and Italian civilian labourers ran through the streets throwing hand grenades, killing and setting fire to the *tukuls* (native huts) with flame-throwers. Scores of inhabitants were unable to escape from their blazing huts and perished in the flames. The confusion was indescribable.'[98] According to another of the legation staff, 'The Legation grounds were invaded several times by excited Blackshirts who demolished and pillaged some of the native huts in the park, in which lived the Legation servants, many of whom have been employed there for years.'[99]

Messages sent across to the British legation confirmed that when the Blackshirts looted the living quarters of the Ethiopian staff at the French legation, they invaded and destroyed the laundry building.[100] The American

68. A strong wind fans the flames across a gully during house-burning at night. This photograph was most likely taken either in the Ghilifaleñ River valley, on the southern perimeter of Jan Méda, or possibly in the Qechené (Genfile) River valley at Serateñña Sefer

consul-general reported that 38 Ethiopian servants were taken away from the French legation during the night,[101] and other reports, confirming the official dispatches, stated that the raiders dragged out and slaughtered Ethiopians seeking refuge there, including two of the legation's oldest servants.[102]

The French were outraged, and M. Bodard made strong representations to the Italian authorities, who sent reinforcements to protect the premises. In place of the few frightened *askaris* they sent detachments of Granatieri, Bersaglieri and *carabinieri*.[103] However, neither the regular troops nor the *carabinieri* seemed willing or able to control the Blackshirts, and the protection provided turned out to be ineffective.

QECHENÉ

During the Hour of Mayhem following the attack at the Governo Generale, as noted earlier, the neighbourhood of Qechené had been a refuge for people fleeing the Circle of Death. But that night the *tukuls* of Qechené itself were extensively burned. They were numerous, including many near the Church of

Qechené Medhané Alem, and hundreds more housing traditional artisans such as blacksmiths, potters and weavers, with their families. Thus many Qechené residents suffered a terrible death on the night of Friday, 19 February. Nonetheless, as we shall see, some of those who fled when they saw the Italians coming, or managed to escape from their burning homes, found sanctuary at the German Hermannsburg Mission (today the Qechené Children's Home), where the head, Hermann Bahlburg, reportedly allowed the compound to become a place of refuge.[104]

The Suburbs

As noted earlier, although the residential areas in the central and northern clusters were the most intensely burned on Friday night, all districts outside the Exemption Zone were affected to some extent, including Qirqos, a residential area behind the railway station. Being several kilometres from Siddist Kilo, the inhabitants had been spared the mayhem of the afternoon and were thus caught completely unawares by the arson of the night. Werqu Welde-Maryam, a young boy at the time, was living with his family not far from the Church of Qiddus Qirqos, and became one of the few Ethiopians to escape from a burning house and live to have his story published after the Liberation. During the day of the attempt on Graziani his mother was hosting a religious feast in the name of St Mika'él, and a priest arrived to bless the event. 'Our area, known as Legahar [a corruption of *la gare*—the railway station], was a heavily treed rural area, or *ager bét*, so people fled into the area to escape from the Italians in the city centre. But I and my sister were busy serving bread and local beer, *tella*, for the guests, until the evening. As children, and being far from the city centre, we were unaware of what had happened during the day.' However, in the middle of the night, Werqu's father suddenly realised that there were Italians setting fire to the house and locking the door from the outside. It was a struggle for him to get his family out alive, but somehow he managed to do so, and the children ran towards Qirqos Church. 'It was difficult to escape and avoid being attacked; [in the process] we became separated. From there my sister and I carried on running on one side of the crowd [of fleeing people], while Mum and Dad ran to the railway station. There we found each other, and as we met, it was the happiest moment for our parents.'[105]

* * *

Not only were the suburbs subjected to house-burning; some of them were also used as killing fields for people fleeing the arson attacks in the city centre.

Temesgen Gebré, who survived and wrote about his ordeal at the Governo Generale and his subsequent detention, later became editor of the government journal *Birhanina Selam* and eventually of the national newspaper *Addis Zemen*. In February 1986 *Addis Zemen* published a summary of an account of the massacre of 70 innocent Ethiopians on the southern outskirts of Addis Ababa on Friday, 19 February 1937, as recounted to Temesgen by the same Werqu Welde-Maryam who escaped his burning home.[106] Temesgen tells how an elderly cleric named *Liqe* Tebebt Iwnetu was rounded up with other civilians who had fled their homes during the arson attacks. Roped together, they were then taken to a place near the Akaki River to be shot. From there *Liqe* Tebebt could see both Mt Wechacha to the south-west of Addis Ababa and the burnt-out remains of his own village. A truck arrived with a detachment of Italian soldiers, who got out and prepared a firing squad. The major in charge called out, 'How many Ethiopians do we have?' to which the response came, 'Seventy.' The major ordered the Ethiopians to face him and move closer to the river, whereupon he opened fire with a machine gun, 'spraying them with bullets, and they began falling into the Awash River, to be swept away in the blood-stained water'.

Liqe Tebebt was shot and also fell, seriously injured, into the water. In his state of shock he saw that the major was trampling on the dead and the dying on the riverbank, and laughing at one of his victims who was in agony and begging to be given the *coup de grâce*. But somehow he managed to struggle out of the water and in a state of fury made his way back to the Italians, where, feeling that life was no longer worth living, he demanded that they finish him off.

Liqe Tebebt's wish was not granted. Instead he was rearrested. Committed to 'one of the worst prison cells in Addis Ababa', he there met the young man who told the story to Temesgen, Werqu Welde-Maryam. Werqu was shocked to see this 'elderly short man covered in blood, with a moustache, and numerous serious injuries all over his body'. It was only then that *Liqe* Tebebt found out from Werqu the cause of all his suffering—that there had been an attack at the Governo Generale. Fortunately, after six days both man and boy managed to get out of prison, and *Liqe* Tebebt left Addis Ababa for Gojjam. Temesgen Gebré, who originally published this testimony, met *Liqe* Tebebt himself in 1942/43 (after the Liberation) in Addis Ababa, when the elderly cleric came to the city to be honoured by Emperor Haile Selassie. By the following year Tebebt had been awarded the title *Aleqa Mel'ake Selam* Tebebt Iwnetu of Dembecha.[107]

The Exemption Zone

The Exemption Zone covered the political-administrative area stretching from the Governo Generale down to the army headquarters at the former Menelik *gibbi*, as noted by the German author Louise Diel.[108] As stated earlier, the eastern part of Beshah Welde Chilot Sefer, together with the area north of the Arat Kilo junction, where Tekle-Maryam Kiflom was living (Upper Arat Kilo), was within the Exemption Zone, and was thus not burned. *Immahoy* Hiruta confirmed this: 'On the night of Yekatit 12, my house [between Siddist Kilo and Arat Kilo] and the surrounding neighbourhood was safe; [things were] fairly quiet.'[109] The decision to limit the arson attacks in this part of the city to Lower Arat Kilo, rather than letting them spread into the upper section, was clearly because, like Siddist Kilo and Amist Kilo, Upper Arat Kilo contained several buildings and institutions of importance to the Italian administration.

As the Italians made their way down to Lower Arat Kilo, Tekle-Maryam, who was still at home, could hear the sound of trucks and shouting. However, unaware, like Welette-Birhan, of the decision to leave his area untouched, he assumed the Blackshirts would attack the village. So he decided that, rather than risk being trapped in the flames, he would hide in a bush outside. Thus he spent much of the night crouching in his garden, shaking in fear with housemates Gebre-Sillassé and Siyum and his neighbours, who had gathered at his house when the trouble started. However, as the flames from the villages of Beshah Welde Chilot Sefer and Sera Bét Sefer to the south lit up the sky, Tekle-Maryam and his companions realised that they could easily be spotted and killed by passing Blackshirts, and so eventually, at around 4.00 am, they gave up their hiding place and went back indoors to await their fate. Outside there was no respite; the holocaust was unrelenting. They could hear the crash of falling trees, and from the general direction of the old *gibbi* they could hear the screams of the victims. But as Tekle-Maryam said, 'There was nothing I could do to avoid death if it came', and he decided therefore to try to get some sleep. As the sun came up, he found he and his friends were still alive. The inferno had passed them by.[110]

In the days that followed, Tekle-Maryam discovered that thousands of people across the city had been burned, stabbed, shot or bayoneted to death that night, but his area had been spared. Looking back in his old age, he attributed his good fortune to the presence nearby of the former Menelik II School, which was being used as the headquarters of the Regia Aeronautica.

To the north of Arat Kilo lay what is today known as Amist Kilo, an area also inside the Exemption Zone. A little to the north-west an Armenian named Yervant Semerjibashian, then aged around 23, was living with his elder brother Johannes, adviser for local affairs at the German consulate-general,[111] in a long, low, single-storey house on the eastern bank of the Qechené River. Yervant's experience during the arson attack of Friday night was similar to that of Tekle-Maryam Kiflom and *Immahoy* Hiruta, who, unaware at the time that their areas had been exempted from attack, were afraid that their homes were going to be deliberately burned or that the thatched roof would catch fire from the general conflagration. He recalled, 'During the Italian occupation I was a driver. I drove a *camion* [truck]. At the time of *Yekatit 12* I was in Addis Ababa, during the massacre Yervant was in Johannes's house at the back of the German School [now the Graduate School of Addis Ababa University], not far from the Church of Qiddist Maryam. 'The Italians were shooting and burning … Johannes's house had a straw roof. We were afraid it might get burned during the massacre, but it did not.'[112]

The Fate of Eritreans

Some Eritreans were caught up and died in the conflagration, but many survived, being subjects of Italy's much-vaunted 'first-born' colony. Typical of such families was that of Éfrém Gebre-Amlak, living on the Gojjam Road. During the massacre they never left their house and, like many other Eritrean households, took precautions: 'We were not allowed outside. [To avoid being sent to Danane concentration camp] my father hid in a bush outside so that when the Italians came they would find only my mother, myself, my two elder brothers and my younger brother. They were all in the house. But the soldiers did not come to our house, because we put our Balilla (Fascist Youth) scarves at the gate, so they left us alone. And my elder brother wrote a notice saying "This house is occupied by Eritreans", and put it on the door. So the Italians went away.'[113]

As the hours of mayhem passed, the repression squads grew tired. Some were doubtless drunk; others' arms ached from throwing hand grenades and using Ethiopians for bayonet practice. Many were weighed down by the silver crosses and bracelets ripped from the necks and wrists of their female victims. So back to their barracks they trekked, some walking, others hitching a ride on the 'Trenta Quattro' trucks swerving to avoid the fallen eucalyptus trees in what remained of the smoke-filled villages, to their garrisons off the Intotto Road. They had had their thrills for one night, but they would be back.

* * *

By 4.00 am a ghostly silence reigned in the city. The survivors were huddled together, wide awake but traumatised into silence. Among them was an eight year old boy named Siyum. The son of an Eritrean father and Ethiopian mother, he was living with his family in the Jan Méda area. The household had previously lived in a house near the Gennete-Li'ul Palace, but had been obliged to move away to avoid a serious social problem that had accompanied the Occupation. Italian soldiers had been continually disturbing the family, coming to the house at night looking for women, despite the protests of his father, Gebre-Igziabhér, who spoke fluent Italian and had told them repeatedly and in no uncertain times to go away, insisting, 'This is a family home!'[114]

Siyum and his sister Abeba had heard explosions and gunshots at noon, and had run back home when they saw people fleeing their homes. By the time they arrived, several houses in Jan Méda had been set on fire, and the family spent the day sheltering in their compound. At night they became worried that Siyum's father had not come home, and, apparently not realising the extent of the slaughter in the city, Siyum's stepmother told him and his nanny, Welette-Tsadiq, to go and look for his father. It was thus at 4.30 am, in total darkness, that Siyum and his nanny left the house, planning to search for Gebre-Egziabher at the houses of *Ato* Zekarius, who lived at the Mekane-Yesus Church compound behind the German School, and *Ato* Cherinet, whose home was near the Catholic Cathedral. This meant a walk of several kilometres through Arada—now very dangerous territory. Indeed, Siyum was lucky to survive his nocturnal adventure. He encountered numerous corpses littering the streets, and it was very frightening to have to inspect them to find out whether his father was among them.

In the event, Siyum did not find his father, and was shocked that some of the family friends in *Ato* Cherinet's compound did not even want to admit that they knew him, for the city was gripped with fear.[115] Dejected at the failure of their mission, they headed for home through the gloom and the debris, but no sooner had they reached Ras Mekonnin Bridge than they were arrested by Italian soldiers and put into a makeshift detention camp situated within the river valley near the bridge. The camp consisted of a narrow compound into which, Siyum estimates, as many as 3,000 detainees—and possibly more—were being held.[116] As we shall see, Siyum and Welette-Tsadiq would spend two terrifying days in detention, but fortunately Siyum's ordeal was relieved somewhat. Being the youngest prisoner there, the Italian guards—probably *carabinieri*—took pity on him and gave him bread and water, which was more than the adult detainees received.

6

THE SECOND DAY

THE MORNING AFTER

As the sun rose on Saturday, 20 February, Dr Ladislas Shashka peered through his window and saw a city devastated. 'Abyssinian families were decimated. Homeless people wandered desperately through the streets seeking their lost relatives. There were notno cries, no loud weeping, no complaints which men could hear ... The horror of the night left men silent.'[1] Edouard Garabedian stated that on Friday evening he slept early, but 'next morning I heard that many Ethiopians had been killed during the night when the Italians were burning their houses.'[2] Indeed, where houses had once stood, little remained. In many cases there were no walls—just piles of ashes surrounding the remains of their inhabitants. In the area around the old *gibbi*, entire streets of houses on the slopes of the Genfile River in Sera Bét Sefer had disappeared. The Italian witness Alfredo Godio told Professor Del Boca that, after passing through the city in the morning, 'from 5 May Square [Arat Kilo junction] to the American Hospital very few *tukuls* survived. And among the rubble there were piles of charred corpses.'[3] Some bodies had been largely consumed by fire, particularly where flame-throwers had been used. Others were complete but charred and rigid. Many were interlocked as families had huddled together with their children in the agony of death. Other victims had been struck down by shovels and daggers, blown up by grenades or bayoneted to death as they tried to flee their assailants. The journalist Ciro Poggiali went to have a look at St George's Cathedral. Entering the building, as he recorded in his diary, he

69. 'Among the rubble there were piles of charred corpses'—Alfredo Godio. On the morning of Saturday, 20 February, across the city, numerous families were found to have been burned alive in their homes. Many of the bodies had been entirely or partially consumed by the fire, and in cases such as in this photograph, only body parts remained

70. Citizens fleeing from the mayhem and arson of the Fascist 'repression squads' had been struck down and died where they fell

found the devastation of the previous day: 'All the paintings have been destroyed. The Holy of Holies has been opened, and the containers of the Tablets of the Covenant have been burned.'[4]

Some quick-thinking housewives who realised what was going on reacted as soon as they knew the repression squads were on their way. Despite being alone without their menfolk, they managed to evacuate their children and their belongings before the arsonists arrived. And in some cases, they were lucky enough to be allowed to do so by their attackers. In the morning these housewives returned to find their homes destroyed, but at least they were still alive.

THE KILLING CONTINUES

But there was more carnage to come. At around 9.00 am, Edouard Garabedian set out from his home in General Wavell Street (Via Asmara), on the southern perimeter of Arada, above the Catholic Cathedral, to go to work in Piazza. However, he did not get very far, for the adrenalin of the killer squads was still coursing through their veins. Not content with their nocturnal orgy, they were again prowling the streets looking for victims. The calm of the early morning was giving way once again to indiscriminate attacks—street killings of any Ethiopians who had ventured out of their hiding places to search for their loved ones. 'There was a great panic and Ethiopians were running from everywhere without self-control. The Italian Blackshirts were pursuing them and beating them.'

But now the Blackshirts were forcing their way into the houses of Europeans. 'When I saw this I decided to return to my house where I found my mother weeping, and a group of Italians who had entered my house. They tried to get hold of our waiter. My mother had hidden him and they could not find him. They left our house and went to our neighbours' houses and did the same thing.'

The Armenian continued, 'Another group entered the house of *Blatta* Ayele Gebré who was at that time my neighbour. They caught him and tried to tear him to pieces. They were doing the same to all our neighbours. I saw the Italians were beating them as much as they could.'[5]

No doubt the early resumption of attacks on any Ethiopians found on the streets or even at home on Saturday was encouraged by a telegram from Minister of Colonies Lessona in Rome that had arrived at the Governo Generale at 6.30 am. Expressing concern about the 'excitement' that news of the *attentato* [attempted assassination] in Addis Ababa would create

19 Febbraio 1937

71. Silhouetted against the still-burning embers of her home, a housewife stands disconsolately amid furniture and kitchen hardware salvaged during the massacre of Addis Ababa. A woman we assume to be a relative or neighbour looks on, while someone—perhaps a colonial policeman—walks past amid the rubble. This photograph shows a mixed-income-level residential area after an arson attack of 12 Yekatit. The absence of any male members of the family would be consistent with their having been taken into detention

among Ethiopians, and calling for a general clampdown, he wrote, 'I am sure that from now on [you] will adopt the most stringent measures that appear necessary locally.'[6] These new instructions from Rome would certainly have removed any residual restraint that there might have been among the Blackshirts, *carabinieri* or even the regular army. In fact, the marauding gangs not only resumed their rampage on Saturday morning, but, according to Lieutenant Meleseliñ, also employed a method of killing apparently little known about, and thus not widely reported: 'The next day [Saturday] the Italians continued their activities by pursuing any passers-by they encountered, either by shooting to kill as they wished, or by collecting individuals in groups, tying their hands behind their backs, then taking them and throwing them alive without mercy into rivers and wells.'[7] As we shall see, the accuracy of this report was confirmed by the discovery in the 1940s in the city's riverbeds and drinking-water wells of no less than 500 human skeletons, which were eventually buried at the Church of the Holy Trinity (Sillassé).[8]

* * *

In the Exemption Zone, as on the previous day, things were rather quieter than elsewhere. Behind the Church of Ta'eka Negest Be'ata, *Dyakon* Dawit Gebre-Mesqel and his two fellow *dyakons* had spent the night at his house, and in the morning, assuming that the massacre was over, his colleagues decided to risk walking up to the Cathedral of the Holy Trinity, which was also within the Exemption Zone. However, because the Blackshirts had threatened to kill Dawit if he stepped outside, he stayed at home.[9]

72. 'The Italian Blackshirts were pursuing them and beating them'—Edouard Garabedian. Indiscriminate killings of Ethiopians continued throughout Saturday. Some were servants dragged to their death from the houses of their employers.

* * *

As if being kept awake on Friday night by the horrors of the burning city below him was not enough for the British envoy, a messenger arrived at his office in the morning with news about a break-in at the French legation by the Blackshirt horde during the hours of darkness. Then there was an urgent message that his translator and local informant, Tefere-Werq Kidane-Weld, had been arrested during the night at his house outside the legation, and taken to prison in chains. Bond was angry and affronted. Although *Ato* Tefere-Werq was not a permanent staff member of the legation, he had proved to be a useful man to have around the place. Taking his chances with what he might encounter outside the legation, the envoy drove through the smouldering city to see the Chef de Cabinet, Colonel Alberto Mazzi, and demand Tefere-Werq's immediate release. The colonel claimed ignorance of the arrest and declared himself helpless to intervene, since, he said, the matter fell within the mandate of public security. Nonetheless, he promised to provide the legation with a full report on the matter, and guaranteed a proper investigation.[10]

By sunrise, when the fires around the American legation had died down somewhat, the intrepid American consul-general decided to go and check on the besieged French minister. Engert and his family had originally planned to spend the weekend as guests of the American couple Herbert and Della Hanson, at their mission school at Addis Alem, west of the city.[11] However, given the circumstances, this was now out of the question, so, venturing out into the city in his official car, he took the road through Piazza and across Siddist Kilo to the heavily treed French legation compound in the north-eastern quarter, where he was received by Bodard. The French envoy recounted the events of the night, describing how the Blackshirts had broken into the legation compound.[12] However, the Governo Generale had reacted quickly to Bodard's appeal, and soldiers were now standing by to prevent further incidents.[13]

The Viceroy's office seems to have been embarrassed by what had happened at the French legation, for, according to the *Daily Telegraph*, they took every possible step to cover it up. The British daily stated that 'strict measures' had been taken to prevent the outside world knowing what had happened, and that for that purpose 'employees of the French railway were specially watched and even searched'.[14]

As he left the French legation, Engert could still hear firing in the city, and concluded that more executions were being carried out. Sure enough, on the journey home he saw not only large trucks carting away the bodies of those killed earlier, but, in addition, 'several fresh corpses strewn along the road'. When he reached the American legation, the envoy sent a strongly worded telegram to Washington. He was outraged by the behaviour of the Italians on Friday night, and his report confirmed the accounts that had been trickling out of Ethiopia to the international press. It was this report that described how the Italians had 'completely lost their heads', had been 'killing all natives in sight including women', and compared the ongoing pogrom with the Armenian massacres.[15]

Later that morning, as if further confirmation was required that peace had not yet returned to the city, Engert witnessed a disturbing incident which was to become the subject of diplomatic protests by the American government. Two *carabinieri* brutally assaulted two foreign missionaries. One was Duncan Henry, an American citizen and member of the American United Presbyterian Mission, who was dragged from his car and struck several times with a rifle on his shoulder, arm and head. He received severe bruises and a scalp wound that bled profusely. His assailants then struck him in the throat, slapped him in the face, and handcuffed him. An Englishman who was with Henry, and who was also a missionary, tried to protest but was himself handcuffed and shackled to Henry.

At that moment Engert happened to be passing in his official car. He stopped, and demanded to know what was going on. Henry's assailants were excited, and were described by the consul-general as 'very incoherent'. They claimed that Henry had 'refused to move on', which was clearly not the case, since, as Henry himself pointed out, it was while his servant was cranking the car to start the engine that the assault occurred. A report by the British consul-general of the same incident suggested that the men were targeted because they had Ethiopians in the car. (It was made a criminal offence under the Italian *apartheid* laws for an Ethiopian to be a passenger in a car driven by a white person.)

Engert accompanied the party to the police station, where he submitted a protest to the officer in charge against ill-treatment suffered by an American citizen.[16] In his telegram to Washington in the afternoon, the consul-general explained: 'He [the police officer in charge] said there must have been a misunderstanding and ordered both Henry and the Englishman released at once. I then took Henry in my car to the Legation and after some first aid I accompanied him to his mission. I then made a verbal protest to the Acting Chief of Cabinet [Colonel Mazzi] and the chief of the *carabinieri* which I shall follow up tomorrow with a written one.'[17]

* * *

Meanwhile, for young Imru Zelleqe, who had watched with horror people being killed at Menelik Square on Friday, the nightmare had only just begun. On Saturday he was arrested at the family home, together with his mother and his two sisters, nine-year-old Ketsela and two-year-old Zéna, and taken to a nearby detention centre. 'We were kept prisoners in the basement of a villa by our property. We passed a horrible and terrifying first night because there were some Italian prisoners that were being interrogated and were screaming in agony (these Italian nationals were probably anti-Fascists or criminals).'[18] As we shall see, the family would be moved again the following day.

* * *

THE TRANSPORT OPERATIONS

As the American consul-general noted, by Saturday morning the Italians had set in motion a major transport operation: collecting the dead. Soon the principal sounds throughout the city were those of lorries being driven to and fro collecting bodies, like dead livestock being taken to market. Three locations had been designated for depositing corpses for collection: the main road outside the Gennete-Li'ul Palace in Siddist Kilo; the Ras Mekonnin Bridge area; and outside St George's Brewery at the beginning of the Jimma Road. The bodies at these collection centres were then picked up by another fleet of trucks, operating in a continuous cycle throughout the day between the collection centres and Gefersa in the suburb of Gulelé, north-west of the city. They were offloaded at an area of open land approximately 100 metres long and 50 metres wide between the front of the Catholic cemetery (which served several foreign communities) and Viale Tevere (the Ambo Road, or Arbeññoch Street), opposite the Church of St Peter and St Paul. However, the bodies were not buried. There were far too

73. Stage i: 'Among the persons who were pulled by the iron rakes many were alive'— Captain Toka Binegid, commanding officer of Addis Ababa fire brigade. Bodies trucked to a collection centre are raked into heaps

many for that. The only solution was mass cremation, which was carried out by strewing scores of corpses at a time on the ground, soaking them in kerosene or benzine, and burning them in the open air.

All aspects of the massacre were, of course, shocking to the Ethiopians. But two aspects in particular appalled them beyond belief, and had a lasting impact on any remaining respect the Ethiopians might have had for the Italians. Mentioned frequently by Ethiopian writers, they are the atrocities committed against women and children, and the treatment of the bodies of the dead. The populace was aghast at the sight of bodies of their loved ones treated 'like sorghum', as one local author put it, and being disposed of without rites or ceremony.[19]

74. Stage ii: Bodies at the collection centre are loaded onto trucks

75. Stage iii: Bodies are unceremoniously offloaded at Gulelé

76. Stage iv: Bodies about to be incinerated. In the background, close to the cemetery wall, are piles of soil

77. Pits are dug for the burial of the remains as more bodies arrive for incineration. Here one burial pit is located

There were basically five stages in the disposal process, as illustrated in the accompanying photographs (Figures 73–78).

Not all the bodies arrived dressed. Some were naked and charred, their clothes having been seared off them when they were burned to death in their homes. The remains of families who had been killed in that manner were trucked to the collection centres, then picked up again and transported to Gulelé. In the process, some were photographed and filmed. Fortunately for posterity, Dr Birhanu Abebe ensured that brief footage of smouldering bodies survived (see Figure 78).

Execution Centres

The trucks offloading at the collection centres were carrying not only the dead; they were also bringing the living, for execution. The administration had designated a number of locations as killing points, to which victims were brought by foot or truck to be shot, beaten or bayoneted to death. These corresponded to the body collection points: Siddist Kilo near the Gennete-Li'ul Palace, Ras Mekonnin Bridge, and outside St George's Brewery.[20]

After execution, the bodies were raked into heaps until there were enough for another truckload. One Italian soldier whose truck was stationed at Menelik Square and who watched the massacre, described the slaughter as 'shameful and horrible'. He testified that so many people were killed that in the streets piles of corpses could be seen against the walls 'as high as one floor', and that bulldozers had to be used to move them.[21] Then the bodies were collected and taken to Gulelé for burning. Alfredo Godio was one of the many Italians who witnessed the hideous sight: 'on the Ambo Road I saw many 634 ['Trenta Quattro'] trucks passing by on which were piled in a horrible tangle, the bodies of Ethiopians killed.'[22]

As Captain Toka Binegid of the fire brigade described in his sworn testimony, the process involved organising the militarised labourers in three groups, with responsibilities for killing, raking together the bodies, and loading them onto the lorries, respectively.

> The Italians divided themselves into different formations: while some of them were murdering, some collected the corpses and threw them onto the trucks ... They were gathering the corpses from the roads with iron rakes. Among the persons who were pulled by the iron rakes many were alive ... Furthermore I saw Italian soldiers being photographed while standing on the dead bodies of their victims.[23]

78. Stage v: 'It was an Abyssinian Guernica'—Italian female witness. The streets of Addis Ababa were strewn with corpses, and reeked with the stench of rotting human flesh. Based on eyewitness accounts, some of the victims had been burned alive. Those pictured here are at either one of the collection centres or, more likely, Gulelé. Soaked in kerosene or benzine, many of the bodies can be seen in this film to be still smouldering in the process of incineration

Gulelé

At Gulelé the scene was one of carnage: blazing oil, smoke and the stench of burning flesh. Here the bodies were not thrown into piles, but strewn over the ground. The Italians then ordered their *askaris* or civilian labourers to pour kerosene or benzine from metal drums onto the bodies, which were then incinerated. It is clear from the photographs that while many of the victims had already been burned to death, others were still dressed and had clearly only recently been killed, for *rigor mortis* had apparently not yet set in. And, according to Captain Toka Binegid's testimony, some were still alive. But families were not allowed near the victims—let alone to attend to them.

The transport operation was to continue throughout Saturday and Sunday. There was no shortage of trucks; the Italians had plenty available, and civilian as well as military drivers. Nonetheless, there were thousands of bodies to be disposed of, and by the time most of the killing was over, the transport operation had run for more than four consecutive days.

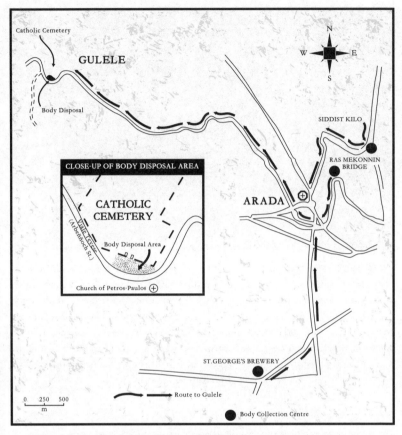

Map 10: Execution and body collection centres

The situation at all three execution and collection centres was appalling, with hundreds of bodies being loaded onto trucks at each centre for dispatch to Gulelé. But the scene at Ras Mekonnin Bridge was particularly gruesome. There, at the *carabinieri* station where more than a thousand hapless Ethiopian detainees were being held, and where prisoners had been thrown to their death, the river was running in blood, and there were corpses both under and over the bridge.[24] Dawit Oquba Igzi'i, still imprisoned at the station, watched the collection gangs climbing down to bring bodies up from the valley below.[25]

Those Italians who remained in Ethiopia under the Fascist regime generally seemed to have difficulty remembering that phase of their life, and those who

171

79. This uniformed man posing in front of a pile of corpses appears in several photographs of the body-burning at Gulelé. The dark flashes and *fascio* badge on the lapels of his jacket, the black tie, and the wide black band around his helmet and under the cockade identify him as a member of the Blackshirt *Centuria Lavoratori*. Many of the victims seen here are still dressed, indicating that they were probably killed during the day while on foot or at home, rather than having been burned to death during the arson attacks of the night. Pits were dug for the remains; note that the pile of excavated soil in the background also appears in Fig. 80

did manage to recall it rarely talked about the atrocities committed or even acknowledged them. An exception to the rule was Signor Marino, who was a soldier at the time of *Yekatit 12*, and stayed on in Ethiopia after the Liberation. In the documentary film *La conquista di un impero* he speaks openly about the massacre. Marino's testimony confirms the eyewitness accounts of what happened. He states that he and his colleagues were *instructed* to kill civilians in retribution for the attack on Graziani. 'We were told to revenge,' he says, explaining that the Blackshirts took the lead in the killing. Asked about the reaction to the massacre, in an interesting reflection on what the Italians thought the Ethiopians believed, he states that the Ethiopians were shocked and demoralised, because they had 'thought that the Italians had come to bring civilisation'.

One item of particular interest that this ex-soldier talked about was the transport arrangements, stating that there were about 100 trucks involved in the

80. Another scene of body disposal at Gulelé, taken to the left of Figure 79. Note the drum of kerosene or benzine to the left of the photograph, and to the right a pile of soil excavated for a burial pit

81. The area used for incineration and disposal of the victims of the massacre of Addis Ababa, viewed from the Ambo Road in 2001

collection of bodies. He said that the fleet worked all through the night, starting on Friday evening after the first wave of killings, that is it was transporting the bodies round the clock. Sergeant-Major Boaglio's account is consistent with this report, speaking of the dead being 'piled up' and being loaded 'in bulk' onto military trucks.[26] Marino explained that the bodies were taken to a cemetery where they were incinerated. He was unable to estimate the total number of Ethiopians killed, but said, 'There were thousands and thousands.'

INSIDE THE MUNICIPALITY

Whether Temesgen Gebré managed to sleep at all on Friday night at the Municipality Building we do not know, but when the sun rose on Saturday morning he saw from where he was sitting at the front of the compound that the Italians were searching the pockets of captives who had been beaten, counting the money, then giving it to their superior officer. However, not only were they stealing the prisoners' money, but, in a procedure that anticipated what the Nazis would do in their death camps, they were removing the rings of the condemned prisoners. 'They were collecting the wedding rings, then threading them on a string, and putting it around their necks like prayer-beads. While one of them counted and weighed them, then presented them to the officer, the others were wearing them around their necks.'

But the Italians did not stop at removing wedding rings; they were also stripping prisoners prior to execution. Temesgen saw a truck arriving full of clothes that had been brought from execution sites; these were sorted out and given to the officers. Temesgen noted that many were not blood-stained, indicating that they had been removed from victims before they were killed. But he was also horrified to see that, as the Italians were sorting out the clothes on the ground, those still wet with blood picked up the dirt. He was not the only one to be appalled by the macabre sight, for one of the prisoners suddenly stood up 'like a madman'. Unable to bear the torment any longer, caution thrown to the winds, he started castigating the Italians in a loud diatribe:

> God has seen this blood mixed with soil, and He will deliver his judgment! You have been killing people with your evil deeds! You have taken the rings of those you killed, and you threaded them on a string and weighed them! You have exhausted the patience of God! The soil has been soaked with our blood! Bodies have been piled up like a haystack! As you kill, so God will judge you! Now you will never rule Ethiopia! And now you are going to kill me![27]

But before the enraged prisoner could finish his tirade, the Italians, panicking, lost their nerve. Pandemonium broke out as they started throwing hand grenades at the captives. According to Temesgen, five grenades were hurled in the murderous assault, and 80 people fell in the explosions. Then transport arrived, and the dead bodies were loaded and taken away.

After the courtyard had been cleared of the remaining body parts, more trucks arrived, ostensibly to take the injured for medical treatment. But this was the trigger for yet another bloodbath. In an extraordinary display of sadism, no sooner had the seriously injured captives reached the gate than an Italian stationed there with a machine gun opened fire and they were killed on the spot.

The crowd was now in turmoil. Realising now what sort of 'medical treatment' they should expect from their captors, those who had suffered less severe injuries tried to disappear among the other prisoners, struggling to hide their wounds from view. But the soldiers pushed their way through the throng to seek out the injured, insisting that they should get treatment. Several were dragged as far as the gate, where they too were mown down as the machine guns burst into life again.

Now there was total uproar. Temesgen described the ghastly scene, the prisoners trying to run and hide: 'The Italians started taking away people who were not injured at all, despite their loud protests: "I am alright! I am not injured!" The Italians were pulling them out, saying, "No! You should get medical treatment, because you are injured!" And when they reached the Municipality Building gate, they held onto the gateposts with both hands and wouldn't let go. But they lined them up alongside a wooden pole and killed them.'[28] How the captives survived another night amid the carnage and without food or water can only be imagined.

The Police Garage

On Saturday, 20 February, the numbers at escalated dramatically, for this was the day when thousands of detainees were taken there. The distinguished diplomat-writer Birhanu Dinqé states that they accepted more and more prisoners until the compound was completely full.[29]

* * *

SATURDAY AFTERNOON

At the British legation, the acting consul-general reviewed the disturbing accounts coming in about the events of the night. Yet even more disturbing was the realisation that the slaughter had by no means come to an end. Although the situation had been relatively quiet in the early morning,

Blackshirts had reappeared on the streets, attacks had been resumed, and by the late afternoon William Bond had compiled several reports for an evening dispatch. 'Italian reaction', he wrote, 'continues to be marked by disgraceful acts of savagery.' He concluded that the rumour that Blackshirts had been given a free hand in carrying out reprisals was true: 'Bands of them continue to roam around the town today as yesterday with staves beating, sometimes to death, any stray Abyssinian found.' Reports of shocking incidents in the city had shaken the consul-general. At that time he could not know how representative they were, but he realised that the sources were dependable, and so the accounts had to be passed on. 'A band of eight were seen beating to death an Abyssinian whose hands were tied behind his back', and passing on information he had received from the American envoy, 'A boy fetching water from a well in the middle of town was beaten and shot before the eyes of the American Consul ... A white American missionary was struck twice and his head was laid open by a *carabiniere* with a rifle-butt while starting his car because he had two Abyssinians in it.'

It is clear from Bond's report that it was not only the Blackshirts who were responsible for the killings. The envoy had noticed that several witnesses reported seeing regular uniformed Italian soldiers and civilians carrying out atrocities. It seemed to be a free-for-all; the city was out of control. 'Italian soldiers and labourers are following this example of the Blackshirts in murdering stray Abyssinians without provocation ... Bayonetting of Abyssinians is also apparently a feature of the present hysteria.'[30]

Even as Bond put together his dispatches for London, members of his staff were dropping in to tell him of continued indiscriminate shooting in the city, and indeed he had heard shots throughout the afternoon. And, to add yet another to the envoy's concerns, there was a new, unsettling development: the trouble was apparently moving out from the centre towards the periphery of the town, and might soon pose a threat to the legation. Bearing in mind the Blackshirt break-in at the French legation, he found it worrying that just a short time before, where the road from the British legation to Arat Kilo turns and crosses the Qebena River, and where Bond himself had passed in the morning en route to the Chef de Cabinet, Colonel Mazzi, a lorry-load of *carabinieri* had been seen firing into the valley. The acting consul-general thought about the handful of guards deployed at the gates of the legation, and sent a message to the authorities requesting additional security.

* * *

At the American legation, Engert's security problems turned out not to have been solved after all. The promised guards had not arrived, and the consul-general was informed that Italian soldiers had brazenly told his staff that, regardless of his requests that there should be no repetition of Friday night, the remaining houses adjacent to the legation compound would be burned that night. Engert appealed yet again to the Chef de Cabinet and the commandant of the *carabinieri*, who again promised a guard and assured Engert that there would be no problem.[31]

* * *

Rosario Gilaezgi observed that during the day on Saturday the Italians were still burning 'small houses' and, in addition, testified, 'On the bigger houses they wrote their names to keep them for themselves ... They said it is "hygienic" to destroy small houses, so they went on destroying.' Judging from the references to both small and large houses apparently in the same area, the district concerned was more likely to be Arada, through which Rosario was driven several times, than the high-density housing around the old *gibbi*. He added that there they could not find a single man to kill: 'the ones who were not killed had been arrested or had run away'.[32]

* * *

Dawit Oquba Igzi'i's evidence confirmed that house-burning continued around the Ras Mekonnin Bridge throughout Saturday. The bridge was close to the Armenian and Greek quarters, and he was to testify, 'Some Greeks and Armenians who had found Ethiopian babies coming from the burning houses came to our compound with these children to ask if their mothers were there. I especially remember one case when an Armenian carried a little baby in her arms, asking for the mother. She was allowed to come to us with the baby and went around the crying crowd (most of them were injured) and tried to find the mother. One woman took care of the child. Whether it was the mother or not, I do not know.' As the houses in front of the *carabinieri* station burned, Dawit watched the arrival of more and more prisoners. On Friday, the station had held a thousand, but the numbers increased so much that the detainees could not move. By the evening, there was literally no room left, and the commander said he could not accept any more prisoners.[33]

Meanwhile, little more than 100 metres south of the Ras Mekonnin Bridge, a young Greek couple, Manoli and Evangelia Fanouris, who had arrived in

Ethiopia as children with their parents a decade earlier, were living at the Greek Orthodox church, in full view of the houses burning along the banks of the Qechené River. They had taken refuge at the home of the priest, Father Irothion, after abandoning their home during the breakdown in law and order that had preceded the arrival of the Italians nine months before. Like most foreign residents, they were appalled at the behaviour of the Italians, but felt helpless to do anything about it. As they recounted later to their daughter-in-law Mellina, they sat surrounded by the sounds of gunfire, crashing masonry, agonising screams and cries for help, and the stench of burning flesh. 'We can't just sit here while those poor people are butchered,' Evangelina exclaimed. 'I can't bear to hear their screams for another night. Holy Mother of God! Why is this happening?'[34]

* * *

Another testimony of Fascist power during the afternoon was the bombing of the city outskirts by the Regia Aeronautica. This was confirmed by Dr Shashka: 'the second night resembled in every way the first, with the difference, as I have said, of some bombing around the town'.[35] Quite apart from the terror and awe that the bombing was clearly designed to inspire, the onslaught was apparently aimed at men who had escaped from the city centre on Friday night into the surrounding countryside. It also followed, as we have seen, the tradition of the Regia Aeronautica being granted an opportunity to participate directly in reprisals.

Meanwhile, for the residents of the city centre who had not fled during the night, and who had been fortunate enough not to have been picked up, it was clear that there was more trouble to come, particularly when they heard that the Fascists were seeking any remaining cameras. 'If any white person ventured onto the streets he was stopped at every corner, and searched to see if he had a camera on him. The houses of white people were visited by Italian soldiers, who confiscated cameras and then went away ...'[36]

But if the confiscation of cameras suggested that more terror was to be unleashed, the Italian authorities themselves dispelled any doubt. As Dr Shashka recalled, 'The hours of daylight which elapsed between the first and the second night of the massacre I shall never forget. We already knew before nightfall that the horror was not at an end. We knew it by proclamations in Italian which appeared in the streets, announcing that more blood would flow.'[37] Written in Amharic and posted up around the city, their message was clear: Tonight will be worse than last night.

Graziani has hitherto shown his good heart to the Abyssinians. Tonight he will show them his immense power.

* * *

MOHAMEDALLY UNDER ATTACK

Ethiopia's largest and best-known trading firm at the time of the Italian invasion was Mohamedally & Co., which had been established in Harar by Mulla Mohamedally Sheikh Sharafally Hararwala during the reign of King Menelik in 1888. The Governor of Harar, *Ras* Mekonnin, invested in the business, and when he was replaced by Goolamally Abdulhusein Paghdiwala, around 1905, the firm was renamed Goolamally Mulla Mohamedally & Co., later abbreviated to Mohamedally & Co.[38]

Hailing from Gujarat, the Mohamedally family was very successful. They opened a branch in Addis Ababa, which quickly became the burgeoning city's leading trading house. The firm also established itself in many of Ethiopia's secondary towns, and went on to thrive as the empire's principal wholesaler and retailer. By the time of the Occupation, Mohamedally & Co. had developed a large complex at the heart of Addis Ababa's commercial district of Arada, consisting of a number of buildings, including a store that was opened during the time of Emperor Menelik, a large family residence, and a parade of shops that still flanks one of Piazza's busy streets (see Figure 82).

From the beginning of the Occupation, Graziani's aim was to close down all foreign companies of any significance, the objective being to 'Italianise' Ethiopia's commercial sector. The firms coming under the most direct attack were the British-owned Arabian Trading Company, the large Anglo-French firm of A. Besse & Co., and G.M. Mohamedally & Co., the last being singled out for special attention because of the Viceroy's conviction that it was involved with the British in activities subversive to the Governo Generale.

However, protests from the British government about the proposed closure of Mohamedally proved an obstacle for Graziani, despite Mussolini himself weighing in, on 26 October 1936, instructing the Viceroy to 'keep a watchful eye on the Indian element which during [League of Nations] sanctions was the greatest enemy of Italy', and adding that it was necessary 'at the opportune moment to expel Mohamedally, the creature and agent of Great Britain'.[39] Thus by the time of *Yekatit 12*, Graziani had failed to get Mohamedally expelled—to his eternal regret, for he became convinced that the company was in some way connected with the grenade attack on the Governo Generale.[40]

82. The Mohamedally shopping complex in 2004. It now houses a post office and several small shops. The original Mohamedally store and the family residence stand inside the block, access to them being through the gap in the street frontage

Although Graziani had at first indicated to the Minister of Colonies in Rome that the grenades thrown at him were of Italian 'Breda' manufacture,[41] some of the military believed that they were British. This belief prompted attacks on Saturday night on the premises of Mohamedally. As reported in the *New Times and Ethiopian News*, 'A bomb was thrown by the Italian military on the premises of the well-known Addis Ababa trading house, Messrs G.M. Mohammed Ali [*sic*] & Co., and more would have followed but for the action of the Italian *carabinieri*. Many Indian and Arab traders were saved by the same force, who took them into custody just in time to save them from being massacred by Italian troops.'[42] In addition, the report went on to state that the mosque near Mohamedally's was bombed and partly destroyed, and that in the process hundreds of Muslims were killed.[43]

While the story of the bomb attack was an accurate report, the death of hundreds of Muslims cannot be substantiated and was probably erroneous. Nonetheless, Mohamedally's business premises were indeed attacked, as reported by the British legation:

A certain amount of damage was done to the Addis Ababa premises of the British Indian firm of Mohamedally, by Italian [illegible] hand-grenades which were thrown at the premises by unknown persons on the night of February 20th [Saturday]. Official regret for this occurrence was expressed [by the Italian administration] to Mr Bond, who reported on February 21st that he had been informed that orders had been given to all Italian troops and other organisations to respect foreign property.[44]

'... the attack on the premises of Messrs Mohamedally & Company in town with hand grenades during the night of February 20th by persons unknown involving damage to the extent of about one hundred pounds ...'[45]

On Sunday morning the British envoy was to hear that some members of the Anglo-Indian community had been arrested. 'On February 21st Mr Bond was informed that, as a result of an Italian soldier at a military post being wounded by a bullet and another being fired at, the neighboring houses had been searched and a large number of British Indians and Arabs, amongst others, were arrested.'[46]

So far as can be ascertained, there was no massacre of Mohamedally staff, nor were there killings of neighbouring Arabs, although some were certainly detained. However, within a few weeks Ethiopia's greatest trading company, Mohamedally & Co., was closed down, and its principals expelled.[47] The company was destined never to return.

* * *

There was also considerable harassment and robbery of foreigners in the city by Blackshirt gangs during the course of the three-day massacre. The French consul-general reported two incidents that most likely took place in Piazza: 'In a pharmacy run by a Levantine, militias entered without any object other than to attack and insult in disgusting terms the foreign customers present. An Egyptian goldsmith, whose shop was closed, saw Fascists trying to enter, in order to rob him.'[48]

However, where the proprietor was dark-skinned, the Blackshirts had no hesitation in committing robbery with violence or murder, as can be seen from this additional report from the same envoy:

As a native confectioner, a British Somali [colonial subject] was leaving his shop, he was stripped by Fascist militia-men of the sum of 20 *thalers*, which constituted his entire fortune. As he protested, the robbers shot him, point blank. The native fell, seriously injured as if he were dead, then, in a burst of energy, he found the strength to drag himself behind his executioners, calling for mercy. Angered by the sight of this being who would not die, the militia finished him off with a revolver, and then, to add to their crime, they rushed to their victim's little shop, and savagely ransacked it, after having plundered it of everything they could take.[49]

* * *

ANOTHER NIGHT OF FIRE AND FURY

Although it is often supposed that the burning of the capital's residential areas would have been less extensive on Saturday night, this is not so. Certainly, fewer people lost their lives, but this was principally because so many had already been killed or been arrested, or had fled the city. The burning was actually very intense, and the killings focused more on women and children. The Italian journalist Ciro Poggiali confirmed that Saturday night was even worse than Friday.

Some of the more outlying districts of the city that had been largely untouched on Friday night now fell victim to the flame-throwers. But in addition, districts already devastated were—incredibly—revisited. While neighbourhoods such as Sera Bét Sefer hung heavy with the smoke of Friday night, and the remaining residents tried to recover from the shock and mourn their dead, the Italians, with a cruelty and barbarity that is difficult to comprehend, actually returned to the same areas to seek out households that had survived the onslaught of the previous night and wreak yet more vengeance on the bereaved, the shocked and the wounded. In fact, almost all the higher-density residential areas suffered repeat attacks on Saturday night.[50]

In the evening the British acting consul-general wrote a report summarising the horrors of the previous night, speaking of 'burning Abyssinian dwellings deliberately set on fire … in every quarter of the town'. Distraught, he added, 'The same thing is happening this evening. Streets are practically deserted except for troops.' In a later confirmation, he wrote, 'again on the evening of the 20th [Saturday], extensive areas in every quarter were ablaze'.[51]

* * *

At about 6.30 pm, as darkness fell, Rosario Gilaezgi and his superior, Della Porta, went out in their official car, passed St George's Cathedral, and saw the result of the previous night's attempt to destroy it: 'We saw the flames from the petrol when they tried to set fire to St George's Cathedral. The windows broke from the heat, but the building resisted.'[52]

The Exemption Zone

At about 9.00 or 10.00 pm on Saturday, as he watched Beshah Welde Chilot Sefer burn from his house in Upper Arat Kilo opposite the Regia Aeronautica headquarters, Tekle-Maryam Kiflom had a visitor. His heart leaped when he heard the noise, but it was not the Blackshirts returning to arrest him; it was his friend Terefe Azage, who had come to see him.

Terefe, who had joined the Patriot resistance fighters, or *arbeññoch*, had come to Upper Arat Kilo to check on his mother, who lived there, to see if she was all right.[53] But much as she was pleased to see him, she was afraid for her son. Fearing he would be found by the Italians, she implored him to leave. Since he did not want to run the risk of being seen outside and leaving what was, in effect, a safe area, he decided to stay at Tekle-Maryam's house. Tekle-Maryam and his housemates offered Terefe dinner. He said he couldn't eat, but he stayed the night.

* * *

As on the previous night, neither Siddist Kilo, nor Amist Kilo, nor Upper Arat Kilo were burned. In Siddist Kilo, at her mother's house, Welette-Birhan and her mother, sister and several children stayed outside the house all day. Soldiers told them they could go back inside since it would not be burned, but, as Welette-Birhan said, 'Burning continued in other areas all Saturday night.'[54]

* * *

Sera Bét Sefer

As noted earlier, being one of the Blackshirts' most popular targets, Sera Bét Sefer was again attacked, and many of its remaining inhabitants killed. This area, which reached down to the Empress Zewditu Memorial Hospital, where the American missionaries Herbert and Della Hanson worked before moving to Addis Alem,[55] had already been extensively burned the previous night.

On the second day of the massacre, the Hansons were expecting the American envoy Cornelius Engert and his family to spend the weekend with them at their Addis Alem mission. When their guests did not show up, they made enquiries and were told that there had been a 'revolution' in Addis Ababa, with many people killed and others fleeing for their lives. The explanation by the local Italian army captain was that there had been a 'fire of purification' in the city. In Herbert Hanson's words, 'A few days later, arriving in Addis Ababa, when we ventured to drive to the city, we found large areas burned that had formerly been covered with inhabited huts.'[56]

We have already noted that on Friday night the burning of Sera Bét Sefer reached across to the Empress Zewditu Hospital, and this was confirmed by

Hanson: 'Even around the hospital walls, where there had been many huts, all was blackened ruins. It made us heartsick to see the devastation, especially when we learned that many of the huts had been burned with their owners inside them.'

Fitawrari Habte-Giyorgis Sefer

In Fitawrari Habte-Giyorgis Sefer, Saturday night saw a repeat of the previous night's performance. In accordance with Minister Lessona's instructions for the Governo Generale to take 'the most stringent measures', it is not surprising that the regular officers once again gave the Blackshirts a free hand. Thus, notwithstanding the assurance that Engert had received to the contrary, burning and shooting in the area started afresh after sunset, and continued throughout the night. On Sunday morning the furious envoy, noting the impunity of the military, asked Washington to contact the Italian government directly:

> I respectfully suggest that the department telephone to Rome in the following sense:
>
> 1. This Legation has for 2 days been needlessly exposed to grave dangers from fire and stray shots due to the activities of the Italian military who have been setting fire to houses and have been shooting down natives in the immediate vicinity of our compound.
> 2. This first happened the night before last [i.e. Friday night] and although I immediately requested the authorities to take steps to prevent a recurrence, Italian soldiers brazenly informed me that the remaining houses adjoining our compound would be burnt that night. I again appealed in person twice to the Commandant of *Carabinieri* and once to the Chief of Cabinet who both assured me that they would not permit it and that a guard would be sent to protect the Legation.
> 3. Despite these promises the burning of huts and shooting of natives close to the Legation were resumed after sunset and continued practically all [Saturday] night. Again if the wind had been stronger our buildings might well have caught fire. Not a single Italian soldier appeared either to prevent the fires or stop them from spreading or to protect the Legation in any other manner. On the contrary we saw the Italians themselves set fire to the very houses that endangered ours.[57]

Feransay Legassion

On Saturday night there was again mayhem in Feransay Legassion district. The French legation itself was again besieged, and, as with the American legation, the regular military once more failed to intervene. Unaware that the reprisals had been authorised, the American consul-general assumed that the Italian High Command had lost control of the rank and file: 'It seems quite obvious that as all the highest officials are wounded ... the Blackshirts and armed laborers have run amuck and are unwilling to obey orders. (The French Minister tells me half a company of Italian regulars were powerless to prevent outrages in his Legation grounds because they were afraid to offend the Blackshirts.)'[58]

East of the Menelik Gibbi

As *carta bianca* grew in intensity, new areas were targeted for attack. *Dyakon* Dawit Gebre-Mesqel told the present author that, although on Friday night there had been no burning in the village immediately east of the Menelik *gibbi* (adjoining the Exemption Zone), on Saturday night that area fell victim to the repression squads. And one particular atrocity affected him deeply.

Not far from Dawit's house, his superior, *Abba* Welde Samiyat, upstairs in his own two-storey residence, heard a commotion outside. The Italians had arrived. Opening the window to find out what was going on, he saw to his horror that his neighbour's house was on fire. But no sooner had he shown his face than he was shot by an Italian soldier. The head priest of Menelik's great Church of Ta'eka Negest Be'ata fell dying to the floor.

Dyakon Dawit thought that the Italians might have picked on the *Abba* because the day before, at the Church of Kidane Mihret, he had been in the Holy of Holies when the Italians burst in, and had challenged them by refusing to leave the sanctuary until he completed his priestly duties. Dawit also believed that the soldiers were particularly annoyed because an Italian Catholic who witnessed the incident told them to let the priests finish mass before being ejected from the church, and 'the soldiers did not like that!'

Dawit dared not venture outside, and he spent a sleepless Saturday night. Kept awake by the screams and sounds of devastation from the nearby village, he prayed and wondered what the morrow would bring.[59]

7

THE THIRD DAY

SUNDAY MORNING

On Sunday morning, following the widespread arson of Saturday night, Addis Ababa was once again strewn with the bodies of those struck down and the charred remains of the victims of the burning squads. Thus, despite the round-the-clock collection of bodies, corpses were still accumulating throughout the city; heaps of them were noted at locations such as Menelik Square. Edouard Garabedian testified: 'On the third day [Sunday] I went to my shop [in Piazza]. This time there were no Ethiopians to be seen in the streets, but many Italians were circulating. I heard many of them saying that they had burnt such and such places and that they had murdered so many Ethiopians.'[1]

While Piazza was now empty of Ethiopians, attacks in other areas were stepped up. This was confirmed in a report reaching London from British Somaliland, from an informant who had arrived in Addis Ababa by train on Sunday. Travelling by car from the railway station, he had reached Jan Méda, turned to the west, and then returned to the station. 'During that journey he witnessed the shooting down by the Italians of every Ethiopian on the road. In one street alone he counted fifty dead. He saw many lorries rushing through the streets collecting the dead bodies.'[2]

The Municipality

By late morning at the overcrowded Municipality compound it was becoming swelteringly hot. Temesgen could see that not all his fellow captives had sur-

83. Killing throughout the city on Sunday resulted in more bodies for disposal, and convoys of trucks continued running throughout the day to carry them all to Gulelé. Judging from their uniforms, some of these soldiers are members of the regular army

vived; there were more corpses in evidence. 'We were in the field of the Municipality prison, surrounded, and very much afraid. We received neither food nor water.' More captives were being brought to the Municipality, among them Tekle-Tsadiq Mekuriya, a 22-year-old Francophone Ethiopian who after Liberation would rise to the position of Minister of Culture. He had been sheltering from the massacre at home (apparently in the Exclusion Zone) with his friend *Grazmach* Kebede. On Sunday morning, tired of sitting in the house, they had decided to go out onto the verandah to get some air, only to see two Italians walking towards the house—presumably regulars or *carabinieri*, since Blackshirts would most likely have attacked them, as the massacre was still under way. Afraid of being spotted, Kebede said, 'Let's get inside!' but Tekle-Tsadiq thought this would look suspicious, as if they were trying to escape, so they stayed where they were. 'Come here!' shouted the Italians. Using a stick from the fence, they ordered the two young men to walk in front of them and drove them forwards. Stepping out onto the verandah had not been such a good idea after all. They were now ensnared in the round-up of Ethiopian men ordered by the administration, and the destination was the

Municipality Building, where they were detained. There they found many 'nobility, civil servants and businessmen, half of whom had been tortured'.[3]

Conditions in the compound were deteriorating rapidly. Temesgen Gebré estimated that by noon 17 of the detainees had died of thirst. As in all the temporary detention camps in the city, theft and extortion were rife among the Blackshirt guards. In order to get the highest possible price for their water, they waited until their captives were dying of dehydration before they offered them a few drops. In some cases the trade began on Sunday; in other cases, on Monday. In the case of the municipality compound it was on the Sunday that the Italians started selling water to the prisoners from their personal water bottles.[4]

Fitawrari Habte-Giyorgis Sefer

In the suburbs beyond Habte-Giyorgis Bridge the troubles continued throughout the day. After transmitting his morning dispatch recounting the events of the previous night, the American minister was faced with yet further problems. The day started with the arrival at the legation of a group of Italian soldiers, who without a word of explanation brought the body of the mother of one of the legation staff. Like many other victims of the slaughter, she had been shot through the head during the night while running out of her blazing house. Then a female legation servant complained that her own mother had gone missing. Engert once again ventured outside the legation, this time to help the young woman in her search, but they were unable to find her mother.[5] However, no sooner had the American envoy returned to the legation than he was confronted with yet another problem. A staff member had been attacked:

> One of our messengers was on his way home when he was savagely attacked by Italian soldiers who knocked him down and beat him with clubs and tore his coat. His back and shoulders show severe contusions. He wore the Legation's uniform whose belt has a brass plate with 'American Legation Addis Ababa' in large letters to which he pointed when he was attacked. He also had identification papers issued by the Italian authorities to all Legation servants. However, soldiers paid no attention to either and shot three natives in his presence.[6]

Engert was outraged by what was going on. According to Professor Sbacchi, what most disturbed the envoy and his wife was witnessing the cruelty with which the Italians beat boys of 14 with the butts of their rifles, and then bayoneted them to death.[7]

84. 'The Italians continued their activities by ... collecting individuals in groups, tying their hands behind their backs, then taking them and throwing them alive without mercy into rivers and wells'—Lt Meleseliñ Aniley. Here Italian military officers in their leather boots stand over the grievously battered bodies of their victims, bludgeoned with their hands tied behind their backs

85. One of the rare photographs that can be attributed to a specific date and time, this image was taken by an Italian soldier in Addis Ababa around midday on 21 February. The bodies of at least nine civilians lie on a river valley path. After Liberation, the rivers would yield hundreds of human skeletons

The Exemption Zone

On Saturday night Upper Arat Kilo had again been exempted from arson attack. By the time Tekle-Maryam woke, his friend Terefe had already left the house, to return to his mother's home nearby. Gebre-Sillassé and Siyum invited Terefe to join them at breakfast, but again he'd said he didn't want to eat.

However, things did not go according to plan for Terefe. No sooner had he left the house than he was challenged by a group of Blackshirts, of whom there were several patrolling the area. They accosted him and asked why he hadn't acknowledged them with the mandatory Fascist salute, which involved stretching out the arm with the palm raised. They started beating him up, and in the scuffle, his hat fell off. Bending down to retrieve it, they kicked him with their heavy boots. 'Get back inside!' they shouted. So Terefe staggered back to Tekle-Maryam's house, where, instead of thanking Tekle-Maryam for providing a refuge from the Blackshirts, Terefe suddenly turned on him and his housemates, berating them for not having begged him to eat his dinner and breakfast in the name of Saint Abo and Saint Tekle Haymanot. 'What sort of house is this', Terefe asked, 'where Abo and Tekle Haymanot are not present?' Was his friend's bizarre behaviour caused by the stress of the massacre? Tekle-Maryam had no idea, but this curious incident stayed forever in his memory.

All three young men stayed at the Tekle-Maryam's house until 11.00 am, when Terefe decided to venture out again to his mother's house. This time he reached his destination, and in due course he joined the Patriots in the countryside.[8]

* * *

'REPRISALS SHOULD CEASE'

On Sunday, although there were fewer houses left to burn and fewer Ethiopians left to kill, Blackshirt bloodlust was still running at fever pitch, and the repression squads were looking forward to the third night—the climax of their rampage. Indeed, it seems likely that had the orgy of death and destruction been left unchecked, it might well have ended with the extinction of Ethiopian life in Addis Ababa. One Armenian Addis Ababa resident who lived through the massacre said, 'The Italians were intoxicated with power. If the massacre had not been stopped, all the Ethiopians would have been killed. They would have destroyed everyone!'[9]

Graziani, who was aware of the urgency of subjugating the Ethiopians before the country could be converted into a resource base for the Italian military, was to reiterate many times that Italian control over Ethiopia must be, and would be, achieved regardless of the cost, without 'sentiment' and without 'false pity'—an echo of Badoglio's insistence a few years before that the Italians would gain control of the Cyrenaica region of Libya 'even if it meant that the entire population of Cyrenaica should perish'. The Viceroy's instructions to his commanders in the field were clear: '[Your work] must conclude with the total submission of Shewa and the elimination of all who refuse to disarm, even if every last house must be razed to the soil' ... 'Remember that every false pity is a crime when dealing with people decidedly against our dominion' ... 'Conquest is conquest ... and its only law is that of an eye for an eye and a tooth for a tooth.'[10] He knew, of course, that able-bodied Ethiopians were needed for the 'black army', but was willing to pay almost any price to achieve the 'pacification' with which he had been charged. It was now more than seven months since Mussolini had instructed him to 'initiate and systematically conduct a policy of terror and extermination' in Ethiopia, but, despite having followed those orders to the letter, he seemed no closer to achieving his goal.

Yet for all his instructions to wage terror and extermination, the Blackshirt massacre was counterproductive for the *Duce*. The longer it went on, the greater was the risk of its becoming public knowledge, and the more public the spectacle, the more likely it was that members of the League of Nations would conclude that Italian control over Ethiopia had not been achieved, and would vote against any recognition of Italian hegemony. Without recognition there was no 'empire', and so late on Sunday morning, while Tekle-Tsadiq was being taken to the Municipality Building, things came to a head. Although the Fascists had already begun their 'fun' for the day, Graziani, who had received a telegram from Mussolini only the day before calling for 'that radical clean sweep which, in my mind, is absolutely necessary in Shewa',[11] received a shock: instructions from Rome to halt the massacre. Outraged over the attempt on his life, and only now beginning to recover, the Viceroy was furious with this interference.[12] However, he needed to show Mussolini that, despite hospitalisation, he was still in control, particularly as he was suffering from pneumonia brought on by the anaesthetic that had been administered on Friday. So he told Cortese that the killings had to stop.

As far as the Blackshirts were concerned, the massacre was far from over, for the three nights of mayhem Cortese had promised the Party faithful had not yet run their course; there was still one more night to go. Thus, not surprisingly, the federal secretary resisted the instruction. In response, Graziani threatened to call in the Military Police to restore law and order.[13]

Faced with the unwelcome prospect of a showdown between the more disciplined and professional *carabinieri*, on the one hand, and his Blackshirt rabble, on the other, Cortese backed down, and reluctantly instructed his office to print notices ordering that the reprisals should cease. Later that morning Dr Giovanni Sindico of the Fascist Party Office sent Graziani's Chef de Cabinet, Colonel Mazzi, an urgent message by phonogram stating that the required orders had been circulated to terminate the massacre (see facsimile in Appendix IV). 'Notice is hereby given for information purposes that the attached order of suspension of the acts of reprisal that had been authorised was issued at 10.30 am this morning.'[14] Shortly afterwards this was followed up by a letter to Mazzi explaining that the notices had been printed in the Fascist Party Office, and enclosing the actual notice shown in Figure 86.[15]

Displayed at key public buildings in the city, including Casa Littoria and Casa Fascio, the announcement read as follows: 'Comrades! I order that starting from 12 noon today, February 21st XV, any act of reprisal should cease. At

CAMERATI!

Ordino che dalle ore 12 di oggi 21 febbraio XV cessi ogni e qualsiasi atto di rappresaglia.

Alle ore 21.30 i fascisti debbono ritirarsi nelle proprie abitazioni.

SEVERISSIMI provvedimenti saranno presi contro i trasgressori. Le auto pubbliche, private, ed i camions (meno quelli in servizio di Governo e Militare) debbono cessare la circolazione alle ore 21.

IL SEGRETARIO FEDERALE

86. Guido Cortese, who launched the massacre of Addis Ababa on Friday evening, was obliged to end it prematurely at noon on Sunday. The official announcements of the end of the massacre, as seen in the specimen above, sent from the Federazione dei Fasci di Combattimento to Colonel Mazzi, were duly stamped, and posted in public places

9.30 pm Fascists must return to their homes. Very severe measures will be taken against transgressors. Public and private cars and lorries (except those in government and military service) must cease circulation at 21.00 hrs. The Federal Secretary.'

The posting of these notices was confirmed by an Italian civilian who spoke to Professor Angelo Del Boca in Addis Ababa in 1965. He said that he saw one of them stuck on the wall of L'Alimentare, a shop in the Corso Vittorio Emanuele [Adwa Avenue, connecting Piazza with Arat Kilo]. 'I read it and reread it. I couldn't believe my eyes. I found it incredible that the authorities had pasted up these notices that proved beyond a shadow of doubt that they had tacitly acquiesced in the massacre.'[16] In fact, Sindico's phonogram, reproduced here in Appendix IV, removes any doubt that the Italian authorities had gone beyond acquiescence; they had actually authorised the massacre, just as they were now bringing it to an end.

* * *

Not having dared to venture outside since the massacre began, Manoli and Evangelia Fanouris, sitting in their room at the Greek Church in Piazza, realised at midday that an eerie silence had descended upon the inner city. 'Nothing stirred. Scattered plumes of smoke rose from among the smouldering ruins ... An army truck came rumbling down the road and stopped where a mother and three children lay in a bloody heap. Two soldiers leapt out and together threw the bodies on the back. The truck moved on.'[17]

Officially, the massacre had indeed been brought to an end. But the repression squads were determined to enjoy their third night of arson, murder and looting. They were still on the rampage, and not even Guido Cortese would be able to stop them.

* * *

SUNDAY AFTERNOON

For the British legation, located on the eastern outskirts of the city, the first sign that the carnage was to cease appeared on Sunday afternoon. Attributing the decision to terminate the slaughter to either 'a surfeit of butchery' or 'the belated awakening of official conscience', the consul-general reported that in the afternoon a *carabiniere* non-commissioned officer said that the *carabinieri* now had orders to shoot on sight any person 'found in the act of incendiaries', indiscriminate shooting or looting, 'whatever the colour of his complexion or his shirt'.

Tekle-Maryam Kiflom stayed at his house in Upper Arat Kilo for the rest of Sunday, and had no more visitors. In the inner city things were generally quieter than they had been on the Friday and Saturday; he himself did not witness any incidents. However, he explained that, despite the termination announcement around midday, killing continued in several parts of the city during Sunday afternoon.[18]

Indeed, the massacre did continue, but the Sunday afternoon attacks were more in evidence in the outer suburbs, far from where Tekle-Maryam was living. The Blackshirts were aware of the directive to stop the killings, and in any case there were few houses left standing in the inner-city *sefers* where the attacks had been authorised, and many families had either been killed or had fled, so that the vigilantes were short of targets. The upshot was that to avoid the *carabinieri*, some of the Blackshirt gangs moved to the outskirts, to which many families had fled. There, homeless women and children took refuge, clinging together in fear in the woods surrounding the city, in river valleys and under bridges. Out of sight of their superiors, the marauding squads sought out these little family clusters and hurled hand grenades into their hiding places. After interviewing eyewitnesses who managed to escape and reach Djibouti a few weeks later, the foreign correspondent Ali Baig reported, 'Intermittently some detonations were heard here and there and at times took the form of a squall. It was when they discovered groups of families hidden under bridges, or in the quarries of Gulelé, or in the clefts of the Akaki River!'[19]

* * *

By Sunday afternoon Graziani had recovered his composure, and had discovered that Cortese's termination notice had not been entirely effective. Thus he confirmed the midday termination order by issuing from his hospital bed another instruction, as Rosario Gilaezgi reported. Rosario, who, as we have seen, was in the company of high officials of the Governo Generale throughout the massacre, testified that an order was received from the Viceroy, stating, 'By the grace of God I am feeling well. Stop the hostilities.'[20] But even Graziani's orders were not enough. The Blackshirts had been promised their three days of fun, and they were determined to enjoy their full entitlement.

At some point during the day, even Cortese, who would certainly have been aware that the instruction for terminating the massacre had come from the *Duce* himself, was getting worried; he seemed powerless to stop the violence he had unleashed. So he asked for help from Ciro Poggiali. In his private diary the newspaper correspondent wrote, 'The *Federale* has asked me to spread the word that the violence must end, and by 9.00 pm all whites should have returned to their homes.' With his own touch of irony, he noted, 'Obviously there are no more chickens or *thalers* left to steal.'[21]

* * *

BLACKSHIRTS OUT OF CONTROL
(SUNDAY NIGHT)

One of the first records we have of prisoners being released following the orders to terminate the massacre relates to the makeshift and overcrowded detention centre at the *carabinieri* station near Ras Mekonnin Bridge. On Sunday evening, prisoners who had been in possession of identity cards when they were arrested were set free. Dawit Oquba Igzi'i was among them. Having been given nothing to eat or drink during their three days in detention, the prisoners were in very poor condition, and if they had not been released at that time, few would have survived. Curiously, and as if to admit the injustice of their incarceration, the *carabinieri* proceeded to hand each man and woman a piece of bread and a little water as they left. As Dawit made his way home, he saw that houses were still burning and in some cases that people had been burned to death in their homes.[22]

By that time Sara's brother, Sibhatu Gebre-Iyyesus, had also managed to get away from the same detention centre, though the circumstances in which this occurred are not clear.[23] Not surprisingly, the prisoners who remained behind did not fare well. Many of them died from thirst and hunger.[24]

Siyum Gebre-Egziabher and his nanny were also released from detention at the Ras Mekonnin Bridge, along with the other women and children.[25] When they arrived home at Jan Méda, Siyum found to his horror that the house had been burned to the ground, and the furniture strewn across the yard. However, he was happy to see his father was alive, albeit 'depressed and sad'. Despite resenting the Occupation, Gebre-Egziabher had managed to get a job translating for the Italians, and had been spared, at gunpoint, after showing his employment papers. Siyum recalled in his memoirs that if it were not for his father's fluent Italian, he would certainly have been killed, as he was on the death list of the soldiers, who had been infuriated by his objections to their hunting for women at his former house.[26]

* * *

On the basis of the written order to terminate the massacre, it has hitherto been assumed that the house-burning was brought to an end by noon on Sunday. However, this was not so. Although the *carabinieri* and the regular military obeyed the Viceroy's order of Sunday morning, the Blackshirts, as noted earlier, were annoyed about the premature termination of their three-day massacre. Having begun the onslaught on Friday night, following the proclamation of *carta bianca*, they were looking forward to a third night of pillage and house-burning. So it comes as no surprise that, where the Blackshirts and Fascist civilians were concerned, the instruction to cease *carta bianca* was by no means universally obeyed. In several parts of the city the burning continued throughout Sunday night, as confirmed by the testimony of Captain Toka Binegid of the Addis Ababa fire brigade: 'The burning of houses and killing of the people which started on Friday at about 6 o'clock continued until Monday morning.'[27]

That the arson attacks were kept up after dark on Sunday was also confirmed by the American consul-general, who reported on Monday morning that on the previous night there had been more burning and shooting: 'Italian authorities finally sent one white soldier and one *askari* to guard the front gate of the Legation at 8 o'clock last night. They would of course have been entirely useless in a serious emergency but they informed me that orders have been issued to the Blackshirts not to burn any more houses. None were in fact burned in our immediate neighbourhood but further away several big blazes were clearly visible and the shooting continued for several hours during the first half of the night.'[28]

Similarly, the French consul-general reported, 'The end of the day of 19th February did not stop these excesses; they continued the next day [i.e. Saturday] and the day after [i.e. Sunday]. Shooting followed shooting. The nights were lit up by the deplorable red of the fires that were still spreading to the horizon.'[29]

Tekle-Maryam was aware that on Sunday the Italians had proclaimed a halt to the massacre, but, like other witnesses, he explained that, despite the instructions, shooting continued across the city, and could be heard throughout Sunday night.[30] Further confirmation of the burning on Sunday night was provided by Welette-Birhan, who pointed out that, while on that day Siddist Kilo was once more free from arson attacks, other districts suffered: 'Despite the fact that the Italians had been forbidden to carry on [the arson attacks], the burning continued on Sunday. There was a lull during the daytime, but the burning was resumed at night.'[31]

From the British legation, the acting consul-general, William Bond, noted that 'conflagrations' could be observed on Sunday night, 'in the outlying parts of the town'.[32] The envoy thought that the continued burning he could see in the periphery of the city might have been due to less effective security patrols in those areas, that is that the burning was carried out by bandits or common criminals. However, that was not the case. The repression squads had simply shifted their burning programme to the suburbs.

After the devastation and arrests of Friday and Saturday, there were so few able-bodied men remaining in their homes by Sunday evening, that, as on Saturday night, most of the victims of the attacks of Sunday night were women, children and the elderly.

* * *

Arada Revisited

Tekle-Maryam recalled the feelings of devastation and despair as he described to the present author how the houses burned in the downtown areas on Friday and Saturday nights were still smouldering on Sunday, and thick, billowing smoke filled the city. 'The flames [in those areas] had stopped after Saturday night, but now the city was full of smoke.' At this point in the interview his friend Tamrat Istifanos, who at the time was living close to Arada, reminded him that on Sunday night Gedam Sefer went up in flames. Watching with his family from their house near the Italian Hospital, Tamrat knew that the burning was not being carried out by bandits; it was the Blackshirts who were still intent on death and destruction, for from his window on Sunday evening he watched them moving into Gedam Sefer, where they proceeded to torch many houses (see Map 11).

Living in the Consolata Mission compound (now the Arbeññoch School) close to the Italian Hospital, Tamrat watched the houses behind the compound burn: 'The Arbeññoch School [district], which was in that area [of the hospital], was burning. The house of the mayor of Addis Ababa, *Kentiba* Tena Gashaw, was there. The house and its surroundings were burned' (see Map 11). And then, he said, he saw smoke pouring out of Dejazmach Yigzew Sefer, just beyond the Arbeññoch School, where Viale Tevere turned west to become the Ambo Road.

Until the notices to terminate the reprisals at midday were posted, no settlements near the Italian Hospital had been burned. Yet Tamrat saw wide-

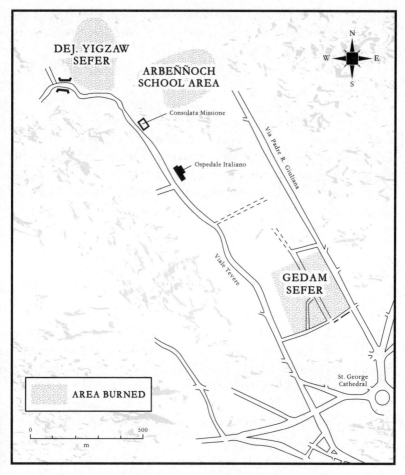

Map 11. Villages within sight of the Italian Hospital (Ospedale Italiano) burned on Sunday night

spread burning on Sunday night—not only on the outskirts, but particularly around the hospital, where Graziani was being treated for his injuries: 'Everything near the hospital was being burned.' He believed that the Blackshirts did so deliberately, to make sure that Graziani would see the flames from his hospital window.[33]

Then there was the question of St George's Cathedral. The unsuccessful Blackshirt attempt to burn it down on Friday was a major embarrassment for the Italians, and it was decided to entrust responsibility to the Regia

Aeronautica. However, following the orders to bring reprisals to an end, the instruction to bomb the cathedral was countermanded. The bomber never took off, and St George's Cathedral survived.[34]

Fitawrari Hapte-Giyorgis Sefer

At 8.00 pm the military finally acceded to the American consul-general's request for assistance: Italian soldiers turned up with a lone *askari* to guard the front gate of the legation. But it was a hollow gesture, for there was no longer any need for a guard—the soldiers admitted that *carta bianca* in the vicinity of the legation had been brought to a close. The Blackshirts had been told that no more houses were to be burned.[35] In any case, there were no houses remaining in the immediate vicinity to burn.

* * *

If the torching of neighbourhoods beyond the Italian Hospital after the official termination of the massacre was a final flourish of defiance by the Blackshirts, it was also intended to show Graziani whom they considered to be in charge. The Fascists also had a similar message for the residents of Addis Ababa, for a third set of announcements started appearing on the walls of the city—clearly posted by the Blackshirts. This time it carried the following declaration in Amharic, in the name of their beloved *Duce*, but with no mention of the Viceroy: 'Mussolini is as mighty as God. They have the same ways. He was angry, but is angry no more. Go home, and continue your daily work.'[36]

A DEADLY NEW DEVELOPMENT

In the smaller detention centres, Sunday afternoon had seen the *carabinieri* releasing captives considered harmless, such as women and children. But by the evening, a different pattern had emerged. Those remaining in the major detention camps such as the Municipality Building were removed and most of them were divided into two groups: those to be sent in the pipeline to prison or concentration camps, and those to be executed. This sudden development clearly reflected a more systematic policy on the part of the occupying forces. How had this come about?

During the course of Sunday, a telegram had been sent by Mussolini to Graziani marked 'Personal'. It contained explicit instructions—brief and to the point: 'No persons arrested are to be released without my order. All civilians and clerics in any way suspect are to be shot without delay. Acknowledge. Mussolini.'[37]

Clearly, implementation of this order had begun. There would be no more discretionary releases by the *carabinieri*, and any Ethiopian 'in any way suspect' was to be shot immediately. There was no question of guilt or innocence. Any degree of suspicion, no matter how slight, meant execution. This was not to be a Blackshirt *carta bianca*; the executions would now be official. Those whose names did not appear on the death lists would be incarcerated in a prison such as Akaki or Alem Bekañ, from which most would then be transferred to serve life sentences outside Ethiopia—in Danane concentration camp in the torrid coastal zone of Italian Somaliland; in the searing heat of Nocra, the notorious penal camp in the Red Sea; or on an Italian prison island.

Since the Municipality Building would have to resume its normal function as soon as possible, it would have to be emptied. Temesgen Gebré was one of those moved out of the compound on Sunday night. He saw much of what was going on because he was near one of the gates, and the Italians were taking the prisoners from the other end of the compound, so it took them time to reach where he was. Suffering from severe hunger and thirst, he watched as a truck arrived, and 30 prisoners were picked out, their names recorded before they were taken away—apparently to another prison.

'I witnessed terrible things,' he recalled. 'At that time there were three pregnant women who had nowhere to go to give birth, and they were trampled underfoot by the prisoners. I personally saw the bodies of these three women with their [unborn] babies. Because of the hunger and thirst, there were so many dead bodies that no one recognised the three women who had been killed.'[38] Temesgen himself had so far managed to evade execution despite being on the Italians' 'wanted' list, but finally he was obliged to get onto one of the trucks.[39] Nonetheless, 'Since they had my name, and they were looking for me to kill me, I gave them a false name when I was boarding the truck.'[40]

So it was that Tamesgen was moved from the Municipality Building. But was he going into long-term incarceration or was he to be executed? He had no idea where he was going or what was to befall him, but, as the truck made its way south-eastwards through Arada, he could see in the darkness that the Addis Ababa he knew had been transformed into a charnel house—a world of suffering, devoid of law and order. He could see that the street was full of dead Ethiopians; they were actually driving on corpses. And 'in the headlight[s] I saw cats pulling off the beards of the dead and eating their flesh.'[41] Finally the truck pulled up at an even more notorious detention centre: the Central Police Station, opposite one of the gates of the Menelik *gibbi*. For Temesgen, the horrors of the Municipality Building were now behind him, but even they would pale beside what he was about to experience.

The Central Police Station stood in a walled compound in the southern reaches of Sera Bét Sefer. A major police station combined with a police garage, today it is known simply as the Police Garage. The site had been commandeered by the Italians as the headquarters of the *carabinieri*. In earlier times this area of the city was associated with Empress Taytu; Lieutenant Meleseliñ speaks of Ethiopians being interned in 'the former prison house along Itégé Taytu Street'. Later it took the name of the nearby gate of the *gibbi*: Fit Ber.

Temesgen would never forget what happened on arrival. The truck stopped at the entrance of Fit Ber, and the captives were ordered off. But as soon as some of them had done so, the Blackshirts, apparently keen to have some 'fun' before handing over the prisoners to the Fit Ber guards, started playing cat-and-mouse with their captives. In a game remarkably similar to what had happened at the Municipality, one of the Blackshirts tossed a grenade at the detainees who had just alighted. There was a terrific explosion, and as the dust cleared Temesgen saw that the victims were dead. The captives still on the vehicle froze in horror at the spectacle. Frightened to dismount, they stayed where they were, and tried to hide. But there was no hiding place. Then another shock: a machine gun opened fire from the front of the truck, killing some of the remaining prisoners. The survivors jumped from the truck and ran into the prison.[42]

That was Temesgen's welcome to the detention camp at Central Police Station, where thousands were suffering and dying in unspeakable squalor, in conditions even worse than those at the Municipality Building. *Immahoy* Hiruta had good reason to recall seeing truckloads of dead bodies coming out of Fit Ber, for the death rate there in the few days following *Yekatit 12* bore comparison with some of the world's most notorious concentration camps. As bodies were going out, more and more prisoners were arriving in trucks, some straight from their houses and others, like Temesgen, from other detention centres. In fact, the transport operation went on through the night until morning.

Having eaten nothing since Friday, the captives Temesgen found at Fit Ber had been reduced to eating the weeds growing in the yard. Temesgen followed suit. Despite the unpleasant taste, they probably saved his life, for the roots contained enough moisture to ward off total dehydration: 'I wondered what they were eating, and went to the people to try to get something to keep me alive. Then I found someone who knew me, and he gave me the root. I took it and shared it with my companions, telling them it would alleviate their thirst ... Some of us chewed the bitter root until 10.00 pm.'[43]

* * *

Meanwhile, Tekle-Tsadiq Mekuriya, who had been detained in the Municipality Building during the day, was among those removed after Mussolini's instructions sentencing all captives to either imprisonment or execution. At 11.00 pm several trucks arrived, and 40 captives were loaded onto each one. He and his friend *Grazmach* Kebede left in one of them; as Tekle-Tsadiq recalled, 'We did not know where we were going or what they would do with us.'

They were driven out of the municipality compound and up the Ambo Road, eventually to Gefersa—an area several kilometres west of the city, where there was a small reservoir. Were they to be executed there? Apparently not, for they were not offloaded; instead, the trucks turned around and returned to the city. Passing through the area known as Filwoha (a field where natural hot springs were situated), the captives thought that the area might be an execution site. However, instead of stopping, the trucks drew up at the entrance of the Central Police Station opposite the grand palace gate known as Fit Ber, where Temesgen Gebré was being held. Hearing the sound of machine-gun fire from within, Tekle-Tsadiq feared the worst, imagining that this was indeed a place of execution. His welcoming committee was less deadly then Temesgen's, but nonetheless terrifying. It consisted of a number of Italian soldiers standing on both sides of the truck. Each held a gun in his left hand while in his right he held a heavy stick with which he beat the captives as they ran the gauntlet to the prison gate. As they entered, Tekle-Tsadiq and Kebede exchanged a few last words; as Tekle-Tsadiq put it, 'We agreed to meet in heaven'. Seeing so many people lying on the ground inside the compound, Tekle-Tsadiq thought his worst fears had been realised, until another prisoner told him, 'Don't worry; these people are alive. They are not dead. They were ordered to lie there. And the shooting that you can hear is the sound of guns being fired into the air.' The young men found that reassuring, but they spent the night without a minute's sleep.[44]

8

THE AFTERMATH

THE BATTLEFIELD

By Monday morning, Addis Ababa looked like a battlefield. According to one eyewitness account, 'Now the appearance of the city is like a field of battle after fighting is over ... everywhere ... a dead calm reigns. There are no more markets, no more victuals ... The population of the environs ... has been invited by leaflets scattered over the countryside from aeroplanes to bring provisions of cereals and cattle for the army. But no-one dare venture into the city which has been turned into the city of death from whence spreads the legend, strengthened by the disembowelling scenes, that there are "man-eaters" there.'[1] Lieutenant Meleseliñ confirmed the general situation, saying, 'On the fourth day—that is, Monday—no Ethiopian was seen on the streets of Addis Ababa, as so many had fled the city.'[2]

The following day, having taking cover at the British legation since the massacre began, a 14-year-old boy named Demissé Hayle-Maryam, who was a member of *Bejirond* Letyibelu Gebré's household, ventured back into the city and made his way home to Letyibelu's house. Describing the journey in con-versation with the present author, he said that he was assailed by the stench of rotting flesh. Evidence of the massacre was everywhere. 'I saw many putrefying bodies, eaten by dogs and hyenas. Around the bridge on the way to Arat Kilo there were so many bodies. All over Siddist Kilo there were bodies. In some cases the Italians had not bothered to remove them; they had burned them where they lay.'[3] And as the Fanouris family observed, 'All around the city,

87. On Monday, bodies still lay strewn throughout the city, many of them still lying in the remains of their homes

bodies lay in the mud-soaked piles prey to the tearing jaws of dogs and ravenous hyenas.'[4]

Owing to the large numbers of corpses still awaiting collection, the Italians had indeed started burning them 'where they lay', as Demissé testified. This is also confirmed by other reports. For example, Lieutenant Meleseliñ recalled the Italians pouring benzine on the corpses 'in every corner of the city', and setting fire to them like the fires in the traditional Ethiopian ceremony of the Finding of the True Cross.[5] This is consistent with the report in the British *News Chronicle*, which announced:

FLAME-THROWER ONSLAUGHT BY BLACKSHIRTS

Thousands of Victims on Petrol Pyres:

Funeral pyres are burning amid the blackened ruins of Addis Ababa … So many thousands of Abyssinian men, women and children were massacred during the three days following the bombing of Viceroy Graziani that they cannot be buried, let alone counted. The authorities are therefore piling the bodies into heaps, which are doused with petrol and set on fire.[6]

The only people to be seen on the streets were Italian troops milling around, as if expecting an imminent attack from a redoubtable adversary. 'The Blackshirts walk around quietly; groups form here, and disperse there. Every militia-man exerts himself to narrate his exploits, counting with satisfaction the number and quality of his victims.'[7] Noting the extent of the burning, British Intelligence reported, 'The Qebena, the area at the Gulelé Race Course [Jan Méda], and the part behind the station along the railway line were completely gutted ... The area between the Menelik Hospital and the small [Gennete-Li'ul] palace of *Ras* Tafari is completely destroyed.'[8] Diplomatic dispatches document, from the foreign community's viewpoint, the gradual recovery of Addis Ababa during the days following the massacre. William Bond at the British legation reported on Tuesday, 23 February, that order had practically been restored and that Ethiopians were just beginning to circulate. This did not, however, apply to some districts of the city, where he termed the conditions 'indescribable,' and said that people were reported to be in a desperate condition for lack of food, water and any form of sanitation.[9]

The following day, the envoy was to report, all 700 of the refugees at the American legation had left, after the American minister obtained full assurances that no harm would come to them, and that food would be provided on their leaving the compound. By the 25th, he said, Ethiopians were moving about freely, with the exception of those still in detention, and those for whom the decisions of the military tribunal were expected on 25 or 26 February.[10]

* * *

88. The Bank of Italy during the Occupation. Previously the Bank of Abyssinia, and today the Central Statistical Office, it was here that Blackshirts changed the silver *thalers* they had stolen from their victims during *carta bianca*

Dr Shashka resumed work at his clinic, but even there, there was no escape from the horrors, for many of the Italians who visited his surgery regaled him with stories of how many people they had killed. Some were very modest and had apparently killed only two; others had killed, or claimed to have killed, eight or ten, and the doctor heard them congratulating themselves for having stolen 400 or 500 *thalers* in the night.[11] Clearly shocked by their impunity, he reflected, 'If anything could increase the horror of such a sight [of defenceless people being murdered], it was the knowledge of the human baseness which accompanied the murder, the knowledge that while the lorries were still collecting the dead bodies from the streets, while the blood was congealing on the ground, Blackshirts were already running to the Bank of Italy to change the *thalers* they had stolen in the night, from the Abyssinian houses they had entered, and the gold and silver ornaments from the necks of Abyssinian women whom they had killed.'[12]

The Italian-educated Dawit Oquba Igzi'i, who had been released from prison the previous day, was so shocked by the thought that the Italians would have actually burned people to death that he went out of his way to find out if it was true. He checked on cases in which he had noticed dead bodies among the charred remains of their homes. 'I made a special investigation on Monday to be sure that they were burnt and not shot', and was horrified to find his worst fears confirmed.[13]

* * *

At the French legation conditions had by no means returned to normal, for on Monday morning, 22 February, the American consul-general informed Washington, 'Thirty-eight native servants of the French Legation who had been forcibly removed from its compound on Friday have not yet returned.'[14] Presumably the majority found their way back, for by Wednesday the Ministry of Foreign Affairs in Paris was asking the French ambassador in Rome to get the Italian government to instruct their representatives in Addis Ababa to secure the release of just two legation employees, who appeared to be at 'great risk of being shot, despite their obvious innocence'.[15]

HORRORS AT THE CENTRAL POLICE STATION

While the city residents who were still at large began to pick up the pieces of their lives, the captives behind the walls of the detention camps continued to suffer. In the early morning light Tekle-Tsadiq saw that there was barbed wire on the gate of the Central Police Station in Fit Ber, and to the right and left were soldiers with machine guns at the ready, 'waiting for the order to shoot'.[16]

In his memoirs, Temesgen stated that the Italians estimated that there were 18,000 prisoners in Fit Ber. Although this is probably an overestimate, the figure was certainly in the thousands, and there is no doubt that he was correct in saying that the captives 'were not able to speak, due to the hunger and thirst. Although alive, they were totally exhausted.' Like the previous day, Monday was quite hot, and in the compound of the Central Police Station, where thousands of prisoners were sitting on the ground, there were no shelters and no shade. So the prisoners took off their clothes and put them over their head.[17]

Tekle-Tsadiq describes a mock execution in which the prisoners were ordered to stand up against the wall. As the soldiers took aim at the crowd with their machine guns, people at the front tried desperately to get to the back. But then the officer who was to give the order to shoot just disappeared, leaving the terrified Ethiopians standing.[18]

Temesgen never forgot the spectacle of a dying man with a bottle begging for water in his delirium. He was in agony, trying to open his mouth, and his 'Please, please' was scarcely audible, as he begged for some urine to drink. He said that two of his brothers had died of thirst, and that he was also on the point of death. Temesgen's companion, Gebre-Medhin Aweqe, replied, saying that not having had any water for days, he could not help. 'For me this is the third day without any water. From where can I get urine?' Exhausted and unable to speak, the delirious man could not carry on begging. 'Resting on the ground with a boulder as a pillow, he lived a little longer, then his head still on the boulder, he died.' On that day, noted Temesgen, by 1.00 pm more than 100 of the inmates at Central Police Station had died of thirst, the dead bodies being taken away on trucks.[19]

Finally, the officer Temesgen refers to as the *Azajh*, or commandant, of the camp, *Tilinti* (Lieutenant)[20] Luigi Corbo, decided that the time had come to start sharing some of his water with the most dehydrated prisoners, and when some of the captives started offering him silver thalers for a drink, Corbo knew he had a good money-making venture on his hands.[21] Temesgen recalled the comments of the prisoners at the time on the manner in which charity became extortion: 'He brought water to hand out free of charge to the most needy, but ended up selling it to the better-off!'

At a rate of one thaler for a quick drink, Corbo soon earned himself 25 thalers—a considerable sum of money for a few minutes' work. Temesgen described the process, and not without a touch of irony and a certain wry humour: 'Then I went to him [Corbo] with money. Since he was the only one selling water, it was difficult to reach him; many people were clamouring to get water. I pushed my way to the place where the water was being sold, and reached *Tilinti* Luigi Corbo. He was only selling in exchange for *thalers*. As for me, I had in my pocket only lire. He refused to accept lire.[22] I was born unlucky—since all I had was lire, I was unable to buy and drink water.'

Temesgen then watched *Tilinti* Corbo, who was armed with a pistol. He was holding his water canteen in his right hand and putting out his left hand to collect the money, which he then pocketed. Then he shifted the canteen from his right hand to his left hand, took out his pistol with his right hand, and put a little water in the mouth of the thirsty prisoner with his left hand.[23] Repeating this procedure for each recipient, Temesgen commented, 'He was getting tired, like someone rowing a boat.' The canteen held 2½ litres, but Corbo was giving very little water—the prisoners desperately needed more. An astonished Temesgen wrote, 'I had never imagined that anyone would ever buy such little water for a *thaler*!' But 'his right hand held the pistol so that no one could grab the canteen'.

Corbo was doubtless looking forward to earning much more before the day was over, when one of the prisoners was desperate enough to grab the canteen. The officer brought the canteen close to the prisoner's face and poured the water into his mouth, but, as he took it back, the thirsty prisoner grabbed hold of the canteen with both hands. A gunshot rang out, and the desperate prisoner fell back, shot by Corbo at point-blank range through the head. '*Tilinti* shot him through the eye, and as he fell down, the water came out [from his mouth] all over his cheeks. Shooting him again and again, *Tilinti* killed him.'

At that point in his account—written not long after the event—Temesgen, the level-headed, highly respected evangelist, who, having chosen to spend his working life with European missionaries, seems not to have had an ounce of racial prejudice in him, had to admit that the brutality he encountered came as a great shock: 'With our suffering in captivity, we saw the cruelty of the Italian people to a greater extent than one could ever learn either in school or from human history. Some people were born to be destructive, and enjoy human suffering.'

Temesgen knew that he himself was also at death's door. Desperate for water, he backed away from the crowd around Corbo. Making his way to where he had been sitting previously, he saw an Italian soldier standing on his own, and offered him 30 lire for a drink. He was turned down, but an increased offer of 100 lire was accepted, so Temesgen paid him and he went away, leaving Temesgen sitting on the ground. In due course the soldier returned with a flask of water, but the price had increased by a further 50 per cent. The soldier was communicating in sign language, and 'was selling water in secret', so that Lieutenant Corbo would not see them, 'for *Tilinti* was not allowing other soldiers to sell water'.

Temesgen had no choice but to pay the additional 50 lire, and earned himself the flask of water—the first drink he had had since Friday morning. Surrounded as he was by thousands of desperate prisoners, it was dangerous for him to be seen drinking water, so 'I sat below his legs and drank the water, while he was protecting me from the other thirsty prisoners with his bayonet'.

Temesgen's next problem was how to get the water left in the flask to his friends: 'I knew that the other prisoners would take the water away if I took the remaining water to my companions. In my pocket I had one coin bearing Menelik's image; I gave it to the soldier and begged him to accompany me to my companions. With his bayonet he accompanied me, protecting me from the thirsty prisoners.' Temesgen reached the place where he had been sitting, but he was too late: 'I found two of my companions dead. I tried to pour water into their mouths, but they were dead.'[24]

Clearly, the Italians were soon going to have thousands of corpses on their hands, and it was at this point that someone in authority decided that it might be a good idea to provide some water at the Central Police Station detention camp. So it was that Captain Toka Binegid of the Addis Ababa fire brigade was ordered to intervene. He duly arranged for water to be taken into the prison, but, in sworn testimony provided later for the War Crimes Commission, he reported that the guards were responsible for very rough treatment—and that in fact there was terrible violence meted out when the water arrived: 'There were at least 10,000 persons detained in Fit Ber prison, deprived of water and food. On the third day after the attempt [i.e. on the Monday] we took drinking water with us and went to visit the prisoners. There, when they were struggling to quench their thirst, the Italians struck them with bludgeons and stabbed them with bayonets.'[25]

Temesgen's account correlates with Captain Toka's testimony; he describes how the captain's fire engine arrived at the compound on Monday and, using a canvas hose, pumped water into 120 *berméls*, or barrels.[26] Tekle-Tsadiq also recalls there having been 'several thousand' prisoners at Fit Ber, mentions the arrival of the water for the prisoners, recounts the confusion and pandemonium as the Italians tried to marshal the crowd into orderly queues, and tells of the desperate crowd surging forward and an unsuccessful struggle by the

Italians to keep control.[27] At that point, Temesgen's report goes into further detail and drama as he describes the death of two Italian officers in the melée and the subsequent killing of many Ethiopians—aspects of the incident not covered by Tekle-Tsadiq's account. Temesgen states that as the desperate prisoners surged forward, Corbo and Marshalo were trampled to death, and that in response the yelling Italians started hurling grenades into the crowd, which became a writhing heap of dying men and women, with body parts flying through the air and into the water, while frantic prisoners at the back tried to clamber through the crowd to the front. Having no containers, some dipped their clothes into the barrels: 'Some of the prisoners soaked their clothes in the water and sucked the cloth like a breast; they also squeezed the cloth into the mouths of their weak companions, thereby becoming their saviours.' This is also confirmed to a similar level of detail by Tekle-Tsadiq. But at this point Temesgen's account again becomes more dramatic than Tekle-Tsadiq's, with machine guns opening fire, resulting in widespread carnage.[28]

According to Temesgen, five trucks arrived to transport the bodies, but five was nowhere near enough, so the trucks had to make many journeys, and the transport operation had to carry on through the night, the corpses and body parts lit up by a floodlight that the Italians were obliged to install. Meanwhile, another officer made arrangements for the orderly distribution of water to surviving prisoners: 'Those who had drunk left on one side, while those who hadn't [drunk] came in from the other side, thus preventing those who had drunk from drinking for a second time. Then they gave us bread and water—after four days without food or drink. We took the bread in an orderly manner, as we did for the water. We ate the bread, we drank the water, and our bodies were at rest.'[29]

But there was no respite from the constant threat of death, for the regime grew harsher, and the hours were filled with horror upon horror such that Temesgen was moved to ask himself, 'What is the point of staying alive while in the custody of Italian Fascists?' Whenever the *carabinieri* or regular officers left the prisoners to the mercy of the Blackshirts, or the 'beasts' as Temesgen sometimes referred to them, life became even more unbearable. This is what happened as soon as the prisoners had received their first food and water, and the departure of the regulars left the Blackshirts to amuse themselves, playing their deadly cat-and-mouse games. 'When the officers who gave us food and water went back to their houses, the Fascists vented their anger on us by starting to throw grenades at us! However, they didn't have any reason to be angry. We pushed and shoved each other in our frantic efforts to escape from the grenades. The grenades did not reach the middle of the crowd; most of the prisoners killed were those on the perimeter.'

Apparently not satisfied with the carnage they were creating among the prisoners, and wanting something more exciting, the Blackshirts decided to bring up the heavy guns. Temesgen claimed, 'Since they were not able to reach the centre of the crowd with their grenades, they opened fire with a machine gun into the centre of the crowd. Those who lay down on the ground to avoid the machine-gun fire were trampled by the others. Those who remained stand-ing were gunned down.' There was no one to help the victims; the suffering and horrors that night can scarcely be imagined, and for Temesgen they were clearly beyond words, for he wrote simply, 'The wounded, the dead and the uninjured spent the night together.'

* * *

The next morning, Tuesday, 23 February, another officer arrived, had the wounded separated from those who were not injured, and started to arrange for the dead bodies to be taken away in a truck.[30] During the process Temesgen noticed that one of the bodies was moving:

> One of the women imprisoned with her baby had been killed by a grenade, and her dead body was lying beside the gate. The baby was not injured. He had been lying on his mother's chest and sucking her breast the whole night, as if she was alive. Although the prisoners were unable to help each other by sharing water, they were heart-broken at the suffering of this baby. The prisoners picked up the baby and gave it to a woman whose own baby had been trampled [to death] the day before, and asked her to breast-feed it.

> But the woman was not happy to receive it as a substitute for her own child. She refused, saying, 'I will not breast-feed [a baby] who will be killed by the Italians tomorrow; I will not suckle the baby for a machine gun and bayonet!' The baby cried, lying on the ground in the heat of the sun. I picked him up and put him on his mother's body, and he stopped crying when he found his mother.

> They carried on taking the bodies away with the truck, and when the Fascists put the body of the mother onto the truck, I saw one of the Fascist officers holding the baby with tears in his eyes.[31] The other Italians [regular officers] felt sorry for the baby, and the officer took him away.[32]

But the humanity that a lone soldier showed in that moment of horror stood in stark contrast to what happened next, when a group of Italian Catholic clergy arrived with a list of Catholic prisoners to be freed. 'Then Catholic clergymen[33] who had come in with the officer started looking for fellow Catholics [among the prisoners]. They called out their names from a list, and had them released.'[34]

But that was not all. The Italian government's repression of foreign Protestant missions, previously conducted at the diplomatic level and limited to the expulsion of missionaries and seizure of their property,[35] now erupted at the lower, brutal level of the military. In a scene that would have done justice to their counterparts in Europe conducting the anti-Jewish pogroms of Nazi Germany, the Italians started pulling out the Protestants pointed out by collaborators, following which they were taken away and shot. 'Those suspected to be Protestants and identified as such by informants were taken and killed with a machine gun at the gate of the prison.'[36]

The executions sent a shock wave through the detainees. From that moment onwards, no one wanted to be known as a Protestant. 'For a few hours they asked [us] questions about religion. Then they asked each prisoner to name [his or her] religion. All the prisoners claimed to be either Catholic or Muslim. There was no one who claimed to be Protestant, with the exception of *Ato* Ar'aya, *Aleqa* of Medhané Alem [church], who was a courageous and devout Christian.'[37]

Here Temesgen, himself a Protestant with a record of close relations with foreign missionaries, was clearly upset when he wrote his memoir, and addressed them rhetorically, as if to ask, 'Can you imagine how he died?' 'The missionaries who were in Addis Ababa, Ethiopia, knew *Ato* Ar'aya. What did they [the Italians] do to him? How did they kill him?' Temesgen himself supplied the answer. The *Aleqa* refused to renounce his faith, so the Italians decided that he should get special treatment. The Catholic clergymen watched, impassive, as the committed Christian was seized and dragged to a military truck. 'After the three days of rampaging in the town, Fascist beasts who had returned from Holetta [military academy] with a truck tied the legs of *Ato* Ar'aya to the back of the truck. Before the vehicle moved, Ar'aya sang a mission song:

Heaven is opening for me to enter
– I will see Jesus there.
I am happy! I am happy!
– I am happy!'

Unmoved, the laughing Blackshirts told him that it would be better for him to listen to their song instead, and chanted their 'war cry': '*Du-ce! Du-ce!*'

Temesgen was not only shocked by the behaviour of the Blackshirts, but also disgusted by the reaction of the clergymen, who raised not a word of restraint while the Blackshirts tied the cleric to the truck. As Temesgen put it, 'They did not oppose the death penalty.' He wrote, 'Each Italian Fascist behaved like a king, and the Catholic monks,[38] with their ropes around their waist, were standing and watching when it was decided to kill *Ato* Ar'aya, and while he was being killed. [Their only reaction was that] they were not impressed with his singing, because *Ato* Ar'aya's voice was weak from hunger and thirst.'[39]

The Blackshirts jumped on board, the engine roared into life, and *Aleqa* Ar'aya crashed to the ground and disappeared in a cloud of dust as the truck sped away. The clergymen then left the detention camp, taking with them their freed Catholic prisoners.

FLIGHT FROM THE CITY

Lieutenant Meleseliñ wrote, 'Leaving the dead behind, [some] survivors migrated from Addis Ababa to the rural areas, following tracks during the night.'[40] It is well attested that many Ethiopians fled the city during the massacre, boosting the resistance to hitherto unknown levels, and bringing about a collapse of local supply markets. The American consul-general reported,

> It is estimated by competent foreign observers that, in spite of stern refusal by the authorities to grant exit permits, between ten and twenty thousand Ethiopians have quietly left the city. The departure of thousands is clearly indicated by half-deserted streets, and concern has been expressed by several Italians over the native exodus. Possibly the Italians realise that they have gone too far and that as the rainy season approached, they will be faced with the problems of scarcity of native labourers and servants, scanty markets, and the menace to Italian convoys and outposts by the banditry of thousands of urban natives driven from their homes.[41]

Engert was absolutely right, although the empty streets were due as much to the number of people in detention as to the flight from the city. He had identified a looming problem for which the Italians were quite unprepared, and which threw them into a panic, particularly as many of the women who had fled the city had been market traders, and many of the men were joining the resistance. Refugees reaching Djibouti told Wazir Ali Baig what was happening, and what the inevitable outcome would be. In turn, Sylvia Pankhurst published their reports and observed that the Italians were desperate to stop the exodus. She stated that by conducting the massacre, 'the Italians have lost anything they gained in Abyssinia. The Abyssinians know that there is nothing left for them but to fight, and the world will presently hear that they are everywhere attacking anew.' She was correct in her analysis, from which she concluded that the massacre would heighten the resistance.[42] Indeed, thousands of able-bodied men left Addis that night, many to join the Patriots. As several members of the resistance informed the present author, they decided that, rather than stay at home and be burned to death, they might as well die fighting the Italians. The result was a great swelling of Patriot ranks, as Sylvia Pankhurst predicted. Dawit Oquba Igzi'i went so far as to put a figure on it: 'One result of the massacre was that the patriot leader, *Ras* Abebe Aregai, who operated some 40 to 50 km from Addis Ababa, had his forces increased immediately, at least by 10,000; also other patriot troops received reinforcements because when people heard of what had taken place in Addis Ababa and that the city was burnt, they also left their homes and went away from the neighbourhood of Addis Ababa. Very few Ethiopians stayed in Addis Ababa.'[43]

Dawit had a tendency to exaggerate when it came to numbers; he went on to suggest that 10,000 Ethiopians were deported to Italy, which is a gross overestimate; the actual number was in hundreds, not thousands.[44] Similarly, 10,000 refugees reaching Abebe Aregay is probably also an overestimate. Many of the refugees were women and children, and, as Professor Shiferaw Beqele pointed out to the present author, many of the men who fled the city did not go further than the outskirts, and several returned.[45] All things considered, the net loss to the city due to able-bodied men joining the *Ras* following *Yekatit 12* was most likely in the thousands, but considerably less than 10,000, as many of the missing men were actually in detention. The question of city population movement and loss during the massacre is revisited in chapter 10.

ADRENALIN RUNS HIGH

Just as some districts of the city suffered burning of residential areas on Sunday well after the order to cease was first announced, many areas experienced continued attacks for several days after the massacre officially ended. If there was any shame or contrition on the part of the Italians it was well hidden; on the contrary, as noted earlier, the Blackshirts, regulars and civilians were often smiling when photographs of atrocities were taken, suggesting that they were proud of what they had done, and were keen to project a posture of arrogance and a position of absolute power.

In this regard an incident involving the American consul-general is of interest, for it suggests that there were at least some Italian officers capable of embarrassment, if not remorse. Having transmitted his Monday morning dispatch setting out the events of Sunday, the envoy was driving through the city the next day, 22 February, in his official car, when he witnessed what he described to Washington as 'a revolting scene.' The car in front of him stopped without warning, and an Italian colonel got out and, without any apparent reason, rushed across to an elderly Ethiopian man standing with two women. Shouting, 'I'll make you beasts crawl in the dust before me!', he started hitting the man's face with a horsewhip 'until he was covered with blood and prostrated himself before him and with outstretched arms begged for mercy'.

> The Colonel then turned on the women who was [*sic*] already kneeling and was beginning to strike them with his whip when I blew the horn of my car (as if wishing to pass his) so loudly that he stopped and noticing the two American flags on my car he looked embarrassed and drove off. In his blind fury he had evidently not seen my car and realized too late that I must have witnessed the entire performance ... Scenes such as this and many much worse have been going on for four days to impress the natives with the civilising mission of Fascist Rome.[46]

Certainly Italian adrenalin was still running high. A long-time Addis Ababa resident, the Armenian Vartkes Bilemjian, told the present author that when his father, Zakar Bilemjian, went outside with an Armenian friend after the massacre, walking from Arada towards the Fitawrari Habte-Giyorgis Bridge, they had their faces slapped by a group of Italian officers on the street, with the warning, 'Next time you pass an officer, make sure you salute!'[47] As the British consul-general later advised the Foreign Office, 'Had the Marshal and others been killed or died of their wounds, it is fairly safe to predict that there would be few Ethiopians left in the town today [1 March 1937], nor, I think, would Arabs and Indians have escaped altogether.'[48] In fact, many foreigners either left Ethiopia or sent their families away to safety. The French consul-general informed Paris, 'Most foreigners, notably Germans and Armenians, afraid of renewed disorders, are preparing to evacuate their families.'[49]

* * *

Many clergy had been killed in the slaughter at the Governo Generale on 12 Yekatit, and their surviving colleagues continued to be targets thereafter, as Graziani intensified his campaign against the Ethiopian Orthodox Church. A shocking example of such targeted attacks was recounted by Dr Shashka:

> There was a venerable Coptic [Ethiopian Orthodox] priest in Addis Ababa who survived the war, the terrible period of the Occupation, and even the massacre of the 19th and 20th of February. He was still alive on the 21st [Sunday], when the Italians finally stopped killing and robbing, although he was one of the men against whom Fascist daggers were aimed. When Italian authorities became aware that he was still alive, Cortese convoked the murderers to the seat of the Fascio. Order was given to Gallini, one of the most able dagger-men, to stab the Coptic prelate.

The priest was surprised in a house where some twenty or twenty-five Abyssinians, mostly women, were assembled after the massacre to offer up a devoted prayer ... While the Prelate was kneeling in prayer, Gallini stabbed him with the dagger from behind, and retired with the satisfaction of one who had done his job.[50]

* * *

Dyakon Dawit Gebre-Mesqel at the Church of Ta'eka Negest Be'ata, well aware of the danger he was in, stayed at home from Friday, 19 February, to Tuesday, 23rd, but the next day he had no choice but to go outside to fetch some water. There was no piped water supply to most of the residents of Addis Ababa, and fetching water had become very risky; many people—particularly children—had been killed by the repression squads while going to their neighbourhood wells. Nonetheless, Dawit took a chance and left his house. In his words, 'There was a water shortage. I needed to fetch water from a well. So on Wednesday [24 February] I went out. I was immediately confronted by an Italian soldier and two Eritrean *askaris*, who surrounded me and led me down the street towards the church [of Ta'eka Negest Be'ata]. As we walked past them, the neighbours saw what was happening and started crying. They assumed the Italians were going to shoot me.' Dawit also thought he was going to be killed, but his humble bearing and the wailing of the women apparently had some effect on his captors because, as he told the present author, 'They seemed to respect me, and let me go.' Dawit went straight back to his house, and lived to tell the tale.[51]

* * *

The reader may recall that Gebre-Sillassé Oda and his brother had fortunately escaped the massacre of Addis Ababa by spending the day of 12 Yekatit at Alem Gena, then sheltering at Daleti village when they discovered that it was not safe to return to the capital. Having watched the city burning from afar on Friday night, they decided to stay with their friends for several more days. Then on Wednesday afternoon, 24 February, they heard that the situation in the city had calmed down, and made up their minds to return home. 'Then we wondered how we should go back, because we were afraid that if they [the Italians] found us they would kill us. So we went to the Captain [who had befriended them earlier] and asked him to give us a soldier to escort us to our home. He said he would do so with pleasure, and he put us on a truck, which took us to our house, accompanied by two soldiers. That is how our lives were saved, and we reached home.'

As they reached the city, the two brothers began to realise the full extent of the horrors that had been perpetrated. 'While we were on our way, accompanied by the soldiers, we saw lots of terrifying things. Since the truck was open, we were able to see on both sides of the roads in the city a lot of dried human blood. When we saw this we were terrified!' They also sensed the air of desolation hanging over the city. 'Even though it was daytime, there were far fewer people on the streets than usual. Those who had not been killed were staying at home because they were afraid. They had nowhere to go. In general, the situation in the city was really miserable.'[52]

* * *

Although there is general agreement that by Wednesday, 24 February, things were beginning to return to normal, according to Lieutenant Meleseliñ it was not until several days later (1 March 1937—eleven days after *Yekatit 12*) that the killings actually came to an end. He adds that the following day a 'decree' was issued, offering an amnesty to all those who had fled the city, to enable them to return.

Many of those who came back found their property stolen, their homes burned to ashes, and their loved ones missing. Those fortunate enough to recover their homes began to pick up the pieces of their life. Some managed to find employment in the construction sector; the only alternatives were typically either petty trade or serving in the Italian military.[53]

* * *

TERROR ON THE OUTSKIRTS

In the aftermath of the massacre, residents living on the outskirts of the city were in despair. Survivors there could be seen wandering around the smoking eucalyptus trees without shelter or food. An eyewitness reflected, 'They will soon be finished off, at the will of the Fascists, or of hunger, for no one comes into the town any longer. There are no more markets, no more victuals, and famine awaits Mussolini's army.'[54] In an effort to prevent the population leaving the city, which would have resulted in near starvation for the occupying forces, the Regia Aeronautica dropped leaflets on the outskirts telling the locals to bring cereals and cattle for the army. However, many of the people on the periphery had gone into hiding, for several of these areas were still being targeted by the Blackshirts.

One such area devastated after the end of the massacre had been officially declared was the northernmost section of Gulelé, west of the Kurtumi River. Here, where the Ambo Road turns left to the west, a road running off to the north towards Intotto Mountain led to a village known locally as Biscutti Fabrica, after the nearby biscuit factory.[55] In this small community nestling high in the foothills of Intotto, near the eucalyptus forest boundary, lived a tailor, Asnake Jembere, his wife, Zenebech Werqineh, and their baby boy. Although their village had not yet been attacked, they were well aware of the massacre, for at night smoke had filled the sky above the city below them, and they had been kept awake by the sound of grenades and shooting. During the day they had watched, aghast, the never-ending convoys of 'Trenta Quattro' trucks piled high with bodies and running with blood, rumbling past along the Ambo Road to the Catholic cemetery.

At first Asnake's family and their neighbours had spent the nights sitting in their houses, thankful that they were not in the inner city, and hoping and praying that the holocaust would not reach them. But, as the repression squads worked their way out to the suburbs, the sounds became louder, and the residents of Biscutti Fabrica began evacuating their homes, to take refuge in the forest.

The community did well not to trust Cortese's termination notices, for on the night of 16 Yekatit (Tuesday, 23 February), two days after the notices had been posted, the dreaded Blackshirts arrived. Having burned the areas immediately north of the Italian Hospital and then Dejazmach Yigzew Sefer, they now reached Biscutti Fabrica.

Watching through the eucalyptus from their hiding place in the forest along with the rest of the community, Asnake and Zenebech saw trucks arriving at the village, and shadowy armed figures with fixed bayonets shouting and running from house to house. One by one the cottages burst into flames, silhouetted against the night sky, and soon the entire village was ablaze. Then, seeing beams of light moving towards the forest, the villagers realised to their horror that, instead of returning to their barracks with their loot, the Blackshirts, clearly furious that they had found the houses uninhabited, were not satisfied. Shining their torches at the forest, the *squadristi* were coming for them.

Slowly and silently the community backed off, retreating further into the darkness of the forest, and watched as the Italians called out to one another and shone their torches into the trees. Then, as a beam of light swung across the forest, one of Asnake's friends, who was wearing a rather visible white sheepskin coat, found himself momentarily bathed in light. Assuming he had been spotted, he thought it best to show himself and appeal to the better nature of the Blackshirts. Stepping out from the trees, he called out, in a gesture of surrender, 'Signori! Signori!' The response was immediate: the Italians opened fire. Fatally injured, he fell to the ground.

Asnake and Zenebech held their breath as the Blackshirts, peering into the undergrowth and failing to spot anyone else, decided not to pursue their quarry further into the forest. They gave up the search, climbed into their trucks and drove back to the city, leaving behind the smouldering remains of what until a few hours before had been the thriving settlement of Biscutti Fabrica.

When the sun rose, the community emerged from the forest and despondently inspected their devastated village. They found only embers. Every house had been burned to ashes, except—amazingly—just one, which stood completely unharmed. By an inexplicable twist of fate or stroke of providence, Asnake and Zenebech found their home untouched, and their belongings intact.

The community held a funeral for the dead, and did their best to rebuild their lives. As for Asnake and Zenebech, they never forgot what happened on 16 Yekatit, and henceforth they celebrated the 16th of every month to remember that night and give thanks for their good fortune.[56]

* * *

Confirmation that attacks by groups of Fascists and the burning of houses continued after the official termination appears in a telegram sent by M. Bodard to the Foreign Minister in Paris on Wednesday, 24 February. He wrote that after a three-day period, which he described as 'close to anarchy', calm was gradually returning to the city. 'The mass reprisals have ceased.' On the other hand, he stated, 'individual actions' were continuing, and 'some burning of native houses set fire to by the Fascists have again taken place during the course of these recent nights'.[57]

* * *

BODY DISPOSAL AT GULELÉ

The principal activity in the city after Sunday was the continued removal of the dead, for Addis Ababa was still scattered with corpses. In some districts they covered the streets and squares, and at Menelik Square the dead bodies formed a veritable pile.[58]

89. The disposal of bodies at Gulelé continued throughout Monday, 22 February

No one was allowed to take the body of his or her relative, and no one was allowed to weep or lament over his or her loved ones, on penalty of being shot, imprisoned or deported to one of the concentration camps. Only the military were permitted to gather the dead, which they did by the lorry-load, to be discharged and burned at Gulelé. *Immahoy* Hiruta recalled, 'They were transporting dead bodies in open trucks. I saw many dead people. People were crying and shouting.'[59]

British Intelligence found that 'For four days, lorries were employed removing corpses which were partly burned to prevent an epidemic and thrown into large pits'.[60]

Some eight or ten days after the slaughter, the lorries were still running to Gulelé, yet there were still bodies lying around awaiting collection. At this time, Dr Shashka was near St George's Brewery—one of the three killing and body-collection centres—which was littered with putrefying corpses. He approached a group of mourners who were homeless. Their house had been burned, but they managed to save a little food. Shashka spoke to the eldest among them: 'Did many of your people die?' The reply served to show the immense scale of the slaughter in the city as a whole, compared with which the old man thought his own loss was minor. 'No, sir,' came the reply, 'only five.' 'But over there,' he said, pointing to the brewery, 'many people living around were killed.'[61]

The London *News Chronicle* commented that the lack of proper burial increased the horror that the massacre had created throughout the country. The only exceptions to the prohibition on interment of the dead were a few burials conducted by foreign religious missions.[62] However, even their mourning could not always proceed in peace. The British acting consul-general was obliged to report to London an incident reflecting the level to which the behaviour of the Italians had sunk. At the compound of a British mission, a body which, like many others, had been exposed for several days and was thus in an advanced stage of decomposition, was in the process of being buried by missionaries when an Italian officer came up, stopped the burial to have the corpse searched for money, and pocketed the dollar or two found on it.[63]

* * *

THE DETAINED

Many of the Ethiopians rounded up on Friday afternoon thought themselves lucky to have escaped the carnage on the streets. However, like Temesgen, they soon discovered that they were in even greater danger in custody, for as the British envoy informed London, 'Large masses of Ethiopians who managed to escape the general massacre were concentrated at the different sectional police headquarters or in other guarded spaces. According to the evidence from one who escaped, the conditions in these places of concentration were indescribable, and captives have been dying for lack of food, water and any kind of sanitary arrangements.'[64]

Unfortunately for the detainees, Mussolini's orders were quite specific; notwithstanding the fact that most of them were being held in locations not capable of sustaining them for more than 24 hours, his instructions were clear: 'No persons arrested are to be released without my order.' That meant that—at least until further notice—the vast majority of them would have to remain in detention. The conditions inside these makeshift detention camps were indeed indescribable, and a significant proportion of the prisoners did not survive. In a telegram to Paris on 24 February, M. Bodard reported that 'Apart from chiefs and notables, more than 3,000 Ethiopians have been arrested and crammed into small enclosures', noting that they included women and children, as well as 'numerous injured'. He added that by that date around 1,000 executions of these captives had been carried out.[65] Lieutenant Meleseliñ also testified that thousands of men and women prisoners were interned within walls and wire fences without food or water. 'Quite apart from the horrors,' he wrote, 'children died from the lack of water.'[66]

* * *

The reader will recall that Tekle-Tsadiq Mekuriya and his friend *Grazmach* Kebede had been arrested and interned at the Central Police Station compound at Fit Ber. In due course the Italians started registering the captives, as they had at the Municipality Building, separating them into those to be executed (principally those named on the death list, nobility, clerics, educated Ethiopians, and anyone even faintly 'suspicious') and those to be imprisoned (meaning all others, with only a few exceptions such as Eritreans and collaborators). As at the Municipality Office, many of the Ethiopians were lulled into thinking that being educated or titled would guarantee them privileged treatment. In fact they were told, 'All of you will be released and will go back to your work. Just tell us your name and title.' Tekle-Tsadiq wondered how they would ever register everybody, and was also worried when he spotted that not only were very few people being released, but those that were had no title. When his friend Kebede was registered, his title, *Grazmach*, was noted. 'Then they took him away, saying that those with a title are required for work in the civil service.'[67]

Tekle-Tsadiq had one great advantage over the vast majority of Ethiopians: he could speak Italian, which he had studied at Alliance Française. He may not have been fluent, but his command was good enough for casual conversation. He also spoke French, but it was not wise to let the Italians discover that, for French-speakers were regarded as the educated elite and were to be executed. Speaking Italian, he could strike up a rapport with the Italians and even be mistaken for an Eritrean. So he engaged in conversation with one of the soldiers and pleaded with him to get him registered and released. He was lucky; the soldier took him to his superior, who told him that the father of a certain *Qeññazmach* Tekle-Marqos was thought to be among the prisoners. 'If you find him,' said the officer, 'I will release both of you.' Aware that *Qeññazmach* Tekle-Marqos was a collaborator and well regarded by the Italians, Tekle-Tsadiq guessed that the request was genuine, and that success might lead to his own freedom. Calling out repeatedly in the crowd for 'the father of Tekle-Marqos', he finally met someone who turned out to be the man he was seeking. He took some persuading to turn himself in, but finally the two went back to the officer, who registered their names, and they were both released.

Tekle-Tsadiq could hardly believe his luck. 'As I was very eager to be released, I went very quickly, squeezing myself between the fence and a machine-gun. I did not look back—even at the other man—I was afraid they might call me back!' He took a narrow path, avoiding the main road, and reached home as fast as he could go. In all, he had spent eight to ten days at the Central Police Station.

Tekle-Tsadiq later found out that *Qeññazmach* Tekle-Marqos had indeed requested the Italians to release his father. He also discovered that his own dear friend *Grazmach* Kebede, who was told by the Italians that he was on his way to a job in the civil service, had been rounded up with other titled men, taken into a forest and shot.[68]

* * *

While some of the smaller detention centres closed down in a matter of weeks, others continued functioning for months, and some of the captives in the prisons stayed there for years—some were still there at Liberation in 1941. None of the centres had been designed to hold large numbers of prisoners, and most of them had not been built to accommodate prisoners at all. Such locations, which typically had no food, no water—in fact, nothing at all—saw very high death rates due to hunger, thirst and violence.

Although torture was not as widespread in the detention centres as in the established prisons, it certainly took place in police stations run by the *carabi-*

nieri, as revealed in an affidavit sworn by Yaqob Gebré, an Ethiopian victim and eyewitness:

> After the attempt on Graziani I was taken prisoner. First I had to stay in a police station for three months. They kept me there without water and food for three days and they threatened me during the examinations, saying they would kill me ... There was cruel treatment of other prisoners. They tortured them and beat them. I saw their wounds, and they told me that Italians used to sprinkle water on them and then they lashed them. I heard cries from other parts of the station when such treatment was going on. We were underfed in that station. We were only given black bread once a day; sometimes we got tea without sugar.[69]

* * *

After *Yekatit 12* part of the military barracks behind the Menelik *gibbi*, known as Tyit Bét, or Bullet House, was converted for use as another temporary detention camp. The former ambassador Imru Zelleqe tells an interesting story about Dr Alemewerq Beyene, who was imprisoned in Tyit Bét.

90. 'In this jail an Italian colonel ... said to me, "No person can enter this jail before he has been flogged", and ordered the brigadier to fetch a whip'—Mika'él Tessema. St George's Prison, in Dejazmach Wibé Sefer, still stands on the steep banks of the Qechené River. It consists of one large block with a number of smaller blocks below. Seen here is the main building in the 1990s, after which it was painted and used as a school, and more recently as a municipal courthouse

Alemewerq had been a leader of the Young Ethiopians, and had overseen the Tiqur Anbessa, or Black Lion, group of former cadets from the Holetta Military Academy during the early months of the Occupation.

> This story is about a remarkable man; it happened in Addis Ababa Tyit Bét (which was converted into a prison), where he was detained. His name was Dr Alemewerq. He was a veterinarian graduate from the UK. The prison authorities had put him in charge of the infirmary. Not only did he not know anything about human ailments, he had no medicine to treat even a headache. His only real function was to register the dead in the prison ledger. So, on the column that said 'cause of death' he wrote in Italian 'Morto per la Patria' (Died for the Country).

> When this was discovered and he was interrogated his reply was that, since he didn't know what caused their death, he thought [it] appropriate to register the real reason for which they were jailed. The Italian authorities were not amused, and they sent him to Nocra prison, where he stayed for five years.[70]

* * *

In the detention centre where Sara Gebre-Iyyesus and her children had been held on the afternoon and early evening of 19 February, Mika'él Tessema, a Ministry of Justice employee who subsequently gave evidence before the War Crimes Commission, was also incarcerated. He was picked up a few days after *Yekatit 12*, and held in a number of different police stations before being imprisoned in a cell at a police station located in *Bejirond* Letyibelu's *adarash*, where he stayed for 32 days. As in all the police stations and small prisons used by the Italians at this time, conditions were appalling, torture was common, and in many cases—particularly where the facility was not normally used for accommodating detainees—no food or water was provided. Mika'él reported, 'In the prison there were many other persons in other cells. While I was in my cell I used to hear them crying out, some of them from torture, and some of them from hunger and thirst.'[71] There were also many smaller, temporary police stations. They were generally commandeered private houses, such as those belonging to *Balambaras* Girma, *Dejazmach* Abachew and Feqade-Sillassé Hiruy.[72]

* * *

After being screened, detainees considered to be actual or potential activists were transferred to a prison—usually either St George's or Central Prison. Like the police stations and temporary detention centres, the prisons had high mortality rates, but the deaths tended to be less from hunger and thirst and more from torture and disease, particularly typhoid, as the prisoners were typically kept indoors, in very cramped conditions.

Located on the western bank of the Qechené River in Dejazmach Wibé Sefer, St George's Prison achieved great notoriety during the Occupation. Run before the Invasion by the Addis Ababa municipal administration as a small, local police station with a few cells below, under the Italians it was expanded by the addition of a number of separate outbuildings. However, it was filled far beyond capacity, with a commensurate deterioration in the conditions in which prisoners were kept. As it was quite close to the Governo Generale, many people rounded up immediately after the attempt of *Yekatit 12* were interned there. Within a few days the number of prisoners had reached more than 1,000, although the official capacity was 600.[73] Conditions in the prison were very harsh; for years afterwards local residents spoke of cries of pain and despair from the prisoners during their daily 20-minute sessions when they were allowed to sit outside in the valley below.[74]

Despite the prisons having better access to water than the temporary detention centres, their conditions after *Yekatit 12* were not widely different. Birhanu Dinqé spoke of water being sold to the inmates at the extremely high price of 10 *thalers* per litre, and 'since demand was very high, many people were struggling to reach the place where the water was being sold, and some of those who were weak were not able to survive'. He described bread given to the prisoners which was so hard that it damaged the prisoners' teeth and 'could not be broken unless it was immersed in boiling water'.[75]

Mika'él Tessema's sworn testimony also spoke of atrocious conditions and torture at St George's. Taken there on the night of Wednesday, 24 February, he was told by the colonel in charge, 'No person can enter this jail before he has been flogged,' and a brigadier was ordered to fetch a whip. 'Then I was put in a little house [one of the Italian-built small blocks] among 250 prisoners. I was kept four and a half months in this jail ... As the room was very small, people had to sit on one another ... A prisoner, before entering the jail, was flogged ... When a new prisoner was admitted, he was thrown on us ... When we went out to take air ... We used to find dead bodies of prisoners who had been tortured during the night.' He also described how a prisoner who attempted to escape was flogged, bitten, and 'then they tied his legs together and turned him upside down, putting his head inside a tin which was filled with human excrement'.[76]

Another prisoner testified in an affidavit that one of the small blocks below the main building contained as many as 300 prisoners, who had to sleep on top of each other. 'Many died because of the conditions in that prison ... Almost everybody caught typhus ... The infected persons were not taken to hospital, and every morning we used to find five or six persons who had died in the night, and sometimes even fifteen or so ... I stayed in that prison for one year. I also caught typhus and was very sick. I can remember that at one time there were about 1,400 prisoners there.'[77]

The prison doctor, Iannuzzi Vittorio, himself testified that in the crowded conditions 'we had four to five deaths daily',[78] and Taddesse Tiruneh, whose brother Sibhat died in prison as a *Yekatit 12* suspect, explained: 'St George's was built as a "local" prison by Haile Selassie. The Italians took it over, and used it as a criminal prison. There used to be over 1,000 prisoners there during the Italian occupation. We used to watch the prisoners when they came outside, into the valley. They were crying out. Conditions were very bad ... There was no escape.'[79]

91. Taddesse Tiruneh and Dr Richard Pankhurst standing in front of the main building during a visit to the former St George's Prison with the present author in December 2004. From left to right, Taddesse Tiruneh, school staff member Gétachew, Richard Pankhurst, unidentified staff member

St George's Prison was often used for 'political' prisoners, and executions were frequently carried out there. The reader may recall, for example, that it was the place of execution of at least one of the sons of Dr 'Charles Martin' Werqineh. While many of the prisoners held at St George's were sentenced to summary execution after *Yekatit 12*, there is no doubt that many other captives incarcerated there died from disease, ill-treatment and unlawful killings.

* * *

The second largest penitentiary in Addis Ababa, known to Ethiopians as Karchale (a corruption of *carcere*, Italian for 'prison'), was the Central Prison, the first modern gaol built by Emperor Haile Selassie before the Italian invasion. Enlarged by the Italians, it stood approximately one kilometre south of

92. This photograph was taken at the Central Prison (later known as Alem Bekañ) in the late afternoon of Friday, 19 February 1937. It shows prisoners—mainly men but also some women—taken from their houses and the streets, and assembled under armed guard to await their fate. Note the *askaris* at the front facing the crowd and armed with batons, and the prisoners queuing up to be searched, registered and screened. The uniformed men wearing shorts (far right) are Italian officers of the regular army

the railway station, just above the Tinishu Akaki River (known to the Italians as the Cataba). Consisting of two tiers of cells arranged around an octagonal courtyard, the prison acquired a fearsome reputation for deprivation and torture during the Occupation. It achieved such notoriety that it was known as *Alem Beqañ*, which can be loosely translated as 'I have had enough of the world!', broadly equivalent to 'Abandon hope all ye who enter here'.[80]

Many of the people rounded up after *Yekatit 12* were held in the Central Prison, and many were interrogated there. Mika'él Tessema, who spent more than six weeks in various prisons after *Yekatit 12*, found himself in the Central Prison en route to St George's. 'I was taken to *Alem Bekañ* prison at midnight and put on the bare cement floor. While I was in this prison, I saw an Ethiopian suffering from the wrapping round of ropes from his feet up to his neck.'[81] A favourite torture technique among the Italians, and used extensively in prisons after *Yekatit 12*, this procedure involved soaking the victim in water to tighten the ropes, causing such pressure on the victim's body that blood would ooze out of the pores of the skin and eye sockets.

There is no doubt that many people lost their lives in the Central Prison after *Yekatit 12*, but in the absence of documentation it is difficult to estimate how many. The total number incarcerated there was most likely at least 1,000, and some of those not released were found to be still there when the liberating forces arrived in 1941. As at St George's Prison, the inmates had had to live in appalling conditions, like animals.

* * *

After being held at one of the Addis Ababa prisons or detention centres, many Ethiopians rounded up after *Yekatit 12* were sent to Akaki, a concentration camp developed by the Italians on the site of a former radio station on the outskirts of Addis Ababa. It was the city's largest penitentiary. Captives were generally taken from Akaki either to execution or to one of two concentration camps intended for long-term incarceration: Danane, near Mogadishu in Italian Somaliland, or Nocra, on one of the Dahlak Islands in the Red Sea.

Akaki had an outer and an inner circle of cells and prison barracks, the inner circle double-storeyed, facing a central courtyard. After *Yekatit 12*, some 3,000 prisoners were held there in tents, cells and barracks surrounded by barbed wire, and eyewitness accounts make horrifying reading. Fortunate to be condemned to life imprisonment rather than death, Mika'él Tessema was interned in Akaki, where he witnessed several atrocities. Relatives bringing food for the prisoners were flogged, and at 2.00 pm daily prisoners were taken away by truck for execution.[82]

The process of being taken to Akaki en route to Danane was also described by another captive, Yaqob Gebré-Li'ul, who testified that, while at St George's Prison, he was summoned to the Political Office about three times. 'The name of the investigator was Marciano ... They sent other persons to Danane; but they kept us, informing us that we should be tried by a proper tribunal and receive our punishment, and they told us that they were sure that the tribunal would sentence us to execution. Then one day we were informed that we should be sent to Danane and they took us from the prison to Kaliti (outside Addis Ababa) [Akaki], a radio station which they had transformed into a concentration camp.'[83]

Young Imru Zelleqe, his mother and his two sisters, who had been arrested the day after *Yekatit 12*, were taken on Sunday to Akaki, where they were detained for a little more than a week before being transferred to Danane, where they met Imru's 22-year-old half-brother, Mesfin Zelleqe, a graduate of Lausanne and Montpellier universities. 'Hundreds of prisoners were brought there from all over Ethiopia. Many of them were country people and simple farmers, they did not know what was going on and why they were there. The camp was a sort of distribution centre from where the prisoners were sifted and sent to various prisons and concentration camps.' As Imru notes, Akaki served for many detainees as a transit camp: 'In the beginning of March 1937, they began sending the detainees to the various destinations where they would be jailed. Some groups were taken to Italy, a small number of intellectuals were sent to Nocra in the Dahlak Islands, the worst prison of all. The bulk of prisoners in Akaki went to the Danane concentration camp in Somalia, forty kilometres south of Mogadishu. We were amongst this last group.'[84]

Death in transit was a very real danger for the Ethiopians sent to the concentration camps of Danane and Nocra, for the conditions of travel were insufferable. Prisoners were transported from Addis Ababa to Danane in covered trucks by night to avoid them being seen.[85] By the time they arrived at Danane, a journey of more than four weeks, several had died of disease and hardships along the way.[86] Imru Zelleqe has clear recollections of the terrible journey, which began in March: 'There were hardly any roads but for tracks made by the army during the invasion. The prisoners were crammed in covered trucks without sides; there were no benches.'[87]

* * *

Tekle-Tsadiq Mekuriya, who, as we have seen was detained then released from Fit Ber, was rearrested and interned in Danane. Looking back, he told the present author, 'One month after the attempt [around 19 March], I was arrested in Addis Ababa.' The Italians had obviously discovered that. despite speaking Italian, he was not an Eritrean. 'Because I spoke French I was considered to be a Patriot. Also, being Amhara, it was assumed that I would not accept Italian rule. We were put into trucks, near the railway station ... There were approximately forty prisoners per truck. They were military trucks with a canvas cover over the top, where we were guarded by two armed Italian soldiers on a seat.'[88]

The military trucks generally carried a maximum of 15 to 20 Italian soldiers, but when prisoners were carried a complement of 40 was common. However, prisoners were usually taken on quite short journeys; with

93. Francophone Tekle-Tsadiq Mekuriya was sent to Danane concentration camp for being an educated Amhara

40 prisoners to a truck on the journey to Danane, taking several weeks, and through intense heat and rains, the conditions were unbearable. The worst part of the journey was crossing the Ogaden after Jijiga. '[The journey from Dire Dawa to Mogadishu] took about three or four weeks. It was a very, very painful thing ... Many people died on the road. Some of them were elderly people, some of them were sick—they just couldn't make it.'[89]

For most of the prisoners at Danane there was never any imputation that they had done anything wrong. They were not convicts, for they had never been convicted of any offence. Thus Danane was not officially a death camp, but, since the captives there were sentenced to life imprisonment, it was clearly intended that they would all die at Danane, sooner or later. Several officials of the Italian administration, which was well known to have been riddled with corruption, had lucrative banana concessions and sugar-cane plantations at a project known as Genale, and ran them using forced labour from Danane.[90]

For Ethiopians accustomed to the mild climate of the highlands, the tropical conditions at Danane were unbearable, and their condition deteriorated rapidly. The sworn testimony of surviving inmates suggests some 51 per cent of the prisoners at Danane died there. Malaria was endemic; almost everyone suffered from gastro-intestinal disorders, and, in the absence of potable water, many were obliged to drink sea water.[91] According to Ali Baig, '17 lorries were filled with the flower of Abyssinian youth who were taken as prisoners to Mogadischu.'[92] With a complement of around 40 prisoners per truck, this would account for some 680 of the 1,100 captives sent to Danane after *Yekatit 12*.[93]

In preparation for the UN War Crimes trials, evidence taken from credible witnesses of atrocities at Danane referred to the killing of sick prisoners and forced medical operations by the camp doctor.[94] Despite not being designed as an extermination centre, the torrid, disease-infested penitentiary in the tropical coastal belt proved to be the graveyard of thousands of innocent Ethiopian men, women and children.[95]

* * *

Originally built as a punishment camp by the Italians in the 1890s, Nocra, on an island in the Red Sea, was to become the most horrific but the least known of all the Italian concentration camps. In one of the hottest places on earth, temperatures on the island frequently reach 50°C and humidity touches 90 per cent. There is hardly any vegetation, and almost no water. Following *Yekatit 12*, many innocent high-level Ethiopian government officials and dignitaries were sent to Nocra, which according to a recent study had a 58 per cent mortality rate.[96]

In all but name, Nocra was a death camp, the inmates being quickly reduced to living skeletons. Upon its discovery by the British in 1941, Nocra achieved notoriety as having been one of the world's most horrific penal settlements of all time. Taken off the island by boat, the starving and diseased surviving inmates arrived at the mainland in an appalling state; many were unable to walk. A stunned British legal adviser said, 'They were a horrible sight. I'm told Devil's Island was a paradise compared with Nocra.'[97]

THE MYSTERY OF ENGERT'S REFUGEES

As we have seen, the American minister, Cornelius Engert, allowed several hundred[98] Ethiopians fleeing the massacre of Addis Ababa to take refuge in the legation compound, and had sought assurances from the Italians that they would not be molested. On the evening of Wednesday, 24 February 1937, the Secretary of State in Washington advised him, 'While the department, for humanitarian reasons, does not desire to instruct you regarding the natives who have taken refuge in the compound, it is obvious that the presence of these persons adds greatly to the danger of you and your staff. It is hoped that you will be able to take steps to remove such refugees as soon as you can do so without placing them in danger of their lives.'[99]

The next day, Engert announced that the refugees had already left:

> The last of the refugees left the Legation last night and have not been molested. Food has been provided by the authorities as promised. By actual account 700 Ethiopians had taken refuge in the Legation between February 19 and 23 of whom 243 [were] men, 262 women and 195 children. Before leaving, a delegation from them very touchingly expressed their gratitude to the United States Government 'for saving our lives'.[100]

William Bond at the British legation informed London that all of Engert's refugees had left after the American minister obtained full assurances that they would be safe: 'Over seven hundred Ethiopians living nearby took refuge in the American Legation. The refugees ... only left on Friday [Wednesday] 24th [February] after the American Minister had obtained full assurances, honoured so far as is known, that no harm would come to any of them and that food would be provided by the Italian authorities on their leaving the compound.'[101] However, the sceptical London *Daily Mail* commented that 'it is not known whether these refugees were butchered after they left the compound'.

Was Engert deceived by the Italians? Or were the *carabinieri* unable or unwilling—as usual—to control the excesses of the Blackshirts? This may have been the case, for there were reports that these refugees—or, at least, many of them—were, in fact, killed shortly after leaving the protection of the American legation. Consequently, one month later, on 25 March, the matter of their fate was raised in the British Parliament. The MP Arthur Henderson drew the attention of the House of Commons to 'the shock that British public opinion had suffered as a result of the Addis Ababa massacres', and stated, 'The American Minister had allowed seven hundred Abyssinians to take refuge in the American compound until he received assurances from the Italians that they would be properly treated and their lives spared. Nevertheless, the natives were butchered like cattle when they left the compound.'[102]

Among the eyewitness accounts of the massacre of Addis Ababa reaching the Ethiopian legation in London was a report on what became of the refugees at the American compound: 'There were also the seven hundred refugees at the American Legation, who were persuaded to leave the Legation compound after the Italians gave their words to the Legation officials that they would not be molested, but all of whom were slaughtered at the very gate of the Legation and under the terrified gaze of the Legation staff.'[103]

Could the Italians have gone ahead and slaughtered the refugees after solemnly promising the American minister that they would not do so? In principle, the answer is certainly yes, for two reasons. Firstly, there were plenty of precedents. During the invasion and occupation of Ethiopia, Graziani was accustomed to guaranteeing Ethiopian military commanders that they would be spared if they surrendered; then he would have them shot. Secondly, any promises made to the American legation were, in effect, void—or, at least, of little or no significance—since Graziani had been informed that Engert was due to leave Ethiopia on 5 March, and the Legation would cease to exist as of 31 March. Thus there would be no one around to hold the Italians accountable for the fate of the refugees. There was, for a few days, one such person: Morris N. Hughes, the young American consul,[104] but he spent his time concentrating on winding down the affairs of the legation, terminating the lease of the premises, closing the office, and leaving the country.[105]

Nonetheless, the day the matter was raised in the British Parliament, the American Secretary of State asked Hughes to 'comment on press reports that refugees were attacked and otherwise mistreated after leaving the Legation'. On 27 March Hughes confirmed that the refugees had remained at the legation 'from 3 to 5 days after the shooting subsided partly because of fear and partly because many of their homes [had been] burned'. He then went on to state that he knew of no cases of attack or mistreatment of the refugees after their departure from the legation, and that on one day the Italians had given them flour, as promised. More significantly, he added that a 'former refugee spokesman stated this morning that none of them had been molested to date'.[106]

Hughes's statement was somewhat reassuring, and at least indicates that the report that the refugees had been killed 'under the terrified gaze of the Legation staff' was almost certainly incorrect. However, it is inconceivable that the former refugee spokesman quoted by Hughes—or anyone, for that matter—could really have known what had, or had not, happened to each of the 700 people who had been dispersed into the city more than a month before. In the circumstances of a devastated urban landscape, a general absence of law and order, and the flight of thousands from the city, no Ethiopians were in a position to account for anyone other than those closest to them. Indeed, Hughes must have been aware of this, for more than three weeks after the outbreak of the massacre, he informed Washington that the situation was still unstable, and that executions were still in progress: 'For two days, the local situation has been superficially quiet, but among Italians and foreigners there is a feeling of gloom and pessimism. There is still some desultory shooting during the night by sentries, and there are daily arrests of so-called suspects and some executions.'[107]

Moreover, Dr Shashka made it clear that many Ethiopians had no idea what had happened even to their own relatives and friends, let alone strangers: 'In those days which followed ... one could see black people meeting in the street, embracing each other and putting a hundred questions. It was a surprise to any Abyssinian in Addis Ababa to know that one or other of his relations or friends was not dead, because there was a greater likelihood of his having been done away with.'[108]

It is clear that there is reason to question Hughes's apparent optimism regarding the fate of the refugees. Furthermore, since he closed the legation shortly after his report on the refugees and left Ethiopia in early April, all communications between Washington and Addis Ababa ceased, thus closing the door on any further follow-up of the matter.

Would it be possible to find out now, more than 75 years after the event, what happened to these refugees? Unfortunately, whereas the names of the hundreds of Ethiopians who sheltered in the American legation grounds during the chaos that occurred on the departure of the Emperor in May 1936 were listed by the legation staff and the records preserved,[109] the present author has not managed to trace any documentation of those who took refuge there to escape the massacre, neither has he knowingly met any of the survivors or their relatives. Thus, until such time as new evidence might come to light, the ultimate fate of the men, women and children who found sanctuary under the American flag from the arson, murder and pillage of 19, 20 and 21 February 1937 is likely to remain unknown.

9

ROMAN JUSTICE

ELIMINATION OF THE UNDESIRABLES

As we have seen, the nocturnal massacre of Addis Ababa was carried out principally by Blackshirts in a clandestine manner following confiscation of cameras from foreigners and closure of the public telegraph system. On the other hand, the execution of 'undesirables' was conducted largely by day, by the regular army and the *carabinieri*. These sections of the military being under Graziani's command, the term 'Graziani Massacre', often used to denote the Massacre of Addis Ababa, would apply more appropriately to the deaths in detention and to the massive countrywide programme of military executions, rather than to the three-day slaughter by the Blackshirts.

Within hours of the outbreak of mayhem on Friday, 19 February, the High Command followed a procedure established at the beginning of the Occupation, involving military 'tribunals' that provided a veneer of due process for the execution of anyone regarded as a potential threat to the consolidation of Italian power in Ethiopia, whether or not they were guilty of any crime. As the American chargé Morris Hughes observed after the American envoy had left Addis Ababa, 'Apparently reports are well-founded that Italian policy is to eliminate all educated and prominent Ethiopians, considering them potential inciters of rebellion.'[1]

Although not always held in public, the proceedings—if any—were presumably intended to provide a record for Rome. The international community was then to believe that the Italians were doing nothing more than seeking an honourable justice following a great wrong perpetrated against them.

The established civilian courts for Ethiopians were often little short of farcical, with so few competent interpreters that the accused often had no idea what was going on. Yet the tribunals were even more basic, dispensing rough military justice in a rudimentary setting. Normally consisting of nothing more than a list of charges followed by sentencing, they were never anything more than a façade.

In this chapter we review the fate of the 'undesirables' whom the Italians decided to eliminate. The present author has not had access to the reports of these tribunals, if indeed they exist. Nonetheless, from oral and published evidence it is possible to present a general picture of what transpired. The victims may be grouped into three broad categories: (1) anyone actually suspected of involvement in the attack of *Yekatit 12*; (2) the educated Young Ethiopians, a group that also included graduates of the Emperor's Gennet (Holetta) Military Academy, as well as some former government officials; and (3) members of the nobility and community leaders, particularly those of Amhara descent.

A word must be said about the first category, the actual suspects. The people named as suspects in this chapter are derived from research presented in

94. Makeshift military 'tribunals' were held in Addis Ababa and the secondary towns

the present author's book *The Plot to Kill Graziani*,[2] and from information on who was interrogated the most severely by the *carabinieri*. The list is similar to the suspects identified by Graziani in his memoirs, written after the collapse of Fascism.[3] The prime suspects turned out to be senior officials of the Emperor's former government, and the throwing of the grenades was believed to have been delegated by them principally to two 'insiders': Eritrean employees of the Governo Generale who were trusted by the Fascists, named Moges Asgedom and Abriha Deboch, and who managed to evade for a long time the wide dragnet put out to catch them.[4]

However, it is worthy of note that none of the *carabinieri* reports on *Yekatit 12* to which the present author has had access mention the names of Moges Asgedom or Abriha Deboch. In particular, the first *carabinieri* report, written by Captain Enrico Marone the day after the attack (and countersigned by Major Giulio D'Alessandro two days later), identified other people as having thrown the grenades from the crowd, as reportedly witnessed by a *carabinieri* commander, Antonio Di Dato. They were named as Beshahwired Habte-Weld, Tefera-Werq [Kidane-Weld], *Fitawrari* Welde-Giyorgis, *Sheikh* Abdulla, Wodajo Ali, and an unidentified Somali.[5] *Sheikh* Abdulla and the unidentified Somali were reportedly killed on the spot. Only one name on the list— Beshahwired Habte-Weld—is recognisable as someone probably involved in the plot, although it seems most unlikely that he actually threw the grenades. The other names provided by Di Dato do not reappear in subsequent police reports seen by the present author, with the exception of Tefera-Werq Kidane-Weld, an employee of the British legation. But even in his case the report is dubious, because he was actually arrested at his house at night, and not at the Governo Generale in the morning, as stated in the report. Furthermore, he was interrogated harshly, but not, in fact, because he had been seen throwing grenades, but in order to find out if British Intelligence was involved in the conspiracy. Thus it seems that most, if not all, of the names of those purportedly caught 'red-handed' by Di Dato rapidly faded in significance, and may have been spurious. The omission of any mention of Moges Asgedom or Abriha Deboch in the first *carabinieri* report was most likely because they threw their grenades from a hidden vantage point. However, the continued omission of these two names from later reports could be put down to the fact that the Governo Generale did not want Rome to know that the attack was an 'inside job'. Further confusion is caused by the fact that, instead of focusing on the handful of people identified (rightly or wrongly) in the *carabinieri* report as the prime suspects, the *carabinieri* and D'Alessandro went on to provide the names of numerous Young

Ethiopians, former Holetta Military Academy cadets and notables, all of whom were to be arrested and executed for involvement in *Yekatit 12*, but with no indication or even suggestion that there was any evidence of their guilt.

The charge in the tribunals was, typically, that of involvement in the attack of *Yekatit 12*. However, in the overwhelming majority of cases this was nothing more than a pretext. Apart from some of the suspects in the first category, who were few in number, there appears to have been no evidence presented to support the charge. This is consistent with Graziani's written instructions, which make it clear that evidence was regarded as unnecessary. The principle was that if all suspects were executed, then at least the guilty ones would most likely be included among them. The Viceroy was simply seizing the opportunity to eliminate the intelligentsia, and was covered by the *Duce*'s order that all civilians and clerics 'in any way suspect' were to be shot without delay.

It may be noted that the three categories of victim were not mutually exclusive. For example, several of the suspects in the first category were also Young Ethiopians or nobility. Similarly, some of the Young Ethiopians in the second category were also members of the nobility.

In virtually all cases, the prisoner was found guilty and a death sentence was handed down. Death was typically by shooting or hanging. The majority of the first and second categories were executed in secret; most of the third category were executed in public. However, the highest-ranking members of this category and their families were sentenced to imprisonment in Italy. In these cases there was no 'tribunal'—or if there was, the victims had no knowledge of it.[6] They were simply rounded up and deported under armed guard.

* * *

THE SUSPECTS

As already noted, the Italians made 'involvement in the attack of 19 February 1937' the charge against hundreds of prisoners, the vast majority of whom could not possibly have known about the plot, let alone be involved in it. In fact, despite Graziani's claims at the time that entire communities were involved in the plot, it is clear from his correspondence and his memoirs that he actually believed that only a handful of people participated. So whom did Italian Military Intelligence really suspect? The list presented here is based largely on a combination of the Italian documents, the Viceroy's memoirs, a letter sent by Mesfin Sileshi to the Emperor in 1938,[7] and research conducted by the present author between 1991 and 2010.[8]

While most victims suffered summary execution shortly after being rounded up, and with a minimum of 'legal' process, a few were kept alive for several days or even weeks, during which time they were subjected to severe interrogation—most likely because they were serious suspects. This group, 18 in number, represents the men regarded by the present author as having been seriously suspected by the *carabinieri* of involvement in the plot of *Yekatit 12*. Of these 18 suspects, so far as can be ascertained, only seven were actually conspirators, and all of those were identified by the Italian Military Police within minutes of the attack. Thus the mass detentions and the thousands of executions and random killings thereafter were entirely opportunistic.

Of the seven who were most likely involved in the plot, three fled the city before they could be traced, and four were subjected to brutal interrogation, following which they either died in custody or were executed.[9] The remaining 11 suspects were also interrogated and executed. The fate of each of the 18 suspects is summarised here.

Plotters who Fled Addis Ababa

BEJIROND LETYIBELU GEBRÉ

Letyibelu Gebré was born in 1893/4 in the village of Manlachesh, Afqera, Gino *qebelé*, Yefat *awraja* in the rugged district of Merhabété. He served the young Teferi Mekonnin (the future Emperor Haile Selassie) on the estate of Teferi's father, *Ras* Mekonnin, at Siddist Kilo.[10] Letyibelu continued to enjoy the favour of the Emperor, eventually earning the title of *Grazmach*, and receiving promotion to Royal Chamberlain.[11] By the time of the Italian invasion he had been put in charge of military supplies, and fought beside the Emperor at the Battle of Maychew.

Letyibelu, who was involved in resistance activities in the early stages of the Occupation with the sons of *Ras* Kassa, returned to Addis Ababa and was asked by members of the Emperor's entourage in exile in London to become the local coordinator of the conspiracy of *Yekatit 12*. To lead the attack on the Italian High Command he recruited two Eritrean employees of the Governo Generale, Moges Asgedom and Abriha Deboch. After the attack he managed to evade an Italian military dragnet and, disguised as a shepherd, trekked to northern Shewa, where he resumed his association with the Patriots. So far as is known, he was the only locally based *Yekatit 12* conspirator to survive the Occupation and live to take part in the Emperor's post-Liberation government. He died in the abortive coup of 1960.

95. The debonair *Bejirond* Letyibelu Gebré, from Afqera in Merhabété, had become a wealthy courtier under Emperor Haile Selassie. He was the only plotter to survive the Occupation

96. Eritrean plotter Moges Asgedom fled Addis Ababa and was executed by the Italians in northern Ethiopia

MOGES ASGEDOM

Moges Asgedom was born around 1912[12] in Akela Guzay, Eritrea. A devout Orthodox Christian who studied at the celebrated 14th-century Monastery of Debre Bizen, he was assisted by friends in the clergy to go to Addis Ababa for further education (secondary education for 'natives' not being permitted by the Italian colonial administration in Eritrea). Around 1928, Moges joined Addis Ababa's Teferi Mekonnin School, where he was regarded as a highly intelligent and diligent student. His fees were paid by the Imperial Palace.

While working in the Cartography Department of the Addis Ababa Municipality Office, which was taken over by the Fascist administration, Moges plotted with a friend named Sibhat Tiruneh (see below) to make an attack against the Governo Generale. In due course Moges was transferred to the Governo Generale as an interpreter, and he persuaded his compatriot and friend Abriha Deboch (see below) to join them in the conspiracy.

Before Sibhat, Moges and Abriha had turned their plans into action, the latter two were introduced by their friend Simi'on Adefris to *Bejirond*

Letyibelu, who headed up a broader-based conspiracy for which, as we have seen, he was seeking to recruit young men to carry out an attack on the Italian High Command.

After the grenades were thrown on 12 Yekatit, Moges and his friend Abriha fled the city with the help of Simi'on Adefris, thus escaping the slaughter that followed the abortive attack. However, they were caught later by the Italian military while en route to the Sudan, and executed at Qwara, near Gondar.

ABRIHA DEBOCH

Abriha Deboch was born in Hamasén Province, Eritrea, in 1913. He attended Italian schools in Asmara, then went to Addis Ababa, where he studied at the Teferi Mekonnin School. Abriha was a clever and bright student, noted for his curiosity, intelligence and mercurial personality. While at school Abriha met Moges Asgedom, with whom he developed a close relationship.

After leaving school, Abriha taught for a time at St George's School for Boys, Addis Ababa. However, he fell foul of the law. During Italy's build-up to the invasion of Ethiopia, he was imprisoned by the Ethiopian government for selling Ethiopian military secrets to the Italian legation in Addis Ababa.

Released from prison at the beginning of the Occupation, in May 1936, he was employed by the Italians in the Governo Generale. Abriha worked in the Political Office, a department concerned with the murky business of working with spies and Ethiopian informers, in order to gather intelligence for the Italian military government. Abriha was highly regarded by Graziani's administration, but when Rome began to introduce a series of racial policies (which later would become legislation), Abriha's career prospects in the Governo Generale evaporated, and he became disgrun-

97. Eritrean plotter Abriha Deboch fled Addis Ababa and was executed with Moges Asgedom in northern Ethiopia

tled. He turned against the Italians, became a double agent, and joined Sibhat and Moges in their quest to make a strike against his employers.

As mentioned above, Abriha fled the city with Moges after the attack of 12 Yekatit, but was eventually arrested and executed by the Italian military along with Moges Asgedom at Qwara.

Suspects Arrested in Addis Ababa

SIBHAT TIRUNEH

Sibhat Tiruneh (actual name Sibhatu) was born in 1901/2 in Debre Tabor *awraja* of Gondar Province, Ethiopia. A Protestant, and one of the first students at the Teferi Mekonnin School, he went on to study at the Swedish Evangelical Mission School on the Intotto Road. In 1930/1 he accepted a

position as resident Amharic teacher at the German Hermannsburg Evangelical Mission behind today's Semien Hotel. The mission moved shortly afterwards to Qechené, where the humble but highly intelligent Sibhat invited his friend Moges Asgedom to share his room. Soon Sibhat's residence became the unofficial meeting place for a group of young Ethiopian intellectuals.

Sibhat inspired Moges to turn against the Italians. The two had been discussing this possibility for several weeks when Moges brought along his former school-friend Abriha Deboch to meet Sibhat.

As Abriha became involved in the discussions, Sibhat began to take something of a back seat in the plot and, after Simi'on Adefris was drawn in, he appears to have more or less withdrawn from direct involvement. Nonetheless, owing principally to Moges's extended period of residence with Sibhat at the Hermannsburg Mission, Sibhat was arrested as an accomplice, and died in prison (possibly St George's, in Dejazmach Wibé Sefer, Addis Ababa).[13]

98. Sibhat Tiruneh, who had earlier inspired Moges Asgedom and Abriha Deboch to strike against the Italians, died in custody

SIMI'ON ADEFRIS

Simi'on Adefris was born to a Catholic family (originally from Ankober) in 1912 in Hararge Province, Ethiopia. As a smart young businessman in Addis Ababa owning two taxis, he became a close friend of *Bejirond* Letyibelu Gebré.

Simi'on played a pivotal role in the plot of *Yekatit 12* by introducing Moges Asgedom and Abriha Deboch to his friend Letyibelu, who needed energetic young men to lead his planned attack on the Italian High Command. The two Eritreans being 'insiders' with permits to be present at the palace among the Italian high officials, Simi'on's role in linking the 'Hermannsburg Mission' cell with Letyibelu's group was critical to the implementation of the conspiracy.

After the attack of *Yekatit 12*, Simi'on drove Moges and Abriha to Debre Libanos, some 100 kilometres north of Addis Ababa. However, on returning to Addis Ababa he was arrested, and suffered severe interrogation before dying in custody in St George's Prison.

One of Simi'on's sisters paid the Italian doctor at the prison to release his body and was much distressed to see that during brutal interrogation her brother's hair and various body parts including fingernails had been wrenched off. Simi'on's remains were subsequently buried by his family in sanctified ground at the Gulelé cemetery.[14]

BESHAHWIRED HABTE-WELD

Beshahwired Habte-Weld, the husband of Sara Gebre-Iyyesus, was born in Shewa in 1895. Educated in India and America, he was Director of Finance and a confidant of the Emperor.

After returning to Addis Ababa in December 1936 from exile in England, where he had been a member of the Emperor's entourage and treasurer for the royal family, he became involved with the conspirators *Bejirond* Letyibelu, Sibhat Tiruneh, Moges Asgedom and Abriha Deboch, and was most likely involved in the plot.

99. Simi'on Adefris died after brutal interrogation at St George's Prison

A close associate of the Anglo-Indian firm of Mohamedally & Co., which was also suspected of involvement in the plot, Beshahwired was executed following brutal interrogation in the basement of the Governo Generale in Siddist Kilo. Figure 101, published by the director of the Itégé Menen School, *Weyzero* Siniddu Gebru, was captioned 'Ato Beshahwired suffered a lot before he was killed'.[15] Despite strenuous efforts by his family after Liberation, Beshahwired's body was never found.

QEÑÑAZMACH BELIHU DEGEFU

Qeññazmach (formerly *Shaqa*) Belihu Degefu had fought with the Emperor at Maychew and, like his friend Beshahwired, went into exile in England with the sovereign.

Belihu was among a small group of people instructed by Haile Selassie to return home and help Viceroy *Ras* Imru relocate the Ethiopian government to Goré in the west of Ethiopia, and foster a resistance movement.

100. Beshahwired Habte-Weld, educated in India and America and confidant of Emperor Haile Selassie, photographed before *Yekatit 12*. He was executed after harsh interrogation

101. Beshahwired Habte-Weld in custody before execution

102. *Qeññazmach* Belihu Degefu before *Yekatit 12*. Executed after harsh interrogation

103. Belihu Degefu in captivity, before interrogation and execution. This photograph appears to have been taken at St George's Prison, the steps running down from the main building

Although the present author has found no proof that Belihu was involved in the *Yekatit 12* conspiracy, Graziani believed he was the organiser, and there is circumstantial evidence that he was involved. He was arrested with Beshahwired immediately after the attack of *Yekatit 12*, and suffered severe interrogation in the basement of the Governo Generale, following which he was executed.[16]

MOHAMMED SAYED

Moges Asgedom and Abriha Deboch are said to have been assisted by others in their execution of the attack of *Yekatit 12*, but the Italian documents of the period are replete with so many purported plotters as to be almost worthless as serious sources for reconstruction of the plot. It is unlikely, for example, that any of the young men mentioned by Captain Marone in his report of 20 February were actually involved in the conspiracy or in its implementation.

On 22 February, Major-General Bernardo Olivieri sent Graziani a summary report of *Yekatit 12* in which he suggested responsible parties—notably

104. Mohammed Sayed in custody before execution

105. *Dejazmach* Welde-Amanuél, who was almost certainly not involved in the plot of *Yekatit 12*, was photographed in custody on the dais at the Gennete-Li'ul Palace before being taken for interrogation and execution

106. *Qeññazmach* Welde-Yohannis Welde-Ab photographed in custody before interrogation and execution. Most likely not involved in the plot

the Young Ethiopians and the former Holetta cadets.[17] However, according to Professor Tekeste Negash, a more detailed report from Olivieri the same day provided some specific names, including a certain Mohammed Sayed. Professor Tekeste states that Mohammed Sayed was reported to have thrown the third grenade.[18] However, little is known about him, other than his being listed by the diplomat-writer Birhanu Dinqé as a notable.[19]

Given that, as part of Italy's divide-and-rule policy in Ethiopia Muslims were ostensibly favoured by the Fascist administration, the involvement of a Muslim in the plot comes as a surprise, though the possibility cannot be ruled out. Curiously, Mohammed's name does not appear in the subsequent Military Intelligence reports on the incident, and neither does it feature in Graziani's memoirs.

DEJAZMACH *WELDE-AMANUÉL HAWAS*

Described as a 'generous-hearted hero', *Dejazmach* Welde-Amanuél Hawas was Commander of the Imperial Household, and Governor of Jimma. He fought the Italians, alongside the military commander *Dejazmach* Nesibu, on the southern war front. He left Addis Ababa with the Emperor in May 1936 and remained in Djibouti until October, when he returned to Addis Ababa and submitted to the Italians.[20]

One of the Emperor's senior courtiers, the *Dejazmach* was almost certainly not involved in the plot of *Yekatit 12*, but apparently had the misfortune of being tipped off in advance by Abriha Deboch that there would be 'trouble' at the Governo Generale on that day. This most likely came about because Welde-Amanuél's son-in-law, the late *Fitawrari* Kelkilé, had become Abriha's adoptive father. *Dejazmach* Welde-Amanuél was reportedly executed for not passing to the Italians the information he had received about the plot.[21]

QEÑÑAZMACH *WELDE-YOHANNIS WELDE-AB*

Qeññazmach Welde-Yohannis Welde-Ab was a provincial nobleman from Maychew, who acted as a guide for the Ethiopian army at the Battle of Maychew. A steward of the Imperial Household in Addis Ababa, he is listed by Birhanu Dinqé with the title *Ye Medfeñoch Aleqa*.[22]

The *Qeññazmach* was reportedly executed along with *Dejazmach* Welde-Amanuél. Alazar Tesfa Michael wrote that he was sentenced for the same reason as the *Dejazmach*: 'failure to warn the authorities'.[23]

KENTIBA *TENA GASHAW BEHABTE*
and his son, *CAPTAIN DESTA TENA*

The son of *Negadras* Behapte (*Negadras* of Harar for *Ras* Mekonnin), Tena Gashaw had served as director of the prison at Ankober, *Kentiba* of the municipality and Governor of Addis Ababa, and subsequently Governor of Jimma at the age of approximately 57.[24] He submitted to the Italians two days before *Yekatit 12.*[25] His son, Captain Desta Tena, is listed in the *carabinieri* report of 20 February 1937 as one of the first ex-Holetta cadets to be arrested after the attack.[26] However, the present author is not aware of any evidence that either *Kentiba* Tena or his son Desta, who were named by *Ras* Mesfin as having been executed after brutal interrogation, were actually involved in the plot of *Yekatit 12.*

LIQE MEQWAS *HAYLE-MARYAM WELDE-GEBRIÉL*
and his brother, QEÑÑAZMACH *TEKLE-MARYAM*

Liqe Meqwas Hayle-Maryam Welde-Gebriél, born around 1901, the son of *Betwedded* Welde-Gebriél, grew up at the imperial palace and was described as 'one of the Emperor's favourites'.[27] So far as is known, the *Liqe Meqwas* and his brother Tekle-Maryam were locally educated. Sara and Welette-Birhan Gebre-Iyyesus told the present author that Hayle-Maryam was present at an ill-fated gathering of dignitaries of the Emperor's government in a private house near the Governo Generale on the eve of *Yekatit 12*, at which, it is thought, the impending attack on the Italian High Command was discussed. Although Letyibelu, Beshahwired and Belihu were at the same function, no evidence has yet come to light that either the *Liqe Meqwas* or his brother was actually involved in the plot of *Yekatit 12.*

KIFLE NESIBU

Kifle Nesibu was the son of *Dejazmach* Nesibu ZeAmanuél, one of the Emperor's leading military commanders during the Italian invasion.[28]

One of the Young Ethiopians, Kifle reportedly studied in France and Alexandria. He became cadet commander at Holetta Military Academy, where he was widely respected and admired for his leadership qualities. Later he became a member of the Black Lion, or *Tiqur Anbessa*, resistance group.[29]

Although he was certainly an activist, the present author has come across no evidence that Kifle Nesibu was involved in the plot of *Yekatit 12.* According to

107. *Liqe Meqwas* Hayle-Maryam Welde-Gebriél, who was most likely not involved in the plot, photographed in custody before interrogation and execution

108. *Qeññazmach* Tekle-Maryam, probably not involved in the plot, photographed in custody before interrogation and execution

the writer Kirubel Beshah, Kifle Nesibu was executed in Addis Ababa, near the Church of Medhané Alem, on the Intotto Road.[30]

GRAZMACH *MESFIN QELEME WERQ*

Mesfin Qeleme Werq was educated at the Teferi Mekonnin School (English stream),[31] and, so far as is known, did not pursue higher education overseas. After *Yekatit 12* he was made to appear before a tribunal. The translator was Rosario Gilaezgi, who testified:

> When I was called as an interpreter to General Olivieri, he started to ask one of the prisoners, Mesfin Qeleme Werq, if he was the man who had sent a telegram to the League of Nations, saying that the Ethiopians would form a government in Goré. And Mesfin Qeleme Werq said that it was he. Olivieri then asked him where his followers were.

> Then I said to Olivieri, 'I have come here to assist at the investigations about the Graziani attempt. If you are going to ask me about what happened before that, I am not going to assist you, and if you are not content with my work, I will return.' And I returned to the house of Della Porta.[32]

109. Kifle Nesibu, one of the leading Young Ethiopians, but who was most likely not involved in the plot of *Yekatit 12*, photographed in custody before interrogation and execution

110. *Grazmach* Mesfin Qeleme Werq, photographed before interrogation and execution. His dispatch of a telegram to the League of Nations incurred the wrath of the Italians. Most likely not involved in the plot

Although *Grazmach* Mesfin Qeleme Werq was a patriot, his name has never arisen among those involved in the plot of *Yekatit 12*. It appears from Rosario's testimony that even if his interrogators failed to establish any connection with *Yekatit 12*, they wanted to eliminate him, like all the other Young Ethiopians, as a potential enemy of the Fascist administration, and *Yekatit 12* provided a convenient opportunity to do so.

TADDESSE MESHESHA

One notable among the suspects—who was also sometimes classified as a Young Ethiopian—was Taddesse Meshesha. A close friend of both Beshahwired Habte-Weld and Belihu Degefu, Taddesse was born in 1905. The son of Meshesha Gebru, he studied at the Lazarist Mission at Harar, and later worked for the Djibouti–Addis Ababa Railway Company. He was then hired by *Ras* Teferi as his private secretary.

Described by the American envoy in 1929 as 'one of the King's most influential Private Secretaries', Taddesse continued to work in that capacity for Teferi Mekonnin as Emperor Haile Selassie, and is said by some sources to have been involved in secret negotiations on the Emperor's behalf with Mussolini's representative.

Taddesse accompanied the Emperor into exile, but returned to Ethiopia in December 1936. He formally submitted to the Italians in February 1937.[33] He is listed in the first *carabinieri* report of 20 February 1937 as having been arrested immediately after the grenades were thrown.[34]

111. Taddesse Meshesha, private secretary to the Emperor, in custody before interrogation and execution. No evidence of his involvement in the plot has yet come to light

MESFIN MENGESHA

Mesfin Mengesha, formerly Governor of the Ogaden, one of the Young Ethiopians who submitted to the Italians on 17 February 1937, was also executed for involvement in *Yekatit 12*. His father, *Dejazmach* Mengesha Wibé, was a distinguished figure in pre-Occupation Ethiopia. So far as is known, Mesfin was not involved in the plot of *Yekatit 12*, but his father certainly knew Abriha Deboch, for, a few months before, he had introduced Abriha to Taddessech Istifanos, who became Abriha's wife.[35]

In addition, the Italians seem to have suspected some other Young Ethiopians of involvement in the plot, such as Yoséf and Binyam Werqineh, sons of the Ethiopian minister in London, Dr 'Charles Martin' Werqineh. However, despite Graziani's accusations, the evidence suggests that they were not serious suspects, and they are assigned here to the category of Young Ethiopians executed principally because they were deemed to be a current or potential threat to the Italian administration. They are thus considered in the next section.

All of the *Yekatit 12* suspects listed above were interrogated severely and executed *in camera*, the majority without 'tribunal' proceedings. A description of the extreme brutality to which these suspects were subjected appears in the Emperor's autobiography.[36] In addition, the Italians are known to have employed electric shock treatment during interrogations. The Patriot Shewareged Gedlé, who was arrested on Saturday, 20th February, at the age of about 39, was subjected to what she referred to as 'third degree', involving securing her with a rubber ring around the neck, tying her wrists, and administering electric shocks through her body that caused bleeding and loss of consciousness.[37]

The Italians prohibited relatives from knowing anything of the fate of their prisoners, and did not allow them to take custody of the bodies or arrange a burial or, indeed, any sort of memorial or commemoration. The only exception to this among the *Yekatit 12* suspects appears to be Simi'on Adefris, whose remains, as we have seen, were secretly taken charge of by his relatives. This makes Simi'on the only *Yekatit 12* collaborator arrested by the Italians to have received a proper burial, so far as can be ascertained.

THE YOUNG ETHIOPIANS

The Young Ethiopians (a term originating from the radical Young Turks of 1908) represented Emperor Haile Selassie's hopes for the future. Ethiopia, the sovereign planned, would no longer be a feudal state run by the reactionary *rases*, with whom he was constantly at loggerheads in his modernisation programmes. The old guard was to have been replaced by a generation of young men from all walks of life whom the sovereign had personally selected and sent overseas for education—at the expense, it might be added, not of foreign aid, but of Ethiopia's own resources.

The extermination by Italy of the Ethiopian intelligentsia in February–March 1937 was one of the 20th century's most carefully orchestrated and cold-blooded pogroms against a nation's educated youth.[38] As a proportion of the population, the educated generation at the time of the Italian invasion was tiny; those who had returned from overseas studies, or had been cadets at Holetta (Gennet) Military Academy, consisted of no more than a few hundred souls. Nonetheless, as they were virtually the only people in the country with a higher modern education, their potential contribution to the nation was beyond measure. As the Ethiopian legation in London reported, 'This category of victims [were those] especially aimed at, who numbered from two hundred to three hundred, most of whom were educated in France, England, Egypt, the United

States, Belgium, Germany and Italy, as well as the few survivors of the Gennet Military School, who under the impetus of the Swedish Military Mission promised to furnish Ethiopia with a list of officers of the first order.'[39] Dr Shashka put his finger on the way the Italians looked at this elite: 'Those cultured, young Abyssinians, with whom our relations were so friendly before the invasion, had to perish for two reasons: first because their learning and their position assured them a certain influence over their compatriots; secondly, because many of them possessed in their homes objects of value, especially from Europe, which the murderers distributed amongst themselves.'[40]

In reality, not all the Young Ethiopians were particularly young. The first batch of students to go abroad to study did so under the auspices of the Emperor in the 1920s while Regent. Others had left in the early 1930s and some, such as Beshahwired Habte-Weld, were already old enough to be in senior positions in government when they joined foreign universities as 'mature students', and were in their forties by the time they returned. Nonetheless, the sponsorship and recruitment of these men, who often came from lowly backgrounds, represented a radical break with the past in terms of the country's education policy, and they were rising stars in what the Emperor had planned would be a 'new Ethiopia'.

The rooting out of the Young Ethiopians was ruthlessly conducted by the *carabinieri*, in line with Mussolini's requirement that the pogrom should be conducted in secret. As noted earlier, the Italians lined up for execution anyone with a high-school diploma, had studied overseas, or had been a Holetta cadet.[41] In addition, any Ethiopian who spoke a foreign language, particularly French, was under suspicion,[42] and Protestants—typically educated by foreign, non-Italian missionaries—were also targeted. When educated individuals could not be identified or traced, they were pointed out by informers and arrested. Some of the victims stood 'trial' in a tribunal; others were simply identified from among groups of people who had been rounded up, taken out and shot unceremoniously.

The 'trials', which were held in a number of venues—and are thus referred to by some writers as the 'flying tribunal'—commenced with an opening session in Addis Ababa on Friday afternoon, 19 February, immediately after the attack at the Governo Generale. However, the purpose of the tribunal was basically not to judge a case, but simply to conduct the formalities for execution. Graziani himself had frequently referred to the need to eradicate the Young Ethiopians with their 'French-like erudition', many of whom were more highly educated than the Viceroy himself, and the strike of *Yekatit 12* gave him the perfect excuse to do so. The Italian High Command was more than willing to oblige, as the very concept of a refined, educated Ethiopian was anathema to those who had characterised Ethiopians as 'vile' and 'barbaric', and had depicted even the Emperor—the very image of a debonair and dignified sovereign—as a grotesque, subhuman creature. As Imru Zelleqe put it, 'The Graziani incident [*Yekatit 12*] was a watershed for the Italian occupation. It revealed the really vicious character of the Fascist colonisers. It gave the Fascists the excuse to carry out what was all along in their mind, to exterminate the traditional leadership and Ethiopian intelligentsia, who had formal education and military training.'[43]

In each case the 'trial' began with a charge being read out by a military judge, which was typically one version or another of 'involvement in the plot of 19 February 1937'.[44] After this came a statement by the military prosecutor, and sometimes an opportunity for the defendant to speak briefly, following which he or she was declared guilty.

It was clear to Rosario Gilaezgi, the Eritrean interpreter employed in the initial tribunal, that although the tribunals were purportedly set up to try members of the plot to assassinate the Viceroy, they were indeed used to eliminate supposed enemies of the Occupation, regardless of whether they had anything to do with the attempt of *Yekatit 12*. 'On Friday evening I was called to the Palace to the President of the Military Court, General Olivieri, to act as interpreter. People who were brought before that court were shot; afterwards I learned that 62 were shot. One asked me what I thought of the attempt against Graziani and I said, "This is something which had been done by some persons, but is not a conspiracy of the people, and because of this you ought not to punish the people en masse."'[45] Rosario testified that he said the same thing to his superiors. Nonetheless, 'involvement in *Yekatit 12*' remained the charge in most, if not all, of the tribunals. In the case of the first sessions attended by Rosario, the majority of the 62 defendants were either Young Ethiopians or nobility, who knew nothing about the plot of *Yekatit 12*.

If any doubt remains about the nature of these tribunals as nothing more or less than a means of eliminating the intelligentsia, the statement by Ciro Poggiali in his secret diary makes the situation crystal clear. As Ethiopian-based correspondent of the *Corriere della Sera*, he was closely engaged with the Fascist hierarchy in Addis Ababa, and thus was well informed, but at the same time his diary reveals a diligent and balanced observer, apparently devoid of the more rabid racism that was seeping into Fascism. In his entry for 24 February, three days after *Yekatit 12*, he wrote that the officials staging the tribunals in the *gibbi* had received official notification that they did not need to ascertain any personal responsibility of the defendants for the actions with which they were charged. The defendants were to be shot anyway, on the principle that this would ensure that, one way or another, the culprits would be dealt with.[46]

On 1 March the British acting consul-general reported, 'Immediately after the attempt ... authorities rounded up and placed under arrest practically every Ethiopian of any distinction in the capital. These included many of the personages who had made their submission only two days earlier. Since then a military tribunal under General Olivieri has been sitting ... a trial, probably on the Kremlin model, followed the hundreds of arrests made ... by process of examination, confession and confrontation, some sort of guilt was established: many executions on the 26th February were the result.'[47] For the initial batch, which contained several of the most well-known Young Ethiopians, the sentences were handed down a week after *Yekatit 12*. Some were delivered on Thursday, 25 February 1937, and others on the following day.[48]

There are a few published references on which an estimate of the number of Young Ethiopians executed can be based. Firstly, the British envoy informed the Foreign Office in London, 'The first batches of these [Young Ethiopians] amounting, I am credibly informed, to eleven lorry loads, were executed on the 26th ultimo in different parts of the town.'[49] Since each truck would normally have carried at least 20 prisoners—and possibly as many as 40—this report indicates that the number of victims had grown considerably since the initial session which led to 62 death sentences. It would imply that between 220 and 440 Young Ethiopians were executed on Friday, 26 February.

A more modest number was suggested by one of the French diplomats who left Addis Abba some days after the massacre: 'The Italians at once arrested all the members of the "Young Abyssinia" Party (numbering between 150 and 200). Most of these were educated in France. They represent the fine flower of Abyssinia, "enlightened individuals" who before the war worked with the Emperor, Haile Selassie, for the modernisation of their country. It is probable that only a handful who happened not to be in the capital at the time remain alive.'[50]

Thirdly, in April the British envoy estimated that more than 200 ex-Holetta cadets had been executed in a second batch. 'Suspicion ... fell on a number of cadets from the former military school which was at one time under Belgian and Swiss officers. Over two hundred of these young Abyssinians were later rounded up and massacred by machine-guns. Moreover, any young Abyssinian who is believed to have any patriotic feelings and thus be capable of fomenting trouble is shot without any form of trial.'[51]

Several more Young Ethiopians were executed in the weeks that followed, and by April, Sylvia Pankhurst in England, relying principally on the reports coming to her through her correspondent in Djibouti, had concluded that they had all been eliminated: 'In the end the authorities made a last enquiry if all the young intellectuals had been suppressed. Not a single one survived! All had been previously dispatched.'[52]

In fact, some of the Young Ethiopians did survive—notably, as suggested by the French report, those who were overseas at the time, or who happened to be outside Addis Ababa, and were not caught up in the dragnet launched in Ethiopia's secondary towns where the 'flying tribunal' also operated. Nonetheless, it is clear that many of the foreign-educated Ethiopians were eliminated during the days following *Yekatit 12*. In fact, after *Yekatit 12* the military went around with lists of Young Ethiopians to be executed, and when they were found they were typically shot out of hand.

Did Graziani really believe that the Young Ethiopians—several of whom were also former cadets of the Holetta Military Academy—were all involved in the *Yekatit 12* conspiracy? Judging from his memoirs, the answer would certainly be no, the conclusion being that the mass executions of these educated youngsters was opportunistic. This is confirmed by Ciro Poggiali's revelation that the members of the tribunal had been told not to bother ascertaining any degree of guilt on the part of the defendants. However, the Viceroy was, as usual, circumspect in his communications with Rome. Putting his usual gloss on the proceedings, he gave the impression that the silence of the defendants under interrogation signalled guilt. Knowing that the defendants had no information to provide, he informed Mussolini that virtually nothing was to be gained by interrogations. Complaining that the captives were 'mute' and demonstrated 'the most complete obstructionism', he wrote, 'Little can be gathered from the mouths of the condemned people that could in any way be useful to trace the origins of the criminal act.' The military historian Professor Rochat confirms that the dignified manner in which the victims went to their death was interpreted as proving their culpability: 'In the prevailing climate of revenge, even the proud attitude of those sentenced to death became evidence of their guilt. Graziani telegraphed: "45 men have been executed on the morning of the 26th and none of them raised his voice in protest against the destiny that awaited them."'[53]

Although the executions were carried out in secret, word got out that when faced with the firing squad, the victims typically denounced the Italians and bravely cried out for the freedom and independence of Ethiopia. Sergeant-

Major Boaglio comments that rumour had it that the Ethiopians exhibited 'heroic behaviour', their cries of freedom cut short only by machine-gun fire.[54]

In his study of the Italian records, including reports, memoranda and telegrams, Professor Rochat found no concrete evidence against the Young Ethiopians. He discovered only 'at the most, prejudicial suspicions', 'rumours', and 'testimonies clearly made up by the investigators'.[55]

Some of the Young Ethiopians executed after 26 February were also former cadets of the Holetta Military Academy who had been captured with *Ras* Imru in late 1936 and released under amnesty.[56] While execution was normally by shooting or hanging, some of the cadets were reportedly thrown alive out of aeroplanes, their wrists and ankles shackled.

The constant repetition of the charge of being involved in the attack of *Yekatit 12*, in hundreds of cases, had the desired effect—at least to some extent, for some members of the foreign community and subsequently some sections of the international press assumed that there must be evidence against the Young Ethiopians and that the charges were genuine, as suggested by the British acting consul-general's report to London: 'From what has been learnt of the proceedings of the military tribunal, the young Ethiopian intelligentsia is suspected of having inspired the plot.'[57]

There is no comprehensive list available of the Young Ethiopians executed during the massacre of Addis Ababa, although some authors have published partial lists. In Appendix I there is as complete a list of the fate of the Young Ethiopians as the present author has been able to draw up from the various lists available.

The following pages contain photographs taken by the Italians of some of the Young Ethiopians on the dais at the Gennete-Li'ul Palace where the hand grenades were thrown in the strike of *Yekatit 12*. After being photographed, these young men, who represent only a fraction of the Young Ethiopians killed, were taken away for interrogation and execution. Although the photographs are of poor quality, and the originals were not available for the present publication, they are nonetheless reproduced here in an attempt to compile as comprehensive a documentary record as possible of the fate of the Young Ethiopians.

* * *

YOSÉF (JOSEPH) 'MARTIN' WERQINEH
and his brother BINYAM (BENJAMIN)

The Fascist newspaper *L'Azione Coloniale* claimed that these two sons of the Ethiopian envoy in London, Dr 'Charles Martin' Werqineh, together with Sirak

Hiruy, the son of the Ethiopian Foreign Minister, had been responsible for the attempted assassination of Graziani, and this was assumed at the time by Ciro Poggiali to be so.[58] However, while the brothers certainly played leading roles in the resistance, neither the present author nor any other published researcher has come across any evidence of their involvement in the plot of *Yekatit 12*.

Yoséf and Binyam Werqineh were often regarded as Dr Werqineh's favourite sons. Yoséf was born in 1912, followed by Binyam around one year later. Both studied at Trent College, England, and then went on to Loughborough College. They were both active in sports, Yoséf becoming captain of the college cricket team.

When their father was appointed minister in London in 1935, both sons joined him as assistants. In October, soon after the launch of the Italian invasion, they returned to Ethiopia to help in the struggle. After the sovereign's departure they joined the Black Lion resistance organisation, then surrendered to the Italians with *Ras* Imru. According to their half-brother Yohannis, their surrender to the Italians indicated misplaced trust: 'Joseph and Ben ... were largely responsible for their own deaths. As young men they fought with

112. Loughborough College cricket team in the early 1930s. Yoséf and Binyam Werqineh are standing second and fourth from left, in the back row

Ras Imru and naïvely surrendered to the Italians. They were victims of their own education and they thought that the Italians were civilized.' He said that after *Yekatit 12* their mother tried to persuade them to join the Patriots, but they decided to stay, because of their education and trust in the Italians. 'At night they were arrested and then shot.'[59]

It was reported in England that Yoséf and Binyam were among a batch of Young Ethiopians shot on Friday, 26 February.[60] However, Poggiali dates the execution of at least one of the two brothers to the next day, for on 27 February he noted in his diary, 'One of the sons of Martin was shot this morning.' Yohannis Werqineh was probably right about his half-brother's misplaced trust in the Italians, for Poggiali noted that, faced with the firing squad, the young man's last words were, 'So this is the civilization you have brought to us! Down with Italy!'[61]

Of the thousands of Ethiopians shot during the massacre, there are very few whose place of execution is known, given Mussolini's orders for the killings to be carried out in secret. The Werqineh brothers, however, are an exception, for Beshahwired Habte-Weld's sister-in-law, Welette-Birhan Gebre-Iyyesus, told the present author that they were killed at St George's Prison.[62] Considering

113. Yoséf Werqineh, son of the Ethiopian envoy in London, and educated in England, in captivity before execution

114. Yoséf Werqineh's brother, Binyam, educated in England, in captivity before execution

that she was well informed, had a wide network of friends, knew the Werqineh brothers personally, was in Addis Ababa throughout the Occupation, and was herself at one point in prison in the city under sentence of death, this information can be regarded as reliable.

FEQADE-SILLASSÉ HIRUY

Feqade-Sillassé, son of Foreign Minister *Blatten Géta* Hiruy Welde-Sillassé, and known to his English friends as 'George', was born in 1907/8.[63] He was educated at Victoria College, Alexandria, and Cambridge University, where he studied political economy. He married Yemiserach, the daughter of *Ras* Imru.

Feqade-Sillassé joined the Werqineh brothers in the Black Lion resistance organisation and, like several other Young Ethiopians, formally submitted to the Italians on 17 February 1937, two days before *Yekatit 12*. He was arrested immediately after *Yekatit 12*,[64] and was shot in March after severe interroga-

115. Cambridge-educated Feqade-Sillassé Hiruy, seen here with his father, *Blattén Géta* Hiruy Welde-Sillassé, preparing for a radio broadcast by the Emperor before the Italian invasion. He was executed by the Italians

tion, for incitement to rebellion and his father's continuation of the diplomatic struggle in exile.[65] The British envoy in Addis Ababa informed London, 'Feqade Sillassé (George) Hiruy ... has almost certainly suffered the same fate [death by shooting]; his mother has been daily at the palace, begging for mercy, and she too is now said to be under arrest.'[66]

LIEUTENANT-COLONEL BELAY HAYLE-AB

Of Eritrean origin, Belay Hayle-Ab attended the Teferi Mekonnin School in Addis Ababa, then rose to a senior position at Holetta Military Academy. Attaining the rank of lieutenant-colonel at an early age, he became chief instructor of the *Tiqur Anbessa*, or Black Lion movement, which he was instrumental in creating—the group of former Holetta cadets presided over by Dr Alemewerq Beyene.[67] Six months after leading a daring attack on the Regia Aeronautica in June 1936 at Boneya, near Neqemté, in Wellega, Belay surrendered to the Italians with *Ras* Imru on 18 December 1936, following which he was freed in an amnesty.

Belay was a friend of Sibhat Tiruneh, Moges Asgedom and Abriha Deboch.[68] However, so far as the present author has been able to ascertain from interviews with some of his associates and contemporaries, including his friend Mehari Kassa and Sibhat's brother, he was not involved in the plot of *Yekatit 12*. Nonetheless, he was arrested and executed shortly afterwards.[69] According to Ciro Poggiali, Belay was shot on 1 March 1937, approximately two weeks after *Yekatit 12*. But the Eritrean resistance fighter's last words indicate that he believed that his execution had nothing to do with *Yekatit 12*: 'You are killing me because I led

116. A former student of Teferi Mekonnin School, Lieutenant-Colonel Belay Hayle-Ab, shown here as a youth, was executed following *Yekatit 12*.

the massacre of Neqemté, but you are unjust, because after that I was with *Ras* Imru and I surrendered with his group. So if my submission was accepted, that implied that I was pardoned.'[70] It is clear that Graziani, who had never agreed with the amnesty granted after the Boneya incident, was simply taking the opportunity to 'get even' with its perpetrators.

MESHESHA GEBRU

Educated at Teferi Mekonnin School, where he was in the English stream,[71] Meshesha Gebru is listed by the Black Lion' historian, Taddesse Mécha, as having been elected by the general assembly of the organisation to be a military trainer.[72]

Siniddu Gebru's caption for the photograph in Figure 147 is 'Meshesha Gebru, killed by the enemy at the age of 19 years'.[73]

ASSEFA ADMASU

Shaleqa ('Major') Assefa Admasu, as he is referred to by Birhanu Dinqé, was the son of *Fitawrari* Admasu of Harar.[74] Educated at Teferi Mekonnin School (French stream),[75] he is listed by Taddesse Mécha as a military trainer of the Black Lion organisation.[76] Siniddu Gebru refers to him as *Lij* Assefa Admasu.[77]

GEBREMEDHIN AWEQE

Ato Gebremedhin Aweqe, who had studied agriculture in England,[78] is identified by Birhanu Dinqé as the former *Shum* of Ambo town.[79] He is also named by Taddesse Mécha as having been an executive committee member of the Black Lion movement.[80]

MEKONNIN HAYLE

Mekonnin Hayle was educated at Teferi Mekonnin School (English stream), following which he was one of twelve students sent to Beirut in October 1926 to study pedagogy.[81] From there he went on to study finance at Cornell University in the United States.[82]

DESTA WELDE-IYYESUS

A former Holetta Military Academy cadet, Lieutenant-Colonel Desta Welde-Iyyesus was the son of *Qeññazmach* Welde-Iyyesus from Wellega.[83] So far as is

117. Meshesha Gebru in custody before execution

118. Assefa Admasu in custody before execution

119. Gebremedhin Aweqe in custody before execution

120. Mekonnin Hayle, a graduate who studied in Beirut and America, in custody before execution

121. Desta Welde-Iyyesus, a former Holleta cadet, in custody before execution

122. Yohannis Boru, educated in England, in custody before execution

123. Captain Mitike Desta of the Holleta Military Academy, in custody before execution

124. Tsigé-Marqos, former employee of the Ministry of Finance, in custody before execution

known, he was locally educated. Desta was listed by Taddesse Mécha as an executive committee member of the Black Lion movement.[84]

YOHANNIS BORU

A Young Ethiopian, Yohannis Boru studied at Victoria College, Alexandria, then went to England to study engineering.[85] He is on record as having written to the British Foreign Office in January 1933 on behalf of all the Ethiopian students in the UK on a letterhead of *The Student Movement House*, asking the Foreign Office to get in touch with the Ethiopian Foreign Office to address the students' financial problems.[86]

CAPTAIN MITIKE DESTA

Captain (*Shambel*) Mitike Desta, the son of *Ato* Desta of Arsi, was a graduate of the Holetta Military Academy,[87] and a military trainer in the Black Lion organisation.[88] Mitike's name does not appear in any of the lists of foreign-educated Ethiopians; so far as is known, he was educated locally.

TSIGÉ-MARQOS WELDE-TEKLE

Listed by Birhanu Dinqé as *Ato* Tsigé Marqos but entitled *Lij* in the Italian photograph in Figure 124, Tsigé-Marqos Welde-Tekle studied economics in England and was employed in the Ministry of Finance.[89] He is also listed by Taddesse Mécha as an executive committee member of the Black Lion organisation.[90]

MOHAMMED SÉYFU

This young man was one of the few Muslim Young Ethiopians, but was nonetheless executed, despite Mussolini's ostensibly favourable posture towards Ethiopian Muslims.

Given that there were few Muslim students educated at Teferi Mekonnin School, and one of them was named Mohammed Séyfu,[91] it is likely that 'Séyfu Mohammed', as written by the Italian administration on this photograph, refers to the same person.

DEBEBE GEBRU

Debebe Gebru was educated at Teferi Mekonnin School (English stream),[92] and was named by Taddesse Mécha as an executive committee member of the Black Lion.[93] Siniddu Gebru's caption of the photograph in Figure 126 of this Young Ethiopian reads, 'Debebe Gebru gave his blood for his country'.[94]

MULUGÉTA ASSEFA

Neither Pankhurst nor Clapham list Mulugéta Assefa among Ethiopians educated abroad since 1936. Thus it is assumed that he was locally educated, although his name does not appear in the list of students at the Teferi Mekonnin School. He is not listed by Taddesse Mécha as a member of the Lions Lion, neither is he listed by Birhanu Dinqé as a Holetta cadet.

TEKLE-BIRHAN DESSALEÑ

According to Birhanu Dinqé, Tekle-Birhan Dessaleñ was the son of the former Minister of Foreign Affairs *Ato* Dessaleñ Habte-Mika'él.[95] Taddesse Mécha entitles him *Aleqa*, and identifies him as a military trainer of the Black Lion organization.[96] Siniddu Gebru's caption for the photograph in Figure 128 reads: '*Lij* Tekle-Birhan, a young man killed by the enemy'.[97]

ASSEFA TEDLA

Sinuddu Gebru identifies the Young Ethiopian in the photograph in Figure 129), on which the name has been partially obliterated, as *Lij* Assefa Tedla.[98] Taddesse Mécha identifies *Lij* Assefa as a former Holetta cadet who was appointed a military trainer in the Black Lion organisation.[99]

Other Young Ethiopians Executed

Many other educated Young Ethiopians died during the pogrom of *Yekatit 12*, of whom no photographs are available. For example, Bahru Keba, who was educated in the French stream at Teferi Mekonnin School,[100] was reported in *New Times and Ethiopia News* as having been killed in the repressions that followed *Yekatit 12*, and described as 'a young Captain of Aviation, educated at the French Military School of St Cyr'.[101]

125. Mohammed Séyfu in custody before execution

126. Debebe Gebru in custody before execution

127. Mulugéta Assefa in custody before execution

128. Tekle-Birhan Dessaleñ in custody before execution

129. Assefa Tedla, a military trainer in the Black Lion organisation, in custody before execution

As we have seen, several of the Young Ethiopians were also Holetta Military Academy cadets, and we are fortunate that the diplomat-writer Birhanu Dinqé published the names of cadets executed in addition to those mentioned above. His list is set out in Appendix I.

LIEUTENANT-COLONEL KETEMA BESHAH

One of the names on Birhanu Dinqé's list is that of Lieutenant-Colonel Ketema Beshah (who was educated at the Teferi Mekonnin School, French stream).[102] His execution was described by his brother, Kirubel Beshah, in his book on the Italian Occupation.[103] Ketema had been a high-ranking officer at Holetta and a senior member of the Black Lion. Kirubel's account is valuable as a historical source because he describes the circumstances of Ketema's execution, which was typical of the casual and often squalid manner in which executions were often carried out by the Italians. Once sentence of death had been passed, the process consisted of tying or chaining a number of victims together, dragging them to a patch of land on the outskirts of the city—often at night—then shooting them. Sometimes the bodies had soil shovelled over them; more often than not, they were left where they fell, at the mercy of hyenas or scavenging dogs, or thrown into a nearby river or drinking-water well.

Ketema was executed together with his friend *Qeññazmach* Kassa Abba Wukaw, whose name appears in the next section, 'The Nobility and Notables'. Kirubel tells how his brother was taken in a vehicle at night, his hands tied behind his back, to a location at the Kurtumi River near his family home in Gulelé, on land belonging to *Grazmach* Tedla Hayle-Giyorgis, and near the

130. The camera captures a lone Ethiopian being led to his death before the firing squad

house of 'Muse' (Monsieur) Samu'él, a Lazarist priest who was told the story by the Italian officer concerned.

Bravely facing his executioners, Ketema was told to turn around, but retorted, 'I will die like a soldier. Shoot at my forehead. I will not turn my back like a thief! ... I may die, but my God and my country will not. One day they will avenge me!' Ketema was shot at the side of the head, as was *Qeññazmach* Kassa Abba Wukaw. Their bodies were presumably left where they fell, for subsequently Ketema's family incurred the wrath of the Italians for requesting permission to bury him.

Apart from those identified here, many other educated Ethiopians went missing during the pogrom, most or all of whom may be presumed executed. Probably numbering more than 150, most of these additional executions were unrecorded, and their photographs before execution—if taken by the Italians—have not come to light. In any case it is likely that only those who faced a tribunal in the days immediately following *Yekatit 12* were identified and photographed. Those killed indiscriminately during the massacre were certainly not documented, and those executed subsequently were most likely not officially photographed. Appendix I contains lists of Young Ethiopians known to have been killed following *Yekatit 12*, and those unaccounted for.

In the final analysis, the programme of extermination of the Ethiopian intelligentsia as organised by Graziani and approved by Rome was quite successful, in that many of the foreign-educated Ethiopians were eliminated, as well as many of those locally educated. However, some escaped the pogrom—including those who stayed outside the country during the Occupation—and, fortunately, there were enough survivors to fill at least some of the key civil service vacancies after the Liberation. Nonetheless, there is no doubt that the Italian liquidation of the intelligentsia, together with the prohibition of any form of secondary education for Ethiopians during the five years of Occupation, had a devastating impact on the subsequent socio-economic and socio-political development of Ethiopia.

* * *

THE NOBILITY AND NOTABLES

Some of the nobles and notables hunted down after *Yekatit 12* had been present at the Governo Generale when the attack took place. They were arrested shortly after the incident, despite the fact that many of them had submitted to the Italians a few days before. Others were found at their houses, and some were identified—sometimes with the assistance of Ethiopian collaborators—among those rounded up and herded into the detention centres and makeshift prisons. The higher-level captives, that is members of the aristocracy (some of whom had submitted to the Italians and had been receiving a salary as collaborators) were deported to Italy, where they were imprisoned.

Notables whom the Italians thought might be a problem in the future (and this included numerous people simply categorised as 'Amhara chiefs') and who were not among those selected for imprisonment in Italy were executed. The most prominent ones who were rounded up immediately after *Yekatit 12* were presented at the Addis Ababa tribunals and shot.

As with the Young Ethiopians, these executions were conducted in secret. There are, however, fragments of information to be found in various contemporary reports and telegrams, one of the earliest being a mention, in the first *carabinieri* report after *Yekatit 12*, of the execution of a certain *Fitawrari* Welde-Giyorgis, who was among the small group of suspects allegedly spotted by Captain Di Dato and arrested moments after the grenades were thrown. The report stated that this *Fitawrari* was 'subservient to the will of Mr Teferi' (i.e. Emperor Haile Selassie), and had received instructions from him to keep alive patriotism among young Ethiopians. The report went on to say that at the time of his arrest the *Fitawrari* 'was found in possession of the documents that are enclosed here, from which emerge the precise instructions he received from the *Negus*'. He was reportedly also found with a large-calibre gun, but during interrogation would not make any statement, nor answer any questions—'not even to defend himself. Being found armed, he was immediately shot.'[104]

Countless other dignitaries and notables were executed, although few of their names, personal histories or photographs are now available, and for very few, if any, would there have been any tangible evidence or complaint. Appendix II contains partial lists of the nobles and notables executed, compiled from the available sources.

Hundreds of aristocrats and notables were put to death, and in addition, many were imprisoned in Italian Somaliland, Eritrea and Italy. As reported at the time by the American envoy, 'It is stated by reliable informants that nearly all prominent Ethiopians have been put to death or transported in groups for internment abroad.'[105]

But these were not the only notables put to death. Despite being a major accomplishment on the part of Birhanu Dinqé, his list hardly scratches the surface of the true extent of the massacre of the notables, for after the executions in Addis Ababa the 'tribunals' proceeded to embark on a macabre tour of the countryside, carrying with them—unbelievably—portable gallows. Like

131. A postcard for the family back home. The Italians built numerous portable gallows in kit form to be carried throughout Ethiopia for rapid assembly and disassembly. Complete with ladder and collapsible platforms, some were designed to hang six victims at a time; others, such as this one, could hang ten

medieval witch-hunters, their fearsome caravans descended on village after village and town after town, in an extraordinary and horrific public slaughter of countless innocent Ethiopian notables, elders and community leaders.

Arriving in convoys of armoured cars, Italian soldiers roared into peaceful, unsuspecting villages, surrounded the area, and started rounding up dignitaries, leaders and elders—the most committed and diligent members of their communities.

While some set up the gallows in the village square, other soldiers and colonial *askaris* shamefully dragged their victims out of their homes and from the arms of their terrified women and children. Often with their arms tied behind their back, they were hanged in full view of the entire community. This grisly and shameful episode in Italy's history was not a wild rampage conducted by a disorderly rabble. Planned and orchestrated at the highest level, and conducted with precision and complete impunity, Graziani made it clear in his written orders that it was designed to destroy all local leadership in Ethiopia and spread extreme terror.

Within little more than ten days of *Yekatit 12* and the launch of this pogrom, Graziani became impatient and ordered the military to speed things up, apparently having decided that shooting was a faster way of achieving his objective than hanging. In a telegram on 1 March he instructed General Nasi regarding Amhara notables as well as ex-army regulars: 'I order that they be immediately shot.—The hour has arrived ... Note that I have already envisaged the complete elimination of chiefs and notable Abyssinians, a measure that Your Excellency must carry out in your territories.—A better opportunity could not be found for doing so. Confirm with the phrase, "Shot."'[106]

As weeks turned into months, the caravans of death continued their inexorable passage from town to town and from village to village, spreading terror in their path with both gallows and guns. By May, the required 'complete elimination of chiefs and notable Abyssinians' was still not over. Indeed, having been discharged from hospital and clearly not satisfied that the exercise had eliminated all remaining leaders from every walk of life, on 12 May 1937, after almost three months of carnage, the furious Viceroy ordered the military to intensify its efforts still further. In another explicit telegram, dispatched to all the military governors, he ordered, 'extermination of all Amhara chiefs, great and small, must be speeded up'. The Viceroy was crystal clear about the objective: 'Once the chiefs are executed, the Amhara will be absorbed by us without difficulty. Everyone must understand that.—Civil functionaries and military commanders, without any false humanitarian pity. We must have before us a single aim: that of consolidating the conquest of the Empire.'[107]

132. Six victims hang from one of the many portable gallows used for execution of community leaders in towns and villages across Ethiopia

133. Italian soldiers line the front of the crowd to get a good view as the hangman carries a child up the steps of the gallows to her death

We do not know the final death toll. There are no records of the deaths from this countrywide pogrom, but it must have been very substantial, for Italian records indicate that by the end of 1937 5,469 Ethiopians had been executed for reasons 'directly related to Graziani's attempt', while no figures are given for the even greater numbers deemed to be 'indirectly related' or those 'suspected'.[108] By the time the slaughter was over, there remained few Ethiopians of note—particularly Amhara—apart from a handful of collaborators and the nobles who, as we shall see, had been deported to island prisons off the coast of Italy or to a horrific fate in concentration camps.

* * *

10

THE RECKONING

WHO GAVE THE ORDER?

Did Graziani initiate *carta bianca* on 19 February 1937? Dawit Oquba Igzi'i, who had studied Italian for five years, was to swear under oath that when he was being held at the *carabinieri* station near the Ras Mekonnin Bridge, he heard from the talk of the *carabinieri* and the *askaris* that Graziani himself had given the order for the massacre. 'They said that when the bomb was thrown and Graziani wounded, somebody approached him and asked if they should make reprisals. Graziani did not say much, but he answered: *"Fate"* (Do so!).'[1]

This suggests that while Graziani may have acquiesced, he might not have initiated the idea. Indeed, most reports indicate that the Viceroy was actually unconscious at the time. This would be consistent with what Rosario Gilaezgi had to say. Well connected with senior officials of the Governo Generale, Rosario stated that authorisation actually came later, by telegram from Rome: 'I have also heard that Graziani in his turn had the order from Mussolini. My superiors Avolio and Della Porta told me so. On Friday [12 Yekatit], someone sent a telegram [to Rome] in Graziani's name [seeking permission for reprisals].'[2]

It is fairly certain, according to the most reliable sources, that when struck down on the dais on Friday, Graziani was in shock, critically ill and probably unconscious when he arrived at the Italian Hospital, and was fully conscious again only after about 48 hours—that is on Sunday (following which he contracted pneumonia and remained as a hospital in-patient for more than 70 days). It is therefore unlikely that he could be said to have personally initiated *carta bianca*. Lieutenant Alberto De Turris, a military lawyer who was on the dais behind Graziani, was to note in his diary that, so far as he was able to ascertain, the orders for the massacre did not come from Graziani, but from Guido Cortese.[3] As we shall see, another Italian there at the time who was interviewed in the 1960s said, 'It is Cortese who unleashed the labourers by saying that Graziani had given the order ... but Graziani had no knowledge, [lying] injured in hospital.'[4]

So who could have sent a telegram in the Viceroy's name? Officially, it should have been Armando Petretti, who had been appointed Acting Viceroy, or possibly General Italo Gariboldi, who had taken command of the military. In reality, it might equally have been one of the other military high officials or Cortese. But in any case, the Blackshirts were pouring out of their barracks long before the *Duce's* response arrived at the Governo Generale. As Rosario testified, 'The answer came on Friday evening or Saturday morning, confirming [permission to proceed with] the killing. They did not wait, however, for the answer from Mussolini.'[5]

Professor Alberto Sbacchi confirms that both Mussolini and his Minister of Colonies, Lessona, ordered vigorous repression,[6] and one of Lessona's instructions is reproduced in Appendix III. Sent on Friday evening while the massacre was under way, it requested the Governors to take 'the most stringent measures that appear necessary locally'. The fact that Lessona sent this instruction directly to the Governors (bypassing the Viceroy), and the fact that Petretti had been appointed Acting Viceroy, suggest that Graziani was incapacitated and therefore probably not in a position to issue orders.

Graziani was in favour of mass executions for any form of opposition to Italian rule; on countless occasions during the Occupation he instructed the military in writing to massacre civilians. Indeed, after *Yekatit 12*, as we have seen, he sought permission from Lessona to execute the entire Ethiopian population of Addis Ababa. Permission not having been granted, on 27 February he decided to intern them all in concentration camps. The following day he sought approval to do precisely that, while at the same time expressing regret that concern about the possible international reaction prevented him from machine-gunning them 'en masse' or setting the entire city on fire. However, Mussolini shrank even from this moderated proposal.[7]

It is not suggested that Graziani would not have given the order for the massacre of Addis Ababa, had he been in a position to do so. But the conclusion is that the massacre carried out by the Blackshirts was basically an initiative of the Fascist Party. The gathering at Casa Littoria on Friday afternoon was definitely a party meeting, and *carta bianca* of the ferocity and barbarity of the Massacre of Addis Ababa was the domain of the Blackshirts rather than the regular army. It may be noted that Cortese had often been at loggerheads with Graziani, and at one point accused him of being anti-Fascist. Now, with the Viceroy in hospital and the ineffectual Petretti—described by Poggiali as a 'type of bureaucratic pine-cone, fastidious and inconclusive'[8]—in command of the Governo Generale, Cortese had, in effect, a free hand.

Interestingly, Graziani claims to have had at least some say in the matter. According to his own account of events, on Friday he was lying in hospital when Cortese came to see him in the evening to tell him that certain 'Fascist elements' wanted to conduct reprisals. If the visit was indeed in the evening, after 6.00 pm, then Cortese had already sent the Blackshirts on their way with his 'Go to it!' speech at Piazza. All the same, apparently sufficiently conscious by that time to be able to conduct a conversation, Graziani claimed to have told Cortese that, as head of the military, Gariboldi was 'the sole arbiter' on the subject. However, he reportedly went on to say that excesses should not be committed 'if you do not want to lose in an instant all that has been achieved'.[9]

How much veracity should be placed on Graziani's version of events we do not know, but it is fairly clear that although Petretti was appointed *de jure* Acting Viceroy, and Gariboldi was in overall command of the military, the moment Graziani fell Cortese, with his parallel party apparatus, took *de facto* control. The French consul-general was explicit in his dispatch to the Minister of Foreign Affairs in Paris, stating that the party chief had assumed authority by putting himself in Graziani's place ('*se substituant à l'autorité régulière*').[10] It is not surprising that at the earliest opportunity, while he was still in hospital, Graziani persuaded Mussolini to repatriate Cortese.[11]

The slaughter that broke out around the palace and during the Hour of Mayhem was indiscriminate and carried out in a wild frenzy by any Italians who happened to be in the vicinity, using any weapons at hand. But, following Cortese's declaration at Casa Littoria, the massacre after dark was premeditated, systematic and organised. It was led by the Blackshirts, supported by colonial troops. In addition, many Italian civilians joined in. For the most part, the regulars did not play a leading role in this phase of the massacre, although, as we shall see, some of them did participate.

In conclusion, the nocturnal 'murder, arson and pillage' phase of the Massacre of Addis Ababa was initiated, ordered and led by the federal party secretary, Guido Cortese, and approved at the highest level of the Italian government. On Sunday morning, Graziani, who had by then recovered consciousness, received orders from Rome to terminate the massacre. He passed on the orders to Cortese, who announced publicly that the massacre should end by noon on that day.

However, the liquidation of the intelligentsia and the executions of Ethiopians who had been rounded up, which took place behind the walls of detention camps, were led by a combination of the regular army, *carabinieri* and Blackshirts. It can thus be reasonably supposed that both of these activities were ordered either by Graziani himself or the acting commander-in-chief of the armed forces, Gariboldi. The inevitable conclusion is that after Graziani became fully conscious on Sunday, 21 February, both activities continued with his consent.

* * *

THE PARTICIPANTS

All published accounts and eyewitnesses of the massacre of Addis Ababa attribute the atrocity to one or more arms of the Italian military government, supported to a greater or lesser extent by Italian civilians. It is not the intention here to reiterate those accounts, but, rather, to provide an overview of the general picture painted by them, illustrated by a few typical extracts from the testimonies.

The Blackshirts

Virtually all witnesses name the Blackshirts as the party responsible for taking the lead in the massacre. Although some Ethiopian witnesses were unable to distinguish between the different types of Italian military, and had no opportunity to assess exactly who was who during the pandemonium, there were others who were aware. One such witness, who knew the difference and lived through the massacre, was Tekle-Maryam Kiflom. He was able to explain in some detail to the present author the differences between the Camicie Nere (Blackshirts) and regular soldiers such as the Bersaglieri, the Alpini and Granatieri, in terms of their background and the uniforms they wore. Tekle-Maryam was specific and definite about the leading role played by the Blackshirts in the massacre, which is consistent with other eyewitness accounts: 'These [the Blackshirts] were Mussolini's "right-hand men". They were full-time soldiers [that is not conscripts]. They received the blessing of the Pope in Rome before embarking for Ethiopia. They were the worst. They usually carried pistols. But when in action, on occasions such as this [massacre], they had rifles with bayonets.'

The overwhelming majority of the Blackshirts in Addis Ababa during the Occupation were members of the 6th Division 'Tevere', which, allowing for attrition through death, injury or sickness, would have been around 13,500 strong by February 1937. This particular division, unlike the other five involved in the invasion, consisted of an odd combination of recruits. It contained three Blackshirt regiments (*legioni*): two composed of volunteer veterans, and one of volunteers from the Italian diaspora. These were:

- the 219th Blackshirt Regiment 'Vittorio Veneto', consisting of the 219th and 319th Blackshirt Battalions made up of First World War veterans—these soldiers were considerably older than those of the regular army; (see Figure 195);
- the 220th Blackshirt Regiment, consisting of a combination of the 201st Battalion of amputees who had fought in the First World War and the 220th 'Arditi' Battalion of former First World War assault troops; and
- the 221st Blackshirt Regiment 'Italiani all'Estero' ('Italians Overseas'), consisting of the 221st and 421st Blackshirt Battalions made up of Italians who had been living abroad, outside Italy, notably in Argentina, Uruguay and Brazil, as well as in European countries such as Albania. Most had little or no military experience.[12]

In addition, unusually, the Blackshirt 'Tevere' Division contained two regular army units and one mixed unit: an Army battalion of university students, known as the Curtatone e Montanara; an artillery army battalion stationed on the Gojjam Road, not far from the Italian Hospital; and a mixed Special Engineers Company, composed of both Blackshirts and army regulars.[13]

The historian Anthony Mockler reckons that overall the 'Tevere' was 'probably Europe's strangest military unit'.[14] It was this motley collection of young and middle-aged men, single, married, educated and uneducated, worldly-wise and homespun, who bear the lion's share of responsibility for the Massacre of Addis Ababa.

Apart from the division badge worn on their left arm by soldiers of the 6th 'Tevere', the various units within the division had little in common, for the three regiments operated quite independently. The divisional command tended to serve only as an administrative organisation, each regiment, or

134. Blackshirts of the 'diaspora' 221st Regiment 'Italiani all'Estero' of the 6th 'Tevere' Division in Ethiopia alight from their 'Trenta Quattro' trucks

legione, taking on its own particular character.[15] Perhaps the most notable—and reputedly the most strongly Fascist—was the 221st Regiment 'Italiani all'Estero', which earned itself a name for creditable performance fighting off Patriot attacks on the Addis Ababa–Djibouti railway line. Many of these expatriate Blackshirts were from Argentina, which had a very large Italian diaspora (around 1.8 million at the time the Fascists took power in Italy). For years they were bombarded with propaganda to advance the Fascist ideology, and they were receptive to it, having had to leave Italy to seek prospects elsewhere owing to the poor state of the economy.[16]

The few Italians resident in Addis Ababa at the time of *Yekatit 12* who remained there after Liberation rarely talked about the massacre; indeed, most of them were unwilling—or at least very reluctant—to do so.[17] Some of the most extensive research into this small community was conducted by Fabienne Le Houérou, who interviewed 28 Italians still living in the city some fifty years after *Yekatit 12*. Most had been Blackshirts, regular soldiers or militarised labourers during the Occupation, and formed a small community of ageing men—and one or two ladies—living in modest circumstances, with some in relative poverty.

When the subject turned to *Yekatit 12*, the majority were more or less in denial about the massacre. Most did not want to respond to the questions, and several claimed that they happened to be absent from the city at the time. Few 'had the courage', as Le Houérou put it, to talk about the massacre, but one of the ladies did. Thirty-six years old at the time of the massacre, she was still filled with shame and contempt for the Blackshirts.

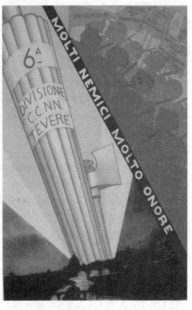

135. 'Many Enemies—Much Honour'—the slogan of the 6th Blackshirt 'Tevere' Division, which was largely responsible for carrying out the massacre of Addis Ababa

> That [*Yekatit 12* massacre] was a shame for the Italians—truly a shame. They killed so many people. I saw with my own eyes, on Ras Mekonnin Bridge, vehicles carrying thousands of corpses—mountains of corpses! This slaughter was something horrible. The Blackshirts were truly little delinquents; for Ethiopia they opened the prisons in Italy ... I had a close friend who had married the leader of the Blackshirts, and during these events [the massacre] they really played 'hunt the Abyssinians'. They were even going inside the houses. Even into the restaurants ... Many Italians were so ashamed of these massacres that they returned to Italy. I remember having heard a conversation between two officers on the Ras Mekonnin Bridge [one of] who[m] was saying, 'How can I leave my wife alone in Addis Ababa after all that has been done, after having decapitated these children?'

The reader may recall this witness adding, 'Since these events I never again saluted a Blackshirt for the rest of my life; especially this friend who was married to Guido Cortese.'[18]

Italian Civilians

It is clear from the journalist Ciro Poggiali's account that the initial slaughter on the streets was launched by Italian civilians within minutes of the incident at the palace, before the Blackshirts appeared on the streets in any substantial numbers. 'In the absence of a military or police presence, all the citizens of

Addis Ababa took on the task of revenge ... in the most authentic *squadristi* manner.'[19] Civilians continued to be involved in the Hour of Mayhem and in attacks throughout the afternoon. As the American envoy stated, 'The streets have been cleared of natives, and all Italians, *including civilian workmen*, go about heavily armed and seem to be thoroughly alarmed' (emphasis added).[20]

Similarly, while the massacre was in progress, the British envoy reported, as did his French counterpart, 'Italian soldiers *and labourers* are following the example of the Blackshirts in murdering stray Abyssinians without provocation' (emphasis added).[21] Later, in his final report on the massacre, he was more specific, stating that on Friday afternoon the indiscriminate killings were carried out by roaming bands of 'Italians in military uniform', 'Blackshirts', and 'members of the labour corps and other Italians', the latter two groups wearing civilian clothes.[22]

Moreover, the civilians did not confine themselves to the daytime onslaught. Lieutenant Meleseliñ was quite specific: 'The killings of Yekatit 12 began on the Friday. As of that day, every white man [that is, Italian], *whether soldier or civilian*, was issued permission referred to as "carta Bianca" to kill any Ethiopian irrespective of age or gender, using whatever means possible. When this instruction reached the *qebele* [local] level, it paved the way for countless Ethiopians to suffer a brutal death' (emphasis added).[23] Several witnesses noted that in the house-to-house rampage the Blackshirts were indeed accompanied by Italian civilians, who enthusiastically joined in the atrocities. Although the Blackshirts tended to take the lead in the arson, murder and pillage, there is no question that the participation of civilians was widespread.

Another of Le Houérou's interviewees held Cortese and the Fascist Party entirely responsible, as though the civilian labourers had no minds of their own: 'It is Cortese who *unleashed the workers*, by saying that Graziani had given them the order ... but Graziani had no knowledge of it, [lying] injured in hospital ...' (emphasis added).[24] As Le Houérou notes, the labourers were all card-carrying Fascist Party members; they needed to be so in order to get work on the construction sites. Furthermore, the party orchestrated to a large extent the lives of the Italians in Addis Ababa, in terms of community activities such as football matches and the cinema. This suggests that the civilians joined in the massacre under the umbrella, so to speak, of the party. We are indebted to Le Houérou for pointing out that it is clear from a statement by Major-General Bernardo Olivieri that the civilian labourers participated in the massacre, and that they were regarded as part and parcel of the party apparatus: 'The masses of labourers, equipped with weapons, were very soon ready for their involvement in the perfect Fascist organization.'[25]

These plaudits for the civilians were echoed by the *Corriere della Sera* on 3 March 1937: 'The Grand Council of Fascism has posted comradely greetings and very best wishes to the Viceroy of Italy, Marshal Rodolfo Graziani, in the certainty that he will be able to apply the right, inflexible law of Rome, and has bestowed a special tribute to the Fascists *and the Italian workers* in Addis Abeba for the attitude they adopted after the attack' (emphasis added).

The Grand Council's commendation of the civilians for their role in the massacre was confirmed in an official publication of the Rome think tank, the Fascist Institute for Italian Africa: 'For their conduct on the occasion of the attack of 19 February 1937, the Fascists earned the praise of the Grand Council. And even when, in other locations, the occurrence of predatory attacks was reported, the Party was ready to align, organize and discipline its legion of *armed civilians*, as in Addis Ababa, Gondar and Dessie' (emphasis added).[26]

It is, moreover, notable that civilian participation in the massacre was not limited to the labourers. As we have seen, Poggiali clearly stated that 'all the civilians in Addis Ababa' took part, and it is clear that members of the Italian middle class also enthusiastically joined in, as Graziani informed Minister Lessona: 'The civil metropolitan population were splendid from all points of view and from all reports. Immediately after the attempt, the bourgeois armies formed repression squads, and effectively cooperated with the *carabinieri* to maintain order.'[27]

Furthermore, Le Houérou notes that Cortese congratulated himself on the 'healthy reaction' of the Italian community during the massacre, and Professor Del Boca received confirmation of civilian involvement from Antonio Dordoni, one of the Addis Ababa-based Italian eyewitnesses whom he met in 1965. While explaining to Del Boca that many of the atrocities committed during the nocturnal arson attacks on Ethiopian families were carried out by civilians, Dordoni's testimony confirmed Poggiali's account: 'They were tradesmen, chauffeurs, officials—people I'd always thought of as law-abiding and respectable, people who'd never fired a shot during the entire war—I'd never suspected that all this hatred was bottled up in them.'[28]

Edouard Garabedian, the Armenian businessman who provided testimony for the UN War Crimes trials, was equally clear: 'I saw them with my own eyes, beating every Ethiopian they met in the streets with anything they could find. *These Italians were civilians*. They were using what they could find, as cudgels etc. This was going on until the circulation of people had finished' (emphasis added).[29]

While most of Le Houérou's interviewees refused to talk about the massacre, or pretended not to know anything about it, the one who chose to do

287

136. Civilians in office attire look at the body of an Ethiopian. The original 1945 caption of this photograph stated that the Italians were torturing the victim to obtain information. However, a separate close-up of the body shows that the victim had been shot or stabbed in the back. The relative absence of blood suggests that death occurred immediately, and that the victim might have been dead by the time this photograph was taken

so confirmed what Professor Del Boca had been told: 'We saw profession-als—the people who worked in the banks—who wore ties—saying, "Let's go and burn the *tukuls* [houses]!" But inside those houses were men, women and children. Even people from good families participated in the reprisals. They became like madmen.'[30]

In the photographs of the massacre showing civilians together with the Blackshirts, most of them are wielding shovels or pickaxes, indicating that they are most likely labourers. But in the photograph in Figure 136 the two civilians looking at an Ethiopian victim who has been stabbed or shot in the back look as if they have just come from the office. Are these two well-dressed civilians really Intelligence officers extracting information, as the original cap-tion suggested? Is one of them smiling? Or are they passers-by shocked by the scene they have encountered? We may never know, but they are clearly in no hurry to render assistance. The fact remains that many Italian civilians—probably the majority of those resident in the city—participated in the massacre, although few, if any, ever admitted having done so.

How can the enthusiastic and widespread involvement of Italian civilians in the massacre be explained? Shocking as it may seem, it should come as no surprise, given that the period from 1935 to 1937 was the golden years of Fascism. Even the doubting Thomases had joined the jubilant crowds in Italy when the 'conquest' of Ethiopia was announced. It was the *Duce*'s finest hour; he was riding on the crest of a wave of popularity. The fact is that at the time of the massacre there was close to a consensus of support among ordinary Italians for Fascism. There was strong and widespread faith in Mussolini, and a belief that he was restoring Italy to her proper place among the Great Powers, that the invasion and occupation of Ethiopia were inevitable and honourable—almost divine—missions, and that whatever methods needed to be used to 'pacify' the 'barbaric and backward natives' were fully justified and ultimately for their own good.

As the reader will understand from the closing chapters of this book, Italy as a nation after the Second World War never came to terms with the exploits of her countrymen during the invasion and occupation of Ethiopia. Following the collapse and discrediting of Fascism, most of the civilians who stayed on in Ethiopia were in a state of denial regarding the atrocities committed, the extent of their own responsibility for them, and even their membership of the Fascist Party. Consequently, it has been difficult for researchers to find Italian residents of Addis Ababa willing to talk about the excesses committed during the Occupation, even though the overwhelming majority of them—if not all—were active party members at the time. Characteristic of this phenomenon is a case recounted to the present author by Tekle-Maryam Kiflom, in which two of his Italian friends turned out long after the Occupation to have been ardent Fascists: 'Some Italian civilians pretended not to have been Fascists ... They stayed on in Ethiopia after the Occupation. Some were professional people. I will give you an example. Long after the Occupation, one such Italian, named Moltalbano, died. At his funeral, as the coffin was being lowered into the grave, an Italian friend named Montori astonished us all by crying out, "Long live Fascism!" We were all astounded. We had no idea that these two Italians had all along been Fascist supporters.'[31]

Ambassador Imru Zelleqe, who, as both a victim and a well-informed observer of the age of Fascism, is as well qualified as anyone to comment on the driving forces behind the massacre, reminded Dr Roman Herzog of the mass hysteria generated by the party and the resultant element of coercion:

The Italians generally are friendly, you know ... When they become frenetic is when they are pushed by some reason. Especially in that era ... the Fascists ... they were very rough ... it was no joke. Even some of the clerks in the bank there, on Sunday, came out in the Piazza in Addis [Ababa], and they had this black uniform and their knives and so forth. And then *saluti Fascisti*, they were 'screaming [blue] murder' there, every Sunday. And every Italian had to go there and parade, no joke! Oh, the Italians had to toe the line. I mean, not all of them were particularly violent ... but they had to follow the line.[32]

Regular Italian Troops

While reports of Blackshirt atrocities in the streets and especially at night are widespread, accusations of the involvement of regular (conscripted) soldiers are considerably less common. Generally, the impression is gained that while the regulars were certainly involved in the daytime raids, the accounts of the systematic massacre carried out at night do not generally incriminate them. As Dr Birhanu Abebe put it, 'There was a difference between the Blackshirts and the regular soldiers. The Blackshirts were the Fascists. Regular soldiers and civilians were not necessarily Fascists, and did not necessarily commit or even condone the atrocities.'[33]

A British Intelligence report went so far as to declare, 'The regular soldiers took no part in it [the nightly house-burning].'[34] Ethiopian accounts sometimes support this position. For example, these reports based on statements from Ethiopians who fled the massacre and reached Djibouti are typical:

He ['our informant'] says that this slaughter was the work of the Blackshirts and labour auxiliaries, and not of the regular troops, totaling one division, still stationed in the capital.[35]

To their credit, the metropolitan troops showed signs of indignation in carrying out the terrible [massacre] order. They hastened to limit their mission to occupying the fortified positions around the city, so as to bar the way to fugitives with the combined fire of artillery and machine guns.[36]

According to Dr Shashka, some regulars actually distanced themselves from the massacre. 'In all fairness I must say that I spoke also to Italian officers and soldiers who were bitterly indignant, who accused their chiefs, and who said that they had nothing to do with the massacre, either with its idea, or with its carrying out.'[37] Indeed, some regulars tried to restrain the Blackshirts. As noted earlier, the French envoy reported that they 'were trying hard to control the Fascist elements'. Interviewed in 1941 by the *Ethiopian Star*, the renowned female Patriot, Shewareged Gedlé, said, 'The Blackshirts were the worst; they were so bloodthirsty that the Italian soldiers and caribineers often tried to stop them killing'.[38]

So can it be said that in general the regulars actively opposed the massacre? Or did they simply stand and watch? The reminiscences of Sergeant-Major Boaglio of the Granatieri di Savoia provide the answer: there was no clear blanket instruction. While the regulars were most likely not ordered to participate, neither were they ordered to restrain the Blackshirts. The choice of trying to moderate the Blackshirts was a matter of personal inclination. He tells how the commander of the Piazza area, General Perego, 'helped in every way to stop the useless carnage', and that Boaglio himself volunteered, in the evening, to become part of 'the first volunteer patrols that were sent to restrain that orgy of blood'.

It was while he was on such a patrol that the simmering tension between the conscripts and the less disciplined but much-vaunted and more privileged Blackshirts bubbled to the surface. During the nocturnal massacre one of his men—a certain Lieutenant Freda—spotted a group of Blackshirts about to set fire to a house to which a telephone cable was connected. Presumably in an attempt to prevent a breakdown in the telephone system, he pulled out his gun and pointed it at the Blackshirt captain concerned, to stop him in his tracks. In response the captain drew his gun and aimed it point-blank at the lieutenant. It was a dangerous impasse. Nobody moved. Then at that moment there occurred what Boaglio termed a tragi-comic incident: a nearby flaming eucalyptus tree came crashing down between the two hot-headed men. They both leapt backwards, bringing the incident to an unexpected and 'providential' end, as Boaglio put it.

Although the majority of the regular soldiers did not join in the massacre, some individuals did. For example, Colonel Azolino Hazon, commander of the *carabinieri*, wrote in a report on the activities of the Granatieri that they were at that time 'gathering together the corpses made ready, and continuing to burn the *tukuls*'.[39] This is consistent with some of the photographs in this book, which show army officers overseeing such activities. It is also significant inasmuch as the Granatieri de Savoia, the 65th Infantry Division of Grenadiers, was the principal regular army force in Addis Ababa at the time of *Yekatit 12*.[40] Thus the report by the commander of the *carabinieri* constitutes compelling evidence that some members of the regular army—notably, the Grenadiers—directly or indirectly supported the nocturnal massacre. It may be recalled that the British envoy, William Bond, reported that during the daylight attacks of 19 February, '*Italian soldiers* and labourers are following this example of the Blackshirts in murdering stray Abyssinians without provocation' (emphasis added).[41] The British envoy's final comment on the subject was that while it might perhaps be true of the soldiers and *carabinieri* that they were less criminal than others, the evidence against them was too convincing to absolve them from serious blame, although it may often have been difficult to differentiate between the regular troops and the militia owing to the similarity of uniforms.[42]

The uniforms were indeed similar; the Blackshirts wore a khaki jacket similar to that of the regular army, and their regulation shirts were often khaki rather than black. But apart from the similarity of the uniforms, it should also be recalled that the 6th Blackshirt Division 'Tevere' contained two regular army battalions and one mixed company.[43] These regulars were thus within a Blackshirt unit, and could therefore have been in action with their Blackshirt colleagues.

It can be concluded that although the regular army as a body was not responsible for the street slaughter or the nocturnal massacre (the majority 'keeping calm', while standing back and watching without intervening), some participated—most likely the regular army battalions, the mixed company attached to the 6th Blackshirt 'Tevere' Division, and the Granatieri de Savoia, to which was attached the 11th Blackshirt Battalion.[44] On the other hand, other Granatieri officers and their men actively attempted to restrain the Blackshirts. In summary, while some regulars participated in the daytime attacks, including arson, few joined in the night-time slaughter, which was led by the Blackshirts.[45]

However, the regular army enforced the curfew. Sergeant-Major Boaglio recounts how the orders were to 'shoot on sight anyone who did not stop, or had a suspicious demeanour'. As he pointed out, this enabled him, if he so desired, 'to kill with impunity any native or European' whom he encountered. Although Boaglio assured his readers that his conscience was clear—that he himself 'never committed any act of cruelty'—it is clear that, with orders like that, some of his more trigger-happy colleagues would have been tempted to do so.

The regulars were also involved in organising the detention centres, the rounding up of captives, imprisoning them in harsh conditions, and carrying out executions. Because these deaths occurred largely out of sight, the true extent of the culpability of the regular army in this widespread civilian slaughter has gone largely unrecognised.

The Carabinieri

The role played by the *carabinieri* in the massacre was somewhat similar to that of the regular army. Some testimonies state that they were involved, but most claim that they were not.[46] Some are ambiguous, such as Graziani's report to Lessona, which stated, 'Immediately after the attempt, the bourgeois armies formed repression squads, and effectively cooperated with the *carabinieri* to maintain order.' It may appear from this statement that the 'repression squads' burned and killed jointly with the *carabinieri*, under the rubric of 'maintaining order'. Did Graziani mean that the *carabinieri* were themselves involved in the work of the 'repression squads'? It is not clear. But whether some of the *carabinieri* participated or not, there is general agreement among the eyewitness accounts that they did little or nothing to stop the massacre. Some *carabinieri* officers, who were generally considered to be royalists rather than Fascists (they were, after all, the 'Royal Carabinieri'), seem to have tried to maintain law and order; others apparently acquiesced in the activities of the Blackshirts. As we have seen, the British envoy believed that the regulars and the *carabinieri* might have been 'less criminal than the others', but the evidence against them 'is too convincing to absolve them from serious blame'.

While the present author encountered no testimonies of *carabinieri* being directly engaged in street-level atrocities or the nocturnal massacre, most of them seem to have either made themselves scarce or stood by and allowed the slaughter to take its course, intervening only on occasions or when ordered to do so. As the eyewitness Antonio Dordoni told Professor Del Boca, 'To my knowledge the police only intervened once when the mob threatened to set fire to Mohamedally's emporium.'[47] However, they certainly ran Akaki concentration camp, and were involved in the running of some of the detention camps in Addis Ababa. The Central Police Station at Fit Ber served as their headquarters, so they cannot be absolved from the atrocities perpetrated there.

ERITREAN ASKARIS

Eritrean *askaris* accounted for a large proportion of the regular Italian troops, and some of them participated in the massacre. In Dr Birhanu's account of the raid on his home in the Tekle Haymanot district of Addis Ababa, he said, 'The Eritrean *bande* were very much involved in the massacre.'[48] However, some refused to participate, and this issue is discussed further in the later section 'Unsung Heroes'.

Somali Askaris

Some writers—notably Birhanu Dinqé—mention the participation of Somali *askaris* (from Italian Somaliland) in the massacre He states that the Somali '*bandas*' burned houses and killed the occupants 'as ordered'.[49] However, the present author has not been able to gather sufficient evidence to reach any broad conclusions regarding the extent of their participation.

Libyan Askaris

Several accounts mention the involvement of Libyan *askaris* in the massacre. Being Muslim, and believing—or having had it drummed into them—that they needed to take revenge on Ethiopian Christians for the actions of Eritrean *askaris* deployed in the past by the Italians in Libya, they often seized the opportunity to do so. Thus the Italians deployed Libyan *askaris* in the colonial battalions in Ethiopia to carry out atrocities, particularly against Christian civilians.

The Libyan *askaris* quickly acquired a reputation for being the most cruel of the perpetrators. Ethiopian refugees from the massacre arriving in Djibouti reported that the Blackshirts and the Libyan *askaris* 'gave themselves up with a joyful heart to the lugubrious business. Revolvers, hand grenades, daggers and clubs were distributed to them freely, and the order *avanti* ("forward!") was given.'[50] Specifically, the Libyans were accused of being responsible for the disembowelling scenes that came to light when the sun rose after the nights of *carta Bianca*. 'The Libyans, whose savage instinct was exalted by the example of their masters, who excited them more by saying this was their day of great vengeance, specialized in cutting the throats of their unfortunate victims or in disembowelling them in cold blood and leaving them to die slowly in terrible agony.'[51]

While not every refugee report can necessarily be taken at face value, it may be noted that this account is consistent with the testimony of the Italian medical officer Manlio La Sorsa, who stated that the Italians deliberately delegated the application of 'barbaric, ferocious and inhuman methods' to the Libyan *askaris*.

Ethiopian Askaris

When the Italians invaded Ethiopia, inhabitants of some regions of the empire who regarded Emperor Haile Selassie as their traditional enemy supported the

Italians, and some Ethiopian soldiers defected to the Italians after being defeated. Thus, by early 1937 the Italian army included a number of platoons made up entirely of Ethiopian soldiers, such a platoon subsequently being referred to as a *banda*, the Italian for 'group' (plural, *bande*). There is testimony that some of these Ethiopian soldiers, or *askaris*, were involved in the massacre, at least in certain districts. For example, Dr Birhanu Abebe told the present author that some of them took part in the nocturnal attack on his family home.[52]

Polizia Coloniale

Some of the Colonial Police, consisting principally of Eritreans, Libyans and Ethiopians, reportedly took part in the massacre. Ambassador Imru, who watched the massacre unfold, was to write, 'Thousands died and were maimed by the Italians who were using guns, bayonets, knives, even picks and shovels to prey on people, indiscriminate of age and gender. The *Camicie Nere* (Blackshirts Fascist cadre), the *Legione di Lavoro* (Workers' Legion) and the *Polizia Coloniale* (Colonial Police) had a field day.'[53]

Ethiopian Civilian Collaborators

In due course the term '*banda*' was popularly used by Ethiopians to mean not necessarily a group of colonial (Eritrean, Somali or Libyan) or even Ethiopian *askaris*, but an individual Ethiopian collaborator or traitor. Some of these '*bandas*' assisted the Italians by pointing out Ethiopians in the detention camps whose names were on Italian death lists. Although Ethiopian witnesses do not often mention this somewhat unpalatable fact, it must be remembered that not all Ethiopians supported the Emperor, and there were many opportunists who defected to the Italians. Dr Birhanu learned from his mother that during the massacre '*bandas*' identified Ethiopians wanted by the Italians, and assisted them by searching for Ethiopians who were in hiding. One nod from the informer, and their fate was sealed.[54]

THE VICTIMS

Who were the victims of the massacre of Addis Ababa? One might suppose that they were principally men, together with a few women and children. But this is not so. Women and children suffered in disproportionately large numbers—particularly in the nocturnal house-burning. The principal reason for this was that thousands of husbands and grown-up sons had been arrested and detained on Friday afternoon, and the situation was exacerbated by the fact that, by the time of the arson of the second night (Saturday), a significant proportion of the remaining men had fled the city. Another factor was that in some cases women were deliberately targeted. A contemporary Ethiopian writer commented on the widespread victimisation of women during the massacre, lamenting, 'Suffering can be normal to the male, but a very large number of females were killed, harassed or imprisoned without having done anything wrong.'[55]

The violence meted out to women and children during the massacre was extreme. Some accounts—impossible to verify, since most witnesses of such atrocities died—speak of the disembowelling of pregnant women.[56] One published report had the attackers whipping women to death in front of their husbands and crushing babies. 'Others [groups of Fascists] entertained themselves by scourging naked women to death under the eyes of their husbands or brothers, who were, of course, first rendered impotent ... Still others derived devilish pleasure out of crushing the little ones made orphans a few minutes previously with their enormous heavy boots (*gadasses*)'.[57] In addition, many children were burned alive, often trapped in the inferno, as the French envoy informed Paris: 'In the midst of the remnants of burned *tukuls* were found the bodies of small children that mothers who had panicked had been forced to abandon, and who had been burned to ashes inside these houses.'[58]

The violence meted out to the youngest victims was particularly shocking; at least one Ethiopian writer compared it with the systematic extermination of children by King Herod.[59] Numerous witnesses testify to having seen babies and small children who had escaped from their burning houses being lifted up and thrown back into the flames. Indeed, this phenomenon was so widespread and so well known as to have been represented clearly in the bronze reliefs on the *Yekatit 12* monument (see Figure 137).

Professor Harold Marcus, who interviewed many Ethiopians, highlighted the extraordinary degree of savagery involved: 'People were beaten and stoned until dead. Women were scourged, men were emasculated, and children crushed under foot; throats were cut—people were disemboweled and left to die, or hung, or stabbed to death.'[60]

Mutilation was certainly commonly practised, as confirmed by the battle-hardened medical specialist Dr Shashka: 'Murder was accompanied by the most horrible mutilation possible to imagine.'[61] The victims were sometimes children, as the French consul-general reported: 'On the road to the British

Consulate, a child of 12–13 years was killed by a bullet then disembowelled with a bayonet, under the eyes of the American Consul, [who was] powerless to stop this act of brutality.'[62]

Together with bayoneting (which was popular with the Blackshirts), decapitation—followed by the display of the victims' heads—was something of a Blackshirt obsession during the Occupation. Moreover, judging from the number of photographs of such scenes left behind by the Italians, decapitation was also popular with both regulars and civilians. There is no reason to imagine that decapitation was not carried out during the Massacre of Addis Ababa; the reader may recall the Italian officer asking his colleague, 'How can I leave my wife alone in Addis Ababa after all that has been done, after having decapitated these children?'

137. Women struggle with the Blackshirts to prevent their children being thrown to their death into the burning houses. Detail, bronze relief on the *Yekatit 12* monument

138. Women with their babies are crushed as their house is demolished by a tank. Detail of bronze relief on the *Yekatit 12* monument

Commenting on the general level of violence employed by the Italians, Imru Zelleqe reflected, 'First, I think they were, let's say, not very violent at the beginning, because they wanted to consolidate. They were not particularly violent during the first few months. And when this thing happened their real character came out, because they wanted to colonise the country, and obviously they were not going to do it with gloves on. So when the occasion came, they showed their true hand, and were extremely violent.'[63]

As Dr Shashka noted, 'There is no means of destroying human life that was not employed on the night of the 19th of February 1937 ... I am reluctant to tell everything. No one in my place, unless he is a monster, could tell these things without a great revulsion, and the necessity of overcoming the natural dislike to reveal that such shameful deeds were done by white men like himself. But it is my duty to speak.'[64]

Among the testimonies are claims of the sexual abuse of women. Such reports are, naturally, difficult to substantiate, since few, if any, Ethiopian witnesses of these atrocities survived. However, the fact is that the Blackshirts had a notorious reputation for abuse of local women at all times—not to mention during a massacre. Eritrean women told horror stories of the sufferings of women in Asmara caught by Blackshirt gangs,[65] and Ethiopian families often complained about their daughters being dragged out of their house by rampaging militia, despite their parents having posted 'Family Home' signs at their gates. Indeed, every Ethiopian house was said to be a potential 'house of pleasure' for the Blackshirts, who sometimes broke into schools and hostels to take away young women to houses used as temporary brothels. Dr Shashka wrote, 'Several times I witnessed the deportation of women to such houses with revolting violence, one girl being attacked by three or four armed soldiers of civilisation!'[66]

Given such reports, one can only imagine the outrages perpetrated by the Blackshirts during the massacre of Addis Ababa, when they were drunk, excited, and told to do as they please. Indeed, Sergeant-Major Boaglio was shocked that colleagues he had come to respect became 'fiercely avid' to rape young girls with impunity during the massacre, as their homes burned to the ground.[67]

Apart from the question of sexual abuse, many Blackshirts certainly used an extraordinary level of violence towards their female victims during the massacre, particularly in the arson attacks. While some showed mercy and allowed women to leave before their homes were set on fire, others took pleasure in bayoneting them or burning them alive. The Italian authorities declared miscegenation to be anti-Fascist, and although the use of Ethiopian women for prostitution was still permitted, cohabitation or any form of affection towards them was outlawed and became a criminal offence.[68] Doubtless these factors would have driven some Blackshirts to avoid showing sympathy towards women, lest their sympathy be misinterpreted by their peers.

Another category of victim that suffered disproportionately was the sick and disabled. The bedridden and immobile, who were unable to flee before their homes were set on fire, were inevitably burned alive, as in this example provided by the French consul-general: 'In front of a property occupied by a Frenchman stood a hut where two native women lived, of which one was blind and the other lame. When the militiamen menacingly appeared, with the help of neighbours the blind one was able to escape somehow. The lame one, unable to move on her own, was burned alive, on her own couch, in the inferno of the hut.'[69]

* * *

UNSUNG HEROES

Even the massacre of Addis Ababa had its bright points—unsung heroes, most of whom will never be known. Who knows how many relatives, friends and even strangers sacrificed their lives in the face of the marauding Fascist mobs, in their desperate efforts to protect the innocent??

Immahoy Hiruta risked her life on several occasions to help people escape from Fit Ber detention camp during the massacre, and no doubt there were many other unsung Ethiopian heroes of whom we have no knowledge. When she arrived at the prison to visit her relatives, the *Immahoy* was told, 'Enter and look for them!' She explained, 'They were making a mark on the forehead and tongue of each visitor. The visitors had to show their tongue at the entrance and exit. If there was no mark, they had to stay behind.' Someone lent her a marker, which she smuggled into the prison while wearing several dresses, one on top of the other. Once inside, she took off some of her clothes and gave them to prisoners. She marked their tongues, and they managed to escape. 'The prisoners were wearing my dresses. [In that way] I got my relatives and neighbours out.'[70]

Several Addis Ababa residents—particularly Armenians and Greeks—hid Ethiopians in their houses, despite door-to-door raids by Blackshirts and *carabinieri*. We have already noted the examples of Mrs Karibian, the Lentakis family and Mr Mavrikos, and there were certainly many more.[71] Another notable case involved an Italian family—notable, because Italians who appeared to oppose the Fascist system in any way were liable to receive particularly harsh treatment, even execution. Dr Iago Bossi, a communications expert, had been conscripted in 1935 into the regular army and subsequently sent to Ethiopia, where he was billeted in Addis Ababa with his wife. During the three-day *carta bianca*, Italian residents, like all foreigners, were expected to hand over their male servants to be rounded up, and this necessarily included Gutama, Dr Bossi's house servant. Dr Bossi's grandson, Nicola Antonio DeMarco, tells the story: 'Rather than hand him over, they hid him, along with a dozen of his relatives, in a shed, and clandestinely fed them during the night until the reprisals ended. My mother [Dr Bossi's daughter], who was ten at the time, recounts seeing twelve terrified faces one night when she happened to go into the shed with her father. For this act my grandparents would themselves have been shot. I am inordinately proud of them.'[72] DeMarco has good reason to be proud of his grandparents, for one recalls the young Imru Zelleqe hearing the screams of Italians regarded as anti-Fascist being tortured in the *carabinieri* cells beneath his family home in Arada.

Apart from individuals who risked arrest to protect Ethiopians in their private houses, there were two cases of large-scale sheltering of Ethiopians. Some were allowed to take refuge at the British legation, but the principal places of refuge were the American legation, under envoy Cornelius Engert, and the German Hermannsburg Mission in Qechené, under Hermann Bahlburg. These two men represented beacons of hope for the desperate men, women and children who sought refuge in their compounds. It would not be too wide of the mark to say that they were Addis Ababa's equivalents of John Rabe, the German who would organise the International Safety Zone during the Massacre of Nanking a few months later, starting in December 1937.[73]

The Western Safety Zone: The American Legation

The only people who were relatively free to venture out into the melée were foreign diplomats. However, this was not without its dangers, because they did not enjoy diplomatic immunity strictly speaking, under the Graziani administration. The most outstanding foreigner in this category was undoubt-ledly Cornelius Engert, the American consul-general, who repeatedly drove out into the city, stood up to the Italians, and tried to restrain them whenever he could.

When Italian high-level officials drove into Fitawrari Habte Giyorgis Sefer during the arson of Friday night, their interpreter Rosario Gilaegzi noted that the American legation had 'assembled all its neighbours in their compound'. Indeed, Engert had taken it upon himself to permit large numbers of Ethiopians from the surrounding districts to shelter in the legation grounds. In his own words, 'Several hundred natives including women and children inhabiting the burning huts surrounding this Legation came into our compound. As they climbed over the fences during the night in order to save their lives I was of course powerless to stop them. However, even if I had been able to keep them out I should not have done so because I felt that the most elementary dictates of humanity and decency required that they be permitted to seek refuge in the only place available to them ... So far the Italians are hardly aware of their exist-ence but should they request that they leave our compound I shall first demand a definite assurance that they will not be hunted down like wild beasts.'[74]

Despite a combination of Blackshirts and armed Italian civilians threaten-ing to enter the compound and drag out the refugees, Engert bravely stood his ground, and continued to resist the Fascist mob for three nights. The American legation became the principal safety zone in Addis Ababa, as it had been during the riots of May 1936, when the Emperor left the city. Finding the safety of his legation and staff threatened by Fascist execution squads and flames from nearby burning buildings, the American minister made repeated requests for assistance, but to no avail.[75]

139. The American consul-general, Cornelius Engert, standing at the entrance of his legation building, flanked by armed guards. Engert insisted on allowing hundreds of Ethiopians fleeing the massacre to shelter in the legation grounds

At 3.00 pm on Tuesday, 23 February, Engert informed Washington that he had called on Colonel Mazzi, the Chef de Cabinet, to inform him that there were 400 or 500 hundred refugees in the compound, whom he would send out only on condition that Mazzi provide 'formal assurance' that no harm would be done to them and that if possible food would be provided temporarily for those who were destitute. Colonel Mazzi said that he would issue the most emphatic orders that none of the refugees should be touched. 'He then called on the acting commandant of the *carabinieri* and instructed him to that effect in my presence, adding that food should be provided and homes found for those needing them and that anybody molesting them should be severely punished. I expect that by tomorrow night most of the natives will have left our compound.'[76]

Many years later, Morris Weerts, manager of A. Besse & Co., was to recall that at the American legation 'truly thousands of refugees took shelter, protected by the US flag until the Fascist authorities might recover their self-control. The firm attitude of Mr Eggerth [*sic*] prevented the arrest and death of many Ethiopians at that time.'[77]

The Northern Safety Zone: The German Hermannsburg Mission

Throughout the massacre, Hermann Bahlburg, head of the German Hermannsburg Mission at Qechené, reportedly sheltered Ethiopians seeking refuge at what was the largest fenced compound in the area. *Carabinieri* went to the mission with machine guns to kill anyone found hiding there, and it took all of Bahlburg's diplomacy and cunning to ward them off. Telling the refugees to carry soil and to claim that they were mission workers if asked, he managed to control the situation. The *carabinieri* and Blackshirts were kept out, and the refugees were allowed to stay. Thus, in a manner not unlike that of Oskar Schindler in Nazi-controlled Poland, Bahlburg is said to have saved the lives of around 200 Ethiopians.[78]

The British Legation

The acting consul-general, William Bond, reported that no Ethiopians took refuge in the British legation grounds, which he attributed to the approaches being well patrolled, and 'probably because the Marshal's house (formerly the Italian legation) is in the neighbourhood'.[79] This was a strange statement to make, because we know from eyewitnesses that in fact the British legation was a safe haven for several residents of the city, as it had been during the breakdown of law and order in May 1936.

We do not know how many people sought—and received—sanctuary at the British legation, but one of them was Demissé Hayle-Maryam, a young relative of *Bejirond* Letyibelu Gebré. In interviews with the present author,

140. Hermann Bahlburg (pictured here in Germany after the war)

303

141. Within these gates, largely unchanged since 1937, 200 Ethiopians are believed to have been given sanctuary by Hermann Bahlburg to escape the marauding Blackshirts during the massacre of Addis Ababa

he described how, as a 15-year-old boy, he walked on the morning of 12 Yekatit to the Church of Yeka Mika'él beyond the British legation.

After the service he learned that there was trouble in the city, and witnessed a clash between Italian soldiers and one of the priests of Yeka Mika'él. In the company of some other men he then ran to the British legation, where the guards opened the gates and let them in. Demissé stayed at the legation. Here he and his compatriots were given shelter, food and water for five days, leaving only when it was relatively safe to do so (on Tuesday, 23 February).

Why the envoy chose to tell London that there were no refugees at the legation is not clear. Furthermore, his comment that the fact that 'the Marshal's house is in the neighbourhood' might have explained the apparent absence of Ethiopian refugees at the legation is also difficult to understand. Although the eastern quarter of the city where the British legation was located also accommodated the Belgian consulate, Graziani's residence (at the former Italian legation) was more than three kilometres' journey from the British legation, and Italian patrols securing his house would not have been in a position to protect the British legation. In any case Graziani regarded the envoys as private individuals, for the instructions from Rome were that they were not to have diplomatic immunity.

In conclusion, it seems possible that Bond was unaware that his guards were allowing Ethiopians to take refuge there. After all, the legation compound covered some 90 acres. In this case it might actually have been the legation guards who were the unsung heroes.

142. Demissé Hayle-Maryam, pictured here in the 1940s, sheltered at the British legation from the massacre of Addis Ababa

Among the Fascists

It may come as a surprise that there were also Fascist heroes. We have seen that there were officers of the Granatieri di Savoia who tried to restrain the Blackshirts, and of course there might have been Blackshirts who did not wholeheartedly agree with what their colleagues were doing, and who in a moment of compassion or remorse might have persuaded them not to consign a woman or child to the flames. Of such cases we will probably never know. But we do know that even within the High Command, the Fascist Party secretary, Guido Cortese, was not entirely unchallenged in launching the three days of unlimited arson, murder and pillage. It is not widely known that two senior officials in the Italian administration attempted to put a stop to it. They were Carlo Avolio and Count Gherardo Della Porta. While it might be an overstatement to describe these two men as heroes, it should be acknowledged that they made an effort to have the massacre brought to an end, and indeed they are the only Italian high officials known to have done so. Both men were senior figures in the Italian High Command. Carlo Avolio was the head of political affairs, and Gherardo Della Porta was a high-ranking official in charge of security at the Governo Generale when the grenades were thrown, and was thereafter never trusted by Graziani.

The Eritrean interpreter Rosario Gilaezgi provided testimony for the UN War Crimes Commission that on Friday evening (the first day of the massacre)

143. Carlo Avolio tried to have the massacre of Addis Ababa brought to an end

Avolio and Della Porta, whom he referred to as his superiors,[80] went to plead with Armando Petretti, Graziani's deputy, who had been appointed Acting Viceroy while Graziani was in hospital. Apparently concerned at the mass hysteria and bloodlust that had taken hold of the Blackshirts and the civilian party members who had joined them in the carnage, Avolio and Della Porta drove through the mayhem for the meeting. 'I followed them in the car to Petretti,' said Rosario.[81]

Upon arrival—presumably at the Governo Generale—Avolio went in to see Petretti to express his shock and plead for restraint, while Della Porta and Rosario waited outside. The fact that Della Porta fell out of favour with the Viceroy's office following the attack at the Governo Generale, and was probably anxious that Graziani might die, could explain why he did not want to meet Petretti.[82]

Shocked at the atrocities being perpetrated, Avolio remonstrated with Petretti: 'See what you are doing!' The Acting Viceroy, apparently sympathetic and willing to cooperate, agreed to go to the Italian Hospital to see Graziani. In due course Petretti reported to Avolio that he had visited Graziani at the hospital, as promised. It is not clear who was at the hospital at that time with Graziani, and it is not known what transpired there. Whether the injured Viceroy took a hard line, whether he would not be moved to prevail over Cortese, or whether he was asleep or unconscious at the time, we may never know, but the upshot was that Petretti failed in his mission.[83] Petretti was not, in any case, a decisive person, was not close to Graziani, and probably had little influence over Cortese.

Nonetheless, Avolio did try again. On Saturday night, as the city was again ablaze, he went to see Petretti once more, but again made no progress. According to Rosario, 'Both on Friday and on Saturday we wanted to find out what Graziani had said.' But although Petretti was formally in overall command, all Avolio could get out of the Acting Viceroy was, 'These men [i.e. the Blackshirts] are barbaric and nothing can be done.'[84]

Eritrean Askaris

It is not widely known that a significant number of Eritrean *askaris* refused to join in the massacre unleashed by *carta bianca*. In 2004 the former soldier *Shaleqa* Éfrém Gebre-Amlak told the present author that from a study he had made it was clear that, although some Eritreans did participate in the massacre of Addis Ababa, there were also many who refused to do so.[85]

The Italians were, of course, aware that there had been defections of their colonial troops to the Ethiopian side during the war of invasion. Despite the stereotype of their 'faithful Eritrean *askaris*' (an image earned largely in action for the Italians in Libya), the Italians were constantly haunted by the spectre of the Eritrean rank and file refusing to shoot their Ethiopian cousins. The boundary between Ethiopia and Eritrea, which ran along the Mereb River, was, of course, an artificial one. Prior to Menelik's granting of the land north of the Mereb to Italy, neither the name nor even the concept of Eritrea existed. There was no particular social distinction between Ethiopians living on either side of the river.[86] Thus many Ethiopians had been born on the northern side of the river, and many Eritreans on the southern side. Indeed, several high-ranking officials of the Ethiopian government were born north of the Mereb, including men such as Lorenzo Ta'izaz, and this was generally not considered in Ethiopia to be strange or problematic. Furthermore, although Italian missionaries had converted many Eritreans to Catholicism, there were still numerous Orthodox Christians in Eritrea.

Such concerns caused the Italians to hesitate to deploy Eritreans—particularly Christian battalions—in sensitive situations involving Ethiopians. For example, this same concern was behind the Italian decision to use a specially created Muslim battalion—the 45th—to carry out the massacre of the Monastery of Debre Libanos in May 1937.[87] According to *Shaleqa* Éfrém, a similar situation arose when Graziani was admitted to the Italian Hospital following the attack of *Yekatit 12*: 'The area immediately around the hospital was evacuated for security reasons and ringed with tanks and about 1,000 soldiers. However, Eritrean soldiers were not assigned to this duty, because some of them had refused to kill Ethiopians.'[88] The *Shaleqa* explained that some of the Eritrean *askaris* protested against *carta bianca*, as a result of which they were shot by the Italians. Showing the present author a photograph of his uncle in Italian military uniform, he said, 'This was my mother's brother. He protested [against *carta bianca*]. His friends [who also protested] were killed, but not him.'

In fact, within a few weeks of *Yekatit 12* information on this issue had reached Sylvia Pankhurst in England, who in April 1937 published a report stating that Eritrean *askaris* refused to join in the massacre, declaring that, being soldiers, they could not be used to slaughter women and children or even defenceless men. 'They were thereupon shut up in their barracks and several among them were shot.'[89]

In 1943 Birhanu Dinqé stated that when the Italians were not looking, some of the Eritrean *askaris* tipped off a number of Ethiopians, warning them to leave before the burning squads took action—a less confrontational but probably more widespread form of resistance.[90]

In conclusion, the true extent of refusal by Eritrean *askaris* to join in the Massacre of Addis Ababa—and Signor Marino, an Italian soldier who remained in Addis Ababa after the Liberation, gives the impression that the rank and file were *ordered* to do so—is unclear. It is, however, reasonably certain that many of them attempted to assist the Ethiopians, and a significant number of them refused point-blank to participate in the massacre, paying for that refusal with their lives.

* * *

THE DEATH TOLL

How many people died in the massacre of Addis Ababa? There have been several published estimates, falling roughly into the following broad ranges:

- 600–2,000 (principally Italian figures);
- 3,000–8,000 (typically European, diplomatic and media estimates);
- 14,000–20,000 (Dr Shashka, Wazir Ali Baig and a number of individual Italians in Addis Ababa at the time; for example, *Shaleqa* Éfrém Gebre-Amlak told the present author, 'An Italian told me that about 20,000 people died in the massacre';[91] and the writer Stephen Mannucci states, 'Many [Italian] soldiers told of *tukuls* burned with women and children inside, and about 20,000 indigenous people massacred in a single night');[92]
- 30,000 (Ethiopian government).

At first sight these figures seem to vary so widely as to render reconciliation almost impossible. However, on closer inspection there is more consistency between the various estimates than is immediately apparent, since a great deal of the variation is due to differences of opinion and perception as to what actually constituted the Massacre of Addis Ababa. For example, the lower estimates generally refer only to the *carta bianca* killings that accompanied the arson of the nights of 19 and 20 February, prior to the announcement of termination. They thus exclude the shooting of the 3,000 in the palace grounds, the unofficial slaughter that preceded *carta bianca*, deaths during the arson of 21 February that occurred after the termination order had been given, the killings that continued for about one additional week, the deaths in detention, and the executions that were carried out in parallel by the military, some of which had a veneer of due process and were thus not regarded by the Italian authorities as part of the massacre.

On the other hand, the much-published high figure of 30,000 of the Ethiopian government appears to have been intended to cover 'the Graziani Massacres', that is not only all aspects of the Massacre of Addis Ababa, but also massacres that took place in parallel in other towns, as well as the pogroms against various segments of Ethiopian society that were triggered by *Yekatit 12* and that continued long after the three days of *carta bianca*.

Thus, before a reasoned and evidence-based estimate can be made, it is necessary to decide what precisely is covered when we speak of 'the Massacre of Addis Ababa'. For the purposes of this analysis, the present author regards the Massacre of Addis Ababa as consisting of the deaths of residents of Addis Ababa that occurred in the city as a direct result of *Yekatit 12*, and that would most likely not have occurred had *Yekatit 12* not taken place. This definition covers the following:

(i) deaths within the grounds of the Governo Generale immediately after the grenades were thrown;

(ii) the Circle of Death—killings in the streets and houses lying within the cordon flung around the perimeter of the Governo Generale;

(iii) indiscriminate killings during the unofficial rampage in Siddist Kilo and Arada, which took place during the Hour of Mayhem;

(iv) those residents of Addis Ababa rounded up during and after the curfew of Friday, 19 February, and on Saturday, 20 February, who died in custody or were taken from detention and executed;

(v) random killings throughout the city during the afternoon of Friday, 19 February;

(vi) victims of the late afternoon and early evening *carta bianca* attacks of Friday, 19 February;

(vii) victims of the authorised nocturnal *carta bianca* arson attacks in Addis Ababa of 19, 20 and 21 February and beyond;

(viii) victims of random daytime attacks in Addis Ababa by Italians, using military weapons such as guns (both shooting and bayoneting) and non-military weapons such as shovels, truncheons, clubs and starting-handles, from Saturday, 20 February, until the end of the month;

(ix)   Young Ethiopians and nobles arrested in Addis Ababa and executed by the tribunals set up on 19 February as a direct result of *Yekatit 12*.

Strictly speaking, the reckoning should also include those who suffered—and, in some cases, later died from—injuries sustained during the massacre. As Dr Birhanu Abebe pointed out to the present author, 'Many people were injured during the massacre. Although we read about the dead, the large numbers of injured are often overlooked.'[93] The numbers of injured can only be guessed at, but, to cover those who died, an additional category is introduced:

(x)   Ethiopians seriously injured during the massacre who died from their injuries later, that is after March 1937, when most of the estimates of the dead were published.

Excluded from this definition of the massacre of Addis Ababa are the following repressions, reprisals and pogroms often included under the general rubric of 'the Graziani Massacres':[94]

• residents of Addis Ababa rounded up and sent to Danane or Nocra concentration camps following *Yekatit 12*, who subsequently died either en route to, or within, one of those concentration camps;
• victims massacred as a result of *Yekatit 12* in towns and districts of Ethiopia other than Addis Ababa, such as Dessie, Harar and Gondar, and at monasteries such as Debre Libanos;
• Ethiopians executed throughout Ethiopia as part of Graziani's general crackdown in the weeks and months following *Yekatit 12*; and
• specific groups of people ordered by Graziani to be eliminated after *Yekatit 12*, but largely outside Addis Ababa, including notables in the rural areas, 'soothsayers', 'musicians' and 'witches'.

The absence of accurate information on the massacre makes any estimate subject to a great deal of uncertainty. Thus, no single method can provide a figure in which much confidence can be placed. For this reason, the approach adopted here is to develop three separate estimates, each based on different data as far as possible. The principle of this triangulation is that if all three results turn out to be similar, it is most unlikely that they would all be wrong. The three methods of estimation are based on:

(A)   an assessment of the number of victims of each of the ten 'phases' of the massacre listed above;
(B)   demographic data; and
(C)   data relating to the transportation of bodies to Gulelé.

(A) Estimation of the Number of Victims of Each of the Ten 'Phases' of the Massacre

Phase i: Killings within the Palace Grounds

It is well attested by both Italian and non-Italian sources that approximately 3,000 people attended the event at the palace to receive alms. It is also well established that almost all of them were killed by the gunfire that broke out, and that the remainder were slaughtered with shovels and batons, the gates having been closed. As the French envoy reported, 'the gates of the Government palace were closed and *all the natives massacred* without pity' (emphasis added). Very few managed to survive the onslaught, and most of those, as we have seen, were killed shortly afterwards by Blackshirts. Thus the best estimate of those killed within the palace grounds is 3,000. To reflect the fact that this figure could not have been exact—it is unlikely that there was ever a count of every individual present—we attach to this estimate a range of 2,900–3,100.

Phase ii: The Circle of Death

The reader will recall Dr Shashka's account of the ground being 'covered with the dead' within a radius of 400 yards (approx. 360 metres) of the palace perimeter, and the Emperor's report that 'Italian military forces encircled the area of the incident. All Ethiopians found therein were killed.' The testimony of Sara Gebre-Iyyesus and her daughter Yeweynishet, who walked through this area while the killing was going on, confirmed these reports. The most specific figure published for the number of victims within the Circle of Death is 1,500, a figure that originated from diplomats in the city at the time. This figure was not produced in the heat of the moment; it was released more than two weeks after the event, and was taken seriously by the international media.[95] But is it possible that so many could have been killed within this area?

The vast majority of the city's Ethiopian population of around 100,000 lived within the rectangle bounded more or less by the Japanese consulate in the north, the railway station in the south, the Menelik Hospital in the east, and the Muslim cemetery in the west, an area of around 21.5 km² (see Map 12). Thus the average density was around 4,500 per km². However, the central, downtown residential areas had a considerably higher density, with lower densities towards the outskirts. A reasonable estimate for the downtown high-density areas would be at least double the average, thus not less than 10,000 per km².

As can be seen from Map 2, the area within the Circle of Death (excluding the Gennete-Li'ul Palace grounds) was around 1 km². Of this district, the sections to the north-west and east were quite densely populated. Even if only half of this area (after deducting part of the open field of Jan Méda, public institutions, and the larger houses of the upper-income group) is assumed to have been attacked, the affected resident population could hardly have been less than 5,000. If we take into account the British Intelligence report and the testimony of witnesses who said that the Circle of Death reached Menelik Hospital, then the figure would include many houses along the Ghilifañ River valley, and would thus most likely account for at least an additional 2,000 people, bringing the total affected population to around 7,000. Taking into account that the event at the palace had drawn in many additional people from other parts of the town, who were watching through the palace fence or attending the market in Jan Méda, the conclusion is that the number of *potential* victims within the Circle of Death at that time most likely exceeded 7,000.

Given witnesses' testimonies that the Italians killed everyone they met, and entered houses and restaurants and killed the occupants, and given that the soldiers from the Regia Aeronautica headquarters at the Menelik II School had just rushed to the palace in response to the alarm when many Italians thought that Graziani might already be dead and an insurrection imminent, there is no doubt that the attack was furious and indiscriminate, and that all Ethiopians in that area at the time were potential victims. We therefore conclude that a figure of 1,500 deaths, representing approximately one in five of the potential victims resident in the affected area, is a plausible figure, and is probably conservative. In order to avoid spurious accuracy, and to reflect the fact that it is only an estimate, not based on records, we allocate it the range 1,400–1,600.

Phase iii: The Hour of Mayhem: Slaughter in Arada

The slaughter that took place in Arada, as the centre of the massacre migrated away from the Circle of Death, mainly affected the Ras Mekonnin Bridge area, the central area around St George Cathedral and the Municipality Office, the areas around today's Arbeññoch Street, and the market (Map 3). These were not all high-density residential areas. Like the district around the Gennete-Li'ul Palace, they were mixed. Part of the Ras Mekonnin Bridge area was built up with permanent houses, and the central area around the cathedral contained several institutions and large residential compounds. Overall, many of the people who died in these areas, which together totalled some 0.5 km², were merchants and visitors on their way to and from Arada—particularly the market—rather than residents of that area.

For this reason many of the deaths in this area were street killings, as the journalist Poggiali observed. Many people walking in these areas, including Welette-Birhan Gebre-Iyyesus, were not yet aware of what had happened in Siddist Kilo and were taken unawares. Although it was horrific to watch these random deadly attacks on innocent people, as Imru Zelleqe did from his house opposite St George Cathedral, and the gruesome manner of execution, such as being run over by heavy vehicles, the slaughter was less intense than within the Circle of Death, and the numbers killed are more likely to have been in hundreds rather than thousands. In the absence of any published estimates for this episode, we suggest an estimate of rather less than 200 people killed in each of the four areas shown in Map 3, totalling 750. To reflect the wide confidence limits on this figure, we adopt a final estimate of the range 500–1,000.

Phase iv: Deaths of Those Rounded Up

Following the curfew of 1.00 pm on Friday, 19 February, and during the course of the afternoon, large numbers of Ethiopians—mainly, though by no means entirely, men—were rounded up, of whom many are reported to have subsequently died. This excludes the deaths of those falling within the groups of the Young Ethiopians and the nobility and notables, which are addressed under phase ix.

The figure of 2,000 arrested appeared in several foreign newspapers, while the New York *Amsterdam News* spoke of an *additional* 1,400 having been shot. This suggests a total of more than 3,400 people having been arrested, a figure that increased steadily during the course of Friday and the weekend. According to Italian records, a total of 4,000 Ethiopians *found in circulation* were detained, to which must be added the thousands picked up from their homes from Friday afternoon onwards. Since the number taken systematically from their homes across the city was far greater than those found in circulation during the curfew, this suggests that the total detained could have been as many as 10,000 or more.

How does this estimate compare with the fragmentary data available on the detention centres?

• Central Police Station (Fit Ber), the largest and most frequently mentioned detention centre. In his affidavit, the fire brigade officer Toka Binegid indicated that it held at least 10,000 prisoners. Given that he had to provide

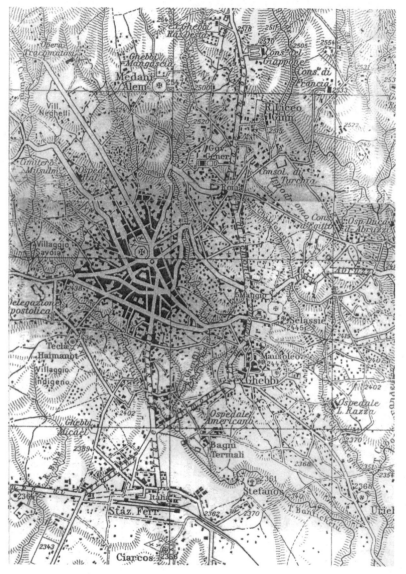

Map 12. Addis Ababa before *Yekatit 12*, showing density of buildings (Based on *Guida dell'Africa Orientale Italiana*, pp. 484–5, a map drawn from aerial photographs taken before *Yekatit 12*)

water for the inmates, it is likely that the Italians told him how many prisoners were being held there—or at least gave him an estimate. Furthermore, the fact that he supplied around 24,000 litres of drinking water on Monday, 22 February, which would amount to 2.4 litres per person, would be consistent with such a figure.[96] On the other hand, Temesgen Gebré stated that the Italians estimated that there were 18,000 captives in Central Police Station. This is a very high figure, though not impossible considering that there were women as well as men, and also considering that Birhanu Dinqé reported that people were crowded into the Fit Ber compound 'until it was completely full'.[97] Nonetheless, one is inclined to place more reliance on Captain Toka's more conservative figure, since he had official communications with the supervising authorities regarding the numbers.

- Central Prison (Alem Bekaña). As noted earlier, the numbers at Addis Ababa's largest purpose-built prison most likely exceeded 1,000.
- St George's Prison. One source mentioned 'more than a thousand' held here, while Birhanu Dinqé wrote that, like Fit Ber, St George's was 'completely full'.[98]
- Municipality Building. No figure is available, but from the evidence available and bearing in mind the size of the compound, which was full, it was most likely not less than 1,000.

Other detention centres included:

- Governo Generale. Around 200 were held here, based on Sara Gebre-Iyyesus's report of the situation inside the palace building, where she was detained.
- Ras Mekonnin Bridge police station. At one point, this was reported to have held 'more than 1,000'.
- *Tyit Bét* military barracks. No figures are available, but they are likely to be small, since it was not designed to hold prisoners.
- Other detention centres are estimated to have held prisoners in the range of 20–30 to 200–300 each.

At Akaki there were reportedly around 3,000 prisoners, but many of these captives had been transferred there from one of the prisons or detention centres already mentioned. Furthermore, they were not all '*Yekatit 12*' prisoners. Moreover, there were frequent transfers of prisoners between the various prisons and detention centres. Thus, if all these figures were to be added together, the result would incorporate a significant measure of double counting. Taking these considerations into account, these reports suggest a total of around 12,000 arrested, most of them being held at the Central Police Station at one time or another, which is consistent with the earlier estimate of at least 10,000.

How realistic is this estimate of a total of 12,000 detainees?

The number of able-bodied adult males (excluding the elderly) in a population of 100,000 (swollen by men who had drifted in seeking employment from the Italians) would most likely have been in the range 20,000–25,000, and the same for able-bodied women. Thus, even allowing for around 10,000 adults fleeing the city, and those who stayed at home, it is quite possible for 12,000 to have been detained. Since these arrests were made simply in door-to-door rounding up, as opposed to targeted arrests of named suspects, one would not expect the foreign diplomats to be informed, and they certainly would not know what was going on in all the 'urban villages'.

Of these 12,000, it is estimated that around 700 Young Ethiopians, nobles and notables were executed—many before the detention centres started filling up (see the analysis for phase ix below)—and 1,100 people who possessed a certain level of education or were from Amhara families (but were not regarded as senior notables, radical Young Ethiopians or Holetta cadets) were dispatched (often via Akaki) to Danane concentration camp. An estimated additional 400 were sent to Nocra Concentration camp,[99] around 200 upper-class 'political' prisoners held at the Governo Generale were deported to prisons in Italy,[100] and a few hundred people (estimated at around 200) regarded by the Italians as 'hard core', criminals or potential troublemakers were kept in prison in the city. These categories account for around 2,600 of the detainees, leaving an estimated 9,400 detainees who were released, or were out of hand (that is without the formality of a 'tribunal'), or died in custody.

How many of these detainees died in custody? Those who did so perished largely owing to the harsh conditions. They died from starvation, thirst or general ill-treatment in the first three days. Based on all the available testimonies, a reasonable estimate of such deaths would be around 10 per cent, suggesting a figure of around 940. This leaves around 8,460 detainees to be accounted for.

Of these remaining 8,460, how many were executed? There were a number of published estimates. One Ethiopian writer claimed that half of those arrested were executed; the London *Times* stated that of those arrested 'the majority were shot'. The British envoy concluded his dispatch of 1 March 1937 stating he had just received a report that there had been 3,200 'officially ordered' executions; and, based on Italian records, the number of official executions 'directly related to Graziani's attempt' reached 5,469 by the end of 1937. However, these figures doubtless included executions outside Addis

Ababa, which are excluded from the present analysis. To these estimates of 'official' shootings, one would have to add the unofficial executions, such as the slaughter of prisoners at the Municipality Building and the massacre at Fit Ber described (and probably exaggerated) by Temesgen Gebré.

However, the general impression gained from interviews of Ethiopians who were there at the time is that a large proportion of the 'Yekatit 12' detainees in Addis Ababa—at least half of them—were released, many of them before Mussolini issued his 'no more releases' order. This suggests that at least 6,000 were eventually set free. Thus, of the 8,460 to be accounted for, the balance of some 2,460 died in custody or while being transferred between detention centres—as happened to many of the prisoners who accompanied Temesgen to Fit Ber.

Table 10.1: Number and fate of detainees in Addis Ababa following *Yekatit 12*

Group	Fate	Number (est.)
Aristocrats and high-ranking nobles	Deportation to prisons in Italy	200
Middle-ranking nobles and notables	Incarceration at Nocra concentration camp	400
Young Ethiopians (see phase ix)	Executed after 'trial' by tribunal	500
'Political notables' who were not also Young Ethiopians (see phase ix)	Executed after 'trial' by tribunal	200
Educated and lower-ranking notables	Incarceration at Danane concentration camp	1,100
'Criminals' and 'hard core'	Retained in prison	200
Elderly and those particularly vulnerable	Died from starvation, ill-treatment or disease	940
Men and women killed 'officially' and 'unofficially' while in custody	Executed or killed while in custody	2,460
Those identified as harmless, including Eritreans, women, children, elderly	Released	6,000
Total (indicative estimate only)		12,000

The various estimates made in this analysis are listed in Table 10.1. The conclusion from this analysis is that the best estimate that can now be made of those rounded up who died in detention (excluding nobles, Young Ethiopians, deportees, those taken to concentration camps, and those kept in prison) is 2,460 + 940 = 3,400.

Phase v: Random Killings during Friday Afternoon

Following the announcement of the curfew, while the *carabinieri* were rounding up men on Friday afternoon, gangs of Blackshirts and civilians made deadly attacks on anyone found on the street. Such attacks were witnessed, for example, by Tekle-Maryam Kiflom, who named several areas as being affected, particularly the Police Garage area (Sera Bét *Sefer*), parts of Arat Kilo, parts of Arada and Gedam Sefer, the Dejazmach Wibé area and Serateñña Sefer (see Map 6).

These were not official killings, and neither were they carried out in the same wild frenzy of the attacks earlier in the Circle of Death. They were conducted by roaming bands of Blackshirts and labourers out to rob their victims and have 'fun' by 'punishing' anyone found breaking the curfew. Not all the victims were killed, but many were injured. Judging from the evidence available, it is suggested that in each of these areas 20–30 people might have been killed in this manner, implying a total of around 120–180 deaths.

Phase vi: The 'Carta Bianca' Daytime Attacks of Friday, 19 February

These attacks occurred between 5.00 and 6.30 pm, immediately after the slaughter was given official sanction, but before dark. They involved many Italian civilians, who realised that they would be unaccountable for their actions. Professor Del Boca points out that many members of the repression squads formed at that time later received medals from Graziani.

The attacks were particularly vicious; the report of the British consul-general described how 'Ethiopians were hunted through the streets and into their dwellings all over the town and were beaten, shot, bayoneted or clubbed to death'. However, despite the gruesome nature of these killings, they were certainly far fewer in number than those carried out at night, which are estimated at 3,000–4,500 on Friday night, over a period of around eleven hours (see phase vii below). This is because the onslaught lasted only one and a half hours, there were no flame-throwers in use at that time, there were fewer military vehicles available compared with the night attacks, and the 5.00–6.30 pm attacks were conducted over a smaller geographical area than the night attacks. For these reasons it is estimated that the 5.00–6.00 pm attacks would have killed perhaps 10 per cent but no more than 20 per cent of those killed on Friday night (see phase vii below), that is between 10% x 3,000 = 300 and 20% x 4,500 = 900, thus between 300 and 900.

Phase vii: The Nocturnal Arson 'Carta Bianca' Attacks of 19, 20, 21 February and Beyond

A secret British Intelligence report containing an eyewitness account of the massacre by a source classified as reliable estimated that between 6,000 and 9,000 men, women and children were slaughtered in the three nights of systematic house-burning.[101] Unlike the earlier lower estimates made by the British and American consuls in Addis Ababa, when neither of them realised the full extent of the area affected, the author of this later report stressed (correctly) that the burning covered districts spread over a distance of between five and six miles.

In order to determine the plausibility of this estimate, we need to examine the housing stock. With an average household size (including servants) of between 5 and 6 (assume 5.5), there would have been around 18,200 Ethiopian houses in Addis Ababa, of which the majority were in the high-density residential areas most affected by the arson, such as Sera Bét Sefer. Thus the published estimates suggesting that 4,000 houses were burned during this 'official', organised phase of the massacre—some 22 per cent of the housing stock, or a little more than 1 in 5—are quite plausible.[102]

Accepting the estimate of 4,000 houses burned, this would have affected around 22,000 occupants, less 4,000 to 5,000 people taken into detention on Friday, 19 February,[103] i.e. leaving around 17,000–18,000 potential victims in the houses. Thus the estimate of 6,000–9,000 people killed would represent between a third and a half of the occupants of the houses burned.

Considering that virtually every witness and every report of the nocturnal *carta bianca* mentions the burning to death of occupants inside their houses and the killing of anyone trying to escape, and considering that weapons of mass destruction such as flame-throwers, machine guns and hand grenades were deployed liberally, a rate of one death for every three occupants would be plausible, and might even be conservative, given statements such as that by the American missionary Herbert Hanson, who wrote, '*many* of the huts had been burned with their owners inside them' (emphasis added). Thus, one death out of three occupants is likely to be a reasonable minimum, particularly bearing in mind that many of the victims were people the Blackshirts came across at random—not necessarily residents of the houses being burned. On the other hand, a death rate of around a half of the occupants is probably an overestimate, because, although the killing was extensive, we know from witnesses that many families were allowed to leave the houses before they were burned, and no reports suggested that the *majority* of the occupants were killed. In conclusion, it seems that a rate somewhere between these two extremes would be consistent with the eyewitness accounts. Thus the British Intelligence estimate of between 6,000 and 9,000 killed during the nocturnal arson is considered credible.

On the basis of the general impression provided by eyewitnesses, it is suggested that, bearing in mind the flight of residents from the city during the massacre, of the total of 6,000–9,000 deaths during the nocturnal arson attacks, around a half (3,000–4,500) of the deaths most likely occurred on Friday night, a third (2,000–3,000) on Saturday night, and the remainder (1,000–1,500) on Sunday night.[104]

Phase viii: Random Daylight Killings from Saturday Onwards

During Saturday, 20 February, and Sunday, 21 February, there were random killings during the day, the Italian Blackshirts and civilians using whatever weapons they could get hold of. Some of the perpetrators of these sporadic attacks photographed their victims. The victims were typically alone or in a small group of two or three walking in the street. Attacked by gangs, they were left for dead. The objective was usually sadistic pleasure and, in the process, to steal whatever the victims might be carrying. In some cases, the victims were dragged out of their employers' houses and killed in the street outside. The reader will recall the American and British envoys personally witnessing and reporting attacks of this type to Washington and London. The random killings continued for several days, albeit at a diminishing rate. Tekle-Maryam Kiflom told the present author that they continued until the eleventh day after *Yekatit 12*, at the beginning of March.

It is difficult to estimate how extensive these attacks were. The only viable method would seem to be to use the nocturnal deaths as a yardstick, and take a small percentage of them, such as 2 per cent. The deaths during the nocturnal arson of Saturday, 20 February, are estimated at 2,000–3,000 (see phase vii analysis); on this basis the number of Saturday's random daytime killings is estimated to be 40–60. For Sunday the figure would be 20–30. As this phenomenon gradually faded after the official termination of the massacre, it is assumed that over the following nine days the rate reduced linearly, the final figures being as follows:

20 February: 40–60;
21 February: 20–30;
Over the next nine days: 9 x average of 10–15 per day = 90–135.
Therefore total killed: 150–225. Mean: 187.

The factor of 2 per cent of the nocturnal deaths is, inevitably, a somewhat arbitrary yardstick, and probably leads to figures that are underestimates, given that several witnesses reported random daytime killings. Thus, a figure of 200 is adopted here as a reasonable estimate, with a range of 170–230.

Phase ix: Young Ethiopians and Nobles[105]

As we saw in chapter 9, the British envoy informed London that eleven lorry-loads of Young Ethiopians were executed on 26 February, representing 'the first batch' of these victims. With a complement of 20 to 40 prisoners per truck, this would suggest a total of between 220 and 440 victims. Later he reported the killing of over 200 ex-Holetta cadets who had been rounded up 'later', implying that they were additional to the first batch of Young Ethiopians, bringing the total to 420–640. Since this is only a rough estimate, and likely to be conservative, we round the figures down to the nearest hundred: 400–600 victims, with a mean of 500.

How realistic is this estimate?

It is usually assumed that the Young Ethiopians were all educated overseas. Using this definition, it is generally believed that there were around 250, of which some were outside Ethiopia in February 1937.[106] Actually, many of the foreign-educated Young Ethiopians survived the repressions of *Yekatit 12*, as Professor Christopher Clapham has determined. However, the Italian definition of Young Ethiopians was wider than those who were educated overseas; it included the ex-Holetta cadets (many of whom were educated locally) and locally educated Ethiopians with a high school certificate or diploma.[107] This means that the category of potential victims known as Young Ethiopians actually extended to more than 1,500 (see Appendix I). Thus the estimate of 400–600 executed is feasible.

It is well established that hundreds of minor nobility and notables (the higher ranks were imprisoned in Italy) were executed after *Yekatit 12*, particularly Amhara notables, who Graziani on many occasions insisted must be eliminated, and many of whom lived in Addis Ababa. The Italian figures extant are dispersed among a number of fragmentary, inconsistent and even self-contradictory memoranda, reports and telegrams, with no complete documentation of the total number of victims. The problem of placing reliance on the numerical data in the Italian sources is an enduring one, as each document tells only part of the story, and the authors—often Graziani himself—were very selective in their use of data. Instead of being presented in a systematic manner, as one would expect in military communications, the data usually appear only fleetingly, and woven into vague and often emotional prose.[108]

Furthermore, Graziani's reports often understate the extent of Italian atrocities. For example, the massacre of virtually the entire assembly of 3,000 Ethiopians at the Governo Generale immediately after the attempt of *Yekatit 12*, which is well attested by all available sources, was apparently not reported to Rome.[109] Further difficulties arise from the fact that the pogrom triggered by *Yekatit 12* was not confined to Addis Ababa. As explained in chapter 9, it evolved into a nationwide slaughter of notables and community leaders, which continued for several months.

In the absence of any published data of the number of Addis Ababa-based 'nobles and notables' killed as a result of *Yekatit 12*, a simple estimate of 200 is proposed, bearing in mind that many have already been covered within the Young Ethiopians category (see Appendix II). Added to the estimate given above for educated Ethiopians, the total of this combined category then becomes 600–800 deaths, with a mean of 700.

Phase x: Deaths from Injuries

Most phases of the massacre of Addis Ababa already examined would have caused serious injuries as well as death (notably phases ii, iii, iv,[110] v, vi, vii and viii, during which an estimated total of around 12,000 were killed). Indeed for each person killed there must have been others seriously injured—but how many?

There are generally no records of such deaths, which would have occurred weeks or even months after *Yekatit 12*. However, the number of seriously injured people must have been substantial, for witnesses reported large numbers of detainees suffering from injuries, and the French envoy noted that 'even among the men, women and children rounded up and detained there were numerous injured'.[111] In typical battle situations, the number of wounded normally exceeds the number killed, but we are concerned here only with injuries from which the victim later died.

Only in isolated cases of notable figures are such deaths documented, such as *Betwedded* Welde-Tsadiq Goshu. Born in 1870, he was an important politician and personality under Emperor Menelik, Empress Zewditu and Emperor Haile Selassie, and at various times held the position of *Kentiba* of Gondar, Minister of Agriculture, Minister of the Interior, and President of the Senate.[112] Appointed by Haile Selassie as President of the Provisional Government at Goré following the Italian invasion, he surrendered to the Italians in November 1936, but suffered serious injuries during the massacre of Addis Ababa, from which he died three months later, in May 1937.[113]

In the absence of documentation of this significant but largely unquantified category of deaths, the best that can be done is to enter an indicative figure. Thus taking a conservative estimate that an additional 10 per cent of deaths occurred later from serious injuries received during the massacre, this would suggest a figure of around 1,200, with a range of 1,000–1,400.

Table 10.2: Estimate of deaths based on an analysis of each phase of the massacre

Phase	Description	Estimated Deaths	
		Mean	Range
(i)	Deaths within the grounds of the Governo Generale immediately after the grenades were thrown.	3,000	2,900–3,100
(ii)	The Circle of Death: killings in the streets and houses lying within the cordon flung around the perimeter of the Governo Generale.	1,500	1,400–1,600
(iii)	Slaughter in Arada: indiscriminate killings during the 'unofficial' rampage in Siddist Kilo and Arada that took place during the Hour of Mayhem.	750	500–1,000
(iv)	Ethiopians rounded up during and after the curfew of 19 February, and on 20 and 21 February, who were taken from detention and executed, or died 'unofficially' in custody.	3,400	3,200–3,600
(v)	Random killings throughout the city during the afternoon of 19 February;	150	120–180
(vi)	Victims of the late afternoon and early evening *carta bianca* attacks of 19 February.	600	300–900
(vii)	Victims of the nocturnal *carta bianca* arson attacks in Addis Ababa of 19,20 and 21 February.	7,500	6,000–9,000
(viii)	Victims of random daytime attacks in Addis Ababa, for eleven days from 20 February until the end of the month.	200	170–230

(ix)	Young Ethiopians (including local students and ex-Holetta cadets) and nobles arrested in Addis Ababa and executed (some following a tribunal) as a direct result of *Yekatit 12*.	700	600–800
(x)	People injured who later died from their injuries.	1,200	1,000–1,400
Total		19,000	17,462–20,538[114]

Summary Total

This analysis of each of the ten phases of the Massacre of Addis Ababa brings the estimated total number of victims to a mean of 19,000, with confidence limits of 17,462–20,538, as shown in Table 10.2. Before adopting this estimate, it needs to be validated against two other, separate estimates, of which the next utilises demographic data.

(B) Estimate of the Total Number of Victims Based on Demographic Data

There was no official population census in Ethiopia, but most estimates of the 1936 Ethiopian population of Addis Ababa are in the range 95,000–100,000. Earlier figures had been around 95,000,[115] but there had been an influx of people from the rural areas seeking work under the Italian administration. Thus 100,000 is adopted here as the estimated population before *Yekatit 12*.

The estimated total population of the city published by the Italians in March 1938 (the time of writing is presumed to have been late 1937) was 90,000, of which 17,301 were Italians and 2,443 were foreigners.[116] This means the Ethiopian population was estimated to be around 70,256, which was substantially less than the population before the massacre.

Part of the drop in population from 100,000 to 70,256 can be explained by the fact that after *Yekatit 12* about 10,000 people fled Addis Ababa, of whom about 5,000 men joined the Patriots or went to Kenya or Djibouti, the remainder returning to the city during the weeks that followed. This means that the net loss due to flight from the city was around 5,000. In addition, as we have seen, approximately 1,100 Ethiopians were deported to Danane concentration camp, 400 to the island penal camp of Nocra, and 200 to prison in Italy.

If we denote the number of people who died in the massacre 'M', then the population of Addis Ababa after the massacre was 100,000—M—5,000— 1,100—400—200: that is, 93,300—M. In the (approximately) six months between *Yekatit 12* and late 1937, when we assume the Italians made their estimate of the Ethiopian population, there would have occurred a population growth rate of around 1.24 per cent (assuming an annual growth rate of around 2.5 per cent). Thus the estimated late 1937 population would have been (93,050—M) x 1.0124. Based on the Italian estimate of 70,256, then M = 93,050—70,256/1.0124 = 23,655. Thus on this reckoning, approximately 23,655 people must have died in the massacre.

There is, however, considerable uncertainty about the number of Addis Ababa residents who fled the city to join the Patriots. Some sources suggest that 15,000 left, of whom an estimated 5,000 returned, suggesting a net loss to the city of 10,000 men (rather than 5,000). Although this figure is probably an overestimate, doubt remains about the figure of a net loss of 5,000. Thus a mid-point figure of a net loss to the Patriots of 7,500 would be a more reasonable estimate. Furthermore, some Addis Ababa residents fled to other venues such as the Sudan in the weeks following *Yekatit 12*. Taking into account these two factors, the net loss of population to the Patriots and to neighbouring countries might be closer to 10,000 rather than 5,000. Furthermore, the pre-*Yekatit 12* population estimate of 100,000 might be high; some sources, as mentioned above, suggest a figure of around 95,000. These two factors would suggest that the estimate of 23,665 can be regarded as a maximum, and that a minimum figure would be approximately 10,000 less, or 13,665.

The conclusion is that the demographic data available suggest that number of deaths in the massacre of Addis Ababa was between 13,665 and 23,665, with a mean of 18,665.

(C) Estimate of the Total Number of Victims Based on Data Relating to the Transportation of Bodies

Here we attempt an estimate of the death toll based on the number of bodies transported.

Number of Bodies per Truck

Alfredo Godio, a witness to the transport of the corpses, said that he watched 'many 634 trucks' heading out of town on the Ambo Road 'each carrying tens of bodies'. This suggests at least 20 adult bodies per truck, and possibly 30 or, based on other eyewitness accounts, 40 or more. In order to verify this, we examine the features of the military trucks concerned.

The most common Italian military vehicle was the Fiat 634N. The overall length of the vehicle was 7.4 m, of which approximately 4.6 m was available for carrying loads. The width was 2.4 m, providing a bed of area of around 11 m^2 for carrying goods. The sides were often extended with a steel or wooden framework to a height of around 1 m, for use as personnel carriers.

With a load stacked 1 m high, the cubic carrying capacity of the 634N was thus approximately 11 m^3. This means that with an estimated three dead bodies per cubic metre, one truck could carry around 33 adult bodies, or more than 40 if several of them were children.[117] With higher sides, additional bodies could be carried. Thus this estimate, arrived at by examining the dimensions of the trucks, corresponds to eyewitness reports. It is clear that with the higher sides attached, these trucks would have had no difficulty carrying 40 bodies each.

Since the payload of the 634N was 7.4 tons, equivalent to around 100 bodies, the weight of the bodies was not a limiting factor.

Number of Trucks

Some trucks took bodies to the collection centres while others took them from the collection centres to Gulelé. Thus, based on Marino's report of 100 trucks used in the transport operation, a reasonable breakdown would be 40 per cent of the trucks used for the Gulelé run (i.e. 40 trucks) and 60 for taking the bodies to the collection centres.

No. of Days of Operation

The trucks were reported as having run for four full days taking bodies to Gulelé: Friday, Saturday, Sunday and Monday. Marino said they started on Friday, and that they worked at night—so it was 'round the clock'. An operation of three to four days is thus assumed. It should, however, be noted that this is a conservative estimate, given that the French envoy reported on Wednesday, 24 February (that is the sixth day of body transportation) that the corpses had not yet all been removed.[118] Furthermore Dr Shashka wrote, 'A week after the massacre there were still places in the town where the corpses had not yet been put away ... Something like eight or ten days after the massacre I was near the brewery ... around the building there were still corpses.'[119]

Number of Trips per Day

This is the least certain parameter. We do not know how long (if at all) the trucks would had to wait at the body collection centres for a sufficient number of corpses to accumulate. The maximum speed of these vehicles was around 40 kph, and the round trip to Gulelé from, for example, St George's Brewery, which was about 15 kilometres from the cemetery on a rough road, could have taken at least one hour, plus offloading time and re-collection time. The overall cycle time could thus have been 3–4 hours. Taking into account driver resting time and shift change over, a conservative estimate would be 3–5 (average 4) trips per vehicle per 24-hour day.

CONCLUSION

Taking a conservative loading of 33 bodies per truck, the 'low' estimate of the number of bodies taken to Gulelé is: 3 days x 40 trucks x 33 bodies/truck x 4 loads/day = 15,840 bodies. The 'high' estimate is based on the same conservative load factor but a full 4-day transport operation: 21,120 bodies.

In addition, as we have seen, the remains of around 500 bodies were found years later, after the Liberation, dumped in rivers and wells. Furthermore, some of the estimated 700 Young Ethiopians and notables were executed after Monday, 22 February 1937, and an estimated 1,200 people died later from their injuries. These categories would account for an additional total of around 2,000 bodies. Thus the final estimated death count based on the transportation of bodies is 17,840–23,120, with a mean of 20,480.[120]

Conclusions

From these analyses we arrive at three estimates of the death toll, as can be seen in Table 10.3. It is striking that these three relatively independent estimates are quite similar; they overlap to a considerable extent. This indicates that it is unlikely that they are very far off the mark.

Table 10.3: Estimates of death toll based on three methods

Method of estimate	Range	Mean
Method based on each phase of the massacre	17,462–20,538	19,000
Method based on demographic data	13,665–23,665	18,665
Method based on transportation of bodies	17,840–23,120	20,480

The estimate that lies within all three of these ranges is 17,840–20,538. That is to say, a range of 17,840–20,538 is consistent with all three methods, with a mean of 19,189. Thus, rounded to three significant figures, the best estimate of the death count of the Massacre of Addis Ababa based on this analysis is 19,200, representing around 19–20 per cent of the pre-*Yekatit 12* population of the city. It should be remembered that this estimate does not include Addis Ababa residents who died later in other locations outside the city (such as in the concentration camps), or in subsequent repressions that were connected with *Yekatit 12* but that continued long after the massacre.

At this point we should seek another validation of the estimate. Is it compatible with the number of Italians actively involved in the massacre? Of the estimated 19,200 who died, 3,000 were killed largely by the regular army and *carabinieri* in the grounds of the Gennete-Li'ul Palace, and between 2,000 and 4,000 were executed by the regular army after 'tribunals' or were simply taken from detention and executed, usually by a military firing squad. This leaves around 12,000–14,000 killed mainly by the 6th Division 'Tevere' Blackshirts during the days and nights, assisted by Fascist civilians and other forces such as the Colonial Police. At the time of the massacre the 6th Division 'Tevere' consisted of around 13,500 Blackshirts. This implies that, on average, each Blackshirt killed one Ethiopian. Considering that some of the soldiers and civilians boasted afterwards of having killed many Ethiopians, this finding is quite feasible, while suggesting that by no means all of the Blackshirts killed their victims; the reader will recall that some of them let the families leave before setting fire to their houses.

Comparison with Other Estimates

In comparing the final estimate of 19,200 dead with those previously published, we note that it does not correspond with the figures suggested by some of the international media at the time (between 3,000 and 6,000), which in the light of the evidence examined are too low. It is, however, quite close to estimates made by well-informed observers such as individual Italian civilians who were there at the time (20,000), Dr Shashka (14,000) and Wazir Ali Baig ('more than 14,000').[121]

According to Sergeant-Major Boaglio, it was commonly reported (presumably by Italian soldiers) that 11,000 had died in the massacre—a figure which he felt unable to confirm or deny.[122] Since the military executions, deaths in detention and later deaths from injuries (which the soldiers would most likely not have included in their estimate) account for an estimated 5,300 deaths, the author's equivalent figure for those massacred in public would be 19,200—5,300 = 13,900, which bears comparison with the figure quoted by Boaglio.

The estimate of Wazir Ali Baig ('more than 14,000') merits attention, because he worked closely with Consul Andargachew Mesay in Djibouti, and they were the only people able to meet on 'neutral' territory and interview a substantial number of Ethiopian refugees fleeing from the massacre, thereby being in a position to reach conclusions about the overall extent of the slaughter. No one else is on record as having done this—neither at the time nor since. Thus the fact that the present author's estimate is consistent with that of Ali Baig lends it considerable support.

But what about the Ethiopian government estimate of 30,000 deaths? The present author's estimate is not necessarily inconsistent with this figure, because, as noted earlier, it was almost certainly intended to cover *all* deaths from the slaughter that followed *Yekatit 12*, countrywide.

The figure of 30,000 appeared in the Ethiopian government submission to the Paris Peace Conference in 1946, within the following list:[123]

Killed in action	275,000
Patriots killed in battle during five years of Fascist occupation	78,500
Children, women, old and infirm people killed by bombing during the occupation	17,800
Massacre of February 1937	30,000
Patriots condemned to death by 'court martial'	24,000
Persons of both sexes who died in concentration camps from privation and maltreatment	35,000
People who died of privations owing to destruction of their villages during the five years' occupation	300,000
Provisional estimates of casualties [Total]	760,000

It is apparent from this list that the victims of the February 1937 massacre in the secondary towns of Ethiopia must be covered under the 'massacre of February 1937' entry, because they are clearly not included under any of the other entries. This view is reinforced by Sylvia Pankhurst's reference to 'the Great Massacre of 19th–21st February, 1937' as having been a 'terrible massacre in Addis Ababa *and other towns* of February 19th, 20th and 21st' (emphasis added).[124] The numbers killed in the other towns is unknown, but it could well bridge the gap between the present author's estimate of around 19,200 deaths in Addis Ababa and the Ethiopian government estimate of a total of 30,000 countrywide.[125]

* * *

ROBBERY WITH VIOLENCE

The massacre of Addis Ababa featured mass murder, arson and theft. The extent of murder and arson has been analysed in this chapter, but the subject of theft has been only touched on. Robbery was, however, one of the primary objectives of the attacks, particularly in the daytime, as is clear from many of the eyewitness accounts. But the full extent of this phenomenon, and the total loss that it represented for the residents of Addis Ababa, will never be known.

What is known is that in thousands of attacks on individuals, money and other property such as watches, rings, bracelets and jewellery were stolen; in fact, all victims, including corpses, were thoroughly searched and robbed. The reader will recall Dr Shashka's description of Blackshirts turning up at the Bank of Italy after the massacre to cash in their ill-gotten gains. Furthermore, it was standard practice for every home entered by the Fascists to be stripped bare of anything and everything of value; as we have seen, Sara Gebre-Iyyesus was robbed of all the valuables she and her family possessed, in room after room, by the soldiers sent to arrest her. The resultant bag of silver looted by the Italians was so heavy that Sara could hardly carry it, and the rest of her possessions, which were loaded onto a military truck, were never seen again.

Many similar cases came to the attention of the foreign diplomats. For example, the French envoy reported, 'The Fascists forced their way into the house of an Abyssinian notable, *Ato* Belachew, the former Controller of *la Legion d'honneur*, inspected the furniture and took a substantial sum, represented by gold or silver coins ... Approximately 6,000 *thalers*, equivalent to 100,000 francs, disappeared from [another] one native house in similar conditions.'[126]

Considering that educated Ethiopians in the city (excluding those working for Graziani's administration) were either executed or deported, and their homes commandeered, it can be safely assumed that in the process they were also looted. In fact, several months later Graziani's administration put a legal gloss on the theft and looting of the assets of the wealthier Ethiopians who had been executed or imprisoned. He legalised by decree the seizure of all movable and immovable assets of 61 individuals accused of being involved in what he now termed 'the massacre'—i.e. the strike at the palace of 12 Yekatit. These included Beshahwired Habte-Weld, Belay Haile-Ab, Feqade-Sillassé Hiruy, Taddesse Meshesha, Yoséf and Binyam Werqineh, and Belihu Degefu. The decree of course made any surviving dependants virtually destitute. Additional decrees ten days later did the same for the assets of another 147 individuals, including *Abune* Petros, Hayle-Maryam Mamo, Abriha Deboch, Moges Asgedom, Letyibelu Gebré, Yemiserach Imru (the daughter of *Ras* Imru, who had married Feqade-Sillassé Hiruy) and Dr Werqineh Isheté, who was still alive but in London.[127] Thus the assets of a significant proportion of the urban elite were stolen by the Fascists during the massacre, amounting to several hundreds of thousands of dollars—and possibly millions—in today's money.

* * *

11

THE COVER-UP

PERFECT TRANQUILLITY

The Massacre of Addis Ababa—the brutal slaughter of a significant proportion of the civilian population of Ethiopia's capital city—rapidly disappeared from the world's collective memory. Why is this so, and why was no one ever held to account?

The cover-up began with the public face that the Italians put on the massacre, which was basically a denial that it ever happened—and if it did, then what occurred was a minor incident which became grossly exaggerated. This denial, which was intended both for the international community and for the Italian general public, was reinforced by a severe crackdown on anyone in Addis Ababa attempting to dispatch reports or photographs of the massacre. For the Ethiopians, the Italian posture was, of course, absurd, as the outraged Dr Shashka wrote: 'Can you imagine a burnt house on which you read an announcement that the house was not burnt? A communiqué hung over heads of still bleeding corpses? Can you imagine with what feeling one reads in the streets in which the smoke of burning houses and the smell of blood can still be seen and felt, that all these things did not happen?'[1]

Such announcements set in motion a cover-up that has continued to the present day. It was facilitated by writers such as the German author Louise Diel, a Fascist sympathiser commissioned by Mussolini in October 1937 to visit his 'new empire' and write a book on her findings. Despite containing quite a detailed study of events of the Occupation and the situation in

Ethiopia at the time of her visit (which lasted several months), and a purport-edly in-depth analysis of the relationship between the occupiers and the occu-pied, Diel's book made not a single mention of the massacre of Addis Ababa—not even an attempt to justify it. Setting a precedent for subsequent Italian literature on the Occupation, Diel referred to the attack on Graziani, but chose not to mention what followed.[2]

For those who knew, or later discovered, the true nature and scale of the massacre, such as the foreign diplomats in Addis Ababa, there was a different tale: the wretched Blackshirt rabble had carried out the atrocity without the approval of the Viceroy, who was beside himself with shock and anger, and wept when he discovered the terrible thing they had done. This story was propagated by the Viceroy's office within days of the event, and was forwarded to London by the acting British consul-general, albeit with considerable scepticism.[3]

The evidence shows that neither of these two tales reflects reality. The mas-sacre was certainly not a minor incident, and, according to none other than his superior, Minister Lessona, Graziani would have continued the slaugh-ter—probably to its bitter end—had he not been prevented from doing so by Mussolini. His missives during the remainder of 1937 reflect his view that the massacre was a healthy lesson for the citizens, and for the remainder of his tenure as Viceroy he had no qualms about continuing merciless retribution against whichever Ethiopian communities he thought might be opposed to his administration.

The complete lack of remorse on the part of the Italian administration is consistent with the authorisation of reprisals after *Yekatit 12*, and indicate that William Bond was correct in his conclusions. Although the British envoy was unaware at the time of the official Italian communications, such as the one in Appendix IV, he gained the distinct impression that the massacre indeed had the blessing of the Italian High Command:

> It was at first thought that the local, surviving authorities [that is those not hospi-talised after *Yekatit 12*] had merely lost their heads or that the rowdier elements had got out of control. If this were the case the authorities might be less blameworthy. It is however difficult to reconcile the sudden imposition of control and its immedi-ate effect after two days of unbridled licence with any such hysteria or impotence; and moreover the conversation of Italians in the street indicates that they were indeed given a free hand to carry out reprisals in any manner they liked ... I myself cannot avoid the conclusion that the reprisals were carried out with the full knowl-edge of the constituted authorities and with their sanction and approval.[4]

Although Graziani projected the massacre as fully justified and a positive achievement, the manner in which the slaughter was orchestrated created problems for him at the time. He had assured Mussolini that all executions would be carried out in secret, whereas the Blackshirts operated in public and had made a spectacle of themselves. Reporting as they did to the party federal secretary, who had his own connections with Rome, they created an embarrassing situation for the Viceroy, who considered himself in charge. The new Roman empire was based on a culture of power and discipline, and civilian massacres, like any other form of military activity, should be commenced and brought to an end at times that he, Graziani, would determine. Instructions from Rome for premature termination undermined his authority in the eyes of his subordinates. And even worse: when he issued his order for the reprisals to cease, the Blackshirts had continued their operations, brazenly ignoring his command, and then had the audacity to follow up with their own, unilateral announcement of termination.

Graziani reacted swiftly and angrily. But his fury was not for the innocent Ethiopian mother watching her children being burned alive before her eyes; it was the anger of a threatened and humiliated commander. The Viceroy made numerous representations to the foreign legations to curtail their newspaper correspondents and, turning openly against the senior local Fascist Party officials, went to the extent of petitioning Rome to recall Cortese.[5]

Meanwhile, the Viceroy went on to portray the massacre in yet another light: it was evidence of victory in an ongoing struggle of good over evil. His office prepared leaflets in Amharic, scattered over the city by the Regia Aeronautica. Making it clear that it was he—Rodolfo Graziani—who had been wronged, and who had consequently wrought justice in God's name, they re-established him as the indisputable and ultimate authority in Ethiopia, a message which he drove home with repeated references to the government.

He also took the opportunity to deny the dangerously accurate rumour going around that the attempted assassination was an 'inside job': appealing to Ethiopians' long-standing suspicion of foreigners, he claimed that the perpetrators had financed the plot using 'foreign gold'. He stated that his military victories which followed the failed attempt by his enemies reflected God's will, and ended his message in traditional Ethiopian vein, with 'Let traders carry on their commerce, and let farmers plough!'—mimicking Emperor Susinius's historic declaration changing the official state religion of the empire back from Roman Catholicism to Orthodoxy in the early 17th century.[6] Finally, he took the unusual step of signing his proclamation as the Viceroy of 'the Emperor of Ethiopia' (meaning King Vittorio Emanuele), with no mention of Mussolini or the party.[7]

People of Ethiopia—Harken!

On February 19th while I was distributing alms to the poor, and contributing to the churches of Addis Ababa to celebrate the birth of His Highness the Prince of Naples, grandson of our great and powerful King and Emperor, Vittorio Emanuele II, a few rascals purchased with foreign gold made an attempt to kill me and the other great officials of the government. God, however, was willing to keep my life and the lives of the others who were with me, and [we] escaped with light wounds. Now justice is taking its course without interruption and decisions are being executed without mercy.

In the city and the whole of Ethiopia there is perfect tranquillity. Furthermore, God has given evidence of His unfailing support of the government: On the day the attempt was made on my life in Addis Ababa, my victorious troops encountered in battle *Ras* Desta, *Dejazmach* Beyene Merid and *Dejazmach* Gebre-Maryam. *Dejazmach* Gebre-Maryam was killed in the fight on February 20th. *Dejajmach* Beyene was made a prisoner on the same day. *Ras* Desta was captured on February 24th and both were executed as rebels.

The enemies of the government who became instruments to carry out this vile attempt are spreading false rumours. Do not believe what they say. Abide by the laws of the Powerful Government and attend to your work. Let traders carry on their commerce and let farmers plough!

Viceroy of the Emperor of Ethiopia: *Rodolfo Graziani*

On 1 March 1937 the British acting consul-general in Addis Ababa wrote a detailed 13-page report confirming that the stories of mayhem and depravity collected by the foreign correspondents and the Ethiopian consul in Djibouti were true:[8] the Blackshirts enjoying the screams of the woman being burned to death in her home as they plunged her children back into the flames; the Italian officer interrupting a burial to rob the putrefying corpse of a dollar—all came to life, in their shame and squalor. Clearly feeling that the diplomatic language in his earlier telegrams had not had the desired effect, the envoy let his views be clearly known in language normally alien to British diplomacy: 'The immediate crisis over, there followed for two and a half days, by ways of reprisals against Ethiopians wherever found and however occupied, an orgy of murder, robbery and arson on the part of the Italians that, if the facts were known abroad in every disgusting detail, should make the name of Italy stink in the nostrils of the civilised world.'[9]

* * *

On 10 March Emperor Haile Selassie, in exile in his villa in the west of England, submitted a request for the League of Nations to initiate a commission of inquiry into the massacre. Reminding the Secretary-General of his previous appeals to the League, he wrote, 'Have you completely forgotten the solemn pledges which you undertook towards the Ethiopian people, and of which I once more demand the fulfillment? ... Will you forget us for ever? ... The massacre of February 1937 will leave on the Italian aggressors a [stigma of] perpetual shame.'[10]

But the Emperor's appeal fell on stony ground; the League took no action. Nonetheless, there was now pressure on London to go public on the issue, and Sylvia Pankhurst organised a protest petition to the Secretary-General of the League of Nations drawing attention to the massacre, signed by an impressive array of distinguished figures. It constituted the trigger for yet another pro-Ethiopia campaign, which would agitate the British Foreign Office mandarins beyond anything they had previously experienced, and—although she had no idea at the time—would run for well over a decade.[11]

However, scant attention was paid in London to the British envoy's dispatches; in fact, the Foreign Office falsely claimed in Parliament to have very little information on the subject of the massacre. Then, as we shall see, posing in its self-righteousness as an honest broker, and supported by America, the British government orchestrated several years of political machinations and intrigue to prevent Ethiopia from succeeding in its quest to bring the guilty to justice.

Finding himself in a dilemma, the Foreign Secretary, Sir Anthony Eden, sought a course of action that would allow the government to continue to withhold all documents on the massacre from public view, while at the same time appearing to be honest and transparent.[12] This approach was well received by Neville Chamberlain, Chancellor of the Exchequer, who would become Prime Minister a few weeks later. Anxious to appease Mussolini and determined to suppress Bond's report, he declared, in a remarkably terse and historic dismissal of the very purpose of the League of Nations, 'There can be no useful outcome to official protests.'[13]

Reports by the American envoy, Cornelius Engert, were as unambiguous as Bond's. Describing the Blackshirts' behaviour as 'ominous', his dispatches should have served as a warning of what Fascism had in store. 'So far as the Italians individually are concerned, these events certainly brought out the man. The veil of idealistic humbug has been torn aside, and the meaning of the self-styled Italian mission of civilization had been revealed in all its ruthless materialism and sham.'[14] Yet Engert's insight into the propensity of Fascism to destroy the established moral order was lost on Washington; the American government joined Britain in sweeping under the carpet the behaviour of the Italians in Ethiopia, in the interests of expediency and appeasement.

The whitewash was facilitated by the departure of Bond and Engert from Ethiopia; both men, who knew the situation in Ethiopia well and had personally witnessed the massacre, were transferred shortly afterwards. Bond's successor called into question the former's reports of the massacre, claimed that the *New Times and Ethiopia News* had exaggerated the nature and extent of the reprisals, and declared that the burning of houses in the city had been confined to the immediate vicinity of the Gennete-Li'ul Palace. His contradictions were so blatant that it seems likely that he was doing as instructed by his superiors, who wanted to close the file on the Massacre of Addis Ababa as quickly as possible. The irony is that Mussolini was actually very worried about the potential reaction of the international community—so much so that he imposed a complete news blackout. As Dr Shashka wrote, 'Since I have been abroad I hear sometimes that Europe was sorry not to be able to do anything. If Europe was not able to do anything, I ask, why were the Italians so much afraid of Europe? Why did they watch over the telegraph and the wireless station for the news from Europe? Why were the murderers afraid that Europe should know?'[15]

The logical conclusion is that the British government would have been in a position to get Mussolini to moderate his henchmen in Ethiopia, if only it had had the moral courage to do so.

A New Viceroy

Following Mussolini's instruction to Graziani to multiply the programme of terror in Ethiopia 'tenfold', the Viceroy did exactly that. In addition to the elimination of the educated Ethiopians, the Amhara nobility and community leaders, 'witches' and 'soothsayers', he ordered his commanders to conduct more civilian reprisals and to step up attacks on the Patriots of northern Shewa, supported by the Regia Aeronautica using asphyxiating gases. It was under Graziani's orders that the congregation of the Monastery of Debre Libanos was wiped out, in a particularly horrifying massacre in May 1937.[16]

However, the climate of terror that Graziani created failed to achieve its goal, for the atrocities it spawned further fuelled the resistance, which continued to be a major obstacle to the 'pacification' of Ethiopia. By the end of 1937 Graziani had been dismissed and replaced by the Duke of Aosta.

338

The new Viceroy pursued a different approach to pacification—what Professor Tekeste Negash terms 'pacification by ethnic partition' and 'pacification by apartheid'.[17] The Duke was more humane than Graziani, but at no point did he revisit the issue of the Massacre of Addis Ababa. He released prisoners he considered were an unnecessary burden on his administration, and attempted to rebuild churches and monasteries devastated by his predecessor. But his ultimate goal was the same as Graziani's: to 'pacify' Ethiopia, an objective that was destined never to be achieved. Thus he set the tone for the final stage of the cover-up—he simply behaved as if the massacre had never happened. It was to be papered over, and forgotten as quickly as possible.

The Duke achieved a measure of success with his 'pacification by ethnic and racial partition'; he certainly minimised the possibility of a united front against the Italians, and to some extent defused—or at least contained—the resistance, which in any case was fragmented and often based on local, rather than national, interests. However, in June 1940, nine months after the outbreak of the Second World War, Mussolini declared war on Britain and France, a move for which the Ethiopians had been hoping and praying.

* * *

THE EMPEROR RETURNS

In April 1939 Fascist Italy invaded and occupied Albania, following which Italy and Germany created a 'Pact of Steel', and Germany invaded Poland, as a result of which Britain declared war on Germany. In June 1940 Italy declared war on Britain and France, and in October invaded Greece.

Britain, now at war with Italy, flew Emperor Haile Selassie to Alexandria and arranged for him to enter Ethiopia at the head of a small military force, while an Allied army supported by Ethiopian Patriots routed the Italians. In May 1941 they liberated Addis Ababa, following which the Emperor was able to enter the city in triumph, albeit operating under the auspices of the British, who, having recognised Mussolini's 'conquest' of Ethiopia, now regarded that country as 'Occupied Enemy Territory'.

In his speech the Emperor dwelt at some length on the atrocities committed by the Italians in their five-year Occupation, and talked about the horrors of the massacre of Addis Ababa:

> How many are the young men, the women, the priests and monks whom the
> Italians pitilessly massacred during those years? You know that in Addis Ababa

alone many thousands perished during the three days following St Michael's Day on Yekatit 12, 1929 [19 February 1937]. The blood and bones of those who were killed with spades and pickaxes, of those who were split with axes and hammered to death, pierced with bayonets, clubbed and stoned, of those who were burned alive in their homes with their little children, of those who perished of hunger and thirst in prison, have been crying for justice.

But, as he spoke, the fear of the thousands of Italians still in the city, who half expected to be massacred in revenge, quickly evaporated. Although the Italians were accustomed to carrying out horrific and cowardly reprisals at the slightest 'injustice' committed to themselves, the Emperor made it clear that, while he was fighting for justice, he was not seeking vengeance. Amid the silence of the vast crowd, the man whom the Italians had demonised and castigated as primitive, barbaric and not fit to rule Ethiopia, instructed his people, 'Do not repay evil with evil. Do not indulge in the atrocities which the enemy has been practising ... Take care not to spoil the good name of Ethiopia by acts that are worthy of the enemy.' Ten thousand terrifying Patriots, long-haired and wild-eyed, who had been fighting under *Ras* Abebe Aregay, had come to town to welcome the Emperor, but, as Professor Del Boca points out, 'Not a single ugly incident occurs, not a hair of an Italian's head is harmed.'[18]

The British overran Danane and released the surviving prisoners who had been incarcerated after *Yekatit 12*, but it was Nocra that eclipsed all other Italian prisons in terms of the appalling conditions and shocking state of the inmates, which were comparable to that of the survivors of the Nazi death camps. The 332 surviving Ethiopian 'political prisoners'—most likely from Addis Ababa—found there on 6 May 1941 were all very ill, and some died before they could even reach the mainland. Of the 114 prisoners who had to be immediately admitted to hospital, 30 per cent could not even walk, and nine of the human skeletons died on arrival at the hospital. Nocra may not have been designed as a death camp, but, as the British authorities put it, 'They could not have expected anyone to live.'[19]

On 19 February 1942—the fifth anniversary of the massacre—a memorial was unveiled in Addis Ababa. The event was reported in a special edition of *Berhanina Selam*, relaunching this important national journal that had ceased publication during the Occupation. Dated 5 May 1942 (27 Miazia 1934), it was published just one year after the Emperor had returned to the city. The monument was erected at the Siddist Kilo junction, where the massacre had begun. It took the form of a simple obelisk surmounted by the three-pointed star of the Trinity, the sole inscription being the date 'Yekatit 12, 1929'.

In his speech the sovereign recalled, 'On this day, five years ago, many children and youths were killed by machine-gun fire in their own country ... deprived of a proper burial, their dead bodies were trampled on, their homes burned, and property was destroyed—it is beyond any reckoning ... Words alone are inadequate to describe your sacrifice—It is your sacrifice that led us to victory. Thus this memorial will be known as 'The *Yekatit 12* Monument ... For those of you massacred like sheep—cut down in the flower of your youth—this is to remember your sacrifice.'[20]

By this time the Axis had invaded much of Continental Europe, and the atrocities they carried out in the European countries they invaded, which closely followed the pattern of civilian abuse established by the Italians in Ethiopia, shocked the Allies into a keener interest in war crimes. In October 1942 the American government announced that it would cooperate with its allies in establishing a commission for the investigation of war crimes, and that punishment would be meted out to those 'responsible for the organised murder of thousands of innocent persons.'[21]

By mid-1943, Mussolini had been arrested on the orders of the King; it appeared that Italy would probably be defeated by the Allies, and the British and Americans governments, looking ahead to Mussolini's possible replace-

144. The unveiling of the *Yekatit 12* Monument at Siddist Kilo, 19 February 1942

ment, favoured Marshal Pietro Badoglio. Their desire was for Italy to be led by someone who would prevent the Communists taking over, and would thus keep the country in the Western fold. This entrenched their opposition to any trial of Badoglio and his compatriots for war crimes in Ethiopia. For as long as the British were effectively in control of the Emperor's administration in Addis Ababa, they could ensure that nothing would be done to facilitate any investigation of Italian atrocities in Ethiopia. President Roosevelt also back-pedalled on the question of sending Italian war criminals to trial. Justice would once again have to give way to expediency.

On 20 October 1943 the United Nations War Crimes Commission was formally established, but Ethiopia was excluded from membership.

Grisly Discoveries

The large number of victims of the massacre of Addis Ababa had made it impossible to dispose of the bodies in the city, and as a result they were taken to Gulelé, soaked in petrol and burned. However, some victims, either dead or alive, had been thrown by the Italians into rivers, latrines and even drinking-water wells, following Graziani's practice of polluting drinking-water wells during the suppression of resistance in Libya.

After the Liberation the re-established municipality of Addis Ababa began to recover these remains, and by 1944 they had collected around 500 complete or partial skeletons. These were taken to the Church of the Holy Trinity—a new church with a burial ground for national figures and martyrs—where they were put in a catafalque below the church, pending ceremonial reburial. The discovery of such remains in various locations in and around the city raised hopes among the general population that the bodies of thousands of missing friends and relatives might come to light. Yeweynishet, whose father, Beshahwired Habte-Weld, had disappeared without trace, said, 'When the mass graves were discovered, many people were very hopeful, because people who had relatives missing gave information as to identification, and so on. So did my mother [Sara Gebre-Iyyesus]. And we tried to find out if my father's remains would be found. Many [others] were found. But we did not find my father's remains ... I was always hopeful when they found some obscure graves somewhere ... my mother said he had a ring with his names on it. [But] nothing ever happened, so we never found it ... what they did with the body, we don't know.'[22]

In June 1944 Rome fell to British and American troops, and Badoglio resigned but continued to receive British support. When it seemed likely that

145. Municipality employees recovering bones of massacre victims from a drinking-water well in the early 1940s

the Italian government—now aligned with the Allies—was about to arrest him, Winston Churchill, who had taken over as British Prime Minister in 1940, and had promoted the return of the Emperor to Ethiopia, dispatched a remarkable telegram to the British ambassador in Rome on 8 December 1944 marked 'Personal and Top Secret'. The instructions to the ambassador placed Badoglio, who had signed the documents of Italian surrender, under the protection of the British government, thus making it clear that there was no question of anyone handing him over for trial. 'You are responsible for the Marshal's safety and sanctuary ... you are not to let him go into any danger or pass out of our safeguarding hands ... military honour is also involved ... you are responsible for his honourable security.'[23]

* * *

IN MEMORIAM

A Cenotaph in Addis Ababa

As the British government strove to shield the facts of the massacre of Addis Ababa from international scrutiny, the Ethiopians were coming to terms with its horrors. On Monday, 15 January 1945 the Emperor, Empress and high officials of the government and Orthodox Church attended a ceremony at the Church of the Holy Trinity in Addis Ababa. The Emperor spoke of the 'grave cruelty' of the Italians, 'especially without regard for women, children and old people—male and female'. Following the fall of Fascism and the surrender of Italy, he was now able to add, 'It is the will of Almighty God that this atrocity was turned back on the Fascists, and the whole world has seen this justice. If we feel that we have gained some relief in this important stage of history, we should thank the Lord that we have seen his unerring judgement take place against this barbarous Fascist enemy.'[24]

The Emperor explained that the bodies of some of the people killed during the massacre had been thrown into wells. Their bones, in the catafalque below the church, were now reburied in a tomb below the cenotaph in the church cemetery. The Emperor unveiled the cenotaph, and he and the Empress laid wreaths. An exhibition of photographs of some of the atrocities was temporarily set up in a building near the cenotaph, 'along with literature telling of the cruelties endured by innocent civilians and youth ... which shall live forever in infamy as among the beastliest eras of Twentieth Century civilisation'.[25]

In the congregation at the church were Sara Gebre-Iyyesus and her daughter Yeweynishet, who was now 13. Her father's remains still not having come to light, the event marked a low period in her young life: 'There was a sort of mass funeral ceremony in the cathedral, and that made me very unhappy and very reflective, even as a child.'[26]

The *Ethiopian Review* of February 1945 described the massacre with heartbreaking fervour:

> In many peaceful villages and on the streets of the cities were seen the unburied bodies of civilians nude and mauled with axes and shovels. Prisoners were bludgeoned to death in the presence of their relatives and the public. With daggers, guns, fire and sword and unimaginable methods—the hangman's rope, bombs, unexpected incendiaries—did this criminal vandalism sweep the land. This the unquenchable blood thirst of Fascist Italy in Ethiopia which could hardly be excelled in the record of memorable infamies of human history! 'Love suffereth long'; but the world, history and civilisation will never forget this tragedy.'[27]

Sadly, the writer who penned those words in 1945 was wrong. Unimaginable as it would have seemed at that time, the world did forget the massacre of Addis Ababa. Despite the speeches, articles and commemorations organised by the Ethiopian government and its supporters, the British government continued to do its best not only to ensure that the international community would forget, but that as far as possible it would not be made aware of the

146. The Church of the Holy Trinity on the day of the burial of the bones of massacre victims

147. The *Yekatit 12* Cenotaph, built over the tomb of the remains of the massacre victims whose bodies were found in rivers and wells

massacre in the first place. In this they were successful, for, in their efforts to bring the perpetrators to justice, the Ethiopians, as we will see, continued to be thwarted at every turn.

Atrocities Revealed

Given the extraordinary lengths to which the British government went to discredit the eyewitness accounts of the Massacre of Addis Ababa, conceal the written evidence in its possession, and obstruct attempts to investigate and document the five years of brutalities, the Italian atrocities might have become nothing more than a legend, had it not been for an important discovery: photographs.

While she was in Ethiopia, Sylvia Pankhurst managed to acquire a collection of photographs of some of the atrocities. Taken by the Italians themselves, they had come to light at Liberation. She took them back to England, and in April 1944 the *New Times and Ethiopia News* published some of them. Later, she published several of them in a pamphlet, *Italy's War Crimes in Ethiopia*.[28]

ITALY'S 1/-
WAR CRIMES

**IN
ETHIOPIA**

148. The cover of Sylvia Pankhurst's 1944–5 pamphlet on Italy's war crimes carried a photograph of Italians displaying the severed head of resistance leader Haylu Kebbede, son and heir of the hereditary ruler of Wag, a royal bloodline dating from the 13th century

Replete with photographs taken by Italians of some of their most cruel and savage acts, including unspeakable horrors such as decapitation and skinning alive, the pamphlet went a long way to create international awareness of the Italian atrocities, and the Massacre of Addis Ababa in particular. It was widely distributed, reprinted, and reached numerous venues, including, in due course, the Paris-based council negotiating the Italian Peace Treaty, where Sylvia's son, Richard, distributed it to the deliberating members.

Determined as they were to conceal the evidence of Italian atrocities, the War Office and the Foreign Office had been outmanoeuvred. Once again, the British establishment had been challenged by one formidable woman and her son, bravely upholding the cause of Ethiopia.

* * *

APPEALS FOR JUSTICE

In mid-1945, as the Second World War came to an end, the Allies, determined to seek justice for Europeans who had suffered at the hands of the Germans and Japanese, became more interested in war crimes, and signed what became known as the London Agreement, for the prosecution and punishment of the major war criminals of the European Axis, and set up an international military tribunal to conduct the trials.[29] In Ethiopia there was an expectation that justice would at last be attained for the victims of Italian atrocities. By a strange twist of fate, Imru Zelleqe, who as a young boy had watched the outbreak of the Massacre of Addis Ababa, and had been interned in Danane, was in England in September 1945 as secretary to the Ethiopian Minister of Foreign Affairs in his efforts to seek reparations.

But the post-war environment was not conducive to generating concern for Ethiopia's cause. Europe was not in a settled state, and Ethiopia was the least of Europe's priorities. Looking back years later, Imru recalled, 'We presented a whole case, but nobody listened to it ... [In] London ... the bombing had just finished, the war had just stopped ... everything was destruction, everywhere you went there was nothing. There was no food ... It was a difficult time for all of them, all of us Ethiopians, the British.'[30]

On 19 February 1946, the ninth anniversary of *Yekatit 12*, Prime Minister Indalkachew Mekonnin conducted the annual commemoration ceremony at Siddist Kilo. In its feature article in the government journal *Ethiopian Review* (the English-language sister publication of *Berhanina Selam*), the writer recalled the horrors of the massacre:

> The Ethiopians tried to escape from the courtyard but hardly a single person got out alive. The invalids, the old and the poor, received bullets instead of alms ... The heads of caught Ethiopians were split with picks and shovels. Blackshirts ran through the streets, looking and seeking for new victims and killing any still breathing ... Another massacre followed during the night and many people were burned alive in their huts ... Ethiopians who tried to escape were stabbed with bayonets and thrown back into the flames of their burning homes.[31]

But the speech also departed from tradition. Exasperated by Britain's intransigence over the Italian war crimes issue, the Prime Minister spoke about how the Ethiopian government had struggled to get recognition in the United Nations for the atrocities, and made a thinly veiled attack on the British government for their double standards and their obstruction of justice: 'All the governments are crying, "peace, peace, peace!" ... It is not enough for the Governments to cry "peace", they must be prepared to act and to make sacrifices to get it ... Now, what kind of peace can they show to the world? *A true world peace must dispense equal justice to all, and forgo self-interest*' (emphasis added).[32]

Clearly reflecting the Ethiopian government's annoyance with the cover-up being perpetrated by London, and Britain's continued insistence on blocking Ethiopia's membership of the United Nations War Crimes Commission, the *Ethiopian Review* added, 'Many gruesome photographs and documents about these [atrocities] and similar events were found in Italian archives ... There are many and sufficient proofs to show that no report whatsoever about barbarism, atrocities and sadistic bestialities committed by the Italians in Ethiopia can be considered as exaggerated. These ghastly proofs, which shock every human being regardless of race or creed, have helped to remove even the slightest doubt of the guilt of a nation once believed to be civilised.'

In line with this renewed determination to seek justice, in May 1946 Ethiopian Imperial Order No. 1784 established the Ethiopian War Crimes Commission,[33] which, according to the rules of the United Nations War Crimes Commission, would—at least in theory—be able to try the defendants.

In 1946 the Ethiopian government strengthened its appeals for justice on the international stage by publishing in French a two-volume compendium of shocking photographs of Italian atrocities, together with Italian telegrams ordering or reporting the summary execution of Ethiopians. Entitled *La Civilisation de l'Italie fasciste en Éthiopie*, the publication declared, 'It is our sacred duty to demand, in the name of all the innocent victims, punishment for the guilty. At this time, when the world is preparing for peace, we feel that its primary task will be to ensure for the dead their justice, and their peace.'[34]

THE FINAL SABOTAGE

Shortly after the agreement on the draft peace treaty with Italy, the Ethiopian Ministry of Foreign Affairs wrote to the War Crimes Commission requesting recognition of Ethiopia's intention to institute criminal proceedings against Italians for war crimes committed as from October 1935—a letter that met strong British opposition. London's strategy was to play for time. Knowing that the commission was to have a limited life, they decided to wind it up.[35] Britain had ensured that the window of opportunity for Ethiopia, which had only just opened, would soon close.

To save time, the Ethiopians decided to select just ten from the fifty suspects they had identified: Badoglio, Graziani, Lessona, Cortese, Generals Nasi, Pirzio-Biroli, Geloso, Gallina and Tracchia,[36] and Enrico Cerulli (chief of the Political Office for East Africa in the Ministry for the Colonies, and Deputy Governor-General of Italian East Africa).

Receiving the Ethiopian submission just in time for its last meeting, on 4 March 1948, the commission concluded that there was sufficient evidence to justify the prosecution of these individuals as war criminals, with the exception of Lessona and Cerulli, who were classified as 'suspects and witnesses'.[37] This was a significant achievement for Ethiopia, but time was running out.

Not surprisingly, the British Foreign Office was displeased by the findings of the commission. One of their officials, Alan Pemberton-Pigott,[38] noted on 28 April 1948 that it would now be difficult for Britain to refuse to surrender the defendants. He wrote, 'We have no direct interest in Graziani', but added that a request for Badoglio to be handed over 'might well cause embarrassment'.[39] One wonders why the Ethiopians, aware of the British government's intransigence on the issue of Badoglio, did not drop him from the list as a price to be paid for a chance of at least getting the other suspects to trial, including Graziani and Cortese.

In the event, the Ethiopian government representatives, finding themselves increasingly short of time, decided to limit their case even further: they chose to proceed with charges against only Badoglio and Graziani. However, not surprisingly, they failed to get the Italians to hand over even these two suspects. The Foreign Office rebuffed Ethiopia's demands, on the grounds that they did not follow the laid-down procedure. The British also adopted a form of diplomatic blackmail, suggesting that if the Ethiopians continued to press the matter, they ran the risk of 'losing' Eritrea, a matter that was the subject of ongoing international deliberations.

La Civilisation

de l'Italie Fasciste en Ethiopie

149. The cover of the Ethiopian government's publication on the atrocities carried a photograph of a group of Italians in civilian dress displaying their collection of the severed heads of Ethiopians

Fury in Addis Ababa

The British rejection of Ethiopia's demands for bringing the war crimes suspects to trial, coupled with Italy's increasingly vociferous demands to have its 'colonies' restored, triggered a sharp reaction in Addis Ababa. On 19 February 1949, at the twelfth anniversary of *Yekatit 12*, Ethiopian Prime Minister Indalkachew Mekonnin went further than before in his attack on the double standards of the Great Powers. After the laying of the wreath at the Martyrs Monument, he abandoned his usual description of the massacre, explaining:

> Shall we say that the Italian people are brutal and savage? I can well understand how many of you who have lost members of your families in the course of the Graziani massacres should firmly hold to such an opinion ... Apart, however, from the bestialities of Graziani, there is yet a deeper significance to these massacres. These atrocities and brutalities were perpetrated ... against the innocent and unarmed—against mothers and children who sought harm against no one.

The report on the ceremony in the *Ethiopian Herald* carried a demand that Graziani be taken to trial, stating, 'He must be brought to trial! His [Nazi] confrères in guilt have received their reward—why shouldn't he?'[40]

The Final Débâcle

Flush with confidence that they had right on their side, and undaunted by Britain's intransigence, the Ethiopians continued to press their case. But the British government made it clear that if the Ethiopians insisted on making a nuisance of themselves, they should not expect a favourable outcome on the issue of Eritrea. When the Ethiopian minister arrived at the Foreign Office, the blackmail was only thinly veiled.[41] Britain's Foreign Office officials had not only played their hand with consummate skill; they had also taken advantage of the post-war trauma and the general lack of international interest in Ethiopia's cause, as reflected in Imru Zelleqe's reminiscences:

> By that time we had little support from anyone, because there was competition between Russia and the West ... So we were in the middle of nowhere. No one listened to us ... We were stuck on our own. We had to pull ourselves up by our own shoe-strings. It was a difficult time for us.[42]

The Ethiopians were clearly not only well aware of the international situation, but it also seems that they had finally 'got the message' regarding Eritrea. Nothing more was heard about the Italian war crimes trials. They had been successfully sabotaged.

* * *

12

REFLECTIONS

'I repeat my authorisation to Your Excellency to initiate and systematically conduct a policy of terror and extermination'

Mussolini to Graziani, 'Secret', 8 July 1936

It is difficult to explain the almost unparalleled degree of savagery involved in the massacre of Addis Ababa, which was remarkable not only for the scale of the slaughter, and for the cruel manner in which the victims met their death, but also for the impunity with which it was carried out. As we noted earlier, it has been argued that, having been perpetrated by a people with a reputation for warm-heartedness and a love of children, the extraordinary bestiality of the massacre—particularly towards women, children and the elderly—can be explained only by the indoctrination and conditioning of Fascism, especially its enthronement of violence and the culture of impunity that it fostered. After all, Mussolini's totalitarianism was designed to create 'new' Italians who would be hated, rather than loved: dagger-wielding killers rather than mandolin-playing 'softies'. It is also often held that Fascism's glorification of suffering and the inflicting of pain had its origins in the horrors of the trench warfare of the First World War, which produced battle-hardened men to whom violence was a way of life, and who were incapable of being reabsorbed into their communities other than as *squadristi* or, in the case of their German counterparts, members of private right-wing armies known as the Free Corps—the precursors of the Nazis.

However, while it is true that disgruntled First World War veterans formed the core of the Blackshirt 'Tevere' Division, which led the massacre of Addis Ababa together with battalions of right-wing students and highly nationalistic members of the Italian diaspora from Argentina, the remarkably similar three-day massacre of Tripoli and the use of brutal penal camps by Italy for civilian internment date to before the advent of Fascism. Thus the extent to which the brutality of the Italian invasion and occupation of Ethiopia should be laid entirely at the door of Fascism is open to debate.[1]

What is not open to debate is that when the sovereign of the first country to fall victim to Fascist invasion warned the world at Geneva, 'Today it is us; tomorrow it will be you', no one was listening. As the world turned its back, Ethiopia became the crucible in which were forged, tried and tested the methods of civilian subjugation and abuse that would follow in Albania, Greece and Yugoslavia, and that foreshadowed the ethnic cleansing practices of the Nazis in much of occupied Europe, particularly Poland and the Baltic states.

Whether attributable to Fascist indoctrination or not, the fact is that with Britain and America holding the veil of silence in place, Italy never had to face examination for triggering the chain reaction that culminated in the Second World War, nor for the misdeeds of its nationals in Ethiopia, in the way that Germany was made to do for that nation's excesses during the Nazi era. Thus Italy escaped the analysis and open public debate that her former wartime ally was obliged to undergo, and that would have gone some way towards creating awareness, recognition and a sense of responsibility and contrition for the horrors of the Occupation.[2]

Far from being exposed to public scrutiny, the Blackshirt massacre of Addis Ababa—a monstrous rampage of mayhem and depravity entirely without justification, in which thousands of innocent civilians were bludgeoned, shot, stabbed or roasted to death—an orgy of cruelty designed to terrorise, abuse, rob and murder defenceless men, women and children and provide entertainment and gratification for its perpetrators—was swept under the carpet. In fact, far from being ashamed of what they had done, the Italian authorities were so proud of the bloodbath that they issued commendations to those who carried it out. Equally, the world turned a blind eye to the horrors perpetrated behind the walls of detention centres and concentration camps and at remote execution sites, as well as the unleashing of military killing squads in the countrywide slaughter conducted by the regular army in its determination to liquidate the ruling and educated classes of Ethiopia. As in the case of the Blackshirts, there was no Judgement Day.

When Mussolini fell from power, and it looked as if Germany might lose the war, it was difficult to find Italians willing to admit or even, apparently, able to remember that they had ever been Fascist. Overnight, the millions who had cheered the *Duce* when Ethiopia fell to the Italian jackboot were nowhere to be found. Fascism was the last thing they wanted to be associated with. Furthermore, Italy having avoided censure for the Fascism to which it gave birth, and for its unprovoked invasion of Ethiopia and of the European nation-states that suffered similar fates in the quest for Fascist–Nazi world domination, the story of Italian Fascism underwent a nostalgic revisionism in which facts were not only denied, but replaced by myths. Fascism was reinvented as having been a relatively harmless and even faintly comical episode— a characterisation encouraged not only by Film Luce's newsreel films of the *Duce's* absurd posturings, but also by Italy's embarrassing failures in battle on a number of occasions when confronted with well-armed and determined enemies. Now, in the 21st century, the military invasion and occupation of Ethiopia have finally begun to command the attention of a wider group of Italian academics, but increasingly under the misleading rubric of 'colonialism', thereby offering a fig leaf of legitimacy to the attempted destruction and annexation of a sovereign state.

The failure to hold even a single person to account for the massacre of Addis Ababa can be attributed largely, as we have seen, to the machinations of the British government of the 1940s to protect their new-found ally. However, the recent attempts to present Fascism as a harmless charade, and the brutal invasion and military occupation of Ethiopia as a benign exercise in paternal colonialism, are home-grown, and they dishonour the memory of the innocents who died in the carnage of February 1937.

* * *

EPILOGUE

The Demise of Mussolini

In an audacious rescue operation on 12 September 1943, Adolf Hitler had Mussolini snatched from where Badoglio had imprisoned him, and flew him to Germany, where the *Führer* and *Duce* arranged the establishment of a new government with Fascist loyalists in an area of northern Italy that they named the Salò Republic. The former Italian Viceroy in Ethiopia, Marshal Rodolfo Graziani, was appointed Minister of Defence, with the former party federal secretary, Guido Cortese, as a high-ranking member of the government

Eventually a combination of the advancing Allies and Italian Partisans, consisting mainly of Communists, Christian Democrats and Socialists, overran the Fascist strongholds. In April 1945 Mussolini was arrested while trying to escape to Switzerland and executed by Partisans, following which his body and those of other Fascist leaders were strung up by their feet at a petrol station in Milan.[1]

The Blackshirts

The Italian invasion of Ethiopia in 1935–6 marked the 'golden years' of the Blackshirts as a military fighting force. Never again would such a large number of them be deployed in a single force, be so well equipped, or face such a poorly equipped enemy.[2] Shortly afterwards many of the Blackshirts who had invaded Ethiopia were sent to join thousands of others deployed in Spain, including, in due course, members of the 6th Blackshirt Division 'Tevere', infamous for their role in the massacre of Addis Ababa, and the 'Curtatone e

Montanara', or university militia.[3] However, in Spain it was a different story. Faced with a modern European army, Blackshirt losses were very high, and many were killed in action.

Thereafter, the Blackshirts fought under regular army command but frequently suffered severe losses. After Spain, they were actively involved in all the other invasions for which Ethiopia had provided the blueprint and for which the League of Nations had been rendered impotent: Albania in 1939, and an attack on France in 1940, followed by an invasion of Greece. They were pushed out of Greece, but in 1941 Blackshirts took part in the invasion of Yugoslavia. In Egypt they were badly defeated, and some battalions were entirely destroyed.[4] In the winter of 1942–3 Blackshirts fought on the Russian front, but again with heavy losses, although military historians identify this episode as the highest point of Blackshirt combat effectiveness. In the final analysis, when pitted against a well-armed and well-trained enemy, Mussolini's Blackshirts did not generally excel as a fighting force. However, they managed to sustain and enhance the reputation they had gained for atrocities against unarmed civilians.

As we have seen, the road from Piazza which becomes the Ambo Road was named Viale Tevere in honour of the notorious 6th Division 'Tevere' (later, ironically, Arbeññoch (Patriots) Street), who led the massacre of Addis Ababa. Following their performance in Ethiopia a medal was cast for members of the Division. It depicted six Blackshirt daggers in clenched fists, inscribed with the names of the units of the division: FASCI ALL'ESTERO, COMBATTENTI, MUTILATI, ARDITI, VOL. DI GUERRA and STUDENTI UNIV. ('Fascists from Overseas', 'Combatants', 'Amputees', 'Assault Troops', 'War Volunteers' and 'University Students'); and, inscribed above, the division slogan, MOLTI NEMICI—MOLTO ONORE (Many Enemies—Much Honour).

By July 1943, when Mussolini fell from power, the Blackshirts were failing in their efforts to repel the Allied invasion of Sicily, and upon Italy's surrender in September they did nothing to support Mussolini, and basically disappeared as an entity, being taken over by the regular army, although some battalions continued to carry the Blackshirt name. In the confusion of the collapse of Fascism and the unrest and violence that followed, many Blackshirts, including the 221st Regiment 'Italiani all'Estero' (of which two battalions had formed a major part of the 6th Blackshirt Division 'Tevere' in Addis Ababa), joined the National Republican Army and fought alongside the Germans under the newly proclaimed Repubblica Sociale Italiana, operating from Salò. However, as the Axis lost its foothold in Italy, thousands of these diaspora Blackshirts were slaughtered by roaming Italian Partisan bands. With that, the Blackshirts finally came to an ignominious end.

While some surviving former Blackshirts wrote about their exploits on the Russian front, which many viewed as a righteous battle against the evil of communism, their infamous role in Italy's bogus 'civilising mission' in Ethiopia, with its atrocities, brutal reprisals, asphyxiating gases, summary executions, mass murders, flame-throwers, village burning, killing squads and concentration camps, faded largely from memory.

The Eritrean Question

The issue of the future of Eritrea, which Britain's Foreign Office had used to dissuade the Ethiopian government from pursuing the Italian war crimes trials, took years to resolve. Regarding Eritrea as a former province of Ethiopia that the Italians had unfortunately acquired during the time of Emperor Menelik, Emperor Haile Selassie expected rapid restoration of the colony to Ethiopia after Liberation. Indeed, pamphlets dropped over the former Italian colony by Britain's Royal Air Force in 1941 had proclaimed that Eritreans 'from this day forward' would be living 'under the shade of the Ethiopian flag'.

Italian demands for sovereignty over Ethiopia, as well as its former colonies of Eritrea, Libya and Italian Somaliland, met with fierce debate in the United Nations after its founding in 1945, following which the Italians had to modify their expectations. They then requested at least a mandate over Eritrea. When this strategy also failed, the Italians preferred, as a 'worst-case' scenario, to see Eritrea independent, rather than as part of Ethiopia.

In Eritrea the various factions engaged in protracted guerrilla warfare. Then in December 1950 it was announced that the UN General Assembly had decided upon federation between Ethiopia and Eritrea. Although not tantamount to his desired annexation, this represented at least a partial victory for Emperor Haile Selassie.[5]

In September 1951 Ethiopia and Italy restored diplomatic relations, although the Italian government representative at the ceremony surprised the Emperor by making no denunciation of the Fascist regime and offering no apology for its crimes—indeed, no reference whatsoever to the past.[6]

War Crimes Evidence

In 1949, when it was clear that the Italian war crimes trials would not go ahead, the Ethiopian government published a number of incriminating Italian telegrams sent between Rome and Addis Ababa selected from the documents submitted to the War Crimes Commission. The Italian text of the telegrams was translated into English, and several of them were reproduced in facsimile. The editors wrote that, as well as being evidence of war crimes, the documents 'will repay examination by students of the recent history of Italy and of the relations of Europeans with Africans'.[7] Along with Volume II (1950), which contained affidavits and extracts from publications, this dossier has indeed proved a valuable source for historians.

Marshal Graziani

The Italian army collapsed in confusion after the Badoglio-headed government which succeeded Mussolini changed sides in the war, as Italian soldiers

DOCUMENTS

ON

ITALIAN WAR CRIMES

SUBMITTED TO THE

UNITED NATIONS WAR CRIMES COMMISSION

BY THE

IMPERIAL ETHIOPIAN GOVERNMENT

VOLUME II

AFFIDAVITS AND PUBLISHED DOCUMENTS

PUBLISHED BY COMMAND OF
HIS IMPERIAL MAJESTY

MINISTRY OF JUSTICE
ADDIS ABABA
1950

150. Cover of Volume II of *Documents on Italian War Crimes*, published in 1950.

who under German command had previously carried out atrocities against Italian soldiers and civilians hostile to the Axis were now themselves attacked and killed. After the war some anti-Fascist elements in the Italian government wanted to bring the Nazi commanders to trial, whereas other, pro-Fascist elements were hesitant to do so because they feared a 'boomerang' effect whereby countries such as Yugoslavia, Albania, Ethiopia and Greece would press for Italian war crimes suspects to be handed over for trial. The result of this ambiguity was a half-hearted prosecution of only a handful of suspects, of whom one was Graziani.[8] Thus in late 1948 Graziani found himself on trial in Italy for treasonable conduct by collaborating with Mussolini and Hitler in the Salò Republic and committing atrocities in 1943, after Germany had become Italy's enemy rather than her ally.

Although crimes committed in Ethiopia were not among the charges brought against Graziani, the subject of the massacre of Addis Ababa was raised during the trial. As noted earlier, the former Viceroy said that it was carried out by Fascist squads while he was in hospital, implying that the Blackshirts acted without his approval. However, writing in the *Ethiopian Herald*, the journalist Homer Smith insisted that although, as Viceroy, Graziani had technically been the representative of the King of Italy, the sovereign was in fact a mere figurehead and Graziani was in reality Mussolini's 'head Fascist' in Ethiopia and, as such, 'could have issued an order for those "Fascist squads" to desist'.[9] Smith pointed out that in any case Graziani's signature appeared on numerous execution orders, and that there were numerous reports of reprisals and atrocities committed on his orders after the three-day massacre of *Yekatit 12*. Nonetheless, the absence of any documentary evidence that Graziani ordered the massacre, or was in a fit state to have done so at the time, exemplifies the difficulties the prosecution would have encountered had he ever gone to trial on that particular charge.

The frustration felt in Ethiopia in the 1940s that Graziani was not being charged with war crimes or crimes against humanity related to that country was reflected in Smith's concluding paragraph: 'This brings us to the end of this series of evidence confirming that Graziani committed as cold-blooded war crimes in Africa as the German Nazis did in Europe. This evidence is only typical and could be continued for weeks. However, it should be sufficient to prove that Graziani left a bloody and horrible record behind him ... and is as much a big war criminal as were those Nazis who were tried and convicted in Nuremberg and elsewhere.'

Graziani was found guilty of treason and sentenced to 19 years in gaol. However, he was released after serving only four months, and during the early

1950s he had some political involvement in an Italian neo-Fascist movement. In January 1955, at the age of 73 years, Rodolfo Graziani died, never having veered from his support for Mussolini and Fascism. It is clear from his memoirs that he had no regrets about his infamous career.

Guido Cortese

By mid-1937, following Graziani's representations to Mussolini after *Yekatit 12*, the young high-flying federal party secretary in Addis Ababa had been relieved of his position, and replaced by Marcello Bofondi. But while he may have ruffled Graziani's feathers, Cortese's career was by no means at an end. On the contrary, he was in the ascendant. He rejoined the Istituto Coloniale Fascista (the Fascist Colonial Institute), where he had worked as secretary-general before relocating to Ethiopia, but this time as president.[10] Within a few months of returning to the institute, his latest work appeared, entitled, appropriately enough, *Problems of the Empire*.[11]

It is clear from the text of *Problems of the Empire* that Cortese was a hardline Fascist theoretician, with strong views about the need for strict racial separation in occupied Ethiopia as well as in Italy's colonies of Eritrea and Somaliland; he recommended 'clamping down with rigour on the absurd cohabitations that are so damaging to national prestige and race'. Such cohabitations, Cortese wrote, 'create sooner or later an indigenous mentality in the white man who undergoes, more easily than one might think, the influence of natives with whom he has excessive familiarity'.[12]

In Rome Cortese received several awards, and served as Prefect of Aquila from 21 August 1939 to 1 August 1943, when he was transferred as Prefect to Cuneo. Then three months later, on 24 November 1943, Mussolini appointed him Director-General of General and Personnel Affairs of the Fascist Salò Republic, in which Graziani was Minister of Defence.[13]

So far as is known, Cortese remained in that position until Mussolini finally fell from power. In due course he was taken to task for his activities with Mussolini and Graziani in the Salò Republic, for which he suffered loss of pension rights in December 1945.[14]

According to the proceedings of Graziani's trial in 1948, Cortese was in hiding at that time. But, as to where he was and what he was doing, nothing is known. At 46 years of age he was still relatively young, but whether like many other senior Fascists he returned to public life or died in obscurity is a mystery.[15] The man who launched the bloodbath of Addis Ababa seems to have disappeared from public view and has long been forgotten.[16]

Achille Starace

Achille Starace, who as Cortese's superior in the Fascist Party hierarchy most likely authorised the massacre of Addis Ababa, lost his position of national party secretary in 1939, and became general commander of the Blackshirts until his dismissal by Mussolini in 1941. After the fall of Fascism he was arrested, and notwithstanding an attempt to regain the *Duce*'s favour at Salò, he was rearrested and imprisoned. Released again and living in Milan, he was spotted in April 1945 by Partisans, shot, and his body was strung up beside Mussolini's.

Aleqa Ar'aya

Aleqa Ar'aya, the devout Ethiopian Protestant clergyman who was last seen tied to the back of a Blackshirt truck as it sped out of the gate of Central Police Station, paid the ultimate price for his defiant resolve. The vehicle was driven to Holetta, the former Ethiopian Military Academy commandeered by the Italians, some 45 kilometres from Addis Ababa. When they arrived, the Blackshirts found that the rough and rocky terrain had made light of *Aleqa* Ar'aya. From the back of the truck hung two solitary legs, which the driver untied and fed to a pack of scavenging dogs.[17]

Temesgen Gebré

On the night of Tuesday, 23 February 1937, following the dragging to death of *Aleqa* Ar'aya, Temesgen Gebré and several other prisoners were put on a truck for execution at Holetta. It seemed to Temesgen that his end had finally come. However, he was to have yet another lucky escape. 'When we arrived there, they took us off the truck in a forest and opened fire at us. When one of the people next to me was hit and fell down, I fell down with him. The Italians left us there, assuming that we were dead. After checking that the truck had left, I crawled out from the dead bodies and went by moonlight to *Itété* ['Auntie'] Bezabish's house. There she dressed me in her clothes, put a scarf on my head, and a *masero* [clay pot] on my back. I set out on my journey to Gojjam by moonlight. Travelling at night and hiding during the day, I made my way along the Blue Nile [gorge] and reached [Debre] Marqos.' In a nearby village Temesgen met up with his mother and sister.[18]

In 1938 Temesgen went to Sudan, where he struck up a friendship with P.A. Hamilton, a British Protestant missionary based in Khartoum. Temesgen became a zealous preacher to Ethiopian refugees, and taught English, Amharic, mathematics, reading, writing and Ethiopian history at the Sudan Government School for Ethiopian refugees at Gedaref. After Liberation he returned to Ethiopia, where he married his wife, Tahka. He died in tragic circumstances in Addis Ababa in 1949.[19]

Gebre-Sillassé Oda

Gebre-Sillassé Oda, who had left Addis Ababa for Alem Gena on the morning of 12 Yekatit, narrowly escaped with his life when he encountered rampaging Italians. He then returned to the capital on 24 February with a military escort, but found life in the city very difficult. So a month later he returned to Alem Gena, where he and his brother settled and set up a small grain-trading business.

After the Liberation Gebre-Sillassé became a successful and well-known businessman and a promoter of national football. In 1964 his company, the Ethiopian Tyre Economy Plant, won the Haile Selassie Prize Trust award for Industry. Gebre-Sillassé Oda published his memoirs in 1992/93.

151. Gebre-Sillassé Oda in 1991/2

Open Wounds

The massacre of Addis Ababa left a legacy of suffering for those maimed, mutilated and mentally scarred, and grief for the loss of loved ones. Ten years afterwards, in 1947, an American journalist in Addis Ababa was struck by the open wound. Commenting on how the Occupation had left thousands of orphans,[20] he wrote, 'Even today, twelve years after Mussolini's Blackshirts began their "master race" invasion of Ethiopia, stark and grim, living reminders of Fascist occupation may be met daily on the streets of Addis Ababa ... At the telegraph office [of the Post Office] a young man who receives foreign telegrams from the public looks sad even today—five of his young friends were burnt alive, he told us, in their benzine-soaked homes during the terrible Graziani massacre in Addis Ababa in February, 1937.'[21]

Almost seven decades after those lines were written, for many of the survivors interviewed by the present author there has still been no apology and no serious attempts at restitution. Moreover, the mortal remains of lost spouses, parents and siblings never having been found, there have been no burials and no closure.

A New Martyrs Memorial

By the mid-1950s the Cold War was steering Emperor Haile Selassie towards the non-aligned movement, among whose leading lights were Marshal Tito of Yugoslavia, Abdel Nasser of Egypt and Pandit Nehru of India. On 21 December 1955 Marshal Tito arrived in Addis Ababa for a state visit, staying at the Gennete-Li'ul Palace.

Despite their differences in political outlook, the two heads of state had quite a lot in common, and the state visit was to be warmly reciprocated, for both countries had been invaded by Fascist Italy and both peoples had suffered similar atrocities during Italian occupation—in several cases at the hands of the same notorious military commanders, such as General Alessandro Pirzio-Biroli, who was responsible for atrocities in both Ethiopia and Montenegro. It was thus fitting that Tito presented Ethiopia with a monument of remembrance for the victims of the Massacre of Addis Ababa. A gigantic obelisk, it supported a double frieze consisting of six massive bronze reliefs depicting the massacre and the funeral held for the victims at the Trinity Cathedral after the Liberation, surmounted by the Lion of Judah. It was erected at Siddist Kilo in place of the previous monument, where it can still be seen today.

Not only was the new monument clad in fine marble, but the bronze reliefs were the work of the two most celebrated Yugoslavian sculptors of the day: Antun Augustinčić, assisted by Frano Kršinić. A specialist in monumental works, Augustinčić, state sculptor of Yugoslavia, had created a bronze statue of Tito at the marshal's birthplace, in addition to numerous other national and international commissions. Kršinić was also a monumental sculptor of international standing, and the fact that the *Yekatit 12* bronze reliefs are the product of a team consisting of such famous sculptors, and are of massive dimensions, makes the monument an international masterpiece. Apart from being a fitting tribute to the first victims of Fascism, the new *Yekatit 12* memorial represents one of Addis Ababa's finest and most valuable public works of art.[22]

The team responsible for the bronzes was so meticulous in the research its members conducted into the massacre, and in its depiction in the relief work, that it has been possible for the present author to refer to several of the bronzes to illustrate and bear witness to various phases of the massacre.[23]

The Valiant Warrior

In 1955 Sylvia Pankhurst, seeing that there was no further need for the anti-Fascist campaigns of *New Times and Ethiopia News*, brought the newspaper to an end, and decided at the age of 73 to move with her son Richard to Ethiopia. *New Times and Ethiopia News* was replaced by the monthly *Ethiopia Observer*. She died in Addis Ababa in 1960, and was buried at the Sillassé Cathedral in the presence of the Emperor in an area allotted to the most distinguished of Ethiopian Patriots, next to the grave of Ethiopia's first Patriarch, *Abune* Basilios. A note found later among her papers read, 'Let me be counted among the citizens of the world who own no barrier of race or nation, whose hopes are set on the golden age of universal fraternity to come.'[24]

152. The new *Yekatit 12* Monument at Siddist Kilo. A gift from Yugoslavia, with bronze reliefs by world-renowned sculptors Antun Augustinčić and Frano Kršinić

Dr Ladislas Shashka[25]

Dr Shashka, the sensitive, humanitarian Hungarian physician, born in 1890, who arrived in Ethiopia with his wife in 1933 to work for *Ras* Desta, and wrote the most extensive eyewitness account of the Massacre of Addis Ababa ever published, left Addis Ababa in July–August 1937 to settle in Arusha, in the British colony of Tanganyika (now Tanzania). He wrote the journal of his experiences during the Invasion and Occupation of Ethiopia between 1937 and 1940 in Hungarian. As a specialist in malaria and cancer, he also conducted important research and discovered several plants, which are named after him.

It is likely that Herbert Jevons, then secretary of the Abyssinian Association in England, had Dr Shashka's text translated into English; the task was given to Menczer Béla, a Hungarian émigré in London who was also writing for Sylvia Pankhurst's *New Times and Ethiopia News*.

After completing his Ethiopia memoir, Dr Shashka remained for several decades in Tanzania and produced a number of monographs, but wrote almost nothing more about his experiences in Ethiopia, apart from a description of how the Italians tried to confiscate his medical office. His reluctance to write may have arisen from a

153. Dr Ladislas Shashka in the 1960s

desire not to be reminded of the personal humiliations and intimidation he suffered from the Fascist authorities on a number of occasions—as did many European residents of Ethiopia, who were generally persuaded to leave or were expelled on some pretext or the other, unless they were willing to submit and work for the occupying forces. Dr Shashka died in 1978.

Tamrat Istifanos

Tamrat Istifanos, who talked to the present author about the hospitalisation of Graziani after *Yekatit 12*, and described the conditions around the Italian Hospital during the massacre, became a member of the Addis Ababa underground resistance—a *yewist arbeñña*. Tamrat's contribution to the Patriot movement was recognised by Taddesse Zeweldé in *Qerin Geremew*.[26] After the Liberation Tamrat went on to enjoy a career with the Djibouti–Addis Ababa railway. He died in 2009.

Tekle-Maryam Kiflom

Tekle-Maryam Kiflom, who watched the massacre unfold, was arrested, imprisoned and released, and survived the arson because he lived in the

154. Tamrat Istifanos became a Patriot

Exclusion Zone marked out of bounds for the flame-throwers; he joined the military and eventually became a Deputy Minister at the Imperial Palace. He died in 2010.

Asnake and Zenebech Werqineh

Like many other Addis Ababa residents, Asnake and Zenebech Werqineh, whose house was miraculously overlooked during the Blackshirt onslaught at Biscutti Fabrica, decided to leave the city. Their destination was Debre Marqos in Gojjam. They chose a village near the town, and moved their effects there a few at a time, so as not to attract the attention of the Italian authorities. They never returned to Addis Ababa. Today their descendants give thanks on the 16th of every Ethiopian month for Asnake's and Zenebech's narrow escape.

Sara Gebre-Iyyesus

Beshahwired Habte-Weld's wife, the redoubtable Sara Gebre-Iyyesus, who was beaten up and arrested minutes after the attack on Graziani, was made to walk through the Circle of Death, was imprisoned and watched Addis Ababa burn, was sentenced to life imprisonment (for no stated reason) and incarcerated in Italy with her children. When asked to sign a form requesting her release under the Duke of Aosta, she refused, saying that, since her permission had not been considered necessary for her imprisonment, it should not be necessary for her release. She was eventually freed and returned to Ethiopia.

A most remarkable woman, Sara Gebre-Iyyesus was articulate and possessed an extraordinary memory. A major contributor to this book, she died in 2011, shortly before her 100th birthday.

Welette-Birhan Gebre-Iyyesus and Yeweynishet Beshwired

Sara's sister, Welette-Birhan Gebre-Iyyesus, who worked as a nurse and met Sara within the Circle of Death, remained in Addis Ababa during the

Occupation. In a case of mistaken identity, she was sentenced to death but managed to effect an eleventh-hour escape from the gallows. Like Sara, she contributed a great deal to this book, but her own adventurous story is yet to be told. Welette-Birhan died in 2008 at the age of 93.

Sara's daughter Yeweynishet, who was with her mother during her arrest and imprisonment in Italy, agreed to numerous interviews during the course of the production of this book, and continues to be of great assistance to the present author in his research into the Occupation.

Taddesse Tiruneh

Taddesse Tiruneh, who shared a room with Moges Asgedom, watched his brother Sibhat, Moges and Abriha Deboch originate and plot the attack that

155. Sara Gebre-Iyyesus in her mid-nineties, in 2005

eventually evolved into the strike of *Yekatit 12*, witnessed the early stages of the Massacre of Addis Ababa and then sheltered at the Hermannsburg Mission, was asked by Hermann Bahlburg's assistant, Hinrich Rathje, to stay on at the mission and help with the school. However, Taddesse, who was upset over the death of Sibhat, turned down the offer.[27]

After a period of residence with a family friend named *Qés* (Priest) Badima Yelaw, Taddesse left Addis Ababa to become a Patriot. In due course he joined the British army and returned victorious to Addis Ababa in 1941. He then pursued a career in government. Taddesse Tiruneh, who engaged in numerous interviews and discussions with the present author, died during the final stages of preparation of this book.

Dr Birhanu Abebe

The distinguished historian, scholar and author Dr Birhanu Abebe (b. 1933), who provided considerable assistance in the research conducted for this book, recounted his mother's reminiscences about the burning of his family home during the massacre, and made available precious film of the burning of houses and of smouldering bodies of victims at Gulelé, tragically died while on an international consulting assignment in Zimbabwe in 2008.

Ambassador Imru Zelleqe

Ambassador Imru Zelleqe, who as a boy watched the unfolding of the massacre in Arada, and was imprisoned with his mother in Akaki and Danane, became a government official, diplomat and an international banker. With an astonishing memory and with immense knowledge of 20th-century Ethiopian history, his reminiscences have constituted valuable contributions to this book. Today Ambassador Imru lives in the United States.

Blatta Mehari Kassa

Blatta Mehari Kassa (b. c.1903), who was a contemporary and close friend of Sibhat Tiruneh and Belay Hayle-Ab, was at school with Moges Asgedom and Abriha Deboch (whom he knew well), and during the massacre took shelter at the Hermannsburg Mission, went on to become a senior civil servant. Married to *Weyzero* Itenat Kassa Nejo, he worked at the Ministry of Commerce and Industry, and was appointed librarian at the Imperial Palace.

156. Welette-Birhan Gebre-Iyessus (left) with her niece, Yeweynishet Beshahwired, in 2005

157. Taddesse Tiruneh in 2004

158. Dr Birhanu Abebe (1933–2008)

159. Ambassador Imru Zelleqe   160. *Blatta* Mehari Kassa in 1960

He also edited books for writers such as his friend Haddis Alemayehu.[28] Interviewed at the age of 101, a spritely *Blatta* Mehari was able to recall in detail his early days with Sibhat Tiruneh, Moges Asgedom, Abriha Deboch and Belay Hayle-Ab, and the Massacre of Addis Ababa. *Blatta* Mehari Kassa died peacefully in Addis Ababa in 2005 at the age of about 102.[29]

Immahoy Hiruta

Immahoy Hiruta (b. c.1921), whose house was invaded by the Blackshirts at the beginning of the massacre, and who helped prisoners escape from the Central Police Station at Fit Ber, converted from Islam to Ethiopian Orthodox Christianity and became a notable figure in the church community in Addis Ababa. She was living in the home for retired nuns attached to the Church of Ta'eka Negest Be'ata when interviewed by the present author in February 2009. *Immahoy* Hiruta is understood to have died in 2011 at the age of around 90.

Dyakon Dawit Gebre-Mesqel

Dyakon Dawit Gebre-Mesqel, who was attached to the Church of Ta'eka Negest Be'ata and was secretary of St George's School for Boys when Abriha Deboch was teaching there, chose not to attend the event of *Yekatit 12*, was

161. Dawit Gebre-Mesqel in his house behind the Church of Ta'eka Negest Be'ata, Addis Ababa, in 2009

162. Demissé Hayle-Maryam in 2004

rounded up with his colleagues at the Church of Kidane Mihret, and narrowly escaped execution during the massacre, continued to live in the same church house for some 75 years until his death in 2010, after a lifetime of devotion to the church, at the age of around 98.

Shaleqa Éfrém Gebre-Amlak

Shaleqa Éfrém Gebre-Amlak (b. c.1923), who in December 2004 assisted the present author by recounting his memories of life in Addis Ababa during the Occupation, including his experiences during the massacre, and the position of Eritrean families both in the military and in Addis Ababa at that time, is understood to have died during the preparation of this book.

Demissé Hayle-Maryam

Demissé Hayle-Maryam, who knew several of the *Yekatit 12* plotters, sheltered at the British legation from the Massacre of Addis Ababa, went on to lead an adventurous life as a Patriot. Demissé joined the British army in a battalion known as 'Army Ethiopia', and eventually returned in triumph to Addis Ababa under General Cunningham. After the Liberation he became a businessman.

Full of memories and good humour, Demissé engaged in many conversations and interviews with the present author over a period of several years during his long retirement in the Ethiopian town of Nazereth. Demissé Hayle-Maryam died in 2014 at the age of 92.

Tekle-Tsadik Mekuriya

Tekle-Tsadik Mekuriya (b. 1914), who in 1998 recounted to the present author his experiences during the Massacre of Addis Ababa, his journey to

163. Historian Tekle-Tsadiq-Meruriya

Danane concentration camp and his two-year incarceration there, survived the Occupation. Fluent in both French and Italian, he was appointed secretary-general of the Ministry of Education in 1945, and in 1952 embarked on a diplomatic career. He served as director of the National Library, rose to the level of Minister of Culture, Sports and Youth, and became known as one of Ethiopia's most prolific and well-loved historical writers. Tekle-Tsadiq Mekuriya died in 2000 at the age of 86.[30]

164. Dr Siyum Gebre-Igziabhér in 2000

Dr Siyum Gebre-Igziabhér

Dr Siyum Gebre-Igziabhér, who as an eight-year-old boy living in Jan Méda accomplished the extraordinary feat of walking through the centre of Addis Ababa during the first night of the massacre of *Yekatit 12* in an unsuccessful search for his father, and ended up being arrested and detained in a detention camp at the Ras Mekonnin Bridge, studied in the United States and worked in a number of public offices in Ethiopia, including that of *Kentiba* (Mayor) of Gondar. After several years as an international civil servant and adviser, Dr Siyum currently lives in the United States.

A Mistake

On 24 November 1997 the Italian President Oscar Luigi Scalfaro, the first Italian leader to visit Ethiopia since the Occupation, concluded his four-day visit with a statement describing the Invasion and Occupation as a mistake. He said that in discussions with Ethiopian President Negasso Gidada and Prime Minister Meles Zenawi he had acknowledged Italy's 'mistakes and guilt' for attacking Ethiopia, and described the Invasion as 'bloody pages' in Italian history.[31] However, he stopped short of an outright apology for the Invasion, the Occupation, or atrocities committed.

The Unsung Heroes

After the defeat of the Italians and the collapse of the short-lived Italian empire, Hermann Bahlburg, the head of the German Hermannsburg Mission, who reportedly saved the lives of many Ethiopians during the Massacre of Addis Ababa by allowing them to shelter at the mission, was detained and imprisoned with Hinrich Rathje by the British in British Somaliland until 1948.[32] In 1948 he returned to the Addis Ababa mission, but tensions within the Hermannsburg Mission organisation raised by suspicions that he might have been a Nazi sympathiser resulted in a ban on his preaching. In response, he resigned. He returned to Germany, where he lived until his death on 19 February 1962—ironically, exactly 25 years after *Yekatit 12*.

In April 2009, following a January meeting in Addis Ababa of the Ethiopian Mekane Yesus Church (which to a great extent had sprung from the pioneering work of the Hermannsburg Evangelical Mission), officials of the Evangelical Lutheran Mission in Germany showed that they had not forgotten Hermann Bahlburg's heroism. They awarded him (posthumously) a medal for saving the lives of the Ethiopians to whom he gave shelter from the Massacre of Addis Ababa, including 12 Orthodox priests thought to have come from the nearby Church of Qechené Medhané Alem. Members of Bahlburg's family received the medal on his behalf.

The award marked the culmination of a period of rehabilitation of Bahlburg's reputation.[33] Thus not long before this book went to press, Bahlburg's heroism, although still unknown to the majority of Ethiopians, was no longer 'unsung'.[34] Bahlburg performed a most charitable and humane service to the residents of Addis Ababa, and it is fitting that this service should have been recognised, albeit belatedly.[35]

The American consul-general and resident minister, Cornelius Engert, who placed no less than 700 Ethiopians under the protection of the American flag during the Massacre of Addis Ababa, was transferred to Iran. He left the city when the legation closed a few weeks after *Yekatit 12*. Nonetheless, he maintained his personal friendship with Emperor Haile Selassie, visiting the sovereign during his exile in England.

Engert pursued his career with the American foreign service until 1945, when he retired. He visited the Emperor again in Addis Ababa in 1948, and continued an active public life until the 1980s, by which time he was recognised by the State Department as by far the oldest surviving retired foreign service officer.[36] Cornelius Engert died in Washington in 1985, at the age of 97. Although many families in Addis Ababa today owe their very existence to him, his heroic service to the city in February 1937 has never been recognised, so far as the present author is aware.

The Jubilee of Yekatit 12

On 19 February 2012, a celebration was conducted at Addis Ababa University for the Jubilee—the 75th anniversary—of *Yekatit 12*. The event was held on the very spot where the attack took place and the massacre began. Facing the dais of the Gennete–Li'ul Palace (now the Institute of Ethiopian Studies of the University of Addis Ababa), a crowd of dignitaries, ageing Patriots, students and the general public watched a re-enactment of the strike of *Yekatit 12* and the turmoil that followed. After the drama and musical performances outside the Palace, a symposium on *Yekatit 12* was held inside.

Among the many in attendance were several residents of the city who had suffered during the massacre, including Yeweynishet Beshahwired; Patriot Demissé Hayle-Maryam, who had sheltered from the massacre at the British legation and trekked afterwards with Letyibelu Gebré to escape the Italian dragnet; and former Patriots representing the Patriots' Association. A guest of honour was Richard Pankhurst, whose mother Sylvia had supported Ethiopia by leading the international lobby against Mussolini, and who himself had distributed his mother's pamphlet on Fascist war crimes to the delegates at the 1947 peace talks in Paris.

On the first floor of the palace an exhibition of photographs related to the massacre was officially opened. Interestingly, several groups of Italian visitors to the photographic exhibition demanded its closure, though on what grounds is not clear.

The Ghost of Graziani

In August 2012 there was an extraordinary development in Italy. The mayor of the small town of Affile, where Graziani spent part of his young life, used public funds to establish a one-acre memorial park dedicated to the former Viceroy, incorporating a monument and a mausoleum. Designed in Fascist style, and surmounted with the inscription 'Fatherland—Honour' in a Fascist font, the complex was officially opened in front of an admiring crowd keen to honour the man they were proud to call 'the son of Affile'. In September and October Ethiopians, Libyans and their supporters staged protests outside the Italian embassies and ambassadorial residences in London and Washington.

165. Students of Addis Ababa University stage a symbolic re-enactment of the strike against the Italian High Command at the Gennete-Li'ul Palace on the 75th anniversary of *Yekatit 12*

For several weeks there was little reaction in Italy, where, not surprisingly, few Italians today—particularly the younger generation—are aware of what their forebears did in Libya and Ethiopia. Indeed, such aspects of modern Italian history are not covered in Italy's school textbooks. Nonetheless, in due course the international reaction to publicity on the internet attracted wider Italian interest, and by November some Italians had reacted. In November 2012 demonstrators descended on Affile, where they daubed anti-Fascist slogans on the monument, held rallies and conducted a torch-light parade to protest against the Graziani memorial park, expressing outrage that their fellow citizens should be honouring someone regarded as one of the greatest war criminals of the 20th century.

At the 76th *Yekatit 12* memorial service in Addis Ababa on 19 February 2013, the Patriots in attendance took the unprecedented step of combining with the ceremony of remembrance a demonstration that made it clear that, despite being nonagenarians, their task was not yet finished. Having lost family and friends in the Massacre of Addis Ababa or in the horrors that followed it, they had been shocked to learn about the Graziani memorial. In the shadow of the monument of *Yekatit 12*, where the killing had begun, Ethiopian children re-enacted the massacre in front of a large picture of the slaughter, which they had painted in traditional Ethiopian style.

Armed with placards reading 'Down with the Followers of Graziani!', 'The Struggle of the Ethiopian Patriots Continues!', 'The Young Generation Will Uphold the Honour of our Forefathers!' and 'We Request the People of Ethiopia to Stand with Us Against Fascism!', the Patriots marched down to the Cathedral of the Holy Trinity, where they assembled at the

166. Former Patriots at the Cathedral of the Holy Trinity in Addis Ababa gather to denounce the Affile monument

great west door, just a few steps away from the Cenotaph of the Martyrs of *Yekatit 12*. Grim-faced, resolute and resplendent in their immaculate uniforms, they honoured the dead and protested against the Graziani memorial in a series of moving speeches.

At the time of going to press, the Affile affair is far from over. Following international protests, public funding for the monument was suspended, and in April 2013 the Ethiopian Minister of Foreign Affairs stated that Graziani should continue to be condemned for his war crimes, genocidal activity and crimes against humanity. However, it is still unclear what the upshot will be. There were expectations that the Italian government would issue a statement denouncing the monument, but to date it remains tight-lipped. Nonetheless, what is clear is that, though the name of Guido Cortese has been forgotten, the world has not yet heard the last of Rodolfo Graziani.

APPENDIX I

YOUNG ETHIOPIANS EXECUTED FOLLOWING *YEKATIT 12*

The term Young Ethiopians here refers to male Ethiopians and Eritreans who attended formal education either in Ethiopia or abroad during the 1920s and the first half of the 1930s. It includes those who were also cadets at Holetta Military Academy, members of the Black Lion resistance organisation, and members of the nobility. The total number of Young Ethiopians killed by the Italians during Graziani's pogrom to liquidate the young intelligentsia following *Yekatit 12* is estimated to be between 400 and 600, with a mean of around 500 (chapter 11, phase ix). While it is not possible at present to be more precise than this, it is possible to identify at least some of those who died, and estimate what the death toll represented as a proportion of the Young Ethiopians.

There are considerably more data on those who went abroad for secondary or tertiary education than there are for those educated in Ethiopia. For this reason these two categories of Young Ethiopian are addressed separately.

YOUNG ETHIOPIANS EDUCATED OVERSEAS

Because the number of young men who went overseas for higher education was relatively small, travel overseas was documented, and many of the students concerned were quite well known, it has proved possible for researchers to compile a considerable amount of data on the subject. The first scholar to attempt an analysis was Richard Pankhurst, who published in *Ethiopia Observer* in 1962 the names of the majority of the students by country of study, with notes on their fate, as gleaned from an analysis of whatever data were available at the time, supplemented by interviews with contemporaries.[1] This was followed by the work of Christopher Clapham, who built on Pankhurst's findings by further in-depth research in 1964 in Addis Ababa, culminating in a longer list,[2] a summary of which he later published in his book *Haile-Selassie's Government*.[3] For half a century Clapham's list has remained the most comprehensive list of Young Ethiopians educated abroad before the Italian invasion.

As noted by Pankhurst, the Ethiopians who went abroad to study can be categorised by country of destination, as follows):[4]

- France: the largest contingent—at least 63 students—attended a variety of institutions, including Saint-Cyr military academy (French being, at the time, Ethiopia's principal foreign language;
- Egypt: at one time 40 students, mainly at the Lycée Français in Alexandria, but also at Victoria College, and some in Cairo (from Egypt some went on to study in Europe or America);
- England: at least 25 students, at a variety of institutions;
- America: at least 8 students, at a variety of institutions;
- Lebanon: at least 20 students, including several from Teferi Mekonnin School, almost all of whom went to the American University of Beirut (from Lebanon some went on to study in France or America);
- Switzerland: at least 10 students, including five women;
- Italy: at least ten students;
- Germany: 2 students;
- Belgium: 2 students;
- Spain: 1 student;
- Greece and Sudan;
- the Vatican: several students went to the Pontificio Collegio Etiopico (est. 1919), which received four Ethiopian students before the mid-1920s, though here we are concerned with subsequent groups, arriving in 1924, 1928, 1931 and 1932, consisting of a total of 27 students;
- a total of 22 students from the Falasha School in Addis Ababa were also sent during the period concerned to a variety of countries, mainly Palestine (Jerusalem) and Egypt.

In total, Pankhurst identified around 210 Ethiopian students who studied overseas during the 'Regent Teferi Mekonnin—Emperor Haile Selassie' period prior to the Italian invasion, of whom 40 were said to still be overseas by December 1934.[5] Clapham expanded the list to a total of 248 students,[6] to which he later added a further four.[7] The present author has supplemented that figure by an additional one, bringing the total to 253. Of these, 23 died of causes other than those attributable to the Italian invasion, occupation or war of liberation, leaving a balance of 230 to be accounted for.

As already noted, there were around 40 students overseas in December 1934, and this figure would have increased during 1935 as more students joined them. On the other hand, a few were recalled. A reasonable estimate of the number of students overseas when the Italian invasion began would be around 50, which leaves 230–50 = 180 to account for in Ethiopia.

How many of these 180 Ethiopia-based graduates survived the Italian period? Clapham shows that of the total 253 foreign-educated graduates identified, at least 137 survived. Since an estimated 50 of these survived because they were outside Ethiopia, the number in Ethiopia who survived is at least 137–50 = 87. If at least 87 of the 180 foreign-educated graduates in Ethiopia survived, then what happened to the remaining 93? Nine are known to have died during the war of invasion, and twenty in the pogrom following *Yekatit 12*, but the remaining 64 disappeared from view.

How can the 64 whose fate was unknown be accounted for? Were they also killed? Most of the foreign-educated survivors were known to Pankhurst's and Clapham's informants, who were contemporaries of these students (and in some cases were included among them), were well connected and had a wide network of contacts. Thus, although some of the graduates, no doubt, deliberately kept a low profile outside Addis Ababa, living in obscurity or dying of natural causes, the inevitable conclusion is that the majority of those whose fate was unknown must have died, undocumented, in prisons or concentration camps. Of the 64 whose fate was still unknown in the early 1960s, it would be reasonable to assume that two-thirds died during the Occupation in prison or in Danane or Nocra concentration camps. This assumption would mean that of the foreign-educated Young Ethiopians identified, an estimated 20 + (64 x 2/3) = 63 died following *Yekatit 12*. However, this estimate has a wide confidence interval: from a minimum of 20 to a maximum of 84.

This estimate is, of course, based on the overseas students who have been identified by name; it does not include those who are not captured in the data available. To cover this, a contingency of 10 per cent is added to these figures. Thus the final estimate is that the number of students who went overseas to be educated was around 253 + 10% = 278, of whom approximately 69 died in the liquidation of the intelligentsia following *Yekatit 12*, with a range from a minimum of 22 to a maximum of 92.

Since there were less than 300 foreign-educated Young Ethiopian graduates, it has frequently been concluded that the death toll of several hundred Young Ethiopians means that virtually all of them were liquidated. This common assumption overlooks the fact that, as we shall see, there were many *locally-educated* Young Ethiopians. As the analysis above shows (and as first revealed by Clapham), although the pogrom was devastating and unconscionable, it actually eliminated less than 100 of the estimated 278 foreign-educated Young Ethiopians, leaving alive a sufficient number to take up key positions in the post-Liberation government.

The names of foreign-educated Young Ethiopians who can be identified as having been executed, together with their place, and subject, of study (where available), are listed below. As will be noticed, the executions were particularly focused on those who were in tertiary education and who had studied in England or France.

- Awdisa Birbisu: Sudan
- Aweqe Ingida: England (politics)
- Ayana Biru: England, Camborne School of Mines
- Bahru Keba: France, Saint–Cyr (military studies)[8]
- Binyam Werqineh: England, Loughborough College
- Beshahwired Habte-Weld: India; USA, Muskingum College, Ohio (economics)
- Feqade-Sillassé Hiruy: England, Cambridge University
- Gebre-Medhin Aweke: England (agriculture)
- Gebre-Iyyesus Gebre-Kidan: France
- Getachew Zawge: France
- Hayle Dilbo: Palestine
- Heywet Wendyrad: France
- Kifle Nesibu: France, Saint–Cyr (military studies)
- Mekonnin Hayle: Lebanon, Beirut; USA, Cornell University (finance)
- Mulugéta Demera: Sudan
- Tedla Hayle: France
- Tsigé-Marqos Welde-Tekle: England (economics)
- Yilma Mengesha: Egypt
- Yohannis Boru: Egypt, Victoria College, Alexandria; England (engineering)
- Yoséf Werqineh: England, Loughborough College

Those who are known to have died fighting the Italians are:

- Abebe Massay: France

- Dañe Wedajo: Egypt, Lycée Français, Alexandria; France, Saint-Cyr
- Gebre-Iyyesus Biratu: Lebanon (literature and journalism)
- Mekonnin Gobew: England (languages)—died as a Patriot in Gojjam, c.1940
- Pawlos Badima: Lebanon (music)—killed during the rioting of 2 May 1936[9]
- Taddesse Mulugéta: France, Saint-Cyr (military studies)
- Wakjira Gobena: France, Saint-Cyr (military studies)
- Yeshitela Hizgias: Germany (carpentry)
- Zewdé Beyen: USA

Those whose fate is unknown, but of whom an estimated two-thirds died in the liquidation of the intelligentsia (through either execution or internment), are:[10]

- Abebe Damtew Ze'amanuél: France
- Abebe Welde-Giyorgis: France (sculpture)
- Abraha Bokru: Egypt
- Alber Muslem: France
- Amlete Afewerq: Italy
- Abraha Sibhatu: Vatican, Pontificio Collegio Etiopico (arr. 1931)
- Abraha Tekle-Sillassé: Vatican, Pontificio Collegio Etiopico (arr. 1931)
- Asfaw Giyorgis: France
- Ayelew Yimmer: Lebanon
- Ayele Welde-Giyorgis: France
- Benega Tesfa-Maryam: Italy (medicine)
- Birhanu Wendim: Lebanon
- Endale Welde-Maryam
- Feleqe Welde-Hanna: Italy
- Gebre-Iyyesus Bitu
- Gebre Mesqel
- Gebre Tsadiq
- Gebre Zewdé[11]
- Gedeon Yoftahé: Sudan
- Gétahun Chekol
- Gelagel Desta: Lebanon, St Joseph's, Beirut; France
- Gobena Ayana
- Hayle-Maryam Birhane: Vatican, Pontificio Collegio Etiopico (arr. 1932)
- Hayle-Maryam Tekle-Birhan: Vatican, Pontificio Collegio Etiopico (arr. 1928)
- Hika Wodajo (or Wodajo Hika): Alexandria, Victoria College

- Ingida Tsege Hanna: Egypt
- Kebede Beyen: Italy
- Ligiam Yishak: Vatican: Pontificio Collegio Etiopico (arr. 1932)
- Mekonnin Chekol: Lebanon
- Mengistu Asgedom: Vatican: Pontificio Collegio Etiopico (arr. 1931)
- Moges Welde-Yohannis: Alexandria, Lycée Français; France
- Mohamed Mehadi: Lebanon; France
- Momecha Yigzew: France
- Mulatu: Sudan
- Mulugéta Gebre-Mesqel: Lebanon; France
- Petros Segid: Vatican: Pontificio Collegio Etiopico (arr. 1924)
- Qashi Gebre-Sillassé: Sweden
- Sabagadis Sibhat
- Samu'él Gebre-Essayas
- Sergut Qal Welde-Tsadiq
- Siyum Retta
- Sileshi Yigzew: France
- Taddesse Bizuneh
- Taddesse Defersha
- Taddesse Mola: France
- Taddesse Tessema: Italy
- Tadla Hayle-Giyorgis
- Tekle-Birhan Germu: France (engineering)
- Tekle-Birhan Tsadiq: Alexandria, Lycée Français
- Tekle-Maryam Tokruray: Vatican: Pontificio Collegio Etiopico (arr. 1931)
- Terefe Bantywalu
- Tesfa Mika'él (brother of Kebede Mika'él): France
- Tesfa-Mika'él Hayle: France, Le Bourget (aviation); Alexandria, Lycée Français
- Welde-Gebriél Welde Sel
- Welde-Giyorgis Tedla
- Wedle Kidane: Alexandria, Lycée Français; France (engineering)
- Welde-Kidan Beyen
- Yacob Mahmud: Vatican, Pontificio Collegio Etiopico (arr. 1919)
- Yilma Beyene
- Yohannis Abraha: Sudan
- Yohannis Gebre-Maryam: Vatican: Pontificio Collegio Etiopico (arr. 1921)
- Yoséf Tekle-Mika'él: Vatican, Pontificio Collegio Etiopico

APPENDIX I

– Zeray Soquar: Vatican: Pontificio Collegio Etiopico (arr. 1931)
– Zewdé Begele

Note: A number of Ethiopian students from Teferi Mekonnin School spent one year at a college in Cairo while their colleagues were in Alexandria. These students do not seem to have been included in the Pankhurst–Clapham lists of foreign-educated Ethiopians, presumably because they were not in Cairo long enough to have completed a course of studies there (with the exception of Iyyasu Mengesha (later General), who went on to study at Saint-Cyr). These include, for example, Abriha Deboch (executed for involvement in *Yekatit 12*), Zewdé Gebre-Hiwott (later, *Shaqa*),[12] Tefera Seyfu, Tefera Sheshu and Welde-Maryam Hayle (later, General).[13]

YOUNG ETHIOPIANS EDUCATED IN ETHIOPIA

If approximately 500 Young Ethiopians were executed, of whom less than 100 were foreign educated, then the balance of more than 400 were locally educated. What does this figure represent in terms of the total number?

By the time of the Italian invasion, 495 students had studied at the Teferi Mekonnin School, the country's leading educational establishment.[14] Other schools for boys, as documented by Richard Pankhurst,[15] were the Menelik II School (est. 1908; 150 pupils by 1935)[16] Lycée Haile Selassie I (est. 1930; 100 pupils), St George's School (est. 1929; approx. 200 pupils), School for the Redeemer for Orphans (est. 1932; approx. 100 pupils) and the Falasha School (1924). Schools catering for foreign communities as well as Ethiopians included Alliance Française (450 students enrolled by 1935) and several mission-run schools, a Boy Scouts School (1934), the Imperial School of Art, and 14 primary schools set up in provincial towns. Although precise figures are not available, it can be estimated that by 1935/6 there were around 1,500 young locally educated Ethiopian males having undergone a *complete* course of education.

Of these, as we have seen, an estimated 278 left for further education overseas, leaving around 1,220 in Ethiopia. Assuming that 9 per cent died from causes unrelated to the Italian invasion (that is, at the same death rate experienced by the overseas students), this leaves approximately 1,130 locally educated Young Ethiopians to be accounted for. Not all of these were necessarily targeted by the Italians after *Yekatit 12*; those to be executed were principally—though not exclusively—those who had *secondary* education. Thus the estimated 400 or more locally educated Young Ethiopians executed represent around a third of the total.

Only a small fraction of those who died can be identified, and most of these were former Holetta cadets, who were easily pointed out to the Italians by informers. There is very little information on the others, presumably because they were relatively unknown. Several of them were killed because they were Protestants, and their fate was sometimes known to foreign missionaries, such as the four Young Ethiopians who worked with Alfred Buxton teaching Bible classes, of whom three were killed after *Yekatit 12* (Temesgen Gebré being the sole survivor), together with 50 (presumably the majority) of their Bible Study students.[17] But the deaths of the majority of locally educated victims remain undocumented.

The following list identifies 27 locally educated former Holetta cadets known to have been executed following *Yekatit 12*. It is an amalgamation of those identified by Birhanu Dinqé (mainly former Holetta cadets and members of Black Lion), Taddesse Mécha (including civilian members of Black Lion), and those listed in chapter 9 as having been executed, but excluding those educated overseas.[18](The abbreviations MT for Black Lion military trainer and ECM for Black Lion executive committee member have been used after many of the names.)

- Assefa Admasu (MT)
- Assefa Tedla (MT)
- Lieutenant Bayu Gebru Yohannis
- Colonel Belay Hayle-Ab (chief instructor, Black Lion)
- Lieutenant Birhanu Hayle (son of *Blatta* Hayle Welde-Kidan)
- Debre Gebru (ECM)
- Desta Bahru (ECM)
- Captain Desta Tenna (son of Mayor Tena Gashaw of Ankober); he is also listed in the *carabinieri* report as one of the first ex-Holetta cadets to be arrested after *Yekatit 12*[19]
- Desta Welde-Iyyesus (ECM)
- Captain Gétachew Belayneh (employed at the hot springs)
- Gétachew Zewuge (ECM)
- Lieutenant Gebre Hiwett (son of *Negadras* Gebre Hiwett)
- Captain Kebede Akale-Hiwett
- Lieutenant Kebede Desta (MT; brother of Captain Mitike Desta)
- Ketema Beshah (Black Lion, senior member)

- Captain Laqew Habte-Mikaél (ECM)
- Captain Matyas Gemeda (ECM; son of *Ato* Gemeda of Wellega)
- Lieutenant Mengesha Gebru (son of *Kentiba* Gebru of Gondar)
- Meshesha Gebru (MT)
- Captain Mitike Desta (MT)
- Mulugéta Assefa
- Siyum Qechené (MT)
- Lieutenant Taddesse Sileshi (son of *Dejazmach* Sileshi of Wello)
- Lieutenant Tefera Yazew[20] (MT; son of *Ras* Yazew)
- Tekle-Birhan Dessaleñ (MT)
- Captain Yohannis Ras Werq (son of Ras Werq, Prior of Afer Bayné Monastery)
- Lieutenant Zegeye Welde-Giorgis (ECM; son of *Ato* Welde-Giyorgis of Harar)

The following two locally educated civilian Young Ethiopians not known to have been Holetta cadets or members of the Black Lion were also executed:

- Mulugéta Assefa
- Mohammed Séyfu

In addition to the above-mentione 30 executed, the fate of several other former Holetta cadets and members of the Black Lion could not be ascertained. In particular, Taddesse Mécha names four other Black Lion military trainers whose fate he was unable to determine:[21]

- *Aleqa* Nigusé Asgedom
- Siyum Habte-Maryam
- Yohannis Afewerq
- Zewdineh Haylé

The *carabinieri* report of 20 February 1937 lists the following additional 34 former Holetta cadets and Young Ethiopians as having been arrested, all of whom are believed to have been locally educated.[22] Their fate is unknown, but it is likely that they were among those executed. (The abbreviation H after many of the names indicates a former Holetta cadet.)

- Abbebe Tefera (H)
- Addunga Faysa (H)
- 'Anchena' (Anteneh?) Bogale
- Asfaw Fiqre-Sillassé (H)

- Banti Welde-Giyorgis Beyene Turé (H)
- Belete Ayele
- Beqele Kiros[23]
- Birhanu Chekol (H)
- 'Chelfe' (Kinfé? Kifle?) Mika'él (H)
- Feleqe Desta (H)
- Galilé Kassay
- Gebre-Maryam Weldeyes
- Gebre-Tsion Negatu
- 'Grebet' Sehale (H)
- Hayle-Maryam Disasé (H)
- Hayle Dagné (H)
- Haylu Mengesha (H)
- Kebebe 'Acalleiot' (Aschilot?) (H)
- Lemma Kassay
- Lemma Mamo (H)
- Lemma Shi'olti?
- Lemma Tessema
- 'Macios' (Mattewos?) Beqele (H)
- Mekonnin Tayé (H)
- Shiferaw Gebru
- Tefera Meshesha
- Tekele Isheté (H)
- Tesfay Beyene (H)
- 'Uguale' (Bogale?) Negatu
- Welde-Maryam 'Abuai'
- Werqu Metaferia (H)
- Yigzew Degefu (H)
- Zelleqe Negatu
- Zewdé Tesfay (H)

Conclusions

An estimated 400–600 Young Ethiopians were executed during the liquidation of the intelligentsia following *Yekatit 12*, the mean of 500 representing approximately a third of the total number of 1,500 educated Young Ethiopians.

Of the total estimated number of 1,500 Young Ethiopians, the foreign-educated contingent accounted for around 278, of whom the number executed was somewhere between 22 and 92, that is a maximum of a third. Many survived the Occupation because they were out of the country at the time, and several of them took up appointments in the post-Liberation government.

The estimated death toll is summarised in Table A.1.

Table A.1: Estimated death toll of Young Ethiopians following *Yekatit 12* (best estimate, followed by approximate range)

	Total educated Young Ethiopians	Executed during the liquidation of the intelligentsia	Died from other causes including the wars of invasion and liberation
Foreign educated	278	69 (22–92)	209 (186–256)
Locally educated	1,222	431 (308–578)	791 (614–914)
Total	1,500	500 (400–600)	1,000 (900–1,100)

APPENDIX II

PARTIAL LIST OF ADDIS ABABA-BASED NOBLES
AND NOTABLES EXECUTED FOLLOWING *YEKATIT 12*

As was noted in chapter 11, some 200 Addis Ababa-based nobles and notables (who were not among the Young Ethiopians identified as being executed) were executed following *Yekatit 12*. Of these, only a few have been identified to date in the following list (which may include a few also classifiable as Young Ethiopians) compiled by Birhanu Dinqé.[1]

- *Fitawrari* Atnaf-Seged Welde-Giyorgis (Governor, Buno Wereda)[2]
- *Qeññazmach* Awulachew (chief storekeeper)
- *Grazmach* Belachew Welde-Qirqos (chief justice, Jimma Province)
- *Ato* Beshiwerq Sahel Dingel (secretary, Ministry of Agriculture)
- *Qeññazmach* Beyene Siyawuqinew
- *Ato* Beyene Tessema (preacher, Hager Fiqir Association); also listed as arrested in the first *carabinieri* report after *Yekatit 12*
- *Fitawrari* Bogale Gebeyehu
- *Bejirond* Birhane Asfaw (servant of *Ras* Birru Welde-Gebriél)
- *Balambaras* Cherinat Ayenew (palace judge)
- *Ato* Demissé Bililiñ (Customs Office employee)
- *Balambaras* Demissé Tekle-Maryam (Governor, Guma Province)
- *Bahtawi* Desta Tedla (son of *Dejazmach* Tedla Guwalu)
- *Ato* Fiqru Gebre-Yohannis (employee, Ministry of Trade)
- *Qeññazmach* Gefa Wessen (*Shum* of Rasgée Bét)
- *Qeññazmach* Hayle Mikaél (deputy chief of staff, Sidama Province); also listed as arrested in the first *carabinieri* report following *Yekatit 12*[3]

- *Qeññazmach* Kassa Abba Wuqaw (Governor of Wellega)
- *Qeññazmach* Kassa Kareru (chief officer, Sidama Province)
- *Qeññazmach* Kifle Welde-Hitsan (Governor, Menagesha Wereda)
- *Ato* Mahtemewerq Isheté (director, Birhanina Selam Printing Press)
- *Balambaras* Mamo Welde-Sillassé (judge, Sidama Province)
- *Fitawrari* Mekonnin Techane (chief officer, Sidama Province)
- *Fitawrari* Mekurya
- *Qeññazmach* Mengesha Yayenew (servant of *Ras* Imru)
- *Ato* Muluneh Gebre-Sillassé (head of finance, Ilubabor Province)
- *Fitawrari* Nigatu Tekle
- *Balambaras* Retta Gebre-Mesqel (justice of the Criminal Court)
- *Aleqa* Sirgew (*Aleqa* of the Church of St Marqos, Upper Gibé [Siddist Kilo Palace])
- *Fitawrari* Tessema Abdi (officer of *Ras* Desta)
- *Qeññazmach* Welde-Giyorgis Bulo (chief groom)
- *Ato* Welde Semaytat (Addis Ababa Customs Office employee)
- *Fitawrari* Werqineh Lemma (head of military barracks, Sidama Province)
- *Ato* Werqu Welde-Tsadiq (preacher, Hager Fiqir Association); also listed as arrested in the first *carabinieri* report after *Yekatit 12*
- *Bejirond* Wubishet Hayle (director, Jimma District)
- *Fitawrari* Yigeremu (chief of staff, Sidama Province)
- *Grazmach* Yilma Nakaré (military commander, Bale Province)

The first *carabinieri* report after *Yekatit 12* lists a number of additional names of notables arrested immediately following the throwing of the grenades.[4] Any names already accounted for here have been removed. However, it is not known which of these additional 22 notables were executed, except where stated.

Notables Arrested Immediately after Yekatit 12

- *Grazmach* Abbebe 'Naichè'
- *Qeññazmach* 'Bellolm' (Belihu?)
- *Ato* 'Benaccio Tadete' (Belachew Taddesse?)
- *Ato* Birhane Marqos (not executed)
- *Fitawrari* Demissé Hapte-Mikaél
- *Bejirond* Fiqre-Sillassé Ketema
- *Grazmach* Hayle-Maryam Gessese
- *Ato* Ibsa

- *Balambaras* 'Immagnu Imer' (Amanuél Yilma or Yemeru?)
- *Ato* Mekonnin Gebrehiwot
- *Dejazmach* Mengesha Wibé
- *Qeññazmach* Molla
- 'Saia Assin'
- *Lij* Seyfu Mikaél
- *Dejazmach* Siyum Desta
- *Ato* Tassew Gossay
- *Grazmach* Tedla Hayle-Giyorgis
- *Ato* Tegeñ
- 'Teremacciò' (Girmachew?) Tekle-Maryam
- Tessema Ali
- *Blattén Géta* Welde-Maryam Haylé

APPENDIX III

Telegram of 19 February 1937 from Minister Alessandro Lessona to Provincial Governors

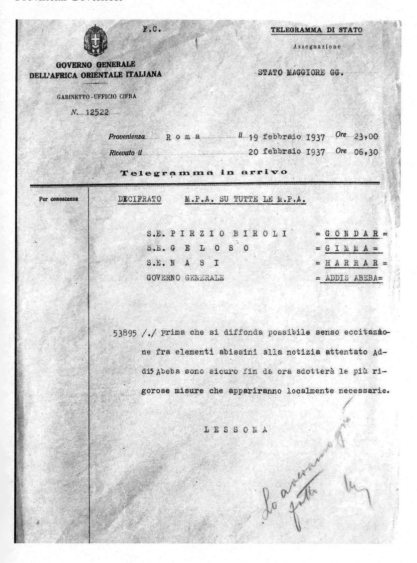

APPENDIX IV

Phonogram of 21 February 1937 from the Fascist Party Office to the Chef de Cabinet

FEDERAZIONE DEI FASCI DI COMBATTIMENTO DI ADDIS ABEBA

n. 12612 di prot.   Addis Abeba 21 febbraio XV°
                                              II° dell'Impero

F O N O G R A M M A   U R G E N T E   a mano

AL CAPO DI GABINETTO DI S.E. IL VICERE'
e per conoscenza :
- Vice Governatore Generale Eccellenza Petretti
- Stato Maggiore - Governo Generale A.O.I. -
- Comando Superiore Reali Carabinieri
- Direzione Superiore AA.CC.PP.

S E D E

SI COMUNICA PER DOVEROSA CONOSCENZA CHE STAMANI ALLE ORE 10,30
E' STATO DIRAMATO L'UNITO ORDINE DI SOSPENSIONE DELLE AZIONI
DI RAPPRESSAGLIA CHE ERANO STATE AUTORIZZATE

                                        d'ordine
                        IL CAPO DELLA SEGRETERIA POLITICA
                           Dottor Giovanni Sindico

allegati : 1

APPENDIX V

PHOTOGRAPHY

Shocked by the barbarity and cruelty of the Massacre of Addis Ababa that he witnessed, and unaware when he put pen to paper that in due course there would be photographs of the event available in the public domain, the Hungarian medical practitioner Dr Ladislas Shashka wrote:

> For the first time in my life I fear to be disbelieved. This is why I wish records had been kept to substantiate what I have said, which is indeed so incredible. I wish many people could see that photograph which a Blackshirt got one of his companions to take of himself. It is a perfect representation of Italian civilization, the Blackshirt, with dagger in hand, surrounded by a dead Abyssinian family, father, mother and three children. Another Blackshirt thought it necessary to preserve himself for posterity on a photographic record, having a severed Abyssinian head in his hand.[1]

In fact, despite the widespread confiscation of cameras before the massacre was launched, many photographs were taken of the slaughter, and a selection of those encountered by the present author is reproduced in this volume. Some found their way into the hands of Italian military correspondents and journalists; for example, in the early 1970s both Ciro Poggiali and Beppi Pegolotti published photographs that they had kept in their possession for more than 30 years. Other images of atrocities carried out during the Invasion and Occupation were found in the Italian military archives and in the possession of Italians when the liberating forces arrived in Addis Ababa in 1941, while others may have hurriedly divested themselves of the incriminating evidence. The upshot was that several of these photographs fell into the hands of the post-Liberation Ethiopian government, were taken to London by Sylvia

Pankhurst in early 1945, and formed the core of her book *Italy's War Crimes in Ethiopia*.[2]

Many of the photographs are close-ups, and could only have been taken by people involved in, or at least closely watching, the massacre. So who took these ghastly images?

They were taken by the Italian military authorities. Most were found in the Italian archives when the British entered the city in 1941, and, as already noted, others were found in the possession of Italian soldiers taken prisoner. In 1999 a number of photographs of the 'repression' of *Yekatit 12* and others associated with it were curated and published by the well-known film director and documentarist Folco Quilici, accompanied by text written by the Italian military lawyer Alberto Luigi De Turris, who collected the photographs in Addis Ababa during and after the massacre, when he was stationed there as a lieutenant of the regular army. In his narrative the lawyer explains that the army General Staff in Addis Ababa documented 'the three days of massacre' with photographs. De Turris was given prints of some of the images by 'officers of the General Staff in charge of documenting the repression', and by July 1937 had left the country, taking the photographs with him.

The official nature of the photography would explain the absence of any apparent shame or contrition on the faces of the perpetrators; indeed, in the case of one of the images, taken in Debre Sina, Quilici comments on the nonchalant attitude of soldiers photographed in front of the Ethiopians they are about to execute, as if they were 'a group on a school trip'.[3] In all of the images the perpetrators cooperated with the photographer by posing confidently and looking straight into the camera with the element of camaraderie normally associated with group photographs; they are often smiling, and are clearly proud of their accomplishments—all features consistent with the presence of an official photographer.

Three of these photographs, together with some previously unpublished images taken by Poggiali and some by De Turris himself, are included in Quilici's publication. The photographs from the official archive were not unidentified pictures casually handed out; in each case there were written captions, and so De Turris and Poggiali were able to record for posterity the details of each of the images they were given. In fact, Quilici notes the 'coldness' of his fellow-countrymen in the matter-of-fact way in which they recorded on the back of each photograph the slaughter of the Ethiopians. Nonetheless, this diligence on the part of the officers in charge of the archive, and particularly De Turris himself, has assisted the present author's documentation of the massacre—while at the same time clearly refuting the suggestion that the massacre took place without the knowledge or agreement of the military authorities.

Apart from officers such as De Turris and official correspondents such as Ciro Poggiali, how did ordinary soldiers also come to have copies of these photographs in their possession when the British reached Addis Ababa? The fact is that the army General Staff went to the extent of making extra prints from the archive negatives to sell to the rank and file, presumably for them to send home as souvenirs. This is confirmed by George Steer: 'For weeks after [the massacre] Blackshirts were touting action pictures [that is, movies]—and stills—round the towns.'[4] Quilici states that the well-known photograph of a dishevelled *Ras* Desta in captivity en route to his execution achieved 'wide circulation thanks to copies that the troops could buy from the photographers of the General Staff'.[5]

Some of these photographic prints would have been mailed to Italy, but equally, many remained with the perpetrators. Steer, who at that time was working for British Military Intelligence, was shocked at how many officers (presumably of the regular army) and Blackshirts taken prisoner during the war of liberation were found to be carrying photographs of atrocities that they had witnessed, and understandably concluded that the Italians used photography 'to convey the sensational joy that the acts of atrocity gave them'. Itemising a selection of the images taken from these prisoners, he mentioned 'an Italian soldier standing guard over a mass of dead Ethiopian civilians after the Graziani massacre of February 1937'. Other photographs included six Ethiopians swinging on a gibbet, and a 'proud owner' sticking a bayonet into an Ethiopian corpse or pointing a knife at a severed Ethiopian head. He also described a picture of the severed head of a Patriot being carried round on a plate with his severed right hand 'set alongside the head in a mock salute'.[6] Some of these prints were doubtless included in the collection given by Ethiopian government officials to Sylvia Pankhurst for publication in England.

Many such photographs reached Italian families of soldiers stationed in Addis Ababa between 1937 and 1941. Some disappeared during the turmoil of the early 1940s after Italy changed sides in the war, and others may have been quietly destroyed during the whitewash of Fascism that took place in Italy during the 1960s and 1970s.[7]

Nonetheless, examples do occasionally surface. In some cases the chilling photographs were made into picture postcards for mailing directly, such as the photograph of a portable gallows, which was reproduced in large quantities and sold as a postcard. Another example is the photograph of a woman in front of the smouldering remains of her house during the Massacre of Addis Ababa—a photograph that was bought in Italy and bears the date of the massacre commercially printed, indicating that it was reproduced in quantity. Most numerous are photographs taken by regular soldiers of the hangings of the ruling classes and community leaders that were carried out across Ethiopia. Almost countless, they can be bought in quantity on the internet, and are testimony to the massive scale of that pogrom.

The names of the military photographers who took photographs of the massacre of Addis Ababa are not known, with a few exceptions. For example, according to Stefano Mannucci, a specialist in photography of the Fascist era, some of the photographs of houses burning during the massacre were taken by Colonel Peter Piacentini.[8]

Apart from the official photographs taken by officers of the regular army, it is believed that some photographs of the massacre were taken—almost certainly clandestinely—by a French official of the Addis Ababa–Djibouti Railway Company. Dr Shashka wrote, 'Hardly any photographic records exist … but as far as I know a French official of the Djibouti railway company succeeded in taking some records of the corpses and the burning houses, and managed to escape the *carabinieri* and to reach the French consulate. As far as I know, these records are in Djibouti.'[9] At least some of the photographs were taken by the Italian photographer Alberto Imperiali.

It is not known if any of the photographs taken by the Frenchman concerned were put together by Ethiopian government staff with those taken from Italian prisoners when Sylvia Pankhurst visited Ethiopia in 1943. It is possible that they were, since a few of the surviving photographs do indeed show burning houses, and appear to constitute a separate series of images of 'townscape' scenes taken from a distance, whereas most of the others are close-ups of victims and their executioners that could hardly have been taken by anyone other than the Italian military.

There also exists brief footage of burning homes and smouldering corpses taken by movie camera. Some of these sequences were kindly loaned to the present author by the late Francophone Ethiopian scholar Dr Birhanu Abebe from his private collection. These were copied (although the copying process led to a reduction in quality), and some of the frames are published in this book. Unfortunately Dr Birhanu died before providing information on the provenance of these sequences, some of which have also been incorporated into various documentary films, such as *La conquista di un impero*, *Mal d'Africa*, and Timewatch's *Fascist Legacy*.

Given Dr Birhanu's background and connections (he was at one time general manager of the Djibouti–Addis Ababa Railway Company), it is possible that these sequences were taken by the French railway official mentioned above. Movie cameras were not common in Italian-occupied Ethiopia, and, having retained a certain degree of autonomy, the staff of the railway would have been more likely to possess such equipment than most foreigners. However, it seems that the Italian military also filmed the massacre, because, as mentioned above, George Steer noted that Blackshirts were selling movie footage of their atrocities. Thus some of the images of smouldering bodies published in this book may originate from military archive footage.

Though the authenticity of the footage used in the three documentary films aleady mentioned is beyond question, caution must be used in attributing some of the images. Upon close inspection by Dr Birhanu, who was involved in the making of at least one of the three films and who was very knowledgeable about the modern history of the Horn of Africa and the events of the Italian Occupation, it became clear that some of these brief film sequences and images do not show the precise subject of the voice-over. For example, in the case of the Massacre of Addis Ababa, some of the film used to illustrate the attack on Viceroy Graziani in *Fascist Legacy* shows him standing on the dais overseeing the alms-giving while wearing a heavy, dark braided jacket and boots. Though genuine, and a legitimate and appropriate illustration of such an event, this footage was actually shot by Film Luce in September 1936—not at the alms-giving of February 1937. On the latter occasion Graziani wore a light-coloured light-weight suit and shoes.[10] A further example is that, judging from the clothes worn by the people being filmed, the sequence in at least one of the documentaries showing adults and children running in panic appears to have been shot in Italian Somaliland.

Apart from the movie footage, Dr Birhanu was also in possession of unpublished photographs of the massacre taken (or acquired) by Boyadjian, the official court photographer to Emperor Haile Selassie. It was not possible to include these in the present volume, but it is hoped that Dr Birhanu's family may make them available for subsequent editions.

Caution must also be exercised in attributing some of the published photographs of individual Italian atrocities in Ethiopia. It is apparent that some show atrocities during the invasion of 1935–6, some depict atrocities of the Occupation (1936–41) other than the massacre of Addis Ababa, and others were taken during the war of liberation (1941). It can be difficult to be precise about the attribution in terms of both location and date. For example, a number of photographs were taken during the mayhem that occurred in Addis Ababa when the Emperor left the city in May 1936, and some of these have been published. These images typically show bodies surrounded by the remains of buildings of modern construction, consisting of cut stone, planed timber, plywood and so on. Materials of this type were utilised for the shops and other commercial buildings in Piazza. However, these images are sometimes mistakenly attributed to the massacre of *Yekatit 12*. In fact, most of the commercial areas of Piazza, which had been earmarked by the Italians as a 'white' area, were not significantly damaged or burned during the *Yekatit 12* massacre. Similarly, there exist photographs of an incident during the war of invasion that are thought to show the remains of Italian airmen whose bodies were mutilated in an incident in the countryside much publicised by the Italian government of the day. These images are sometimes mistakenly attributed to the massacre of *Yekatit 12*.

The attribution of photographs to a particular time or district of Addis Ababa is difficult, but there are some general guidelines. For example, only a few roads of the city were paved, and these were concentrated mainly in Arada. Many areas were densely planted with eucalyptus trees. Steep gradients and gulleys are found where there are river valleys; other areas of the city are relatively flat, except for the roads in the foothills of Intotto Mountain. Photographs showing activities in an open, treeless environment have typically been taken in the countryside—not in Addis Ababa. Images taken in the capital showing tree species other than eucalyptus will often have been taken either in a church compound or on the outskirts of the city. Photographs of the massacre showing weapons in the hands of Italians tend to follow the following broad pattern:

- Shovels are seen mainly in the daytime of Friday, 19 February, when most Blackshirts were off duty and taken unawares. They had not yet been issued with guns.
- Rifles with fixed bayonets are seen mainly during the evenings and nights of Friday and Saturday, 19 and 20 February, when the guns had been issued following the official announcement of *carta bianca*.
- Daytime attacks were carried out mainly by small gangs consisting of a combination of Blackshirts and civilians, and often resulted in individual corpses, or two or three in close proximity. The main aim was often robbery, particularly when the gangs entered Ethiopians' houses in areas such as Siddist Kilo.

- Attacks after dark were conducted mainly by Blackshirts in large gangs, committing mass murder and arson. Theft was significant but less extensive than during the daytime, because the perpetrators' hands were full, carrying their weapons, and the houses were typically those of the lowest income group. Theft in these areas was focused mainly on personal items carried by the victims, that is cash and jewellery.

Indicators such as these help in the attribution process, though of course they are not foolproof.

* * *

NOTES

FOREWORD

1. I.L. Campbell, *The Massacre of Debre Libanos: The Story of One of Fascism's Most Shocking Atrocities*, Addis Ababa University Press, 2014.
2. I.L. Campbell, *The Plot to Kill Graziani: The Attempted Assassination of Mussolini's Viceroy*, Addis Ababa University Press, 2010.

INTRODUCTION

1. There is another copy of his report in the National Library of Budapest (personal communication, Professor Richard Pankhurst). As this book went to press, Dr Shashka's account in English as published by *New Times and Ethiopia News* was edited by the historian Szélinger Balázs and published in full: Sáska László (aka Ladislas Sava), *Fascist Italian Brutalities in Ethiopia, 1935–1937: An Eye-witness Account*, Trenton, NJ: Sea Press, 2014. The present author adopts the spelling 'Shashka' of the doctor's family name, corresponding with the way he transliterated it into Amharic on his official stamp.
2. Sbacchi, A., 1997, p. 177.

1. BACKGROUND

1. Pétridès, S.P., 1988, p. 83.
2. Bahru Zewde, 1991, pp. 56–7; Triulzi, A., 2005, p. 151.
3. For a comprehensive and very readable account of the Battle of Adwa, see Jonas, R., 2011.
4. Duggan, C., 2013, p. 117.
5. Great Britain, Public Record Office, Captured Italian Documents, No. 112809, cited in Pankhurst, R.K., 2001, p. 220, fn. 2.
6. Aloisi, P., 1957, p. 382, cited in Knox, M., 1986, pp. 34–5; Mussolini's draft directive of 30 Dec. 1934, see Rochat, G., 1971, pp. 102–4, and doc. 92. See also

Robertson, E.M., 1977, pp. 112, 227 n. 65, and see Adamthwaite, A.P., doc. 14, for an English translation of the directive.

7. Mussolini to Min. of Colonies, Under-Secretaries for War, Navy and Air Force, and Chief of Gen. Staff, 10 Aug. 1934, Adamthwaite, A.P., doc. 12 (tr.).

8. Del Boca, A., 1969, p. 21.

9. Virgin, E., tr. Walford, N., 1936, pp. 88–90.

10. There being very few Italians in Addis Ababa, and no significant Italian commu-nity outside the capital, the consulates, which Italy had set up under a treaty of friendship with Ethiopia, were used to disseminate propaganda and collect infor-mation on what was happening in Ethiopia.

11. In Libya, Italy had been the world's first nation to carry out aerial bombardment of civilians, albeit not on the scale adopted in Ethiopia.

12. Haile Selassie I, ed. Ullendorf, E., 1976, pp. 235, 273; Del Boca, A., 1969, pp. 104, 165; Mockler, A., 1984, p. 76.

13. Steer, G., *The Spectator*, cited in *New Times and Ethiopia News*, 10 April 1937.

14. Germino, D.L., 1959, p. 10.

15. Crociani, P. and Battistelli, P.P., 2010, pp. 8–9.

16. A 7th division was held in reserve in Libya. For the early history of the Blackshirts, see Crociani, P. and Battistelli, P.P., 2010, pp. 4–5.

17. Crociani, P. and Battistelli, P.P., 2010, p. 19.

18. Governo Generale, Stato Maggiore, A.O.I., 1939A, p. 14. See also Report No. T.27, from Major R.A. (Military Attaché, Addis Ababa) to His Majesty's Chargé d'Affaires, Addis Ababa, 18 July 1936, stating that 'the greater part of the 6th (Tevere) Blackshirt Division has now arrived from Dire Dawa'. Great Britain, Public Record Office, File FO/371/20167, p. 6.

19. Del Boca, A., 1969, p. 26.

20. Duggan, C., 2013, pp. 256–7, citing Archivio Diaristico Nazionale, DG/99, Espedito russo, 'Diario 1935–36', 3 Oct. 1935.

21. Ben-Ghiat, R. and Fuller, M., 2008, p. 4.

22. For an in-depth analysis of Italy's primacy in the use of large-scale internment of civilian populations, see Labanca, N., 2008.

23. See, for example, McCullagh, F., 1912.

24. Labanca, N., 2008, pp. 27–8. Later, many more concentration camps of the same type, in which thousands were held in abominable conditions, were built and oper-ated by the Italians throughout the Balkans. All the territories invaded by Italy featured concentration camps, and by the early 1940s the Italians were operating approximately 200 in a variety of locations including Italy, Yugoslavia and Albania. It is estimated that around 150,000 deportees passed through the camps set up in Italy, and that 10% of the population of Slovenia was interned in such camps. See, for example, Walston, J., 1997, pp. 173–6.

25. Del Boca, A., 1988, p. 178; Walston, J., 1997, p. 181.

26. 'Book Reviews', *Ethiopia Observer*, Vol. IV, No. 3, April 1960, p. 86, citing Maxwell, *The Ten Pains of Death*, London: Longmans, 1960.

27. Duggan, C., 2013, p. 270, citing Archivio Diaristico Nazionale, Pieve Santo Stefano, DG/95, Manlio La Sorsa, 'Il mio viaggio in Africa', 21 May 1936.

28. Rochat, G., 2008, p. 38.

29. Ministry of Justice, Ethiopia, 1950, p. 24, quoting Italian sources. For a detailed review of the use of gas by the Italians in Ethiopia, see Del Boca, A., 1996.

30. Spencer, J.H., 1987, pp. 46–7. See also Baudendistal, R., 2006.

31. Duggan, C., 2013, p. 254, citing ACS, Segreteria particolare del Duce, Carteggio ordinario, Sentimenti per il Duce, b. 2806, 'Un fascista', late Sept. 1935.

32. Duggan, C., 2013, p. 254, citing ACS, Segreteria particolare de Duce, Carteggio ordinario, Sentimenti per il Duce, b. 2806, 'Goliardi Bolognesi', early Oct. 1935.

33. Ministry of Justice, Ethiopia, 1949, Doc. 44, p. 26.

34. Baudendistal, R., 2006, pp. 112–13, citing an interview with Dr Borra on 12 April 1996 in Alba, Italy.

35. Ibid., 2006, pp. 130–9.

36. Ibid., 2006, pp. 112–13, citing an interview with Dr Borra on 12 April 1996 in Alba, Italy.

37. Ibid., pp. 228–9.

38. Ibid., pp. 227–8.

39. Sáska László (aka Ladislas Sava), ed. Szélinger Balázs, 2014, p. 42.

40. Baudendistal, R., 2006, p. 223, citing ACS, fondo Graziani, carta 19, f. 21, Graziani to field commanders, 18 April 1936.

41. Ibid., 2006, p. 231.

42. Duggan, C., 2013, p. 263, citing Fondazione Mondadori, Archivio Bottai, b. 62, f. 2739, letters to wife, 28 Oct. 1935, 24 Feb. 1936.

43. Finaldi, G., 2012A.

44. Ministry of Justice, Ethiopia, 1949, Doc. 33, p. 20.

45. Del Boca, A., 1969, p. 5.

46. Duggan, C., 2013, p. 303.

47. Lé Houérou, F., 1994A, pp. 825–6.

48. Ibid., 1994A, p. 828.

49. Telegram, Mussolini to Graziani, 5 June 1937, Départment de la Presse et de l'Information du Gouvernement Imperial d'Ethiopie, c.1945, p. 11.

50. Del Boca, A., 1969, p. 214, citing *New Times and Ethiopia News*, 6 June 1936.

51. Anon., 1936, quoting McCullagh, F., 1912. See also Pankhurst, R.K., 2007; Pankhurst, R.K., 2012.

52. Anon., 1936.

53. US Government Printing Office, 1953, pp. 307–8.

54. See Campbell, I.L., 2010, pp. 142–3.

55. For a discussion of the possible motives behind *Yekatit 12*, see Campbell, I.L., 2010, pp. 375–82.

56. General Armando Petretti was appointed Acting Viceroy when Graziani was admitted to hospital.

2. THE TRIGGER

1. Meleseliñ Aniley, 1947 EC, pp. 27–8. In 1937 there was an inner courtyard surrounded by railings of which today only the main gate remains. See Campbell, I. L., 2010, p. 215.

2. *Attentato contro S.E. il Vice Re*, Report No. 184-2-39, Addis Ababa, 20 Feb. 1937 (forwarded 22 Feb.), XV [year of Fascism], ACS, fondo Graziani, busta 48, fascicolo 42, sottofascicolo 7, p. 5.

3. Meleseliñ Aniley, 1947 EC, pp. 27–8.

4. Crociani, P. and Battistelli, P.P., 2010, p. 24.

5. 'True Story of the Attempt on the Life of Marshal Graziani', *New Times and Ethiopia News*, 6 March 1937; Tamasgen Gabre, 1945, p. 1.

6. Meleseliñ Aniley, 1947 EC, pp. 27–8.

7. Witnesses differ somewhat in their recollection of the precise time of the attack. Based on the interviews of several informants, the present author has arrived at 11.40 am as the most likely time. See Campbell, I.L., 2010, pp. 196–200.

8. Tamasgen Gabre, 1945.

9. Boaglio, A., 2010, p. 62

10. *The Ethiopia Star*, 23 Nov. 1941.

11. Meleseliñ Aniley, 1947 EC, pp. 27–8.

12. 'The Massacres of Addis Ababa', Ethiopian legation report, *New Times and Ethiopia News*, 10 April 1937, p. 1.

13. Poggiali, C., 1971, p. 179.

14. 'Rapport confidentiel: au sujet du recent attentat contre le maréchal Graziani et de répresailles italiennes qui ont suivi', A. Bodard, 24 Feb. 1937, Affaires Étrangères, série K. Afrique 1918–40, sous-série Éthiopie, Microfiche 103/104, p. 2.

15. *Carabinieri* report, Group Commander, Addis Ababa, No. 184-2-39, 20 Feb. 1937.

16. Del Boca, A., 1986A, p. 83. Diplomat-writer Birhanu Dinqé claims that Madame Graziani 'became aggressive' and ordered the military to slaughter the Ethiopians. Although Madame Graziani was certainly in Addis Ababa at the time in question, the present author has been unable to verify the truth of this report. Birhanu Dinqé, 1937 EC, p. 47.

17. Anon., no date (written 1933 EC; published later), pp. 8–9. The author was Kirubel Beshah, the brother of Lieutenant-Colonel Ketema Beshah, who was killed by the Italians. Cited by Dr Birhanu Abebe in Anon., 1974 EC, p. 43.

18. 'The Massacres of Addis Ababa', Ethiopian legation report, *New Times and Ethiopia News*, 10 April 1937, p. 1.

19. *Carabinieri* report, Group Commander, Addis Ababa, No. 184–2–39, 20 Feb. 1937.
20. Asefa Chabo, 1991 E.C., p. 11. It would have been relatively easy for Mekonnin Denneqe to jump over the railings in this area, as the ground level inside the palace grounds at this point was (and still is) considerably higher than it was outside. In any case, the outer fence was incomplete; security was provided mainly by the inner fence, consisting of railings and gates that at that moment had not yet been closed. Mekonnin Denneqe enjoyed a successful career as a leading national security figure in the post-Liberation government of Emperor Haile Selassie.
21. Report of 1 March, 1937, Great Britain, Public Record Office, File FO371/20927, para. 2.2.

3. AN HOUR OF MAYHEM

1. Marchiso Theodili, Sudan Intelligence Report, Secret, No. 54, ref. J2110/44/1, 24 April 1937, Great Britain, Public Record Office, File FO/371/20930, p. 7.
2. The Regia Aeronautica had commandeered as their headquarters the Menelik II School building on the Intotto Road, a few metres north of the Arat Kilo junction.
3. Taddesse Zeweldé, 1960 EC, p. 322. Also *The Times*, 3 March 1937, and the *News Chronicle*, 6 March 1937.
4. Anon., no date (written 1933 EC, published later), pp. 8–9.
5. *The Times*, 3 March 1937.
6. Paris correspondent, *News Chronicle*, 6 March 1937.
7. Sava, L., 1940A. See Pankhurst, S., p. 542, fn. 1.
8. Dispatch 64, 21 Feb. 1937 (written 20 Feb.), Great Britain, Public Record Office, File FO 371/20927.
9. Haile Selassie 1, ed. Marcus, H., 1994, p. 35.
10. Del Boca, A., 1986A, p. 83, fn. 21.
11. *Shaleqa* Yohannis had been released by the Italians after being captured with an Eritrean-born resistance fighter, Belay Hayle-Ab.
12. Interview, Tekle-Maryam Kiflom, Addis Ababa, 2 Nov. 2004.
13. Interviews, Sara Gebre-Iyyesus, Addis Ababa, 16 Jan. 2005 and 7 June 2006.
14. Interview, Sara Gebre-Iyyesus, Addis Ababa, 16 Jan. 2005.
15. Interviews, Yeweyishet Beshahwired, Addis Ababa, in 2004, 16 Jan. 2005 and 13 Jan. 2010.
16. Interview, Welette-Birhan Gebre-Iyyesus, Addis Ababa, 15 Jan. 2005.
17. After the Liberation, Mika'él Tessema of the Ministry of Justice testified to being held in a cell at Letyibelu's *adarash* for 32 days following *Yekatit 12*. Ministry of Justice, Ethiopia, 1950, p. 11.
18. Interview, Sara Gebre-Iyyesus, Addis Ababa, 16 Jan. 2005.

19. A reference to the black tasselled fez commonly worn by off-duty Blackshirts.
20. Interview, Welette-Birhan Gebre-Iyyesus, Addis Ababa, 15 Jan. 2005.
21. This house is now occupied by the Ethiopian Association for the Blind. Battistoni, M. and Chiari, G.P., 2004, p. 126.
22. Like Sara's husband Beshahwired, *Qeññazmach* Belihu (more commonly known by his earlier title of *Shaqa*) had left Ethiopia with the Emperor and returned to Ethiopia. Campbell, I.L., 2010, pp. 283–6.
23. Poggiali, C., 1971, p. 182.
24. Tamasgen Gabré, 1945.
25. Interview, *Immahoy* Hiruta, Addis Ababa, 28 Feb. 2009.
26. Meleseliñ Aniley, 1947 EC.
27. Battistoni, M. and Chiari, G.P., 2004, pp. 129–30.
28. Affidavit, Captain Toka Binegid, Ministry of Justice, Ethiopia, 1950, p. 8.
29. Sudan Intelligence Report, Secret, No. 54, ref. J2110/44/1, 24 April 1937, Great Britain, Public Record Office, File FO/371/20930, p. 7.
30. 'The Massacres of Addis Ababa', Ethiopian London legation report, *New Times and Ethiopia News*, 10 April 1937, p. 1.
31. Affidavit, Edouard Garabedian, Ministry of Justice, Ethiopia, 1950, p. 8.
32. Temesgen Gebré, 1945.
33. In the 1940s *Blatta* Dawit Oquba Igzi'i described the *carabinieri* station as being 'where the Police Station No. 2 is nowadays'. Affidavit, *Blatta* David Oqbazqui, Ministry of Justice, Ethiopia, 1950, p. 9.
34. Affidavit, *Blatta* David Oqbazqui, Ministry of Justice, Ethiopia, 1950, p. 9.
35. Parts of Arada near St George's Cathedral had been settled principally by Amhara soldiers and their families during the time of Emperor Menelik.
36. Tamasgen Gabre, 1945, p. 4.
37. Ibid., 1945, p. 4.
38. Temesgen Gebré, 2001 EC, p. 92. This account by Temesgen, published by his daughter in 2011/2, begins roughly where his article published by the *Ethiopian Herald* in 1945 leaves off. However, there is one break in continuity: the explanation about which building was burned in this incident, its location and the capture of the occupants, is missing.
39. Personal communication, Ambassador Imru Zelleqe, 19 Dec. 2012. See also Imru Zelleke, 2009.
40. Interview, Imru Zelleqe, 11 July 2012, conducted by Dr Roman Herzog, www.campifascisti.it.
41. Imru Zelleke, 2009.
42. Telephone interview, Ambassador Imru Zelleqe, conducted by Jeff Pearce, 8 Oct. 2012.
43. Imru Zelleke, 2009.
44. Weerts, M.L., 2003.

45. Affidavit, Captain Toka Binegid, Ministry of Justice, Ethiopia, 1950, p. 8.

46. Poggiali, C., 1971, pp. 179–83.

47. Interview, Welette-Birhan Gebre-Iyyesus, Addis Ababa, 15 Jan. 2005.

48. Interview, Vahak Karibian, Addis Ababa, 19 Nov. 2004.

49. Anon., 1933 EC, pp. 8–9.

50. The school for Ethiopian boys was in separate premises from the school for white children, on the opposite side of the road.

51. Interviews, Taddesse Tiruneh, Addis Ababa, 26 Nov., 5 Dec., 6 Dec. 2004, 2 Jan., 26 March 2005.

52. Now commonly known as the Gojjam Road.

53. Interview, *Shaleqa* Éfrém Gebre-Amlak, Addis Ababa, 12 Dec. 2004. The Opera Nazionale Balilla, for children between the ages of 6 and 14 years, had become part of the educational system. All school children in Addis Ababa were expected to join.

54. Interview, *Shaleqa* Éfrém Gebre-Amlak, Addis Ababa, 12 Dec. 2004.

55. This event predated the celebration for 'natives' on 12 Yekatit. Dispatch No. 38, 19 Feb. 1937, Great Britain, Public Record Office, File FO 371/20927.

56. Report of 1 March 1937, Great Britain, Public Record Office, File FO371/20927, para. 5.

57. Telegram 61, 19 Feb. 1937, Great Britain, Public Record Office, File FO371/20927.

58. Cornelius Van H. Engert Papers, Georgetown University, Washington, DC. See also Engert, J.M., 2006.

59. Engert to Secretary of State, No. 453, 6 July 1936, and subsequent correspondence, US Government Printing Office, 1953, pp. 296–304.

60. Secretary of State to Engert, No. 353, 14 Sept. 1936, US Government Printing Office, 1953, p. 311.

61. Wallace Murray, Division of Near Eastern Affairs, to Tom Wilson, Division of Foreign Service Personnel, 17 Sept. 1936, cited in Engert, J.M., 2006, p. 213.

62. Data on location of military barracks are based on Governo Generale, Stato Maggiore, A.O.I, 1939, 'Rete delle linee telegrafoniche urbane di Addis Abeba'. The identity of the concerned divisions is taken from Nicolle, D., 1997, Crociani, P. and Battistelli, P.P., 2010.

63. 'Rapport confidentiel: au sujet du recent attentat contre le maréchal Graziani et de représailles italiennes qui ont suivi', A. Bodard, 24 Feb. 1937, Affaires Étrangères, série K. Afrique 1918–40, sous-série Éthiopie, Microfiche 103/104, p. 2.

4. DEATH IN THE AFTERNOON

1. Affidavit, Rosario Gilaegzi, Ministry of Justice, Ethiopia, 1950, p. 6.

2. Sava, L., 1940A.

3. At that time Hiruta was a Muslim; she converted to Christianity several years after the Liberation. Interview, *Immahoy* Hiruta, Addis Ababa, 28 Feb. 2009.

4. Interview, *Immahoy* Hiruta, Addis Ababa, 28 Feb. 2009.

5. *Immahoy* Hiruta, Interview, Addis Ababa, 28 Feb. 2009. Meleseliñ Aniley, 1947 EC.

6. Meleseliñ Aniley, 1947 EC.

7. Telephone interview, Imru Zelleqe, conducted by Jeff Pearce, 8 Oct. 2012.

8. The officers of both Blackshirt and regular units were typically regulars; those commanding Blackshirts were often members of one of the Granatieri regiments.

9. Temesgen Gebré, 2001 EC, p. 92.

10. Ibid., 2001 EC, p. 92.

11. Tamasgen Gabre, 1945, p. 4; Temesgen Gebré, 2001 EC, pp. 92–3.

12. Temesgen Gebré, 2001 EC, p. 95.

13. Temesgen Gebré, 1945, p. 4.

14. Engert to Secretary of State No. 47, 11.00 am, 20 Feb. 1937, US Government Printing Office, 1953, p. 680.

15. Interviews, Tekle-Maryam Kiflom, Addis Ababa, 7 Sept. and 6 Nov. 2004.

16. The Police Garage is opposite the present-day Sheraton Hotel.

17. Tamasgen Gabre, 1945.

18. Lentakis, M.B., 2006, pp. iv, 61–2.

19. *Amsterdam News*, New York, cited in 'Addis Ababa Massacre Reports', *New Times and Ethiopia News*, 13 March 1937, p. 7.

20. *The Times*, 3 March 1937.

21. Anon., no date (written 1933 EC, published later), pp. 8–9.

22. However, Dawit knew nothing of the plot. Interview, Dawit Gebre-Mesqel, Addis Ababa, 24 Feb. 2009.

23. Interview, Dawit Gebre-Mesqel, Addis Ababa, 24 Feb. 2009.

24. Sava, L., 1941B.

25. Affidavit, Captain Toka Binegid, Ministry of Justice, Ethiopia, 1950, p. 8.

26. Sava, L., 1941A.

27. 'The Attempt on the Life of Marshal Graziani', *New Times and Ethiopia News*, 6 March 1937, p. 2.

28. Sava, L., 1940B.

29. Ibid., 1940B.

30. 'The Massacres of Addis Ababa', Report of eyewitness received at the Ethiopian legation in London, *New Times and Ethiopia News*, 10 April 1937, p. 1.

31. Barker, A.J., 1971, pp. 66–7.

32. Gentilli, R., 1992, pp. 198–9.

33. Barker, A.J., 1971, pp. 66–7; Gentilli, R., 1992, pp. 199–200.

34. 'The Massacres of Addis Ababa', Report of eyewitness received at the Ethiopian legation in London, *New Times and Ethiopia News*, 10 April 1937, p. 1.

35. *News Chronicle*, London, 6 March 1937.

36. Telegram, Engert to Secretary of State, 4.00 pm, 19 Feb. 1937, US Government Printing Office, 1953, p. 679. See also American legation telegram, paraphrased, 19 Feb. 1937, Great Britain, Public Record Office, File FO/371/20928.

37. M. Bodard, to Paris, 19 Feb. 1937, 4.00 pm, Telegrams 65–71. Affaires Étrangères, série K. Afrique 1918–40, sous-série Ethiopia, Microfiche 103/104.

5. CARTA BIANCA

1. 'Ethiopian Wounded Burned Alive: Confession by an Italian Soldier', *New Times and Ethiopia News*, 8 May 1937.

2. Affidavit, Edouard Garabedian, Ministry of Justice, Ethiopia, 1950, p. 8.

3. Data based on www.prefettura.it; Cifelli, A., 2008, pp. 6, 16; www.ssai.interno.it.

4. Cortese, G., *Tripolitania*, Istituto Coloniale Fascista, Rome, 1931; Cortese, G., *Eritrea: traccia storico politica della conquista*, Istituto Coloniale Fascista, Rome, 1934.

5. Guido Cortese's appointment as *Federale* of Addis Ababa was announced in *Foglio di disposizioni del P.N.F.* No. 2, 22 June 1936, cited in Steiner, H.A., 1936, p. 886.

6. Van Kessel, T.M.C., 2011.

7. Weerts, M.L., 2003, p. 9.

8. Affidavit, Rosario Gilaezgi, Ministry of Justice, Ethiopia, 1950, p. 6.

9. Report, 1 Mar. 1937, Great Britain, Public Record Office, File FO 371/20927, #9.

10. Affidavit, Rosario Gilaezgi, Ministry of Justice, Ethiopia, 1950, p. 6.

11. Affidavit, Edouard Garabedian, Ministry of Justice, Ethiopia, 1950, pp. 8–9.

12. Affidavit, Rosario Gilaezgi, Ministry of Justice, Ethiopia, 1950, p. 6.

13. *The Times*, London, 3 March 1937; George Steer, 'Ethiopia in the Press', *New Times and Ethiopia News*, 17 July 1937, p. 7. Steer was a journalist, war correspondent and (later) British Intelligence agent.

14. Sava, L., 1940A.

15. *The Times*, 3 March 1937.

16. The New York *Amsterdam News*, undated (cited in *New Times and Ethiopia News*, 13 March 1937).

17. Affidavit, Rosario Gilaezgi, Ministry of Justice, Ethiopia, 1950, p. 6.

18. Interview, Alemash Sibhatu, Asmara, 30 Jan. 1998.

19. Dispatch, Bodard to Minister of Foreign Affairs, Paris, 10 March 1937.

20. Report of 1 March 1937, Great Britain, Public Record Office, File FO371/20937, para. 7.

21. Sava, L., 1940B.

22. 'The Massacres of Addis Ababa', Ethiopian London legation report, *New Times and Ethiopia News*, 10 April 1937, p. 1.

23. 'Rapport confidentiel: au sujet du recent attentat contre le maréchal Graziani et

de représailles italiennes qui ont suivi', A. Bodard, 24 Feb. 1937, Affaires Étrangères, série K. Afrique 1918–40, sous-série Éthiopie, Microfiche 103/104, p. 3.

24. Steer, G., 2009, p. 40.

25. Del Boca, A., 1986A, p. 85.

26. Affidavit, *Blatta* David Oqbazqui, Ministry of Justice, Ethiopia, 1950, p. 9.

27. Report of 1 March 1937, Great Britain, Public Record Office, File FO371/20927, para. 7.

28. Dispatch, Bodard to Minister of Foreign Affairs, Paris, 10 March 1937.

29. Anon., no date (written by Kirubel Beshah in 1940/1, published later), pp. 8–9.

30. Steer, G., 2009, p. 40.

31. 'The Massacres of Addis Ababa', Report of eyewitness received at Ethiopian legation, *New Times and Ethiopia News*, 10 April 1937, p. 3.

32. Interview, Dawit Gebre-Mesqel, Addis Ababa, 24 Feb. 2009.

33. Gebre-Sillassé Oda, 1985 EC, pp. 21–4.

34. Sava, L., 1940A, p. 4.

35. Sava, L., 1940A.

36. A team of two men was required for each flame-thrower. One man carried the weapon on his back and operated it, while the other man carried on his back the necessary supplies. The flame-thrower consisted of two cylinders, a length of reinforced and flexible tubing, and a jet or flame tube, to which was attached the trigger and the ignition arrangement. The cylinders were identical, each containing nitrogen under pressure and fuel oil that was typically a mixture of benzine or kerosene and light motor oil. The fuel was usually ignited by an electrical current at the base of the jet, by a coil and spark gap. The current was produced by a dry-cell battery. Sometimes the fuel was ignited by means of a friction tube and a wick. US Military Intelligence, Dec. 1942.

37. *Intelligence Bulletin*, US Military Intelligence, Dec. 1942.

38. Del Boca, A., 1965, pp. 221–2.

39. Sudan Intelligence Report, Secret, No. 54, ref. J2110/44/1, 24 April 1937, Great Britain, Public Record Office, File FO/371/20930, p. 7.

40. Report of 1 March 1937, Great Britain, Public Record Office, File FO/371/2927, para. 5.

41. *The Times*, London, 3 March 1937.

42. 'Massacre in Addis Ababa', *Manchester Guardian*, 24 March 1937.

43. 'The Massacre of Addis Ababa', Ethiopian London legation report, *New Times and Ethiopia News*, 10 April 1937, p. 1.

44. *Daily Telegraph*, undated, quoted in *New Times and Ethiopia News*, 13 March 1937, p. 7.

45. Report of 1 March 1937, Great Britain, Public Record Office, File FO371/20927, para. 5.

46. Shashka, L., 1940A.

47. Boaglio, A., 2010, pp. 62–3.
48. 'Rapport confidentiel: au sujet du récent attentat contre le maréchal Graziani et de représailles italiennes qui ont suivi', A. Bodard, 24 Feb. 1937, Affaires Étrangères, série K. Afrique 1918–40, sous-série Éthiopie, Microfiche 103/104, p. 3.
49. Report of 1 March 1937, Great Britain, Public Record Office, File FO371/20927, para. 5.
50. Addis Zemen, 1979 EC, p. 3.
51. Anon., no date (written 1933 EC, published later), pp. 8–9.
52. Married to *Ras* Ayelu, Maniyilushal, whose brothers had been executed by the Italians, was suspected of urging the people of Selalé to rise up against the occupiers. Sbacchi, A., 1997, p. 148. *Dejazmach* Belay Kebbede was a Wello leader said to have betrayed the Emperor at Maychew. Greenfield, R., 1965, p. 219.
53. Interview, Sara Gebre-Iyyesus, Addis Ababa, 16 Jan. 2005.
54. The terrace is now closed in and accommodates part of the library of the Institute of Ethiopian Studies, Addis Ababa University.
55. Interview, Welette-Birhan Gebre-Iyyesus, Addis Ababa, 15 Jan. 2005.
56. Sava, L., 1940C.
57. Sava, L., 1940B.
58. Boaglio, A., 2010, p. 64. Boaglio comments that bullets had previously been a form of currency alternative to coins, and so as the houses burned there was 'an incessant crackling' from bursting bullets. Many people traditionally possessed them—in some cases hidden underground in their houses from the distant past.
59. Sava, L., 1940A.
60. Sava, L., 1940B.
61. Sava, L., 1940C.
62. Le Houérou, F., 1994B, pp. 79–80.
63. Gebre-Sillassé Oda, 1985 EC, p. 23.
64. Affidavit, Edouard Garabedian, Ministry of Justice, Ethiopia, pp. 8–9.
65. Affidavit, David Oqbazqui, Ministry of Justice, Ethiopia, 1959, p. 9.
66. Opposite today's Sheraton Hotel.
67. See Battistoni, M. and Chiari, G.P., 2004, pp. 45, 48.
68. 'Direct News of Addis Ababa Massacre', Djibouti correspondent, 11 March 1937, *New Times and Ethiopia News*, 3 April 1937, p. 2.
69. Interview, *Immahoy* Hiruta, Addis Ababa, 28 Feb. 2009.
70. Following the laws promulgated in 1937 to establish an apartheid system, the Italians relocated the market in Fitawrari Habte-Giyorgis Sefer (now known as Mercato), to rid the city centre of market traders and their customers.
71. The area within the customs compound and other adjoining areas also seem to have been used by market stalls.
72. Much of the material burned in the market belonged to Arab and Indian traders. Wazir Ali Baig reported, 'Fifteen Indian and about fifty Arab traders were arrested

during the disorders, because the cloth market was on fire. The British Consul-General secured the release of the Indians.' 'More News of the Massacre', *New Times and Ethiopia News*, 27 March 1937, quoted in 'The Ethiopian Patriots as Seen at the Time', *Ethiopia Observer*, Vol. III, No. 11, p. 357.

73. Affidavit, Rosario Gilaezgi, Ministry of Justice, Ethiopia, 1950, pp. 6–7.

74. Lentakis, M.B., 2006, p. 61–2. The Grar Hotel was on John Melly Street, leading down towards Piazza.

75. Duke of Harar Street, as this street was named after the Liberation, was named Via Padre R. Guiliani by the Italians. During the Derg period it was renamed Belay Zelleke Street, and is now often popularly referred to as the Gojjam Road. However, in 1937 this road did not reach Gojjam; it ended 2.7 km from St George's Cathedral.

76. Ministry of Justice, Ethiopia, 1950, pp. 6–7.

77. Poggiali completely repudiates the suggestion that the burning of St George's Cathedral was ordered because machine guns had been found in the cathedral. Poggiali, C., 1971, p. 184.

78. Dr Shashka blamed a certain Madame Dabbert, a 'sinister' Russian resident of Addis Ababa, for informing Italian officers about the treasure trove in the cathedral while masquerading as a devoted friend of Ethiopia. Sava, L., 1941B.

79. Sava, L., 1941B; Le Houérou, F., 1994B, p. 80.

80. Affidavit, Captain Toka, Ministry of Justice, Ethiopia, 1950, p. 8. Although some sources suggest the burning of the cathedral took place on Saturday, Poggiali clearly entered it in his diary of Friday, and both Captain Toka and Dr Le Houérou also attribute it to Friday night. According to Professor Alberto Sbacchi, based on Italian sources, 20 mines were placed to blow up the cathedral. Sbacchi, A., 1997, p. 85. However, if this is true, they were either not detonated or else were ineffective, for the building survived intact.

81. Poggiali, C., p. 183; Del Boca, A., 1986A, p. 85.

82. The cathedral was redecorated after the Liberation by well-known artists Ime'alaf Hiruy and Afewerq Tekle.

83. Poggiali, C., p. 183; Del Boca, A., 1986A, p. 85.

84. Report and Covering Memorandum 147/30/37, 1 March 1937, Great Britain, Public Record Office, File FO/371/20927, p. 4, para. 5.

85. Birhanu Dinqé, 1937 EC, p. 51.

86. Temesgen Gebré, 2001 EC, p. 93.

87. Ibid., 2001 EC, p. 93. After Liberation in 1941, the remains of several hundred skeletons were found in the latrines, wells and rivers of the city.

88. Temesgen Gebré, 2001 EC, p. 93.

89. Ministry of Justice, Ethiopia, 1950, pp. 6–7.

90. Engert to Secretary of State No. 47, 11.00 am, 20 Feb. 1937, US Government Printing Office, 1953, p. 680.

91. So called because some of the Italians taken prisoner after the Battle of Adwa in 1896 had been accommodated in this part of the city.
92. Meleseliñ Aniley, 1947 EC, pp. 28ff.
93. Lieutenant Meleseliñ states that they fought for about half an hour.
94. Meleseliñ Aniley, 1947 EC, pp. 28ff.
95. Interview, Welette-Birhan Gebre-Iyyesus, Addis Ababa, 15 Jan. 2005.
96. Del Boca, A., 1986A, p. 85, citing testimony of D. Cerutti.
97. Engert to Secretary of State, No. 47, 11.00 am, 20 Feb. 1937, US Government Printing Office, 1953, p. 680.
98. *News Chronicle*, 6 March 1937.
99. French diplomat's eyewitness account, *News Chronicle*, London, 6 March 1937; 'The Massacres of Addis Ababa', Ethiopian legation report, *New Times and Ethiopia News*, 10 April 1937, p. 3.
100. Dispatch 64, 21 Feb. 1937, Great Britain, Public Record Office, File FO/371/20927 (written on 20 Feb.).
101. American legation telegram, 10.00 am, 22 Feb. 1937, paraphrased, Great Britain, Public Record Office, FO/371/20928.
102. *Daily Mail*, London, 6 March 1937; *Daily Telegraph*, London, undated, cited in *New Times and Ethiopia News*, 13 March 1937.
103. French diplomat's eyewitness account, *News Chronicle*, London, 6 March 1937.
104. Commenting on the Hermannsburg Mission report that the main gate of the mission compound remained closed at the time, Pastor Jürgen Klein pointed out to the present author that these Ethiopians might have entered the compound through the fence separating it from the compound of the Church of Qechené Medhané Alem. Addis Ababa, 27 June 2015.
105. Addis Zemen, 1979 EC.
106. Addis Zemen, 1979 EC, p. 2. Temesgen's orginal article is stated in *Addis Zemen* to have been first published in 1936 EC (1943/44).
107. Ibid., p. 2. It appears from Temesgen Gebré's autobiography, published posthumously in 2008/9, that the story of *Liqe* Tebebt Iwnetu was originally written in historical novel format. Thus while the account is based on a true story, it may not be accurate in all details, and '*Liqe* Tebebt Iwnetu' may be a pseudonym.
108. Diel, L., 1939, p. 41.
109. Interview, *Immahoy* Hiruta, Addis Ababa, 28 Feb. 2009.
110. The neighbours were a young man named Mekonnin Abat, a woman whose name Tekle-Maryam could not recall, and a man named Isheté and his wife and children. Interview, Tekle-Maryam Kiflom, Addis Ababa, 6 Nov. 2004.
111. Johannes Semerjibashian joined the German legation as dragoman in 1925, and was later promoted to Oriental Secretary. He became adviser for local affairs in 1936 after the legation was reduced to the status of a consulate-general. In his house he produced an underground newspaper for the resistance, but, despite

being decorated by the Emperor after the Liberation, he is generally believed to have been murdered by Ethiopian government agents. Bairu Tafla, 2010.

112. Interview, Yervant Semerjibashian, Addis Ababa, 29 Nov. 2007.

113. Interview, Éfrém Gebre-Amlak, Addis Ababa, 12 Dec. 2004.

114. Syoum Gebregziabher, 2012, pp. 32–5, 60.

115. Information provided by Siyum Gebre-Egziabher, 26 Oct. 2015.

116. Syoum Gebregziabher, 2012, pp. 60–1. This was almost certainly a part of, or an extension to, the camp where young Sibhatu Gebre-Iyyesus was also being held, although the two boys did not know each other.

6. THE SECOND DAY

1. Shashka, L., 1940B.

2. Affidavit, Edouard Garabedian, Ministry of Justice, Ethiopia, 1950, p. 9.

3. Alfredo Godio, interview with Professor Angelo Del Boca, Borgosesia, 13 Nov. 1979. Del Boca, 1986, pp. 85–6.

4. Poggiali, C., 1971, p. 183.

5. Ministry of Justice, Ethiopia, 1950, p. 9. Ironically, *Blatta* Ayele Gebré, formerly a distinguished figure in the Ethiopian judiciary, had submitted to the Italians, and was selected the following day by the Italians administration to sit on the official committee appointed to investigate the assassination attempt.

6. Telegram No. 12522, Lessona to Biroli, Geloso, Nasi and Governo Generale, 19 Feb. 1937, ACS, fondo Graziani, busta 48, fascicolo 42, sottofascicolo 7. See Appendix III.

7. Meleseliñ Aniley, 1947 EC.

8. See chapter 11, section 'In Memoriam'.

9. Interview, Dawit Gebre-Mesqel, Addis Ababa, 24 Feb. 2009.

10. Dispatch 63, 21 Feb. 1937 (written 20 Feb.), Great Britain, Public Record Office, File FO 371/20927. After the restoration of Emperor Haile Selassie, Tefere-Werq Kidane-Weld joined the Emperor's service, eventually becoming Minister of the Imperial Palace. Pankhurst, R.K., 2004.

11. Hanson, H.M. and D., 1958, p. 55.

12. Telegram, Engert to Secretary of State, 11.00 am, 20 Feb. 1937, US Gov. Printing Office, 1953, p. 680.

13. *Daily Telegraph*, London, undated citation in *New Times and Ethiopia News*, 13 March 1937.

14. Ibid., London, undated citation in *New Times and Ethiopia News*, 13 March 1937.

15. Telegram, Engert to Secretary of State, 11.00 am, 20 Feb. 1937, US Gov. Printing Office, 1953, p. 680.

16. Telegram, Engert to Secretary of State, 2.00 pm, 20 Feb. 1937, US Gov. Printing Office, 1953, pp. 680–1; Dispatch 64, 21 Feb. 1937 (written 20 Feb.), Great Britain, Public Record Office, File FO/371/20927.

17. Telegram, Engert to Secretary of State, 2.00 pm, 20 Feb. 1937, US Gov. Printing Office, 1953, pp. 680–1; Dispatch 64, 21 Feb. 1937 (written 20 Feb.), Great Britain, Public Record Office, File FO/371/20927.

18. Imru Zelleke, 2009.

19. Welde-Giyorgis Welde-Yohannis, 1939 EC, p. 23.

20. Shashka, L., 1940B.

21. 'V.B.', interviewed by Dr Irma Tadia. Pasquali, M.C., 2015, p. 79, citing Taddia, I., 1988.

22. Alfredo Godio, interview with Professor Angelo Del Boca, Borgosesia, 13 Nov. 1979. Del Boca, 1986, pp. 85–6.

23. Affidavit, Captain Toka Binegid, Ministry of Justice, Ethiopia, 1950, p. 8.

24. Shashka, L., 1940B.

25. Affidavit, *Blatta* David Oqbazqui, Ministry of Justice, Ethiopia, 1950, p. 9.

26. Boaglio, A., 2010, p. 64.

27. Temesgen Gebré, 2001 EC, p. 93.

28. Ibid., 2001 EC, p. 94.

29. Birhanu Dinqé, 1937 EC, p. 51.

30. Dispatch 64, 21 Feb. 1937 (written 20 Feb.), Great Britain, Public Record Office, File FO/371/20927.

31. Telegram, Engert to Secretary of State, 9.00 am, 21 Feb. 1937, US Gov. Printing Office, 1953, p. 681. See also American legation report, Feb. 21, 9.00 am, paraphrased, Great Britain, Public Record Office, File FO/371/20928.

32. Affidavit, Rosario Gilaezgi, Ministry of Justice, Ethiopia, 1950, p. 7.

33. Affidavit, *Blatta* David Oqbazqui, Ministry of Justice, Ethiopia, 1950, p. 9.

34. Fanouris, M. and L., 1995, p. 68.

35. Shashka, L., 1940C.

36. Ibid., 1940C.

37. Shashka, L., 1940B.

38. Zervos, A., 1936, pp. 189–90; Pankhurst, R., Sohier, E. and Smidt, W., 2007. Note that on the company's official documents the name of the firm is spelt 'Mohamedally', not 'Mohamed Ali'.

39. USA, National Archives, Microcopy, No. T 821, Roll 472, p. 162, cited in Pankhurst, R.K., 1971, p. 66, fn. 54.

40. See Campbell, I.L., 2010, pp. 384–9.

41. Breda was a leading Italian arms manufacturer. The identification of the grenades as of 'Breda type' was made by Captain Marone of the *carabinieri* on Saturday, 20 Feb. Report No. 184–2–39, Captain Enrico Marone, 20 Feb. 1937, *Attentato contro S.E. il Vice Re*, ACS, fondo Graziani, busta 48, fascicolo 42, sottofascicolo 7.

42. 'Direct News of Addis Ababa Massacre', Djibouti correspondent, 11 March 1937, *New Times and Ethiopia News*, 3 April 1937, p. 2.

43. 'Direct News of Addis Ababa Massacre', Djibouti correspondent, 11 March 1937, *New Times and Ethiopia News*, 3 April 1937, p. 2.

44. 'Note on the Events in Addis Ababa Subsequent to the Attempt on Marshal Graziani's Life on February 19th', 2 March 1937, Great Britain, Public Record Office, File FO/371/20927.

45. Report of 1 March 1937, Great Britain, Public Record Office, File FO/371/20927.

46. 'Note on the Events in Addis Ababa Subsequent to the Attempt on Marshal Graziani's Life on February 19th', and Dispatch No. 5, 21 Feb. 1937, both in Great Britain, Public Record Office, File FO/371/20927; 'Direct News of Addis Ababa Massacre', Djibouti correspondent, 11 March 1937, *New Times and Ethiopia News*, 3 April 1937, p. 2.

47. See Campbell, I.L., 2010, pp. 304–5, 384–9.

48. 'Rapport confidentiel: au sujet du récent attentat contre le maréchal Graziani et de représailles italiennes qui ont suivi', A. Bodard, 24 Feb. 1937, Affaires Étrangères, série K. Afrique 1918–40, sous-série Éthiopie, Microfiche 103/104, p. 4.

49. Dispatch, Bodard to Minister of Foreign Affairs, Paris, 10 March 1937.

50. Although the present author has been unable to verify the account, an Ethiopian writer, 'M.T.', tells a moving story of how her uncle's mother, who as a young woman was having an affair with a member of the Italian military, managed to get her home area (then known locally as Bella Haile Selassie, now known simply as Bella) between the Italian legation and Menelik II Hospital exempted from burning during *carta bianca*. M.T., 2004.

51. Dispatch 64, 21 Feb. 1937 (written on 20 Feb.), Great Britain, Public Record Office, File FO/371/20927; 'Report, 1 March 1937', Great Britain, Public Record Office, File FO/371/20927, para. 5.

52. 'The Massacres of Addis Ababa', Ethiopian legation report, *New Times and Ethiopia News*, 10 April 1937, p. 1; Ministry of Justice, Ethiopia, 1950, p. 7.

53. Terefe Azage was apparently associated with Patriot leader Hayle Maryam Mamo. Interviews, Tekle-Maryam Kiflom, 7 Sept. and 6 Nov. 2004.

54. Interview, Welette-Birhan, Addis Ababa, 15 Jan. 2005.

55. Also known as the Seventh-Day Adventist Hospital, and referred to by the Italians as the American Hospital, this hospital was located in the compound of what is now the National ('Jubilee') Palace. It was later moved to its present site north of the Filwoha Hotel, on the other side of the new road that was constructed running beside the Jubilee Palace.

56. Hanson, H.M. and D., 1958, pp. 55–6.

57. Telegram, Engert to Secretary of State, No. 49, 9.00 am 21 Feb. 1937, US Government Printing Office, 1953, pp. 681–2. See also American legation report, 21 Feb. 1937, 9.00 am, paraphrased, Great Britain, Public Record Office, File FO/371/20928.

58. Telegram, Engert to Secretary of State, No. 49, 9.00 am, 21 Feb. 1937, US Government Printing Office, 1953, pp. 681–2; American legation report, 21 Feb.

1937, 9.00 am, paraphrased, Great Britain, Public Record Office, File FO/ 371/20928.

59. Interview, Dawit Gebre-Mesqel, Addis Ababa, 24 Feb. 2009.

7. THE THIRD DAY

1. Affidavit, Edouard Garabedian, Ministry of Justice, Ethiopia, 1950, p. 9.

2. *New Times and Ethiopia News*, 24 April 1937.

3. Tekle-Tsadiq Mekuriya, 2008 EC, p. 60.

4. Temesgen Gebré, 2001 EC, p. 94.

5. The woman's son was also missing. Telegram, Engert to Secretary of State, 10.00 am 22 Feb. 1937, US Government Printing Office, 1953, pp. 682–3.

6. Engert to Secretary of State, No. 51, 10.00 am 22 Feb. 1937, US Printing Office, 1953, pp. 681–2. See also American legation report, Feb. 22, 10.00 am, para-phrased, Great Britain, Public Record Office, File FO/371/20928.

7. Sbacchi, A., 1997, p. 220, citing MAI/Pol. 66/110, MAE to MC, 10 March 1937, SHAT/7N3267, Guillon: *Au sujet de l'attentat contre le Viceroy*, 3 March 1937.

8. Interview, Tekle-Maryam Kiflom, Addis Ababa, 7 Sept. 2004.

9. Interview, Vartkes Bilemjian, Addis Ababa, 11 Nov. 2007, quoting his mother.

10. See, for example, Graziani to Lessona, 13 May 1937, telegram no. 24923, in Stato Maggiore de Governo Generale, *Il secondo anno dell'impero*, 5 Vols., Ufficio topo-cartografico, Addis Ababa, 1937–38, pp. 58–9, cited in Rochat, G., 1988, p. 214. Translation based on quotation in Labanca, N., 2008, p. 33.

11. Pankhurst, R.K., 1970, pp. 45–6. See also *New Times and Ethiopia News*, 14 and 21 Dec. 1940.

12. Interview, Alemash Sibhatu (daughter of Graziani's interpreter, Sibhatu Yohannis), Asmara, 1998.

13. Rochat, G., 1988, p. 196.

14. Sindico to Chief of Cabinet, *Fonogramma urgent a mano*, No. 12612, 21 Feb., XV [year of Fascism]. ACS, fondo Graziani, busta 48, fascicolo 42, fottofascicolo 7.

15. Letter, Sindico to Chef de Cabinet, with notice terminating the massacre, 21 Feb. XV [year of Fascism]. ACS, fondo Graziani, busta 48, fascicolo 42, sottofascicolo 7. See also Rochat, G., 1988, p. 196.

16. This interview of 'Signor D.' took place in Addis Ababa, 26 March 1965. Del Boca, A., 1965, pp. 221–2.

17. Fanouris, M. and L., 1995, p. 69.

18. Interview, Tekle-Maryam Kiflom, Addis Ababa, 7 Sept. 2004.

19. 'The Massacres of Addis Ababa', Ethiopian legation report, *New Times and Ethiopia News*, 10 April 1937.

20. Affidavit, Rosario Gilaezgi, Ministry of Justice, Ethiopia, 1950, p. 7.

21. Poggiali, C., 1971, pp. 185–6.

22. Ministry of Justice, Ethiopia, 1950, p. 9.
23. Interview, Welette-Birhan Gebre-Iyyesus, Addis Ababa, 15 Jan. 2005.
24. Ministry of Justice, Ethiopia, 1950, p. 9.
25. The men being held in that part of the camp were not set free at that time, and Siyum never knew what happened to them. Syoum Gebregziabher, 2012, p. 61.
26. Syoum Gebregziabher, 2012, p. 61.
27. Captain Toka actually gave the time as '12 o'clock, Ethiopian time'. Affidavit, Captain Toka Binegid, Ministry of Justice, Ethiopia, 1950, p. 8.
28. Engert to Secretary of State, No. 51, 10.00 am, 22 Feb. 1937, US Printing Office, 1953, pp. 682–3. See also American legation report, Feb. 22, 10.00 am, paraphrased, Great Britain, Public Record Office, File FO/371/20928.
29. 'Rapport confidentiel: au sujet du récent attentat contre le maréchal Graziani et de représailles italiennes qui ont suivi', A. Bodard, 24 Feb. 1937, Affaires Étrangères, série K. Afrique 1918–40, sous-série Éthiopie, Microfiche 103/104, p. 4.
30. Interview, Tekle-Maryam Kiflom, Addis Ababa, 7 Sept. 2004.
31. Interview, Welette-Birhan, Addis Ababa, 15 Jan. 2005.
32. 'Note on the Events in Addis Ababa Subsequent to the Attempt on Marshal Graziani's Life on February 19th', 2 March 1937, and Report of 1 March 1937, para. 13, Great Britain, Public Record Office, File FO3271/20927.
33. Interview, Tekle-Maryam Kiflom and Tamrat Istifanos, Addis Ababa, 6 Nov. 2004.
34. Ministry of Justice, Ethiopia, 1950, p. 7.
35. American legation report, 22 Feb. 1937, 10.00 am, paraphrased, Great Britain, Public Record Office, File FO/371/20928.
36. Sava, L., 1941A.
37. Telegram 93980 of 21 Feb. 1937. See also ACS, Graziani, 33 and 60, 'Direttive per l'azione politico-militare', cited by Knox, M., 1986, pp. 4, 301.
38. Temesgen Gebré, 2001 EC, p. 94.
39. Temesgen had been arrested by the Italians early on in the Occupation, in July 1936, and apparently sentenced to be shot, from which he had a lucky escape. The reason for his arrest appears to have been related to his role as one of four Ethiopians who had been running Bible classes and preaching under the auspices of the British Protestant missionary Alfred Buxton. As such, they were regarded as subversives and listed for execution. Two of the others were executed following *Yekatit 12*, together with a third because his name, Tegeni, was mistaken for that of Temesgen. It appears that the Italians had recognised their mistake and had put Temesgen's name back on the death list. See Grubb, N., 1943, pp. 152–3; Hamilton, P.A., 1949.
40. After Liberation, Temesgen told Tekle-Tsadiq Mekuriya that he had changed his name because he would have been killed if the Italians had realised he was a pastor. Tekle-Tsadiq Mekuriya, 2008 EC, pp. 62–3.
41. Temesgen Gebré, 2001 EC, p. 95.

42. Temesgen Gebré, 2001 EC, p. 95. Whereas Temesgen generally uses the term 'Italians' when referring to the officers at Fit Ber (typically *carabinieri* or regulars), he usually uses the term 'Fascists' when referring to the Blackshirts.

43. Temesgen Gebré, 2001 EC, p. 95.

44. Tekle-Tsadiq Mekuriya, 2008 EC, p. 60.

8. THE AFTERMATH

1. 'The Massacres of Addis Ababa', *New Times and Ethiopia News*, 10 April 1937, p. 3.

2. Meleseliñ Aniley, 1947 EC.

3. Interview, Demissé Hayle-Maryam, Nazereth, 30 Aug. 2005.

4. Fanouris, M. and L., 1995, p. 68.

5. Meleseliñ Aniley. 1947 EC.

6. 'The Massacres of Addis Ababa' Ethiopian legation report, *New Times and Ethiopia News*, 10 April 1937, p. 3; Alazar Tesfa Michael, 1948; *News Chronicle*, London, 6 March 1937.

7. 'The Massacres of Addis Ababa', Ethiopian legation report, *New Times and Ethiopia News*, 10 April 1937, p. 3.

8. Sudan Intelligence Report, Secret, No. 54, ref, J2110/44/1, 24 April 1937, Great Britain, Public Record Office, File FO/371/20930, p. 7.

9. 'Note on the Events in Addis Ababa Subsequent to the Attempt on Marshal Graziani's Life on February 19th', 2 March 1937, Great Britain, Public Record Office, File FO 371/20927.

10. *Daily Mail*, 8 March 1937.

11. Sava, L., 1940C.

12. Sava, L., 1940B.

13. Affidavit, *Blatta* David Oqbazqui, Ministry of Justice, Ethiopia, 1950, p. 9.

14. Engert to Secretary of State, No. 51, 10.00 am, 22 Feb. 1937, US Government Printing Office, 1953, pp. 682–3.

15. Telegram, Minister of Foreign Affairs, Paris, to French ambassador, Rome, 24 Feb. 1937, Affairs Étrangères, série K. Afrique 1918–40, sous-série Éthiopie, Microfiche 103/04.

16. Tekle-Tsadiq Mekuriya, 2008 EC, p. 61.

17. Temesgen Gebré, 2001 EC, p. 96.

18. Tekle-Tsadiq Mekuriya, 2008 EC, p. 61.

19. Temesgen Gebré, 2001 EC, p. 96.

20. Temesgen's *Tilinti* is presumably a corruption of the Italian *tenente*, meaning 'lieutenant'.

21. Temesgen uses the term 'birr', meaning 'silver', i.e. a Maria Theresa 'thaler'. The price of 1 thaler per drink is consistent with Birhanu Dinqé's account of conditions in

the prisons at that time, which put the price of water at 10 birr (thaler) per litre. Birhanu Dinqé, 1937 EC, p. 51.

22. Temesgen writes 'liré', which was presumably how he pronounced 'lire'. The Italians knew that the lira was not readily accepted by traders in Ethiopia, who preferred the traditional silver thaler that the Ethiopians had used for centuries.

23. Temesgen writes 'they' here, suggesting that there was another Italian soldier with the commandant at the time.

24. Temesgen Gebré, 2001 EC, pp. 97–8. In his autobiography, Tekle-Tsadiq Mekuriya's account concurs with Temesgen's; he also describes prisoners at Fit Ber sucking the moisture from the roots of weeds, begging for urine to drink, and having to buy water from the Italians. Tekle-Tsadiq Mekuriya, 2008 EC, pp. 60–1.

25. Affidavit, Captain Toka Binegid, Ministry of Justice, Ethiopia, 1950, p. 8.

26. Most likely oil drums; each *bermél* typically had a volume of around 200 litres, totalling some 24,000 litres of water.

27. Tekle-Tsadiq Mekuriya, 2008 EC, p. 61.

28. Temesgen Gebré, 2001 EC, p. 98. It should be noted that, while most of Temesgen's published memoir is by his own hand, certain sections appear to have been reconstructed posthumously, based apparently on his notes and memories of his family. Thus some parts of the narrative covering his detention may not be as accurate in issues of detail compared with Tekle-Tsadiq's, which can be entirely relied upon.

29. Temesgen Gebré, 2001 EC, pp. 98–9. Tekle-Tsadiq also confirms bread being handed out, but states that it was very salty, which made the prisoners even thirstier.

30. Temesgen Gebré, 2001 EC, p. 99.

31. The officers of the Blackshirt units were normally drawn from the regular army.

32. Temesgen Gebré, 2001 EC, pp. 99–100.

33. Temesgen uses the term *kahnat*.

34. Temesgen Gebré, 2001 EC, p. 100.

35. For political reasons the expulsions excluded the German Hermannsburg Mission and a few individual American missionaries.

36. Following expulsion of the foreign missionaries, until 19 Feb. 1937 Ethiopians connected to Protestantism had been allowed to continue to practise their faith and in some cases to take over mission buildings. However, following the attempt on Graziani, the Italians launched an anti-Protestant pogrom in which many Protestants were sent to concentration camps or execution. Lass-Westphal, I., 1972, p. 99. The involvement of Catholic priests in the separation of Protestant and Catholic prisoners and the promise of freedom for converts are noted in a number of sources, e.g. Quinton, A.G.H., 1949, pp. 28–9.

37. Temesgen Gebré, 2001 EC, p. 100. The present author is not aware of a Protestant church in Addis Ababa during the Occupation named Medhané Alem. It is likely

that *Ato* Ar'aya was *aleqa* of an Orthodox Church of Medhané Alem with which the Bible Churchmen's Missionary Society (BCMS) was working, under Temesgen's friend Alfred Buxton. The BCMS was unique among the Protestant missions in adopting a policy of working with the Ethiopian Orthodox Church, with the intention that all evangelisation would be carried out by the latter. Launhardt, J., p. 65; Mikre-Sellassie G/Ammanuel, 2014, pp. 39–40.

38. Temesgen uses the term *menekosat*.

39. Temesgen Gebré, 2001 EC, p. 100.

40. Meleseliñ Aniley, 1947 EC.

41. American legation report via London, 22 Feb. 1937, 3.00 pm, paraphrased, Great Britain, Public Record Office, File FO/371/20928.

42. 'Direct News of Addis Ababa Massacre', Djibouti correspondent, 17 March 1937, *New Times and Ethiopia News*, 3 April 1937, p. 2.

43. Affidavit, *Blatta* David Oqbazqui, Ministry of Justice, Ethiopia, 1950, p. 9.

44. Sbacchi, A., 1997, pp. 128–31.

45. Personal communication, Professor Shiferaw Beqele, Addis Ababa, 11 Feb. 2013.

46. Engert to Secretary of State, 3.00 pm, 23 Feb. 1937, US Government Printing Office, 1953, p. 684. See also American legation report via London, 22 Feb. 1937, 3.00 pm, paraphrased, Great Britain, Public Record Office, File FO/371/20928.

47. Interview, Vartkes Bilemjian, Addis Ababa, 11 Nov. 2007.

48. Report attached to memorandum 147/30/37, 1 March 1937, Public Record Office, File FO/371/20927, p. 6, para. 10.

49. Dispatch, Bodard, to Foreign Affairs, 24 Feb. 1937, Telegrams 79–81. Affaires Étrangères, série K. Afrique 1918–40, sous-série Ethiopia, Microfiche 103/104.

50. Sava, L., 1941A.

51. Interview, Dawit Gebre-Mesqel, Addis Ababa, 24 Feb. 2009.

52. Gebre-Sillassé Oda, 1985 EC, pp. 23–4.

53. Meleseleñ Aniley, 1947 EC.

54. 'The Massacres of Addis Ababa', Ethiopian legation report, *New Times and Ethiopia News*, 10 April 1937, p. 3.

55. Also known as the 'egg factory', eggs being used in the biscuit production process.

56. Interview, Asnake Jembere's son, Dr Abraham Asnake, with his cousin, *Ato* Mengesha Werqineh, Addis Ababa, 26 Oct. 2013.

57. Dispatch, Bodard, to *Affaires Étrangères*, 24 Feb. 1937, Telegrams 79–81. Affaires Étrangères, Série K. Afrique 1918–40, Sous-Série Éthiopie, Microfiche 103/104.

58. 'The Massacres of Addis Abba', Ethiopian legation report, *New Times and Ethiopia News*, 10 April 1937, p. 1.

59. Interview, *Immahoy* Hiruta, Addis Ababa, 28 Feb. 2009.

60. Sudan Intelligence Report, Secret, No. 54, ref. J2110/44/1, Great Britain, Public Record Office, File FO/371/20930, p. 7.

61. Sava, L., 1940C.

62. *News Chronicle*, London, 6 March 1937.

63. Report of 1 March 1937, Great Britain, Public Record Office, File FO371/20927, para. 7.

64. Report of 1 March 1937, Great Britain, Public Record Office, File FO/371/29027.

65. Telegram, Bodard to Foreign Affairs, Paris, 24 Feb. 1937, via Djibouti. Affaires Étrangères, série K. Afrique 1918–90, sous-série Éthiopie, Microfiche 103/104.

66. Meleseliñ Aniley, 1974 EC.

67. Tekle-Tsadiq Mekuriya, 2008 EC, p. 62.

68. Ibid., pp. 62–3.

69. Affidavit, Yaqob Gebré Li'ul, Ministry of Justice, Ethiopia, 1950, p. 14.

70. Imru Zelleke, 2009.

71. Affidavit, Mika'él Tessema, Ministry of Justice, Ethiopia, 1950, p. 11.

72. Affidavit, Jacob Gabrie Leul, Ministryo of Justice, Ethiopia, 1950, p. 14.

73. Affidavit, Ianuzzi Vittorio, Ministry of Justice, Ethiopia, 1950, pp. 15–16. The capacity of 600 referred to the situation following the expansion carried out by the Italians, who built a number of separate small blocks containing additional cells.

74. Interview, Taddesse Tiruneh, Addis Ababa, 26 March 2005. See also Affidavit, Mika'él Tessema, Ministry of Justice, Ethiopia, 1949, p. 12.

75. Birhanu Dinqé, 1937 EC, p. 51.

76. Affidavit, Michael Tessema, Ministry of Justice, Ethiopia, 1950, p. 12.

77. Affidavit, Jacob Gabrie Leul, Ministry of Justice, Ethiopia, 1950, p. 14.

78. Affidavit, Iannuzzi Vittorio, Ministry of Justice, Ethiopia, 1950, pp. 15–16.

79. Interview, Taddesse Tiruneh, Addis Ababa, 26 March 2005.

80. It remained in continuous use until 2007–8, when it was demolished to make room for the new African Union headquarters.

81. Affidavit, Michael Tessema, Ministry of Justice, Ethiopia, 1950, pp. 11–13.

82. Ibid., p. 11.

83. Affidavit, Jacob Gabrie Leul, Ministry of Justice, Ethiopia, 1950, p. 14.

84. Imru Zelleke, 2009.

85. Sbacchi, A., 1997, p. 132.

86. See, for example, Affidavit, Michael Tessema, Ministry of Justice, Ethiopia, 1950, p. 13.

87. Imru Zelleke, 2009.

88. Interview, Tekle-Tsadiq Mekuriya, Addis Ababa, 10 Feb. 1998.

89. Interview, Imru Zelleke, 11 July 2012, conducted by Dr Roman Herzog, www.campifascisti.it.

90. www.zadigweb.it/amis/schede.asp?idsch-115&id=7: Museo Virtuale delle Intolleranze e degli Stermini.

91. Sbacchi, A., 1977, p. 217.

92. 'Latest News from Ethiopia', Djibouti, 9 April 1937, *New Times and Ethiopia News*, 1 May 1937, p. 8.

93. In April 1937, *New Times and Ethiopia News* quoted a report from British Somaliland stating that someone en route to Ethiopia from Mogadishu had seen 130 lorries 'full of Ethiopian prisoners, including women and children'. *New Times and Ethiopia News*, 24 April 1937, cited in Pankhurst, S., 1959, p. 389. While there is no reason to disbelieve the sighting, the number of vehicles may be an overestimate, for the trucks are known to have been tightly packed, and 130 of them would imply several thousand prisoners, which probably exceeds the number sent to Danane at any one time. Some of the prisoners were possibly destined for prisons in Mogadishu.

94. Affidavit, Michael Tessema, Ministry of Justice, Ethiopia, 1950, p. 13.

95. Affidavit, *Blatta* Bekele Hapte Michael, judge at the High Court of Ethiopia, Addis Ababa. Ministry of Justice, 1949, p. 69; Ministry of Justice, 1950, Doc. 18, pp. 16–17; Sbacchi, A., 1997, p. 132.

96. Baudendistal, R., 2006, p. 222, citing Ottolenghi, G., p. 174, but cautioning that Ottolenghi is not always clear about his sources.

97. British Military Administration in Eritrea and Somalia, 1944, p. 28.

98. Engert did not count or name the refugees while they were in the legation compound until they left the premises. Thus their number is variously estimated in the reports as 'four to five hundred', and 'several hundred', etc. until their departure, when it was reported that the headcount was precisely 700. Engert to Secretary of State, 25 Feb. 1937, US Government Printing Office, 1953, p. 686.

99. Secretary of State to Engert, 24 Feb. 1937, US Government Printing Office, 1953, p. 686.

100. Engert to Secretary of State, 4.00 pm, 25 Feb. 1937, US Government Printing Office, 1953, p. 686.

101. Report of 1 March 1937, Great Britain, File FO371/20927, para. 12.

102. Melbourne *Argus*, 27 March 1937, p. 8.

103. 'The Massacres of Addis Ababa', Ethiopian legation report, *New Times and Ethiopia News*, 10 April 1937, p. 3.

104. Morris N. Hughes (b. 13 January 1901) was a career diplomat who arrived in Addis Ababa in 1936 from his previous posting as 3rd Secretary in Tokyo. He left Addis Ababa on 8 April 1937 to take up the position of 2nd Secretary in Albania. Denshaw, W.R. and Truman, H.S., 1957.

105. US Government Printing Office, 1953, pp. 689–95.

106. Secretary of State to Hughes, 25 March 1937, US Government Printing Office, 1953, pp. 696–7.

107. American legation report, 14 March 1937, Great Britain, Public Records Office, File FO/371/20928.

108. Sava, L., 1940C.

109. The lists of refugees sheltering at the American legation in May 1936 are available among the Cornelius Van H. Engert papers at Georgetown University Library, Washington DC.

9. ROMAN JUSTICE

1. Telegram, Hughes (chargé in Addis Ababa) to Secretary of State, 10.00 am, 14 March 1937, US Government Printing Office, 1953, p. 695.
2. Campbell, I.L., 2010.
3. Graziani, R., 2001.
4. Campbell, I.L., 2010, pp. 213–19.
5. *Attentato contro S.E. il Vice Re*, Report No. 184–2–39, Addis Ababa, 20 Feb. 1937, XV [year of Fascism], ACS, fondo Graziani, busta 48, fascicolo 42, sottofascicolo 7.
6. For example, Sara Gebre-Iyyesus did not face a tribunal before being imprisoned with her children in Italy, neither was she aware of any such proceedings.
7. Haile Selassie I, ed. Marcus, H., 1994, pp. 79–85.
8. The findings of which are set out in Campbell, I.L., 2010.
9. For a more detailed analysis of the roles, responsibilities and demise of the *Yekatit 12* conspirators, see Campbell, I.L., 2010.
10. Interview, Letyibelu Gebré's relatives Amsale Letyibelu and Habtu Welde-Medhin, Addis Ababa, Sept. 2005. Confirmed in Letyibelu Gebré's obituary, Anon., no date (c.1960).
11. Anon., no date (c.1960)
12. Although documentary evidence indicates that Moges was born in 1912, information recently gathered by his relatives, who have been most helpful in the present author's research, suggests that he was actually born several years earlier.
13. According to a letter written at the time by Hermann Bahlburg (the head of the Hermannsburg Mission in Qechené), and shown to the present author by his son Cord, Hermann Bahlburg believed that Sibhat, whom he described as 'always a valuable employee', died from a combination of harsh interrogation and being incarcerated in 'a typhus-contaminated prison'—possibly Akaki—in late April 1937. See also http://hermannbahlburg.name/. Sibhat's brother Taddesse, who shared a room with Sibhat and Moges Asgedom, has been one of the key informants for the present author's research into the plot of *Yekatit 12*.
14. Information provided by Simi'on's nephew, His Holiness *Abune* Berhane-Yesus Derimew Surafa'él, Metropolitan Archbishop (now Cardinal) of the Catholic Church in Ethiopia. In 1997 Simi'on's surviving sister, attending a lecture by the present author at Addis Ababa University, confirmed this account. See also Sáska László (aka Ladislas Sava), ed. Szélinger Balázs, 2014, pp. 66–7.
15. Siniddu Gebru, 1942 EC, p. 35. See also Birhanu Dinqé, 1937 EC, p. 47, and Campbell, I.L., 2010, pp. 283–6.
16. *Attentato contro S.E. il Vice Re*, Report No. 184–2–39, Addis Ababa, 20 Feb. 1937,

XV [year of Fascism], ACS, fondo Graziani, busta 48, fascicolo 42, sottofascicolo 7, p. 5; Birhanu Dinqé, 1937 EC, p. 47; Siniddu Gebru, 1942 EC, p. 11.

17. *Risultanze di carattere generale circa I fatti del 19 corrente*, Report No. 1101, B. Olivieri to Viceroy, 22 Feb. 1937 XV [year of Fascism], ACS, fondo Graziani, busta 48, fascicolo 42, sottofascicolo 7.

18. Tekeste Negash, 1986, p. 64, citing Olivieri to Graziani, 22 Feb. 1937, fondo Graziani, busta 48, fascicolo 42.

19. Birhanu Dinqé, 1937 EC, p. 48.

20. 'Terrible News from Addis Ababa', *New Times and Ethiopia News*, 3 April 1937, p. 1; 'The Massacres of Addis Ababa', Ethiopian legation report, *New Times and Ethiopia News*, 10 April 1937, p. 3; Dispatch, 9 March 1937, Great Britain, Public Record Office, File FO/371/29028.

21. Haile Selassie I, ed. Marcus, H., 1994, pp. 80–1.

22. Ibid., p. 80; Birhanu Dinqé, 1937 EC, p. 48.

23. See also 'The Massacres of Addis Ababa', Ethiopian legation report, *New Times and Ethiopia News*, 10 April 1937, p. 3; Alazar Tesfa Michael, 1948, p. 2.

24. Haile Selassie I, ed. Marcus, H., 1994, p. 80, fn. 140, citing *Records of Leading Personalities in Abyssinia*, 4 May 1937, FO 371/20940/00401.

25. Dispatch No. 41, 26 Feb. 1937, Great Britain, Public Record Office, FO. 371/20917.

26. *Attentato contro S.E. il Vice Re*, Report No. 184–2–39, Addis Ababa, 20 Feb. 1937, XV [year of Fascism], ACS, fondo Graziani, busta 48, fascicolo 42, sottofascicolo 7.

27. Haile Selassie I, ed. Marcus, H., 1994, p. 80, fn. 141; Birhanu Dinqé, 1937 EC, p. 49.

28. 'The Massacres of Addis Ababa', Ethiopian legation report, *New Times and Ethiopia News*, 10 April 1937, pp. 2–3; American legation report, 14 March 1937, Great Britain, Public Record Office, File FO/371/20928.

29. Taddesse Mécha, 1943 EC, p. 31.

30. Anon., no date (written 1933 EC; published later).

31. Birhanina Selam, 1942 EC, p. 53.

32. Affidavit, Rosario Gilaezgi, Ministry of Justice, Ethiopia, 1950, p. 7.

33. Bahru Zewde, 2002, p. 98; 'The Massacres of Addis Ababa', Ethiopian legation report, *New Times and Ethiopia News*, 10 April 1937, p. 3; Dispatch, 9 March 1937, Great Britain, Public Record Office, File FO/371/29028.

34. *Attentato contro S.E. il Vice Re*, Report No. 184–2–39, Addis Ababa, 20 Feb. 1937 (forwarded 22 Feb.), XV [year of Fascism], ACS, fondo Graziani, busta 48, fascicolo 42, sottofascicolo 7, p. 4.

35. Campbell, I.L., 2012, pp. 86–8.

36. Haile Selassie I, ed. Marcus, H., 1994, pp. 79–85.

37. Interview, Shewareged Gedlé, *The Ethiopia Star*, 23 Nov. 1941.

38. For information on the number of Young Ethiopians executed after *Yekatit 12*, see chapter 11 and Appendix I.

39. 'The Massacres of Addis Ababa', Ethiopian legation report, *New Times and Ethiopia News*, 10 April 1937, p. 3.

40. Sava, L., 1941A.

41. Dugan, J. and Lafore, L., 1973, p. 323.

42. Interview, Tekle-Tsadiq Mekuriya, Addis Ababa, 10 Feb. 1998.

43. Imru Zelleke, 2009.

44. Before *Yekatit 12*, the most common charges leading to summary execution were 'being in possession of a photograph or picture of the Emperor or Foreign Minister Hiruy Welde-Sillassé', or 'being suspected of providing guns or bullets to the Patriots'. Meleseliñ Aniley, 1947 EC.

45. Affidavit, Rosario Gilaezgi, Ministry of Justice, Ethiopia, 1950, p. 7.

46. Poggiali, C., 1971, p. 187.

47. Dispatch, 9 March 1937, Great Britain, Public Record Office, File FO/371/28028.

48. See 'Note on the Events in Addis Ababa Subsequent to the Attempt on Marshal Graziani's Life on February 19th', 2 March 1937, Great Britain, Public Record Office, File FO 371/20927.

49. Report of 1 March 1937, Great Britain, Public Record Office, File FO/371/29027.

50. Based on a French diplomat's report, *News Chronicle*, 6 March 1937.

51. 'The Massacres of Addis Ababa', Ethiopian legation report, *New Times and Ethiopia News*, 10 April 1937, p. 3.

52. Ibid.

53. Rochat, G., 1988, p. 200, citing Graziani to Lessona, 28 Feb. 1937.

54. Boaglio, A., 2010, p. 64.

55. Rochat, G., 1988, p. 200.

56. Dispatch, 9 March 11937, Great Britain, Public Records Office, File FO/371/28028.

57. Report of 1 March 1937, Great Britain, Public Record Office, File FO/371/2902, para. 15.

58. 'Attempt to Excuse Fascist Murder of Dr Martin's Sons', *New Times and Ethiopia News*, 10 April 1937, p. 5; Poggiali, C., 1971, p. 187.

59. Garretson, P.P., 2012, pp. 245–50.

60. Dispatch, 9 March 1937, Great Britain, Public Record Office, File FO/371/28028.

61. Poggiali, C., 1971, p. 188. It is also likely that the execution of the Werqineh brothers was also retribution for their involvement with Colonel Belay Hayle-Ab in the Boneya incident, in which senior officers of the Regia Aeronautica were killed and their aircraft destroyed. See the report of the death of Colonel Belay, below.

62. Interview, Welette-Birhan Gebre-Iyyesus, Addis Ababa, 26 Jan. 2005.

63. Bahru Zewde, 2002, p. 71.

64. *Attentato contro S.E. il Vice Re*, Report No. 184–2–39, Addis Ababa, 20 Feb. 1937

(forwarded 22 Feb.), XV [year of Fascism], ACS, fondo Graziani, busta 48, fascicolo 42, sottofascicolo 7, p. 5.

65. Bahru Zewde, 2002, p. 87.
66. Dispatch, 9 March 1937, Great Britain, Public Record Office, File FO/371/28028.
67. Taddesse Mécha, 1943 EC, pp. 31–2; Bahru Zewde, 1993, p. 281; Bahru Zewde, 2002, pp. 203–4.
68. Campbell, I.L., 2010, pp. 79–80, 128.
69. Mockler, A., 1984, p. 177.
70. Poggiali, C., 1971, p. 189. Poggiali identifies the leader of the Boneya incident as Colonel Beicalcià. Given the many misspellings in his book in his transliteration of Ethiopian names into Italian, and given the fact that Belay Hayle-Ab's role at Boneya is well known and attested, it is reasonably safe to assume that Poggiali is referring to Colonel Belay Hayle-Ab.
71. Birhanina Selam, 1942 EC, p. 53.
72. Taddesse Mécha, 1943 EC, p. 28
73. Siniddu Gebru, 1942 EC, p. 50.
74. Birhanu Dinqé, 1937 EC, p. 50.
75. Birhanina Selam, 1942 EC, p. 55.
76. Taddesse Mécha, 1943 EC, p. 28
77. Siniddu Gebru, 1942 EC, p. 14.
78. Clapham, C., 1964, p. 3.
79. Birhanu Dinqé, 1937 EC, p. 49.
80. Taddesse Mécha, 1943 EC, p. 27.
81. Birhanina Selam, 1942 EC, pp. 53, 63.
82. Clapham, C., 1964, p. 4. Birhanu Dinqé has him studying political economy in America. Birhanu Dinqé, 1937 EC, p. 50.
83. Birhanu Dinqé, 1937 EC, p. 50; Anon., no date (written 1933 EC; published later), p. 10.
84. Taddesse Mécha, 1943 EC, p. 27.
85. Pankhurst, R.K., 1962, p. 272; Clapham, C., 1964, p. 7.
86. Bahru Zewde, 2002, p. 87; Pankhurst, R.K., 1962, p. 272.
87. Birhanu Dinqé, 1937 EC, p. 50.
88. Taddesse Mécha, 1943 EC, p. 28.
89. Birhanu Dinqé, 1937 EC, p. 49; Pankhurst, R.K., 1962, p. 275; Clapham, C., 1964, p. 6.
90. Taddesse Mécha, 1943 EC, p. 27.
91. Birhanina Selam, 1942 EC, p. 53.
92. Ibid., p. 57.
93. Taddesse Mécha, 1943 EC, p. 27.
94. Siniddu Gebru, 1942 EC, p. 42.
95. Birhanu Dinqé, 1937 EC, p. 50.

96. Taddesse Mécha, 1943 EC, p. 28.
97. Siniddu Gebru, 1942 EC, p. 24.
98. Ibid., p. 26.
99. Taddesse Mécha, 1943 EC, p. 28.
100. Birhanina Selam, 1942 EC, p. 54.
101. 'The Massacres of Addis Ababa', Ethiopian legation report, *New Times and Ethiopia News*, 10 April 1937, p. 3. Christopher Clapham lists him as having studied 'Military and Aviation'. Clapham, C., 1964, p. 2. According to Richard Pankhurst, he was one of Ethiopia's first airforce pilots. Pankhurst, R.K., 2011.
102. Birhanina Selam, 1942 EC, p. 57.
103. Anon., no date (written 1933 EC; published later), pp. 11–13. Ketema Beshah was the son of *Ato* Beshah Chekol of Menz. Birhanu Dinqé, 1937 EC, p. 50. Kirubel Beshah was also educated at Teferi Mekonnin School (French stream) and returned to teach advanced arithmetic there after the Liberation. Birhanina Selam, 1942 EC, pp. 57, 67.
104. *Attentato contro S.E. il Vice Re*, Report No. 184–2–39, Addis Ababa, 20 Feb. 1937, XV [year of Fascism], ACS, fondo Graziani, busta 48, fascicolo 42, sotto-fascicolo 7, p. 3.
105. American legation report, 14 March 1937, Great Britain, Public Record Office, File FO/371/20928.
106. Telegram 2860, Graziani to Nasi, 1 March 1937, Départment de la Presse et de l'Information du Gouvernement Impérial d'Ethiopie, 1946, pp. 57–8. See also Mockler, A., 1984, p. 178.
107. Telegram 8370/24709, Graziani to all Governors, 12 May 1937, Départment de la Presse et de l'information du Government Imperial D'Ethiopie, 1946, pp. 120–1. See also DEL BOCA, A., 1969, p. 225, fn. 31.
108. Sbacchi, A., 1989, p. 192.

10. THE RECKONING

1. Affidavit, Dawid Oqbazqui, Ministry of Justice, Ethiopia, 1950, pp. 12–13.
2. Ibid., p. 7. Michael Lentakis, a member of the Greek community of Addis Ababa at the time of the massacre, states in his autobiography that Mussolini ordered an inquiry into who had organised the massacre, and that, in addition to Cortese, General Petretti and General Gariboldi were implicated. He also implies that for this reason they were repatriated. However, Lentakis provides no sources for his information, and the present author has not come across the evidence supporting this claim. Lentakis, M.B., 2006, p. 61.
3. De Turris, A.L., 1999, p. 130.
4. Le Houérou, F., 1994B, p. 78.
5. Affidavit, Rosario Gilaezgi, Ministry of Justice, Ethiopia, 1950, p. 7.
6. Sbacchi cites memorandum from Lessona to all Governors of AOI, 19 Feb. 1937

(ACS, fondo Graziani 33); Mussolini to Graziani, 20 Feb. 1937 (ACS, fondo Graziani); Graziani to Lessona, 21 Feb. 1937 (ACS, Diarii Emilio De Bono, Diary No. 35, 21 March 1930); Mussolini to Graziani, 21 Feb. 1937 (ACS, fondo Graziani); Graziani to Mussolini, 22 Feb. 1937 (MAI, Gab 258/III-7). Sbacchi, A., 1997, p. 200, fn. 60.

7. Telegram, Graziani to Lessona, 28 Feb. 1937, cited in Rochat, G., 1988, pp. 200–1; Sbacchi interview of Lessona in 1972, cited in Sbacchi, A., 1989, p. 190, and confirmed in Rochat, G., 1988, p. 204. See also Sbacchi, A., 1997, p. 177, and Campbell, I.L., 2010, p. 284.

8. Pankhurst, R.K., 1997, p. 25.

9. Graziani, R., 2001, p. 78.

10. Dispatch, Bodard to Minister of Foreign Affairs, Paris, 10 March 1937, p. 2.

11. Rochat, G., 1988, p. 203, fn. 64, citing fondo Graziani, busta 32.

12. Crociani, P. and Battistelli, P.P., 2010, p. 10.

13. Lucas, E. and De Vecchi, G., 1976, pp. 63–116; Governo Generale, Stato Maggiore, A.O.I, 1939B, 'Rete delle linee telegrafoniche urbane di Addis Abeba'.

14. Mockler, A., 1984, p. 55.

15. Moher, J., 1996.

16. Aliano, D., 2008, p. 3.

17. Nonetheless, Professor Angelo Del Boca managed to interview a few witnesses during his visit to Addis Ababa in the 1960s, and their comments are covered in the present book.

18. Le Houérou, F., 1994B, p. 79.

19. Poggiali, C., 1971, p. 182.

20. American legation telegram, paraphrased, 19 Feb. 1937, Great Britain, Public Record Office, File FO/371/20928.

21. Dispatch 64, 21 Feb. 1937 (written on 20 Feb.), Great Britain, Public Record Office, File FO 371/20927.

22. Report and covering memo 147/30/37 of 1 March 1937, Great Britain, Public Record Office, File FO/371/20927, p. 6, para. 10.

23. Meleseliñ Aniley, 1947 EC.

24. Le Houérou, F., 1994B, p. 78.

25. Le Houérou, F., 1994B, p. 78, citing ACS, fondo Graziani, busta 48–42, Ufficio Giustizia Militare, report of 22 Feb. 1937.

26. Giglio, C., 1938, p. 9, cited in Dominioni, M., 2008, p. 319, fn. 112.

27. Le Houérou, F., 1994B, p. 80.

28. Del Boca, A., 1965, pp. 221–2.

29. Affidavit, Edouard Garabedian, Ministry of Justice, Ethiopia, 1950, p. 8.

30. Le Houérou, F., 1994B, p. 78.

31. Interview, Tekle-Maryam Kiflom, Addis Ababa, 7 Sept. 2004.

32. www.campifascisti.it: interview, Imru Zelleke, 11 July 2012, conducted by Dr Roman Herzog,

33. Interview, Dr Birhanu Abebe, Addis Ababa, Nov. 2004.

34. Sudan Intelligence Report, Secret, No. 54, ref. J2110/44/1, 24 April 1937, Great Britain, Public Record Office, File FO/371/20930, p. 7.

35. 'The Massacres of Addis Ababa', Ethiopian legation report, *New Times and Ethiopia News*, 10 April 1937, p. 3.

36. 'The Massacres of Addis Ababa', Ethiopian legation report, *New Times and Ethiopia News*, 10 April 1937, p. 3.

37. Shashka, L., 1940B.

38. *The Ethiopian Star*, 23 Nov. 1941.

39. Le Houérou, F., 1994B, p. 80, citing ACS, fondo Graziani, busta 48–42–8, Synthèse d'Azolino Azon de l'ufficio politico.

40. This division had been created on 12 October 1936, principally from the 10th and 11th Regiments 'Granatieri', and the 6th Regiment Field Artillery. It was deployed to defend Addis Ababa and 'pacify' the governorate of Shewa: http://www.regioesercito.it.

41. Dispatch 64, 21 Feb. 1937 (written on 20 Feb.), Great Britain, Public Record Office, File FO 371/20927.

42. Report and covering memo, 147/30/37, 1 March 1937, File FO/371/20927, p. 9, para. 17.

43. Crociani, P. and Battistelli, P.P., 2010, p. 20.

44. www.comandosupremo.com/blackshirts.html/4: Camicie Nere (The MVSN & CCNN Combat Units).

45. The London *Daily Telegraph* correspondent drew the same distinction: 'Regular troops, it is stated, set fire to the "tukuls" or native wooden cabins in several parts of the town, the inhabitants in many cases being burned. In the evening the Blackshirts were let loose.' *Daily Telegraph*, 'Italian Terrorism in Addis Ababa', quoted in 'The Ethiopian Patriots as Seen at the Time', *Ethiopia Observer*, Vol. III, No. 11, Oct. 1959, p. 357.

46. Birhanu Dinqé suggests that the *carabinieri* were ordered to burn homes and kill the occupants. Birhanu Dinqé, 1937 EC, pp. 50–1.

47. Del Boca, A., 1965, pp. 221–2.

48. Interview, Dr Birhanu Abebe, Addis Ababa, 9 Nov. 2004.

49. Birhanu Dinqé, 1937 EC, pp. 50–1.

50. 'The Massacres of Addis Ababa', Ethiopian legation report, *New Times and Ethiopia News*, 10 April 1937, p. 3.

51. 'The Massacres of Addis Ababa', Ethiopian legation report, *New Times and Ethiopia News*, 10 April 1937, p. 1.

52. Interview, Dr Birhanu Abebe, Addis Ababa, 9 Nov. 2004.

53. Imru Zelleke, 2009.

54. Interview, Dr Birhanu Abebe, Addis Ababa, 9 Nov. 2004.

55. Anon., no date (written 1933 EC; published later), pp. 8–9.

56. See, for example, Bahru Zewde, 2002, p. 170.

57. 'The Massacres of Addis Ababa', Ethiopian legation report, *New Times and Ethiopia News*, 10 April 1937, p. 3.

58. Dispatch, Bodard, to Foreign Affairs, 10 March 1937, Affaires Étrangères, série K. Afrique 1918–40, sous-série Éthiopie.

59. See, for example, Welde-Giyorgis Welde-Yohannis, 1939 EC, p. 23.

60. Marcus, H., 1994, p. 149.

61. Shashka, L., 1940B.

62. Dispatch, Bodard, to Foreign Affairs, 10 March 1937, Affaires Étrangères, série K. Afrique 1918–40, sous-série Éthiopie.

63. Interview, Imru Zelleqe with Jeff Pearce, telephone, 8 Oct. 2012.

64. Shashka, L., 1940B.

65. 'They were vulgar guys, scoundrels, jailbirds, and they raped women. We girls could no longer go out at night'. Barrera, G., 1996, pp. 51–2, quoting Maria Messina, an Italo-Eritrean woman born in Asmara in 1917.

66. Barrera, G., 1996, pp. 51–2, quoting Dr Shashka, *New Times and Ethiopian News*, 21 Sept. 1940.

67. Boaglio, A., 2010, pp. 62–3.

68. Furthermore, the party had the power to expel its members for speech or actions deemed not in compliance with 'Fascist behaviour', and had its spies everywhere.

69. Dispatch, Bodard, to Foreign Affairs, 10 March 1937, Affaires Étrangères, série K. Afrique 1918–40, sous-série Éthiopie.

70. Interview, *Immahoy* Hiruta, Addis Ababa, 28 Feb. 2009.

71. This is not to say that all foreign residents were sympathetic to the Ethiopians. Lieutenant Meleseliñ states that some of them tipped off the Italians as to where some of the wanted Ethiopians could be found, resulting in more imprisonments. Meleseliñ Aniley, 1947 EC.

72. Information provided by Signor DeMarco to Richard Pankhurst, and kindly passed to the present author on 2 Oct. 2012.

73. For an account of the work of John Rabe, see Chang, I., 1997, pp. 105–39.

74. Engert to Secretary of State, No. 49, 9.00 am, 21 Feb. 1937, US Government Printing Office, 1953, pp. 681–2. See also American legation report, 21 Feb. 1937, 9.00 am, paraphrased, Great Britain, Public Record Office, File FO/371/20928.

75. *Daily Mail*, London, 8 March 1937, quoting British United Press; 'Direct News of Addis Ababa Massacre', Djibouti correspondent, 17 March 1937, *New Times and Ethiopia News*, 3 April 1937, p. 2. Later reports show that the promised assistance did not, in fact, arrive until the massacre was over.

76. Engert to Secretary of State, No. 55, 3.00 pm, 23 Feb. 1937, US Government Printing Office, 1953, p. 684.

77. Weerts, M.L., 2003.

78. Launhardt, J., 2004, p. 78.
79. Report of 1st March 1937, Great Britain, Public Record Office, File FO371/20927, para. 12.
80. Rosario was Della Porta's interpreter.
81. Affidavit, Rosario Gilaezgi, Ministry of Justice, Ethiopia, 1950, p. 7.
82. Some of the resentment directed in the Viceroy's memoirs towards what might be termed the 'liberal caucus' in the Governo Generale (consisting of men such as Avolio and Della Porta, of whom Graziani was very suspicious) could have arisen from the fact that none of them was physically close enough to Graziani to have sustained any injuries at the strike of *Yekatit 12*. Graziani, R., 2001, pp. 77–81.
83. Affidavit, Rosario Gilaezgi, Ministry of Justice, Ethiopia, 1950, p. 7.
84. Ibid.
85. Interview, *Shaleqa* Éfrém Gebre-Amlak, Addis Ababa, 12 Dec. 2004.
86. In this regard, it is notable that after the Battle of Adwa in 1896, the Ethiopian government treated the Eritrean *askaris* who had fought the Ethiopian army as traitors. Although the punishment for treason (mutilation) in Ethiopia was lighter than the death sentence then generally applicable for the same offence in Europe, its application to the *askaris* was held up in Italy as evidence of Ethiopian barbarism.
87. See Campbell, I.L., 2014, pp. 93–4, 126.
88. Interview, *Shaleqa* Éfrém Gebre-Amlak, Addis Ababa, 12 Dec. 2004.
89. 'The Massacres of Addis Ababa', Ethiopian legation report, *New Times and Ethiopia News*, 10 April 1937, p. 3.
90. Birhanu Dinqé, 1937 EC, pp. 50–1.
91. Interview, *Shaleqa* Éfrém Gebre-Amlak, Addis Ababa, 12 Dec. 2004.
92. Mannucci, S., no date, citing Colarizi, S., 2000, pp. 223–5.
93. Interview, Dr Birhanu Abebe, Addis Ababa, 9 Nov. 2004.
94. See, for example, Ministry of Justice, Ethiopia, 1949, pp. 16–20.
95. Paris correspondent, *News Chronicle*, London, 6 March 1937.
96. 120 berméls each holding 200 litres = 24,000 litres of water.
97. Birhanu Dinqé, 1937 EC, p. 51.
98. Birhanu Dinqé, 1937 EC, p. 51.
99. In 1941 the British found 332 Ethiopian 'political prisoners' still alive at Nocra, suggesting that a total of at least 500–600 were originally incarcerated there, of whom a substantial proportion would have come from Addis Ababa after *Yekatit 12*. British Military Administration in Eritrea and Somalia, 1944, p. 28.
100. Sbacchi, A., 1997, p. 129. The present analysis includes only those arrested shortly after *Yekatit 12*.
101. Sudan Intelligence Report, Secret, No. 54, ref. J2110/44/1, 24 April 1937, Great Britain, Public Record Office, File FO/371/20930, p. 7. However, Birhanu Dinqé estimates 9,000 deaths on Friday night alone. Birhanu Dinqé, 1937 EC, p. 47.

102. According to Professor Alberto Sbacchi, more than 4,000 homes were burned down. Sbacchi, A., p. 177. Sera Bét Sefer could have accounted for 10–15% of the city's population, housing some 1,820–2,730 households. Given Alfredo Godio's statement that 'from 5 May Square [Arat Kilo junction] to the American Hospital [near today's Finfine Hotel] very few *tukuls* survived', it is clear that this residential area was virtually wiped out, which alone would have accounted for a large proportion of the estimated 4,000 homes destroyed.

103. Many more residents were rounded up on Saturday and Sunday.

104. Although there was considerable house-burning in the suburbs during the nights following Sunday, 21 February, the majority of the occupants had by this time fled. Thus the number of deaths was relatively small, and has been absorbed here into the figure for Sunday night.

105. For more details on the Young Ethiopians and nobles executed, see Appendices I and II, respectively.

106. See Appendix I for more details on the Young Ethiopians.

107. Dugan, J. and Lafore, L., 1973, p. 323.

108. In his essays on the treatment of the Ethiopian aristocracy, Professor Alberto Sbacchi, who conducted the most in-depth analyses of the statistics of the Occupation, discusses the aristocrats imprisoned in Italy and those incarcerated in Danane and Nocra, but surprisingly makes no mention of the large number of (particularly Amhara) notables shot and hanged. The fact that Sbacchi's research relied principally on Italian documentary sources suggests that although the instructions for the elimination of Amhara notables appear in many surviving telegrams, no systematic documentation of these deaths exists.

109. See, for example, Rochat, G., 1988, p. 194. For a discussion of the problem of relying on Italian sources, see Campbell, I.L., 2004.

110. The 'unofficial' killings in detention centres, which would have caused injuries to bystanders, are assumed to have accounted for around 50% of these deaths.

111. Dispatch, Bodard to Foreign Affairs, Paris, 24 Feb. 1937, Affaires Étrangères, série K. Afrique 1918–40, sous-série Éthiopie, Microfiche 103/104.

112. Rubinkowska, H., 2010.

113. Mahteme Sillassé Welde Mesqel, 1961 EC, pp. 71–2.

114. This range is not the sum of all the minima and the maxima, which would be most unlikely to occur coincidentally. It is based on the assumption (sufficiently valid for present purposes) that the range for each phase represents 95% probability of occurring, and that the figures for each phase estimate are independent and follow a 'normal' probability distribution. The formula employed is that the variance of the sum of the ten variables is equal to the sum of the variances, i.e. Var. $(\sum X_i) = \sum$ Var. (X_i), for i = 1 to 10. The confidence limits on the mean are then $\pm 2\sigma$, where $\sigma = \sqrt{\text{Var.}(\sum X_i)}$.

115. Shortly before the Invasion, Dr Zervos estimated the population of Addis Ababa as 'over 100,000'. Zervos, A., 1936, p. 27.

116. Consociazione Turistica Italiana, 1938, p. 476.
117. Based on the frequently reported figure of 40 live prisoners per truck, there was little more than 1 m² for four people, which meant standing room only, which is consistent with the accounts provided by Ethiopian prisoners. When used for transporting Italian soldiers, the loading was typically 12–15 per truck for long journeys, and 15–20 for short journeys.
118. Telegram, Bodard to Foreign Affairs, Paris, 24 Feb. 1937, via Djibouti. Affaires Étrangères, série K. Afrique 1918–40, sous-série Éthiopie, Microfiche 103/104.
119. Shashka, L., 1940C.
120. This could be a conservative estimate, since (a) many bodies were burned in the houses, and when collected consisted only of body parts, and (b) in addition to the Fiat 634N, the military also operated some larger, heavy-duty trucks.
121. 'More Tragic News of Ethiopia', Djibouti correspondent, 9 April 1937, *New Times and Ethiopia News*, 1 May 1937, p. 7.
122. Boaglio, A., 2010, p. 64.
123. 'Italy's War Crimes in Ethiopia'—evidence for the War Crimes Commission reproduced in Kali-Nyah, I., 2001, p. 112, citing Sylvia Pankhurst's original *Italy's War Crimes in Ethiopia*. Also published in Pankhurst, S., 1955, p. 548.
124. Pankhurst, S., 1955, p. 542.
125. Birhanu Dinqé estimated that the countrywide death toll *exceeded* 30,000, and Imru Zelleqe is of the same opinion. Birhanu Dinqé, 1937 EC, p. 52; Imru Zelleke, 2009.
126. Dispatch, Bodard to Minister of Foreign Affairs, Paris, 10 March 1937. Bodard's report refers to Belachew Yadeté, one of the foreign-educated generation close to educated fellow-Catholics such as Tesfayé Tegeñ, Ayele Gebré and Birhane-Marqos Welde-Tsadiq. Belachew had returned to Addis Ababa after accompanying the Emperor to Djibouti. M. Bethe Selassié, 2009, p. 131. He had served the British as interpreter at the Harar consulate and at the Addis Ababa legation. He became secretary to the Controller of the Djibouti–Addis Ababa Railway Company, *Lij* Mekonnin Endelkachew, in 1923, and was eventually appointed Controller. In 1934 he was appointed director-general of Posts. Bahru Zewde, 2002, p. 98. The case of the looting of Belachew's house as reported by Bodard is particularly interesting in that Catholic Ethiopians were usually given more consideration during the Occupation than Orthodox Christians.
127. Decree Nos. 738, 15 Oct. 1937; 751, 25 Oct. 1937; 752, 25 Oct. 1937, Governo Generale dell'A.O.I., no date (c.1938), pp. 468, 527–8.

11. THE COVER-UP

1. Sava, L., 1941A.
2. Diel, L., 1939, pp. 62–3.
3. Report attached to covering memorandum 147/30/37, 1 March 1937, Great Britain, Public Record Office, File FO/371/20927, para. 17.

4. Ibid., p. 8, para. 14.

5. Graziani filed a charge of corruption against Cortese. Rochat, G., 1988, p. 203, fn. 64, citing fondo Graziani, busta 32. By 1 March 1937 the British acting consul-general was informing London that Cortese 'appears to have been recalled to Rome'. Report attached to covering memorandum 147/30/37, 1 March 1937, Great Britain, Public Record Office, File FO/371/20927.

6. 'Let the clergy return to the churches, and set up their own altars for the Sacrament; let the people follow their own Liturgy, and may their hearts be glad!' Doresse, J., p. 159.

7. Dispatch, 9 March 1937, Great Britain, Public Record Office, File FO/371/29028, attachment.

8. Report attached to memorandum 147/30/37, 1 March 1937, Great Britain, Public Record Office, File FO/371/20927.

9. Report attached to memorandum 147/30/37, 1 March 1937, Great Britain, Public Record Office, File FO/371/20927, p. 3, para. 5.

10. Pankhurst, R. K., 2003, p. 59; Haile Selassie I, ed. Marcus, H., 1994, pp. 33–7.

11. Pankhurst, R. K., 2003, p. 59.

12. Letter, Anthony Eden to Prime Minister Stanley Baldwin, 5 April 1938, Great Britain, Public Record Office, File FO/371/20918.

13. Letter, Neville Chamberlain to Foreign Secretary Anthony Eden, 12 April 1937. Great Britain, Public Record Office, File FO/371/20928.

14. American legation report of 1 March 1937. Great Britain, Public Record Office, File FO/371/20927, para. 21.

15. Sava, L., 1940B.

16. See Perret, M., 1986; Campbell, I.L., 2014.

17. Tekeste Negash, 1986, pp. 58–61.

18. Del Boca, A., 1969, p. 259.

19. British Military Administration in Eritrea and Somalia, 1944, p. 28.

20. 'Girmawi Janhoy 12 Yekatit hawulet mireqa ye-tenagerut diskur' ['The Speech of His Majesty Janhoy on Yekatit 12'], *Berhanina Selam*, No. 1, Addis Ababa, 27 Miazia, 1934 EC, pp. 25–6.

21. *The Times*, 8 Oct. 1942, cited in Pankhurst, R.K., 1999, p. 84.

22. Interview, Yeweynishet Beshahwired, 18 April 2010, conducted by Dr Roman Herzog, www.campifascisti.it.

23. Pankhurst, R.K., 2003, p. 204, citing Foreign Office to British Embassy in Rome, 8 Dec. 1944, FO, T. 2291/4.

24. 'Feast of Selassie—Unveiling of the Cenotaph—and Views of Fascist Atrocities in Ethiopia', *Ethiopian Review*, Addis Ababa, Vol. 1, No. 7, Feb. 1945, p. 11.

25. Ibid.

26. Interview, Yeweynishet Beshahwired, 18 April 2010, conducted by Dr Roman Herzog, www.campifascisti.it.

27. 'Feast of Selassie—Unveiling of the Cenotaph—and Views of Fascist Atrocities in Ethiopia', *Ethiopian Review*, Vol. 1, No. 7, Feb. 1945, p. 11.

28. Subsequently republished in an expanded edition by the Ethiopian Holocaust Remembrance Committee, Chicago. See Kali-Nyah, I., 2001, pp. 108–35.

29. Pankhurst, R.K., 1999, p. 109, citing Great Britain, Command Paper No. 6668 of 1945.

30. Interview, Imru Zelleqe, 11 July 2012, conducted by Dr Roman Herzog, www. campifascisti.it.

31. '19th February 1937', *Ethiopian Review*, Jan.–June 1946, p. 10.

32. Ibid.

33. Pankhurst, R.K., 1999, p. 109, citing Great Britain, Public Record Office, File FO 372/4385, Doc. T. 19415.

34. Departement de la Presse et de l'Information du Gouvernement Imperial d'Ethiopie, 1946, following p. 143.

35. Memoranda, F. Garner, D. Riches, A. Ross and W. Beckett, 29–31 Jan. 1947, Great Britain, Public Record Office, File FO/371/66571, Doc. U162, cited in Pankhurst, R.K., 1999, p. 121.

36. Curiously, the list omitted General Maletti, who was responsible for carrying out the massacre of Debre Libanos, one of the greatest single atrocities of the Occupation.

37. List No. 80 (May 1948) of the United Nations War Crimes Commission, Ministry of Justice, Ethiopia, 1949, pp. 1–3.

38. Foreign Office official, Alan Desmond Frederick Pemberton-Pigott (b. 1916, d. 1972).

39. Memorandum, A. Pemberton-Pigott, 28 April 1948, Great Britain, Public Record Office, File FO/73180/Z2900, cited in Pankhurst, R.K., 1999, p. 128.

40. *The Ethiopian Herald*, 21 Feb. 1949, p. 2.

41. Foreign Office Minute, 17 Sept. 1949, Great Britain, Public Record Office, File FO/371/79515, Doc. Z6218, cited in Pankhurst, R.K., 1999, p. 134.

42. Interview, Imru Zelleke, 11 July 2012, conducted by Dr Roman Herzog, www. campifascisti.it.

12. REFLECTIONS

1. For a discussion of the extent to which the Occupation and the brutality that accompanied it could be put down to the new implacable philosophy of Fascism, see Finaldi, G., 2008, pp. 79–81; Finaldi, G., 2012B.

2. Neither were those responsible ever held to account for Italian atrocities in Libya, Albania, Greece or Yugoslavia.

EPILOGUE

1. For an account of the last days of Mussolini, see Evans, D., 2005, pp. 163–73.

2. Crociani, P. and Battistelli, P.P., 2010, p. 20.

3. 'Camicie Nere: The Blackshirts (MVSN & CCNN Combat Units)', http//:wargaming.info/1996/.

4. Crociani, P. and Battistelli, P.P., 2010, pp. 10–16.

5. Eritrea would remain federated with Ethiopia until January 1963, when annexation was finally announced.

6. Del Boca, A., 2012, p. 234.

7. Ministry of Justice, Ethiopia, 1949, Preface, p. iii.

8. For an in-depth discussion of these trials, see Battini, M., 2007.

9. Smith, H., 1948.

10. Cifelli, A., 2008, pp. 6, 16.

11. Cortese, G., *Problemi dell'impero*, Pinciana, Rome, 1938.

12. Forgacs, D., pp. 80–1, citing Cortese, G., 1938, p. 292. See also Le Houérou, F., 1994B, pp. 94–6.

13. Cortese's director-general position fell under the Ministry of Interior, http://www.prefettura.it//aquila/generali/48599.htm; Cifelli, A., 2008, pp. 6, 16, 50, 59 n. 170, 198 n. 5; http://web.tiscali.it/RSI_ANALISI/24nov.htm.

14. Cifelli, A., 2008, pp. 6, 16.

15. According to the historian Michael Thöndl, Cortese died in 1976. Thöndl, M., 2008, p. 473, fn. 72.

16. It should be noted that the Guido Cortese who was Fascist Party secretary in Addis Ababa is not to be confused with the well-known Italian liberal politician of the same name.

17. Temesgen Gebré, 2001 EC, pp. 100–1.

18. Temesgen Gebré, 2001 EC, p. 101. A footnote to Temesgen's account makes it clear that the story of his getting assistance and advice from *Itété* Bezabish, and subsequently walking to Gojjam, was told by Temesgen to his wife, who in turn passed the story on to her daughter, Sister Kibre Temesgen, the publisher of her father's autobiography in 2009.

19. Hamilton, P.A., 1949. This obituary written by Hamilton was republished in Temesgen Gebré, 2001 EC, pp. 156–62, citing *New Times and Ethiopia News*, No. 664, 5 Feb. 1949.

20. The Hermannsburg Mission in Qechené had been converted by Empress Menen into an orphanage to help address this problem.

21. Hall, C., 1947.

22. Augustinčić was also responsible for the statue of *Ras* Mekonnin in Harar and a monument to Ethiopian Patriots at Holetta Military Academy.

23. Several eyewitnesses of the massacre confirmed that the images of the atrocity on the Martyrs Memorial are accurate; Sibhatu Yohannis, Graziani's interpreter, told his family, 'Everything depicted there is true.' Interview, Alemash Sibhatu, Addis Ababa, 30 Jan. 1998.

24. Pankhurst, R., 2003, pp. 249–51.

25. For this information on Dr Shashka, the present author is indebted to historian Dr Szélinger Balázs. Sáska László (aka Ladislas Sava), ed. Szélinger Balázs, 2014, pp. 1–9, 32.

26. Taddesse Zeweldé, 1960 EC, foll. p. 533.

27. Hermann Bahlburg reportedly made an unsuccessful approach to General Olivieri to have Sibhat released; http://hermann.bahlburg.name/.

28. Information provide by Mehari Kassa's friends, Sennayt Siyum and her uncle, Seged Abriha, Dec. 2009.

29. Mehari Kassa is named by Richard Pankhurst as also having translated a book on hygiene into Amharic. Pankhurst, R.K., 1962, pp. 5, 131, citing Comba, P., *Inventaire des livres amhariques figurant dans la collection éthiopienne à la bibliothèque de l'University College d'Addis Ababa*, 1961, p. 71.

30. Wolk, E., 2010.

31. Ofcansky, T.P. and Shinn, D.H., 2004, pp. 89–90.

32. Information provided by Taddesse Tiruneh, Dec. 2004. The imprisonment of Bahlburg and Rathje is confirmed in Hermannsburg Mission, 2003, p. 9. See also Launhardt, J., 2004, p. 86.

33. See Ev.-Luth. Missionswerk in Niedersachsen (ELM) and Gremels, G., 2008.

34. http://hermann.bahlburg.name/.

35. Interestingly, both Oskar Schindler, who saved many Jews from the Nazi death camps by employing them in his enamelware factory, and John Rabe, who saved the lives of thousands of Chinese by sheltering them in the International Safety Zone he established during the Massacre of Nanking in December 1937, were members of the Nazi Party.

36. Engert, J.M., 2006, p. 259.

APPENDIX I: YOUNG ETHIOPIANS EXECUTED FOLLOWING *YEKATIT 12*

1. Pankhurst, R.K., 1962. An updated summary of this information was published in *Economic History of Ethiopia*. Pankhurst, R.K., 1968, pp. 678–9, and esp. 681–2.

2. Clapham, C., 1964. The present author acknowledges Professor Clapham's generosity in providing copies of his data for the purposes of the present analysis.

3. Clapham, C., 1969, pp. 18–21.

4. Pankhurst, R.K., 1964, pp. 271–8, and Pankhurst, R.K., 1968, p. 681.

5. Pankhurst, R.K., 1964, pp. 271–2.

6. Clapham, C., 1969, p. 20.

7. Clapham, C., 1964.

8. Information provided by *Lij* Imru Zelleqe, Washington, Nov. 2015.

9. Killed by a stray bullet during rioting that broke out due to impending arrival of the invading army.

10. The names of Bahru Keba, Taddesse Zeweldé and Menqir Gebre-Iyyesus have been removed from Clapham's 'fate unknown' list, since the first was killed following *Yekatit 12*, and the latter two are known to have survived.

11. Gebre Zewde and Mekonnin Desta, who is believed to have survived, may be one and the same person, 'Mekonnin Desta' possibly being a pseudonym. Clapham, C., 1964, p. 3.

12. Interview, *Dejazmach* Zewdé Gebre-Sillassé, Addis Ababa, 30 Dec. 2005.

13. Aklilu Habteweld, tr. Getachew Tedla, 2010, pp. 110–12.

14. Birhanina Selam, 1942 EC, pp. 52–8.

15. All data in this paragraph are taken from Pankhurst, R.K., 1962, pp. 279–83, unless otherwise stated.

16. Pankhurst, R.K., 1968, p. 676.

17. Grubb, N., 1943.

18. Ibid., p. 50; Taddesse Mécha, 1943 EC, pp. 27–8.

19. *Attentato contro S.E. il Vice Re*, Report No. 184–2–39, Addis Ababa, 20 Feb. 1937, XV [year of Fascism], ACS, fondo Graziani, busta 48, fascicolo 42, sottofascicolo 7, p. 5.

20. Kirubel Beshah refers to him as Captain Teferi Yazew. Anon., no date (written 1933 EC; published later), p. 10.

21. Taddesse Mécha actually names seven Black Lion members about whose fate he had no information (Taddesse Mécha, 1943 EC, pp. 27–8). But two of them (Mekonnin Hayle and Mitike Desta) were listed by Birhanu Dinqé as having been executed. Birhanu Dinqé, 1937 EC, p. 50.

22. *Attentato contro S.E. il Vice Re*, Report No. 184–2–39, Addis Ababa, 20 Feb. 1937, XV [year of Fascism], ACS, fondo Graziani, busta 48, fascicolo 42, sottofascicolo 7, pp. 5–6. The names are transliterated, but where the meaning is not clear the name appears as written, in inverted commas, followed wherever possible by the suggested most likely meaning in parenthesis.

23. Thought by Clapham to have been educated in France and survived the Occupation.

APPENDIX II: PARTIAL LIST OF ADDIS ABABA-BASED NOBLES AND NOTABLES EXECUTED FOLLOWING *YEKATIT 12*

1. Birhanu Dinqé, 1937 EC, pp. 48–50. This list may include some who were executed outside Addis Ababa.

2. It is not known if this is also the person referred to in the *carabinieri* report of 20 Feb. 1937 (forwarded on 22 Feb.) as '*Fitawrari* Welde-Giyorgis' (above).

3. *Attentato contro S.E. il Vice Re*, Report No. 184–2–39, Addis Ababa, 20 Feb. 1937 (forwarded 22 Feb.), XV [year of Fascism], ACS, fondo Graziani, busta 48, fascicolo 42, sottofascicolo 7, p. 5.

4. *Attentato contro S.E. il Vice Re*, Report No. 184–2–39, Addis Ababa, 20 Feb. 1937, XV [year of Fascism], ACS, fondo Graziani, busta 48, fascicolo 42, sottofas-

cicolo 7, pp. 4, 5. The names are transliterated from the Italian, but where the meaning is not clear the name appears as written, in inverted commas, followed wherever possible by the most likely meaning in parenthesis.

APPENDIX V: PHOTOGRAPHY

1. Sava, L., 1940B, p. 1.
2. Several original photographs that came into the possession of Sylvia Pankhurst were kindly provided to the present author by Richard Pankhurst for publication in this book. Many other items from the Pankhurst collection were donated several years ago to the Institute of Ethiopian Studies, Addis Ababa University.
3. De Turris, A.L., 1999.
4. Steer, G., 2009, p. 40.
5. De Turris, A.L., 1999, p. 135.
6. Steer, G., 2009, p. 40.
7. The official history in the Archives of the Historical Unit of the Army Staff, Rome (S.M.E., Ufficio Storico Archivio—Registro dei diari storici della guerra italo-etiopica, D-6, fondo 644, AUSSME) covers activities of the 6th Tevere Blackshirts at sites outside Addis Ababa, but is silent on what they were doing between 19 and 21 Feb. in Addis Ababa. Personal communication, Professor Pompeo Volpe, 10 Oct. 2014.
8. Mannucci, S., 2005, fn. 12.
9. Sava, L., 1940B, p. 1.
10. The Istituto Luce internet website no longer carries film of either of these events, although a few years ago it carried the one of September 1936.

BIBLIOGRAPHY

1. Italian Atrocities in 1911 was written by Hakim Werqineh Isheté. See Pankhurst, R.K., 2007 and Pankhurst R.K., 2012.
2. Ke-Hulum Tikit was written by Kirubel Beshah. Personal communication, Dr Birhanu Abebe.
3. This Derg-period article was written anonymously by Dr Birhanu Abebe. Personal communication, Dr Birhanu Abebe.
4. Finaldi, G., 2012A is listed under Internet Sources.

BIBLIOGRAPHY

Published Books and Articles Cited

Abera Jembere, 1997 EC (A), *Bichenyaw Sew: Tsehafé Ti'ezaz Tefera Werq Kidaneweld* (Amharic), Addis Ababa: Shama Books.

———, 1997 EC (B), *Abagest—Ras Abbebe Aregay* (Amharic), Addis Ababa: Shama Books.

Adamthwaite, A.P., 1977, *The Making of the Second World War*, London: George Allen & Unwin.

Addis Zemen, 1979 EC, 'Ye Yekatit ilqitina ye tarik miskiroch: Professor Pankrist Richard na leloch' (Amharic), *Addis Zemen*, Addis Ababa, 12 Yekatit, 1979 EC, Vol. 45, No. 445, pp. 2–3.

Aklilu Habteweld, tr. Getachew Tedla, 2010, *YeAklilu Mastawesha—Aklilu Remembers* (Amharic and English), Addis Ababa: Addis Ababa University Press.

Alazar Tesfa Michael, 1948, 'Eritrean Heroes', *New Times and Ethiopia News*, No. 632, 26 June 1948, pp. 1–2.

Aliano, D., 2008, *Identity in Transatlantic Play: Il Duce's National Project in Argentina*, Dissertation for PhD, unpublished, City University of New York.

Aloisi, P., 1957, *Journal (25 juillet 1932—14 juin 1936)*, Paris.

Aman Worji, 1988, *From Palace to University: A History of Addis Ababa University Main Campus*, Thesis for Bachelor of Arts in History, unpublished, Addis Ababa University, May 1988.

Anon, 1936[1], *Italian Atrocities in 1911* (English and Arabic), London: St Clement's Press.

Anon., 1937, 'Arrest Everybody', *Time*, 1 March 1937.

Anon., no date (written 1933 EC, published later)[2], *Ke-Hulum Tikit* (Amharic), Addis Ababa.

Anon., no date (c.1960), *Kibur Dejazmach Let Yibelu Gebré* (Amharic), unidentified bilingual Ethiopian magazine, Addis Ababa, p. 35.

Anon., 1974 EC[3], 'And Ye-Jegninet Mi'araf—Abriha Debochna Moges Asgedom' (Amharic), *Dehnenet*, Hamle, 1974 EC, Addis Ababa, pp. 41–8.

Asefa Chabo, 1991 EC, 'Qale-Meteyq' (Amharic), *Tobia*, Vol. 7, No. 1, Addis Ababa, pp. 10–13.

Ashetu Assefa, 1977 EC, 'Awqo Lemasawq' (Amharic), *Ye Zareytu Etyopya*, Nehase 25, 1977, Vol. 35, No. 25, Addis Ababa.

Baer, G.W., 1976, *Test Case: Italy, Ethiopia and the League of Nations*, Stanford: Hoover Institution Press.

Bahru Zewde, 1988, 'The Historical Context of the Dogali Encounter', in *The Centenary of Dogali: Proceedings of the International Symposium, Addis Ababa—Asmara, January 24–25, 1987*, Institute of Ethiopian Studies, Addis Ababa: Addis Ababa University, pp. 103–12.

———, 1991, *A History of Modern Ethiopia 1855–1974*, London: James Currey.

———, 1993, 'The Ethiopian Intelligentsia and the Italo-Ethiopian War 1935–1941', *International Journal of African Historical Studies*, Vol. 26, No. 2, 1993, pp. 271–95.

———, 2002, *Pioneers of Change in Ethiopia: The Reformist Intellectuals of the Early Twentieth Century*, Oxford: James Currey.

———, 2008, *Society, State and History: Selected Essays*, Addis Ababa: Addis Ababa University Press.

Bairu Tafla, 1985, 'The Forgotten Patriot: The Life and Career of Johannes Semerjibashian in Ethiopia', *Armenian Review*, Summer 1985, Vol. 38, pp. 13–39.

———, 2010, 'Semerjibashian, Johannes [Hovhannes]', *Encyclopaedia Aethiopica*, Vol. 4, O–X, ed. S. Uhlig, Wiesbaden: Harrassowitz, pp. 613–14.

Barker, A.J., 1968, *The Civilising Mission: A History of the Italo-Ethiopian War of 1935–1936*, New York: The Dial Press.

———, 1971, *Rape of Ethiopia 1936*, New York: Ballantine Books.

Battini, M., 2007, *The Missing Italian Nuremberg: Cultural Amnesia and Postwar Politics*, New York: Palgrave Macmillan.

Battistoni, M. and Chiari, G.P., 2004, *Old Tracks in the New Flower: A Historical Guide to Addis Ababa*, Addis Ababa: Arada Books.

Baudendistel, R., 2006, *Between Bombs and Good Intentions: The Red Cross and the Italo-Ethiopian War, 1935–1936*, New York and Oxford: Berghahn Books.

Bauerochse, E., 2005, 'Die Hermannsburger Mission in Äthiopien im Zeitalter des Totalitarismus', in *Die Hermannsburger Mission und das 'Dritte Reich': Zwischen faschistischer Verführung und lutherischer Beharrlichkeit*, ed. G. Gremels, Münster: Lit Verlag, pp. 127–40.

Ben-Ghiat, R. and Fuller, M., 2008, Introduction, *Italian Colonialism*, ed. R. Ben-Ghiat and M. Fuller, New York: Palgrave Macmillan, pp. 1–12.

Berhanou Abebe, 1998, *Histoire de l'Éthiopie d'Axoum à la révolution*, Addis Ababa: Centre Français dés Études Éthiopiennes.

Berihun Kebbede, 1993 EC, *Ye-Atsé Hayle-Sillassé Tarik* (Amharic), Addis Ababa: Artistic Printers.

Birhanina Selam, 1942 EC, *Ye Teferi Mekonnin Timhirt Bét Achir Tariq: Short History of Tafari Makonnen School* (Amharic and English), Addis Ababa: Berhanina Selam Printing Press, 19 Miazia, 1942 EC.

Birhanu Dinqé, 1937 EC, *Ye-Amistu Ye-Mekera Ametat Acher Tarik* (Amharic), Addis Ababa: Birhanina Selam Printing Press.

——, 1942 EC, *Ke-Welwel Iske Maychew* (Amharic), Addis Ababa: Birhanina Selam Printing Press.

Boaglio, A., 2010, *Plotone chimico: cronache abissine di una generazione scomoda*, Milan: Mimesis Edizioni.

Borusso, P., 2001, 'La crisi politica e religiosa dell'impero etiopico sotto l'occupazione fascista (1936–1940)', *Studi Piacentini*, 29, Piacenza, pp. 57–111.

British Military Administration in Eritrea and Somalia, 1944, *The First to be Freed: The Record of British Military Administration in Eritrea and Somalia, 1941–1943*, London: His Majesty's Stationery Office.

Buonasorte, N., 1995, 'La politica religiosa italiana in Africa orientale dopo la conquista (1936–1941)', *Studi Piacentini*, 17, Piacenza, pp. 53–114.

Burdett, C., 2005, 'Colonial Associations and the Memory of Italian East Africa', in *Italian Colonialism: Legacy and Memory*, ed. J. Andall and D. Duncan, Bern: Peter Lang, pp. 125–42.

——, 2011, '*Nomos*, Identity and Otherness: Ciro Poggiali's *Diario AOI 1936–1937* and the Representation of the Italian Colonial World', *Papers of the British School of Rome*, 79, pp. 329–49.

Buxton, D., 1957, *Travels in Ethiopia*, London: Ernest Benn.

Campbell, I.L., 1999, 'La repressione fascista in Etiopia: il massacro segreto di Engecha', *Studi Piacentini*, 24–5, Piacenza, pp. 23–46.

——, 2004, 'Reconstructing the Fascist Occupation of Ethiopia: The Italian Telegrammes as Historical Sources', *International Journal of Ethiopian Studies*, Vol. 1, No. 2, Winter/Spring 2004, Hollywood: Tsehai Publishers, pp. 122–8.

——, 2007, '*Yekatit 12* Revisited: New Light on the Strike against Graziani', *Journal of Ethiopian Studies*, Vol. XL, Nos. 1–2, June–December 2007, Addis Ababa: Institute of Ethiopian Studies, Addis Ababa University, pp. 135–54.

——, 2010, *The Plot to Kill Graziani: The Attempted Assassination of Mussolini's Viceroy*, Addis Ababa: Addis Ababa University Press.

——, 2014, *The Massacre of Debre Libanos: The Story of One of Fascism's Most Shocking Atrocities*, Addis Ababa: Addis Ababa University Press.

Campbell, I.L. and Degife Gabre-Tsadik, 1997, 'La repressione fascista in Etiopia: la ricostruzione del massacro di Debra Libanos', *Studi Piacentini*, 21, Piacenza, pp. 79–128.

Canevari, E., 1947, *Graziani mi ha detto*, Rome: Maji-Spinetti.

Cifelli, A., 2008, *L'istituto prefettizio dalla caduta del Fascismo all'Assemblea costituente: i prefetti della liberazione*, Rome: Scuola Superiore dell'Amminstrazione dell'Interno.

Clapham, C., 1969, *Haile-Selassie's Government*, London and Harlow: Longmans.

Colarizi, S., 2000, *L'opinione degli italiani sotto il regime 1929–1943*, Rome: Laterza.

Consociazione Turistica Italiana, 1938, *Guida dell'Africa orientale italiana*, Milan.

Cortese, G., 1931, *Tripolitania*, Rome: Istituto Coloniale Fascista.

———, 1934, *Eritrea: traccia storico politica della conquista*, Rome: Istituto Coloniale Fascista.

———, 1938, *Problemi dell'impero*, Rome: Pinciana.

Crociani, P. and Battistelli, P.P., 2010, *Italian Blackshirt 1935–45*, Warrior Series No. 144, Oxford and New York: Osprey Publishing.

De Turris, A.L., 1999, 'L'attentato a Rodolfo Graziani: immagini della repressione italiana in Etiopia', *Nuova Storia Contemporanea*, Vol. III, No. 4, Rome: Luna Editrice, pp. 129–38.

Del Boca, A., 1965, *La guerra d'Abissinia, 1935–1941*, Milan: Giangiacomo Feltrinelli Editore.

———, 1969, *The Ethiopian War 1935–1941*, tr. P.D. Cummins, Chicago and London: University of Chicago Press.

———, 1986, *Gli italiani in Africa orientale*, Vol. III, *La caduta dell'impero*, Rome: Laterza.

———, 1987, 'Un lager de fascismo: Danane', *Studi Piacentini*, 1, Piacenza, pp. 59–70.

———, 1988, *Gli italiani in Libia*, Milan: Mondadori.

———, 1996, *I gas di Mussolini: il fascismo e la guerra d'Etiopia*, Rome: Editori Riuniti.

———, 2003, 'The Myths, Suppressions, Denials, and Defaults of Italian Colonialism', in *A Place in the Sun: Africa in Italian Colonial Culture from Post-Unification to the Present*, ed. P. Palumbo, Berkeley: University of California Press, pp. 17–36.

———, 2005, *Italiani: brava gente?*, Vicenza: Neri Pozza.

———, 2012, *The Negus: The Life and Death of the Last King of Kings*, Addis Ababa: Arada Books.

Denshaw, W.R. and Truman, H.S., 1957, *10,000 Famous Freemasons from A to L*, Part 1, Whitefish, Montana: Kessinger Publishing.

Département de la Presse et de l'Information du Gouvernement Impérial d'Éthiopie, 1946, *La civilisation de l'Italie fasciste en Éthiopie*, Addis Ababa.

———, c.1946, *La civilisation de l'Italie fasciste en Éthiopie*, Vol. II, Addis Ababa.

Diel, L., 1939, *'Behold Our New Empire': Mussolini*, London: Hurst & Blackett.

Dominioni, M., 2008, *Lo sfascio dell'impero: gli italiani in Etiopia 1936–1941*, Rome and Bari: Laterza.

Doresse, J., 1967, *Ancient Cities and Temples: Ethiopia*, London: Elek Books.

Dugan, J. and Lafore, L., 1973, *Days of Emperor and Clown: The Italo-Ethiopian War 1935–1936*, New York: Doubleday & Co.

Duggan, C., 2013, *Fascist Voices: An Intimate History of Mussolini's Italy*, New York: Oxford University Press.

Dwyer, P.G. and Ryan, L., 2012, *Theatres of Violence, Mass Killing and Atrocity Throughout History* (International Studies in Social History), New York: Berghahn Books.

Elkins, C., 2005, *Imperial Reckoning: The Untold Story of Britain's Gulag in Kenya*, New York: Henry Holt & Co.

Engert, J.M., 2006, *Tales from the Embassy: The Extraordinary World of C. Van H. Engert*, Maryland: Heritage Books.

Ev.-Luth. Missionwerk in Niedersachsen (ELM) and Gremels, G., 2008, *Der Weg einer heilsamen Erinnerung: Hermann Bahlburg 1892–1962: Zwischen Missionsdienst und Predigtverbot*, Hermannsburg: Ludwig-Harms-Haus.

Evans, D., 2005, *Mussolini's Italy*, London: Hodder Education.

Fanouris, M. and L., 1995, *Meskel: An Ethiopian Family Saga 1926–1981*, Nairobi: Jacaranda Designs.

Farago, L., 1935, *Abyssinia on the Eve*, London: Putnam.

Fasil Giyorghis and Gérard, D., 2007, *The City and Its Architectural Heritage: Addis Ababa 1886–1941—La ville: patrimoine architectural*, Addis Ababa: Shama Books.

Finaldi, G., 2008, *Mussolini and Italian Fascism*, Harlow: Pearson Education.

———, 2012B:[4]. 'Method in Their Madness: Understanding the Dynamics of the Italian Massacre of Ethiopian Civilians', in *Theatres of Violence: Massacre, Mass Killing and Atrocity Throughout History*, ed. P.G. Dwyer and L. Ryan, New York: Berghahn Books, pp. 245–57.

Fitur Abriham, 1937 EC, *Arménéw Fashist* (Amharic), Addis Ababa: Merha Tebeb Press.

Forgacs, D., 2014, *Italy's Margins: Social Exclusion and Nation Formation since 1861*, New York: Cambridge University Press.

Garima Teferi, 1949 EC, *Ye-Gondare Begashaw* (Amharic), Addis Ababa.

Garretson, P.P., 2012. *A Victorian Gentleman and Ethiopian Nationalist: The Life and Times of Hakim Wärqenäh, Dr Charles Martin*, Woodbridge: James Currey.

Gebre-Sillassé Oda, 1985 EC, *Tizita Lemetasebiya* (Amharic), Addis Ababa: BeEtiopya Nigd Mikir Bét Metamiya Bét.

Gérard, D., 2006, *Ras Teferi—Haile Selassie: visages du dernier empereur d'Éthiopie*, Forcalquier: L'Archange Minotaure.

Germino, D.L., 1959, *The Italian Fascist Party in Power: A Study in Totalitarian Rule*, Minneapolis: University of Minnesota Press.

Goglia, L., 1985, *Storia fotografica dell'impero fascista 1935–1941*, Rome and Bari: Laterza.

Governo Generale dell'A.O.I., n.d. (c.1938), *Giornale ufficiale del governo generale dell'Africa orientale italiana, 1937*, Addis Ababa: Servizio Tipografico del Governo Generale dell'A.O.I.

BIBLIOGRAPHY

Governo Generale, Stato Maggiore, A.O.I., 1939A, *Il l'anno dell'impero*, Vol. III, *Testo*, Addis Ababa: Superiore Topocartografico.

——, 1939B, *Il l'anno dell'impero*, Vol. III, *Allegati*, Addis Ababa: Superiore Topocartografico.

Graziani, R., 2001, *Una vita per l'Italia: 'Ho difeso la patria'*, Milan: Mursia.

Greenfield, R., 1964, 'Remembering the Struggle', *Makerere Journal*, Kampala, Vol. 9, pp. 7–32.

——, 1965, *Ethiopia: A New Political History*, London and Essex: Pall Mall Press.

Grubb, N., 1943, *Alfred Buxton of Abyssinia and Congo*, London and Redhill: Lutterworth Press.

Haile Selassie I Military Academy, 1950 EC, *Ye-Qedamawi Hayle-Sillasé Tir Timhirt Bet Tarik ke 1927 iske 1949 a mi* (Amharic), Addis Ababa: Nigd Matemiya.

Haile Selassie, Qedamawi, 1965 EC, *Hiyweté-na ye Ityopya Irmijja*, Vol. I (Amharic), Addis Ababa: Birhanina Selam Printing Press.

Haile Selassie I, ed. Ullendorf, E., 1999, *The Autobiography of Emperor Haile Selassie I, Volume 1*, Barbados: Research Associates School, Times Publications.

——, ed. Marcus, H., 1994, *My Life and Ethiopia's Progress: Haile Selassie I, King of Kings of Ethiopia, Vol. Two, Addis Ababa, 1966 EC*, East Lansing: Michigan State University Press.

Hall, C., 1947, 'Fascists Gone, but Scars Remain', *The Afro-American: The Afro Magazine*, 22 March 1947, p. M-8.

Hamilton, P.A., 1949, 'Tamasgn is Dead', *New Times and Ethiopia News*, No. 664, 5 Feb. 1949.

Hanson, H.M. and D., 1958, *For God and Emperor*, Mountain View, California: Pacific Press Publishing Association.

Hermannsburg Mission, 1932, *Hermannsburger Missionblatt* (Bulletin of the German Hermannsburg Mission), Hermannsburg: Hermannsburg Mission.

——, 2003, *75th Anniversary of German Hermannsburg Mission (GHM) in Ethiopia, December 30, 1927—December 30, 2002*, Addis Ababa: Hermannsburg Mission.

Hywet Hidaru, 1967 EC, *Yachi Qen Teresach* (Amharic), Addis Ababa.

Jonas, R., 2011, *The Battle of Adwa: African Victory in the Age of Empire*, Cambridge, Mass.: The Belknap Press, Harvard University Press.

Kali-Nyah, I., 2001, *Italy's War Crimes in Ethiopia (1935–1941); Evidence for the War Crimes Commission*, Chicago: The Ethiopian Holocaust Remembrance Committee.

Kebbede Tessema, 1962 EC, *Ye-Tarik Mastawesha* (Amharic), Addis Ababa: Artistic Printers.

Kiflayesus, A., 1973, *The Career of Liul Ras Imru Hayla Silassie*, Essay for the degree of Bachelor of Arts, unpublished, Addis Ababa University.

Knox, M., 1986, *Mussolini Unleashed 1939–1941: Politics and Strategy in Fascist Italy's Last War*, Cambridge: Cambridge University Press.

Labanca, N., 2003, 'Studies and Research on Fascist Colonialism, 1922–1935: Reflections on the State of the Art', in *A Place in the Sun: Africa in Italian Colonial Culture from Post-Unification to the Present*, ed. P. Palumbo, Berkeley: University of California Press, pp. 37–61.

———, 2008, 'Italian Colonial Internment', in *Italian Colonialism*, ed. R. Ben-Ghiat and M. Fuller, New York: Palgrave Macmillan, pp. 27–36.

Lass-Westphal, I., 1972, 'Protestant Missions during and after the Italo-Ethiopian War, 1935–1937', *Journal of Ethiopian Studies*, Vol. X, No. 1, January 1972, Addis Ababa: Institute of Ethiopian Studies, Addis Ababa University, pp. 89–101.

Launhardt, J., 2004, *Evangelicals in Addis Ababa (1919–1991) with Special Reference to the Ethiopian Evangelical Church Mekane Yesus and the Addis Ababa Synod*, Münster: Lit Verlag.

Le Houérou, F., 1994A, 'Portrait of a Fascist: Marshal Graziani', in *New Trends in Ethiopian Studies Ethiopia 94: Papers of the 12th International Conference of Ethiopian Studies*, Vol. I, ed. H. Marcus, Lawrenceville, New Jersey: Red Sea Press, pp. 822–96.

———, 1994B, *L'Épopée des soldats de Mussolini en Abyssinie 1936–1938: les 'ensablés'*, Paris: L'Harmattan.

Lentakis, M.B., 2006, *Ethiopia: A View from Within*, London: Janus.

Lucas, E. and DeVecchi, G., 1976, *Storia delle unità combattenti della MVSN 1923–1941*, Giovanni Volpe Editore.

Mahtämä-Sellas. W.ld. M.sq.l, Blattén Géta, 1969, 'Source Material: A Study of the Ethiopian Culture of Horse-Names: YeEtyopya Bahel Tinat (Ch. Belew)' (Amharic; introduction in English), Journal of Ethiopian Studies, Vol. VII, No. 2, July 1969, Addis Ababa: Institute of Ethiopian Studies, Addis Ababa University, pp. 195–303.

Mahteme Sillass. Welde Mesqel, 1961 EC, Ché Belew (Amharic), Addis Ababa: Nigid Matemiya.

Mallett, R., 2015, *Mussolini in Ethiopia, 1919–1935: The Origins of Fascist Italy's Africa War*, New York: Cambridge University Press.

Marcus, H.G., 1969, 'Ethiopia 1937–1941', in *Challenge and Response in Internal Conflict*, Vol. 3, ed. Doris Condit and Bert Cooper, Center for Research in Social Systems, the American University.

———, 1995, *Haile Selassie I: The Formative Years 1892–1936*, Trenton, New Jersey: Red Sea Press.

Martha Nasibu, 2006, *Memorie di una principessa etiope*, Vicenza: Neri Pozza.

McCullagh, F., 1912, *Italy's War for a Desert: Some Experiences of a War Correspondent with the Italians in Tripoli*, London: Herbert & Daniel.

Meleseliñ Aniley, 1947 EC, *Balefut Amist Ye-mekera Amatat Fashistoch be Etyopya* (Amharic), Addis Ababa: Merha Tebeb Press, No. 890.

Michaël Bethe Selassié, 2009, *La Jeune Éthiopie: un haut-fonctionnaire éthiopien: Berhanä-Marqos Wäldä-Tsadeq (1892–1943)*, Paris: L'Harmattan.

Mikre-Selassie G/Ammanuel, 2014, *Church and Missions in Ethiopia during the Italian Occupation*, Addis Ababa: Artistic Printing Enterprise.

Ministry of Culture and Sports Affairs, Ethiopia, 1990, *Historic Buildings of Addis Ababa: Preservation in Town Planning*, Addis Ababa: Ministry of Culture and Sports Affairs.

Ministry of Justice, Ethiopia, 1949, *Documents on Italian War Crimes Submitted to the United Nations War Crimes Commission by the Imperial Ethiopian Government, Volume I: Italian Telegrams and Circulars*, Addis Ababa: Ministry of Justice.

———, 1950, *Documents on Italian War Crimes Submitted to the United Nations War Crimes Commission by the Imperial Ethiopian Government, Volume II: Affidavits and Published Documents*, Addis Ababa: Ministry of Justice.

Mockler, A., 1984, *Haile Selassie's War: The Italian-Ethiopian Campaign, 1935–1941*, New York: Random House.

Mondadori, A., ed., 1939, *Gli annali dell'Africa italiana*, Vol. II,—No. 2, Rome: Mondadori.

Montanelli, I. and Cervi, M., 1980, *L'Italia dell'Asse*, Milan: Rizzoli.

Moraitis, J., 2001, *Ethiopia My Home: The Story of John Moraitis*, Addis Ababa: Shama Books.

Mosley, L., 1964, *Haile Selassie: The Conquering Lion*, London: Weidenfeld and Nicolson.

Mulu Sew Meteku, 1937 EC, *YeArbeññoch Tegel keFashist Gar: keShewa Iska Sudan Teref* (Amharic), Addis Ababa: Berhanina Selam Printing Press.

Neilson, K., 2010, 'Orme Sargent, Appeasement and British Policy in Europe, 1933–39', *Twentieth Century British History*, Vol. 21, No. 1, pp. 1–28.

New Times and Ethiopia News, Sudan Correspondent, 1937, 'True Story of the Attempt on the Life of Marshal Graziani: An Italian General in Flight', New Times and Ethiopian News, 6 March 1937.

Nicolle, D., 1997, The Italian Invasion of Abyssinia 1935–36, Men-at-Arms series, No. 309, Wellingborough: Osprey.

O'Kelly, S., 2003, *Amadeo: The True Story of an Italian's War in Abyssinia*, London: HarperCollins Publishers.

Ottolenghi, G., 1997, *Gli italiani e il colonialism: i campi di detenzione italiani in Africa*, Milan: Sugarco.

Pankhurst, R.K., 1962, 'The Foundations of Education, Printing, Newspapers, Book Production, Libraries and Literacy in Ethiopia', *Ethiopia Observer*, Vol. VI, No. 3, Addis Ababa, pp. 241–90.

———, 1968, *Economic History of Ethiopia 1800–1935*, Addis Ababa: Haile Selassie I University Press.

———, 1969A, 'The Ethiopian Patriots and the Collapse of Italian Rule in East Africa, 1940–41', *Ethiopia Observer*, Vol. XII, No. 2, Addis Ababa, pp. 92–127.

———, 1969B, 'Fascist Racial Policies in Ethiopia 1922–1941', *Ethiopia Observer*, Vol. XII, No. 4, Addis Ababa, pp. 270–86.

——, 1970, 'The Ethiopian Patriots: The Lone Struggle 1936–1940', *Ethiopia Observer*, Vol. XIII, No. 1, Addis Ababa, pp. 40–56.

——, 1971, 'A Chapter in Ethiopia's Commercial History: Developments during the Fascist Occupation 1936–41', *Ethiopia Observer*, Vol. XIV, No. 1, Addis Ababa, pp. 47–67.

——, 1977, 'The Secret History of the Italian Fascist Occupation of Ethiopia, 1935–1941', *African Quarterly*, Vol. XVI, No. IV, April 1977.

——, 1999, 'Italian Fascist War Crimes in Ethiopia: A History of Their Discussion, from the League of Nations to the United Nations (1936–1949)', *Northeast African Studies*, Vol. 6, No. 1–2 (New Series), pp. 83–140.

——, 2001, *The Ethiopians: A History*, Oxford: Blackwell Publishers.

——, 2002, 'Hakim Wärknëh, Propagandist for Ethiopia at the Time of the Fascist Invasion', in *Ethiopian Studies at the End of the Second Millennium, Proceedings of the XIVth International Conference of Ethiopian Studies, November 6–11, 2000, Addis Ababa*, Vol. I, ed. Baye Yimam, R.K. Pankhurst, D. Chapple et al., Addis Ababa: Institute of Ethiopian Studies, Addis Ababa University, pp. 435–50.

——, 2003, *Sylvia Pankhurst: Counsel for Ethiopia. A Biographical Essay on Ethiopian Anti-Fascist and Anti-Colonialist History, 1934–1960*, Hollywood: Tsehai Publishers and Distributors.

——, 2007, 'Historical Notes on Books, 2: Hakim Warkneh, Ethiopia, and the Libyan War', *Capital*, Vol. 9, No. 464, 4 November 2007, Addis Ababa.

——, 2011, 'Who were the "Young Ethiopians" or Abyssinians? An Historical Enquiry, Part 3', *Capital*, Vol. 13, No. 655, 3 July 2011, Addis Ababa.

——, 2012, 'Ethiopia and Tripoli: Hakim Warkneh's Condemnation of Italian Action in Tripoli in 1911: Ethiopian Authorship of a Now-Forgotten Pamphlet', *International Journal of Ethiopian Studies*, Vol. VI, Nos. 1 and 2, Los Angeles: Tsehai Publishers, pp. 189–93.

Pankhurst, R.K. and Pankhurst, R., ed., 1962, 'Ethiopian Appointments', *Ethiopia Observer*, Vol. V, No. 4, Addis Ababa, pp. 378–80.

Pankhurst, R., Sohier, E. and Smidt, W., 2007, 'Mohamedally and Company', *Encyclopaedia Aethiopica*, Vol. 3, He–N, ed. S. Uhlig, Wiesbaden: Harrassowitz, pp. 986–7.

Pankhurst, S., 1945, *Italy's War Crimes in Ethiopia*, Woodford Green: New Times and Ethiopia News.

——, 1955, *Ethiopia: A Cultural History*, Woodford Green: Lalibela House.

——, 1959, 'Fascist Foreign Policy and the Italo-Ethiopian War', *Ethiopia Observer*, Vol. III, No. 11, October 1959, Addis Ababa, pp. 339–40.

Pasquali, M.C., 2015, *Addis Ababa: End of an Era*, Addis Ababa: Shama Books.

Pedaliu, E.G.H., 2004, 'Britain and the "Hand-over" of Italian War Criminals to Yugoslavia, 1945–48', *Journal of Contemporary History*, Vol. 39, No. 4, Special Issue: 'Collective Memory', pp. 503–29.

Pegolotti, B., 1971, 'L'attentato a Graziani', *Storia Illustrata*, Vol. XV, No. 163, pp. 94–101.

Perret, M., 1986, 'Le Massacre de Däbrä Libanos', in *La Guerre d'Éthiopie et l'opinion mondiale 1934–1941*, Actes du Colloque de l'INALCO, Paris, 14 December 1984, Paris: Colloques Langues O'.

Pétridès, S.P., 1988, 'Alula and Dogali, Their Place in Ethiopian History', in *The Centenary of Dogali: Proceedings of the International Symposium, Addis Ababa—Asmara, January 24–25, 1987*, Addis Ababa: Institute of Ethiopian Studies, Addis Ababa University, pp. 59–90.

Poggiali, C., 1971, *Diario AOI (15 giugno 1936—4 ottobre 1937)*, Milan: Longanesi.

Puglisi, G., 1952, *Chi è? dell'Eritrea 1952: dizionario biografico*, Asmara: Agenzia Regina.

Quinton, A.G.H., 1949, *Ethiopia and the Evangel*, London: Marshall, Morgan & Scott.

Robertson, E.M., 1977, *Mussolini as Empire Builder: Europe and Africa, 1932–36*, London: Macmillan Press.

Rochat, G., 1971, *Militari e politici nella preparazione della campagna d'Etiopia: studio e documenti, 1932–1936*, Milan.

———, 1988, 'L'attentato a Graziani e la repressione italiana in Etiopia 1936–1937 (1975)', in *Guerre italiane in Libia e in Etiopia: studi militari 1921–1939*, ed. G. Rochat, Treviso: Pagus, pp. 177–214 (originally published in *Italia Contemporanea*, No. 118 (Jan.–March 1975), pp. 3–38).

———, 2008, 'The Italian Air Force in the Ethiopian War (1935–1936)', in *Italian Colonialism*, ed. R. Ben-Ghiat, and M. Fuller, New York: Palgrave Macmillan, pp. 37–46.

Ruffolo Editore, 1948, *Processo Graziani* (3 vols.), Rome: Ruffolo Editore.

Rubinkowska, H., 2010, 'Wäldä Şadəq Goššu', *Encyclopaedia Aethiopica*, Vol. 4, O–X, ed. S. Uhlig, Wiesbaden: Harrassowitz, pp. 1107–8.

Salerno, E., 1979, *Genocidio in Libia: le atrocità nascoste dell'avventura coloniale 1911/31*, Milan: Sugarco.

Salome Gabre Egziabher, 1969, 'The Ethiopian Patriots 1936–1941', *Ethiopia Observer*, Vol. XII, No. 2, 1968–9, Addis Ababa, pp. 63–91.

Sáska László (aka Ladislas Sava), ed. Szélinger Balázs, 2014, *Fascist Italian Brutalities in Ethiopia, 1935–1937: An Eye-witness Account*, Trenton, New Jersey: Red Sea Press, 2014.

Sava, L., 1940A, 'Ethiopia under Mussolini's Rule', *New Times and Ethiopia News*, 14 Dec. 1940, p. 1.

———, 1940B, 'Ethiopia under Mussolini's Rule', *New Times and Ethiopia News*, 21 Dec. 1940, p. 1.

———, 1940C, 'Ethiopia under Mussolini's Rule', *New Times and Ethiopia News*, 28 Dec. 1940, p. 1.

——, 1941A, 'Ethiopia under Mussolini's Rule', *New Times and Ethiopia News*, 4 Jan. 1941, p. 1.

——, 1941B, 'Ethiopia under Mussolini's Rule', *New Times and Ethiopia News*, 11 Jan. 1941, p. 1.

Sbacchi, A., 1977, 'Italy and the Treatment of the Ethiopian Aristocracy 1937–1940', *International Journal of African Historical Studies*, Vol. X, No. 2.

——, 1989, *Ethiopia under Mussolini: Fascism and the Colonial Experience*, London: Zed Books.

——, 1997, *Legacy of Bitterness: Ethiopia and Fascist Italy, 1935–1941*, Lawrenceville, New Jersey: Red Sea Press.

——, 2008, 'Poison Gas and Atrocities in the Italo-Ethiopian War', in *Italian Colonialism*, ed. R. Ben-Ghiat and M. Fuller, New York: Palgrave Macmillan, pp. 47–56.

Seltene Seyoum, 1999, *A History of Resistance in Gojjam (Ethiopia): 1936–1941*, PhD thesis, Addis Ababa: Addis Ababa University, School of Graduate Studies, May 1999.

——, 2000, 'Emperor Haile Selassie I and the Ethiopian Resistance: 1936–1941', in *Ethiopian Studies at the End of the Second Millennium, Proceedings of the XIVth International Conference of Ethiopian Studies, November 6–11, 200, Addis Ababa*, Vol. I, ed. Baye Yimam, R.K. Pankhurst, D. Chapple et al., Addis Ababa: Institute of Ethiopian Studies, Addis Ababa University, pp. 477–98.

——, 2003, 'Review of the Literature on Ethiopian Resistance with Particular Emphasis on Gojjam: 1936–1941', *Journal of Ethiopian Studies*, Vol. XXXVI, No. 2, December 2003, Addis Ababa: Institute of Ethiopian Studies, Addis Ababa University.

——, 2006, 'The Role of National and International Missions in the Ethiopian Resistance: 1938–1940', in *Proceedings of the XVth International Conference of Ethiopian Studies*, Hamburg 2003, ed. S. Uhlig, Wiesbaden: Harrassowitz, pp. 364–71.

Shiferaw Bekele, 2013, 'Preliminary Notes on Ethiopian Sources on the Italian Invasion of the Country and the Subsequent Occupation', in *L'impero nel cassetto: l'Italia coloniale tra album privati e archivi pubblici*, ed. P.B. Farnetti, A. Mignemi and A. Triulzi, Milan: Mimesis, pp. 31–6.

Siniddu Gebru, 1942 EC, *Ye-Libé Metshaf, KeHizbachew Wafiqot Yetederese* (Amharic), Addis Ababa: Birhanina Selam Printing Press.

Smith, H., 1948, 'Graziani in the Dock in Rome as War Criminal, Attempts to Defend Himself', *Ethiopian Herald*, 18 Oct. 1948, p. 2; 25 Oct., p. 4; 1 Nov., p. 3.

Spencer, J.H., 1987, *Ethiopia at Bay: A Personal Account of the Haile Selassie Years*, Algonac, Michigan: Reference Publications.

Steer, G.L., 1936, *Caesar in Abyssinia*, London: Hodder and Stoughton.

——, 2009, *Sealed and Delivered: A Book on the Abyssinian Campaign*, London: Faber and Faber.

BIBLIOGRAPHY

Steiner, H.A., 1936, 'The Government of Italian East Africa', *American Political Science Review*, Vol. 30, No. 5, October 1936, pp. 884–902.

Syoum Gebregziabher, 2012, *Symphony of My Life: The Challenging Times and Many Variant Experiences from Ethiopia, Bhutan, Tanzania, and the United States*, Trenton, New Jersey: Red Sea Press.

Taddesse Mécha, 1943 EC, *Tiqur Anbessa* (Amharic), Asmara: Corriere Eritreo Printing Press.

Taddesse Zeweldé, 1955 EC, *Ye-Abalashiñ Zemen* (Amharic), Addis Ababa: Berhanina Selam Printing Press.

———, 1960 EC, *Qerin Geremew: YeArbeññoch Tarik* (Amharic), Addis Ababa: Berhanina Selam Printing Press.

Taddia, I., 1988, *La memoria dell'impero*, Manduria and Bari: Lacaita Editore.

———, 1996, *Autobiografie africane: il colonialismo nelle memorie orali*, Milan: Franco Angeli.

Tamasgen Gabre, 1945, 'Hell on Earth', *Ethiopian Herald*, 24 February, 1945, p. 4.

Tekeste Negash, 1986, 'Pax Italica and Its Ethiopian Enemies, 1936–1940', in *No Medicine for the Bite of a White Snake: Notes on Nationalism and Resistance in Eritrea, 1890–1940*, ed. Tekeste Negash, Uppsala: University of Uppsala, pp. 55–72.

Tekle-Tsadiq Mekuriya, 2008 EC, *YeHiyweté Tariq* (Amharic), Addis Ababa: Eclipse Printing Press.

Temesgen Gebré, 2001 EC, *Hiyweté (Gile Tariq)* (Amharic), Addis Ababa: Sister Kibre Temesgen.

Tesema Ta'a, 1997, 'The Bonayyaa Incident and the Italian Occupation of Naqamte: 1936–1941', in *Ethiopia in Broader Perspective: Papers of the XIIIth International Conference of Ethiopian Studies, Kyoto, 12–17 December 1997*, Vol. I, ed. K. Fukui, E. Kurimoto and M. Shigeta, Kyoto: Shokado Booksellers, pp. 263–83.

Thöndl, M., 2000, 'Mussolinis ostafrikanisches Imperium in den Aufzeichnungen und Berichten des deutschen Generalkonsulats in Addis Abeba (1936–1941)', *Quellen und Forschungen aus italienischen Archiven und Bibliotheken*, Rome: German Historical Institute.

Triulzi, A., 2005, 'Adwa: From Monument to Document', in *Italian Colonialism: Legacy and Memory*, ed. J. Andall and D. Duncan, Bern: Peter Lang, pp. 143–63.

US Government Printing Office, 1953, *Foreign Relations of the United States: Diplomatic Papers 1936*, Vol III: *The Near East and Africa*, Washington: US Government.

———, 1954, *Foreign Relations of the United States: Diplomatic Papers 1937*, Vol II: *The British Commonwealth, Europe, Near East and Africa*, Washington: US Government.

Van Kessel, T.M.C., 2011, 'Cultural Policy and Colonial Conquest: The Dante Alighieri Society in Abyssinia and the British Council in Egypt', in *Cultural Promotion and Imperialism: The Dante Alighieri Society and the British Council Contesting the Mediterranean in the 1930s*, Amsterdam: University of Amsterdam.

Virgin, E., 1936, *The Abyssinia I Knew*, London: Macmillan & Co.

Walston, J., 1997, 'History and Memory of the Italian Concentration Camps', *Historical Journal*, Vol. 40, No. 1, pp. 169–83.

Weerts, M.L., 1970, 'The Late Mr Antonin Besse and the Ethiopian Resistance during the Years 1935 to 1940', *Journal of Ethiopian Studies*, Vol. VIII, No. 2, July 1970, Addis Ababa: Institute of Ethiopian Studies, Haile Selassie I University, pp. 171–80.

———, 2003, 'The Late Mr Antonin Besse and the Ethiopian Resistance during the Years 1935 to 1940', *Addis Tribune*, 18 July 2003, p. 9.

Welde-Giyorgis Welde-Yohannis 1939 EC, *Tarik Yallew Aymotin* (Amharic), Addis Ababa.

Wolk, E., 2010, 'Täklä Şadəq Mäkʷəriya', *Encyclopaedia Aethiopica*, Vol. 4, O–X, ed. S. Uhlig, Wiesbaden: Harrassowitz, pp. 842–3.

Zervos, A., 1936, *L'Empire d'Éthiopie*, Alexandria: l'École Professionnelle des Frères.

Unpublished Manuscripts

Clapham, C., c.1964, *Foreign Educated Ethiopians before 1936*, private collection, Professor Christopher Clapham.

Internet Sources

Aleme Eshete, 2005, *Failure of Fascist 'Legge Organica' to Kill Shoa: Rising Patriotism in Spite of Brutal Repression, Mass Execution, Wholesale Burning and Gas Poisoning*, www.tecolahagos.com/origin_tribal_partIII.htm.

Finaldi, G., 2012A, 'Method in Their Madness: Understanding the Dynamics of the Italian Massacre of Ethiopian Civilians in Addis Ababa', *Abstracts of Papers from an International Interdisciplinary Symposium at Newcastle, Australia, September 2008*, http://www.newcastle.edu.au, pp. 5–6.

Imru Zelleke, 2009, *On the Fascist Invasion of Ethiopia, Danane, Memoir of Former Ambassador*, http://dir.groups.yahoo.com/group/ESAi.

Kindie, D., 1991, 'Dr Lorenzo Taezaz and the Italo-Ethiopian War (1935–1941)', *Ethiopia Review*, May 1991, http://ethiopianreview.homestead.com/ProfileDaniel KindieMay91.html.

Mannucci, S., 2005, *La fotografia strumento dell'imperialismo fascista*, http://www. storiaxxisecolo.it/fascismo/fascismo17e.htm.

Moher, J., 1996, *Camicie Nere: The Blackshirts (MVSN & CCNN) Combat Units*, http://wargaming.info/1996/.

Museo Virtuale delle Intolleranze e degli Stermini, 2013, 'Le misure repressive ideate da Graziani', www.istoreto.it.

M.T., 2004, 'Faccetta Nera', *Selada*, Vol. II, Issue VIII, www.selada.com/feb01/faccetta_nera.shtml.

BIBLIOGRAPHY

Paggi, L., 2006, 'The Colonial Camp and "Population Policy" in Libya (1923–1931)', in *Italian Colonialism and Concentration Camps in Libya 1929–1943*, Tripoli, 12–13 Dec. 2006, Associazione per la Storia e le Memorie della Repubblica, www.storiaememorie.it.

Pankhurst, R.K., 2007, *Hakim Worqneh, Ethiopia and the Libyan War*, aheavens, citing *Capital* newspaper, Addis Ababa. www.Richardpankhurst.wordpress.com.

———, 2010, 'Who were the "Young Ethiopians" (or "Young Abyssinians")? An Historical Enquiry', *Ee-JRIF Ethiopia e-Journal for research and Innovation Foresight*, Vol. 2, No. 2 (2010), Education Issue: pp. 121–38, www.nesglobal.org.

Sommaruga, M. (2013), *Graziani, Carneficina Fascista in Addis Ababa*, http://www.storiain.net/arret/num55/artic5.html.

www.campifascisti.it.

www.comune.biella.it/sito/index.php?polo-bibliotecario.

www.feldgrau.com/rsi.html.

www.Hermann.Bahlburg.name.

www.prefettura.it.

www.regiosercito.it.

www.ssai.interno.it.

Newspapers, Journals and Bulletins Cited

Afro-American, The Argus, Melbourne.

Berhanina Selam, Addis Ababa.

Capital, Addis Ababa.

Corriere della Sera, Milan.

Daily Mail, London.

Daily Telegraph, London.

Dehnehnet, Addis Ababa.

Ethiopia Observer, Addis Ababa.

Ethiopia Star, The, Addis Ababa.

Ethiopian Herald, The, Addis Ababa.

Ethiopian Review, Addis Ababa.

Hansard Parliamentary Debates, London.

Intelligence Bulletin, US Military Intelligence.

London Gazette, London.

News Chronicle, London.

New Times and Ethiopia News, Woodford Green.

Singapore Free Press and Mercantile Advertiser, The, Singapore.

Time, New York.

Times, The, London.

Twentieth Century British History, Oxford.

BIBLIOGRAPHY

Public Archives Consulted

Archivio Centrale dello Stato, Rome.
Archivio Storico del Ministero dell'Africa Italiana.
Great Britain, Public Record Office, Kew.
Microfilm Library, Institute of Ethiopian Studies, Addis Ababa University.
US National Archives II, Maryland.

INDEX